SIXTH EDITION
MATHEMATICS OF FINANCE

Petr Zima
University of Waterloo

Robert L. Brown
University of Waterloo

Steve Kopp
University of Western Ontario

 McGraw-Hill
Ryerson

Toronto   Montréal   Boston   Burr Ridge, IL   Dubuque, IA   Madison, WI   New York
San Francisco   St. Louis   Bangkok   Bogotá   Caracas   Kuala Lumpur   Lisbon   London
Madrid   Mexico City   Milan   New Delhi   Santiago   Seoul   Singapore   Sydney   Taipei

The McGraw·Hill Companies

McGraw-Hill
Ryerson

Mathematics of Finance
Sixth Edition

ISBN-13: 978-0-07-0951617
ISBN-10: 0-07-095161-6

1 2 3 4 5 6 7 8 9 10 TCP 0 9 8 7

Printed and bound in Canada

Editorial Director: Joanna Cotton
Publisher: Lynn Fisher
Marketing Manager: Joy Armitage Taylor
Developmental Editor: Jennifer Bastarache
Editorial Associate: Stephanie Hess
Senior Supervising Editor: Margaret Henderson
Copy Editor: Edie Franks
Senior Production Coordinator: Andrée Davis
Cover Design: Greg Devitt Design
Cover Image: © Getty Images
Interior Design: Dave Murphy/Valid Design and Typesetting
Page Layout: S R Nova Pvt Ltd., Bangalore, India
Printer: Transcontinental Gagne

Library and Archives Canada Cataloguing in Publication

Zima, Petr, 1941–
    Mathematics of finance/Petr Zima, Robert L. Brown, Steve Kopp. — 6th ed.

Includes index.
ISBN-13: 978-0-07-095161-7
ISBN-10: 0-07-095161-6

    1. Business mathematics. I. Brown, Robert L., 1949– II. Kopp, Steve, 1959– III. Title.

HF5691.Z55 2007   650.01'513   C2006-906491-1

Brief Contents

Preface   ix

Chapter 1   **Simple Interest and Simple Discount**   1

Chapter 2   **Compound Interest**   30

Chapter 3   **Simple Annuities**   75

Chapter 4   **General and Other Annuities**   115

Chapter 5   **Repayment of Debts**   145

Chapter 6   **Bonds**   193

Chapter 7   **Business Decisions, Capital Budgeting and Depreciation**   237

Chapter 8   **Contingent Payments**   266

Appendix 1   **Exponents and Logarithms**   289

Appendix 2   **Progressions**   297

Appendix 3   **Linear Interpolation**   305

Glossary of Terms   309

Answers to Problems   313

Index   329

Summary of Notations   335

Contents

Preface   ix

| Chapter 1 | **Simple Interest and Simple Discount**   1 |

Section 1.1   Simple Interest   1
Section 1.2   Discounted Value at Simple Interest   8
Section 1.3   Equations of Value   14
Section 1.4   Partial Payments   20
Section 1.5   Simple Discount at a Discount Rate   23
Section 1.6   Summary and Review Exercises   27

| Chapter 2 | **Compound Interest**   30 |

Section 2.1   Fundamental Compound Interest Formula   30
Section 2.2   Equivalent Compound Interest Rates   37
Section 2.3   Discounted Value at Compound Interest   41
Section 2.4   Accumulated and Discounted Value for a Fractional Period of Time   44
Section 2.5   Determining the Rate and the Time   47
Section 2.6   Equations of Value   53
Section 2.7   Compound Interest at Changing Interest Rates   59
Section 2.8   Other Applications of Compound Interest Theory, Inflation, and the "Real" Rate of Interest   63
Section 2.9   Continuous Compounding   68
Section 2.10   Summary and Review Exercises   72

Chapter 3 **Simple Annuities** 75

Section 3.1   Definitions   75
Section 3.2   Accumulated Value of an Ordinary Simple Annuity   76
Section 3.3   Discounted Value of an Ordinary Simple Annuity   83
Section 3.4   Other Simple Annuities   91
Section 3.5   Determining the Term of an Annuity   100
Section 3.6   Determining the Interest Rate   105
Section 3.7   Summary and Review Exercises   111

Chapter 4 **General and Other Annuities** 115

Section 4.1   General Annuities   115
Section 4.2   Mortgages in Canada   124
Section 4.3   Perpetuities   128
Section 4.4   Annuities Where Payments Vary   134
Section 4.5   Summary and Review Exercises   140

Chapter 5 **Repayment of Debts** 145

Section 5.1   Amortization of a Debt   145
Section 5.2   Outstanding Balance   156
Section 5.3   Refinancing a Loan — The Amortization Method   162
Section 5.4   Refinancing a Loan — The Sum-of-Digits Method   169
Section 5.5   Sinking Funds   176
Section 5.6   The Sinking-Fund Method of Retiring a Debt   179
Section 5.7   Comparison of Amortization and Sinking-Fund Methods   183
Section 5.8   Summary and Review Exercises   187

Chapter 6 **Bonds** 193

Section 6.1   Introduction and Terminology   194
Section 6.2   Purchase Price to Yield a Given Investment Rate to Maturity   195
Section 6.3   Premium and Discount   202
Section 6.4   Callable Bonds   210
Section 6.5   Price of a Bond Between Bond Interest Dates   213
Section 6.6   Determining the Yield Rate   220
Section 6.7   Other Types of Bonds   228
Section 6.8   Summary and Review Exercises   234

Chapter 7

Business Decisions, Capital Budgeting and Depreciation 237

Section 7.1 Net Present Value 237
Section 7.2 Internal Rate of Return 243
Section 7.3 Capitalized Costs 248
Section 7.4 Depreciation 253
Section 7.5 Summary and Review Exercises 262

Chapter 8

Contingent Payments 266

Section 8.1 Probability 267
Section 8.2 Mathematical Expectation 276
Section 8.3 Contingent Payments with Time Value 280
Section 8.4 Summary and Review Exercises 286

Appendix 1

Exponents and Logarithms 289

Section A1.1 Exponents 289
Section A1.2 Laws of Exponents 289
Section A1.3 Zero, Negative and Fractional Exponents 290
Section A1.4 Exponential Equations — Unknown Base 291
Section A1.5 Basic Properties of Logarithms 291
Section A1.6 Computing with Logarithms 292
Section A1.7 Exponential Equations — Unknown Exponent 294
Section A1.8 Exercises — Appendix 1 294

Appendix 2

Progressions 297

Section A2.1 Arithmetic Progressions 297
Section A2.2 The Sum of an Arithmetic Progression 298
Section A2.3 Geometric Progression 299
Section A2.4 The Sum of a Geometric Progression 299
Section A2.5 Applications of Geometric Progressions to Annuities 300
Section A2.6 Infinite Geometric Progressions 301
Section A2.7 Exercises — Appendix 2 302

Appendix 3   **Linear Interpolation**   305

Section A3.1   Exercises — Appendix 3   308

Glossary of Terms   309

Answers to Problems   313

Index   329

Summary of Notations   335

Preface

It is more than 25 years now since the publication of the first edition of *Mathematics of Finance*, and over 30 years since we started teaching this material. Financial mathematics continues to grow in importance, and this book is an excellent tool to equip yourself with the knowledge needed to operate in a world of growing financial complexity. The effects are everywhere, including the interest earned by a school child in his or her first bank account, the investment earnings of a pension fund, the interest rate charged on a credit card or mortgage loan, or rates in the short-term money market used by multinational corporations.

This text is designed to provide readers with a generic approach to appreciate the importance of understanding financial mathematics with respect to a wide range of financial transactions, including annuities, home mortgage and personal loans, bonds, and the assessment of future investment projects. A variety of interest rates are used in the solved examples and in the hundreds of exercises available to the student.

While finance and business students at colleges or universities can readily use the text, it is also appropriate for others who wish to gain a better understanding of these issues. A limited level of mathematical knowledge is assumed at the start of the text, thus permitting introductory chapters on algebra to be omitted. Nevertheless, the appendices include detailed explanation of logarithms, progressions, and linear interpolation, which cover the major requirements.

The text also includes spreadsheet examples. Spreadsheets are a very powerful tool in financial calculations as they permit complicated models to be developed and many calculations to be completed very quickly. As well, we like to emphasize the use of calculators in problem-solving techniques. However, it is essential that the fundamental principles of financial mathematics be appreciated before any spreadsheet is developed or calculator is used.

Our interest in the mathematics of finance remains undiminished. It is our hope that this text provides the reader with improved understanding of the calculations that underlie most financial transactions.

What's New in the Sixth Edition?

Learning Objectives — New to the Sixth Edition are introductions at the beginning of each chapter that outline the learning objectives for studying that chapter.

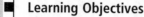

Learning Objectives

In chapter 1, we learned how to perform financial calculations using simple interest. However, most financial transactions involve compound interest rates. Beginning with this chapter, the rest of this textbook is devoted to financial calculations using compound interest. And, once you understand how compound interest works, you will have a powerful tool at your disposal that will allow you to do many financial calculations yourself which will help you in making more informed financial decisions without having to rely on others.

Section 2.1 begins with the concept of interest earned in a given period being added to your principal and thereafter earning interest. This leads to the fundamental formula for accumulating with compound interest. Section 2.2 discusses how interest rates with different compounding periods are related. Section 2.3 shows how to calculate discounted or present values under compound interest. Long-term promissory notes are shown as an application.

Current Dates and Interest Rates — We have updated the dates and many of the interest rates used in the examples and exercises to reflect a more current perspective in finance at the time this text was revised.

New Spreadsheet and Financial Calculator Applications — Spreadsheets are introduced much earlier in the text and spreadsheet examples are now given in chapters, 2, 3, 5, 6, and 7. We have included many more examples of how to use financial calculators to perform calculations. Examples of how to use calculators are now given in chapters 2, 3, 5, 6, and 7.

	A	B	C	D	E
1	Years	6%	8%	10%	12%
2	5	13,488.50	14,898.46	16,453.09	18,166.97
3	10	18,193.97	22,196.40	27,070.41	33,003.87
4	15	24,540.94	33,069.21	44,539.20	59,958.02
5	20	33,102.04	49,268.03	73,280.74	108,925.54
6	25	44,649.70	73,401.76	120,569.45	197,884.66
7	30	60,225.75	109,357.30	198,373.99	359,496.41
8	35	81,235.51	162,925.50	326,386.50	653,095.95
9	40	109,574.54	242,733.86	537,006.63	1,186,477.25
10					
11	Principal=	$ 10,000			

New Exercises — Some new exercises have been added to the sections to reflect much of the new and updated content. The book has plenty of exercises to help students put the concepts learned in each section to practise. **Part A exercises** are designed to help students understand the major concepts. These exercises are fairly straightforward and should be attempted by all students. **Part B exercises** provide more difficult problems and include some advanced material. These exercises are a bit more challenging and are designed for students who are looking to obtain a deeper understanding of the material.

Exercise 2.2

Part A

1. Determine the annual effective rate (two decimals) equivalent to the following rates:
   a) $j_2 = 7\%$; b) $j_4 = 16\%$; c) $j_4 = 8\%$;
   d) $j_{365} = 12\%$; e) $j_{12} = 9\%$.

2. Determine the nominal rate (two decimals) equivalent to the given annual effective rate:
   a) $j = 6\%$ determine j_2;
   b) $j = 9\%$ determine j_4;
   c) $j = 10\%$ determine j_{12};
   d) $j = 17\%$ determine j_{365};
   e) $j = 4.5\%$ determine j_{52}.

3. Determine the nominal rate (two decimals)

9. Bank A has an annual effective interest rate of 10%. Bank B has a nominal interest rate of $9\frac{3}{4}\%$. What is the minimum frequency of compounding for bank B in order that the rate at bank B be at least as attractive as that at bank A?

Part B

1. Determine what is the current best and worst interest rate available on 5-year guaranteed investment certificates by checking three different financial institutions. Calculate the difference in compound interest earned using the best and the worst rate available if you buy a $2000, 5-year certificate.

Solved Examples —
Financial mathematics
is easier to explain and
understand through
the use of examples,
and, for this reason,
most sections include
a number of updated
solved problems.

EXAMPLE 1 Three months after borrowing money, a person pays back exactly $200. How much was borrowed if the $200 payment includes the principal and simple interest at 9%?

Solution We have $S = 200$, $r = 0.09$, and $t = \frac{3}{12}$. We can display this on a time diagram.

P? → discount at $r = 9\%$ for 3 months → $S = 200$

0 ... 3 months

$$P = S(1 + rt)^{-1} = \frac{S}{(1 + rt)} = \frac{\$200}{1 + 0.09(\frac{3}{12})} = \$195.60$$

CALCULATION TIP:

When calculating unknown yearly rates of interest, carry all decimal digits and then round off your final answer to the nearest hundredth of a percent.

**Calculation Tips
and Observation
Boxes —**
Calculation Tips
and Observation
Boxes have been
enhanced and
are easier to
identify within
the text.

OBSERVATION:

Since a perpetuity is an annuity with $n \rightarrow \infty$, we may develop formulas for the discounted value A of other simple perpetuities as in section 3.4:

$A = \frac{R}{i}(1 + i) = \frac{R}{i} + R$ for a simple perpetuity due

$A = \frac{R}{i}(1 + i)^{-k}$ for a simple perpetuity deferred k periods.

New Case Studies — Five new and up-to-date case studies have been added to the text.

CASE STUDY 3   *Scholarships*

A scholarship is set up that makes two payments a year. The first payment is $750 and the second payment, made exactly 6 months later, is $1500. This payment scheme continues forever. If money can be invested at $j_1 = 9\%$, how much money is needed to fund this scholarship six months before the first payment is to be made?

Other Key Features

Each chapter concludes with a set of review exercises. The authors emphasize that one of the most important aspects for the student is visualizing the problem with the help of a **timeline** diagram to assist the student in setting up the solution. A **glossary** at the end of the text contains definitions for key financial terminology. **Answers to all exercise problems** are located in back of the text. For easy reference, the inside front cover includes an index of formulas.

Payment Number	Monthly Payment	Interest Payment	Principal Payment	Outstanding Balance
				$1000.00
1	88.85	10.00	78.85	921.15
2	88.85	9.21	79.64	841.51
3	88.85	8.42	80.43	761.08
4	88.85	7.61	81.24	679.84
5	88.85	6.80	82.05	597.79
6	88.85	5.98	82.87	514.92
7	88.85	5.15	83.70	431.22
8	88.85	4.31	84.54	346.68
9	88.85	3.47	85.38	261.30
10	88.85	2.61	86.24	175.06
11	88.85	1.75	87.10	87.96
12	88.84	0.88	87.96	0
Totals	1066.20	66.20	1000.00	

Updated Visuals — Tables, graphs, and Web sites have all been updated in this edition of the text.

Summary and Review Exercises — Key points, concepts, formulas, and summaries are found at the end of each chapter in the form of a bulleted list that continues to serve as a review feature for students. These points are followed by a wealth of review exercises covering the chapter material.

Section 8.4	**Summary and Review Exercises**

Chapter 8 introduced the concept of risk to the evaluation of future payments.

- $E(X) = x_1 p(x_1) + x_2 p(x_2) + \cdots$ is the expected value of x.
- pS is the expected value of a payment, S, to be paid with probability, p.
- $pS(1 + i)^{-n}$ is the present value of pS.
- When the probability of default is $(1 - p)$ every period, the probability, p, and the present value factor, $(1 + i)^{-1}$, can be combined by finding a new rate of interest, j_1, such that:

$$1 + j_1 = \frac{1+i}{p}$$

A series of contingent payments can now be evaluated using basic compound interest theory at rate j_1.

SUMMARY OF NOTATIONS

Chapter 1

P = principal = present value of S = discounted value of S
I = simple interest
r = annual simple interest rate
S = accumulated value of P = future value of P
t = term of the investment in years
D = simple discount
d = annual simple discount rate

Summary of Notations — A new feature of the Sixth Edition is the **Summary of Notations**, which summarizes the notation and definitions from each chapter. The summary can be found at the back of the textbook.

Updated coverage and organization of topics — The Sixth Edition features new coverage of topics requested by the reviewers and other material deemed necessary by the author team. Some of the more specific improvements are outlined below.

Chapter	Important Changes / Additions
1. Simple Interest and Simple Discount	• Gives a clearer picture of how to determine the number of days between two dates. • Covers the topic of Treasury Bills with a few examples. • Offers examples of how to handle equations of value where there are two interest rates.
2. Compound Interest	• Provides a better explanation of fractional interest periods (section 2.4). • Introduces the "Rule of 70" (section 2.5) as a quick way to determine how long it will take an investment to double.
3. Simple Annuities	• Discusses the use of the "blocking technique" to solve annuity problems where the interest rate or payment amount changes over time. • Offers two new and up-to-date case studies on Car Loans and Car Insurance Premiums.
4. General and Other Annuities	• Adds new examples and exercises on how to calculate mortgage payments using payment schedules other than monthly. • Offers three new and up-to-date case studies that cover Lottery Winnings and Scholarships.
5. Repayment of Debts	• Shows an easier method to determine the outstanding balance of a loan when using the Sum-of-Digits method. • Adds some context to the Sinking-Fund method of repaying a debt.
6. Bonds	• Adds context to the section on bond premium and discount to aid in the understanding of bond amortization/accumulation tables.
7. Business Decisions, Capital Budgeting, and Depreciation	• Compares the net present value and internal rate of return methods for making business decisions. • Emphasizes the depreciation methods used in Canada (section 7.4).
8. Contingent Payments	• Offers more finance-related examples and exercises in the probability and contingent payment sections to give students a better idea of how probability is used in financial mathematics.

Superior Service

Service takes on a whole new meaning with McGraw-Hill Ryerson and *Mathematics of Finance*. More than just bringing you the textbook, we have consistently raised the bar in terms of innovation and educational research — specifically in financial mathematics and generally in education. These investments in learning and the education community have helped us to understand the needs of students and educators across the country, and allowed us to foster the growth of truly innovative, integrated learning.

Integrated Learning. Your Integrated Learning Sales Specialist is a McGraw-Hill Ryerson representative who has the experience, product knowledge, training, and support to help you assess and integrate any of our products, technology, and services into your course for optimum teaching and learning performance. Whether it is helping your students improve their grades or putting your entire course online, your *i*Learning Sales Specialist is there to help you do it. Contact your *i*Learning Sales Specialist today to learn how to maximize all of McGraw-Hill Ryerson's resources!

***i*Learning Services.** McGraw-Hill Ryerson offers a unique *i*Services package designed for Canadian faculty. Our mission is to equip providers of higher education with superior tools and resources required for excellence in teaching. For additional information, visit www.mcgrawhill.ca/highereducation/iservices.

Teaching, Learning & Technology Conference Series. The educational environment has changed tremendously in recent years, and McGraw-Hill Ryerson continues to be committed to helping you acquire the skills you need to succeed in this new milieu. Our innovative Teaching, Learning & Technology Conference Series brings faculty together from across Canada with 3M Teaching Excellence award winners to share teaching and learning best practices in a collaborative and stimulating environment. Pre-conference workshops on general topics, such as teaching large classes and technology integration, will also be offered. We will also work with you at your own institution to customize workshops that best suit the needs of your faculty.

Research Reports on Technology and Student Success in Higher Education. These landmark reports, undertaken in conjunction with academic and private sector advisory boards, are the result of research studies into the challenges professors face in helping students succeed and the opportunities that new technology presents to impact teaching and learning.

Teaching and Learning Package

We have developed supplements for both teaching and learning to accompany this text, available at the **Online Learning Centre** located at **www.mcgrawhill.ca/ olc/zima**. The Online Learning Centre is the text Web site providing many resources for students and instructors including the following:

For Instructors

- **Instructor's Manual.** Prepared by the authors, the Instructor's Manual includes full solutions to the problems and exercises in the text.
- **Question File.** Contains approximately 35 new multiple-choice questions for each chapter along with all exercise questions from the student text. This file is available in a Word document and can be used by instructors to build their own tests.

For Students

- **Student Solutions Manual.** Access to the Student Solutions Manual can be purchased on the Online Learning Centre or through your local bookstore. Instructors, please contact your local *i*Learning Sales Specialist for details on how you can package access to the online Student Solutions Manual with the text.

Course Management

Create a custom course Website with **PageOut**, free with every McGraw-Hill Ryerson textbook.

To learn more, contact your McGraw-Hill Ryerson publisher's representative or visit www.mhhe.com/solutions

Pageout. McGraw-Hill Ryerson's course management system, PageOut, is the easiest way to create a Web site for your *Mathematics of Finance* course. There is no need for HTML coding, graphic design, or a thick how-to book. Just fill in a series of boxes in plain English and click on one of our professional designs. In no time, your course is online!

www.blackboard.com

For the integrated instructor, we offer *Mathematics of Finance* content for complete online courses. Whatever your needs, you can customize the *Mathematics of Finance* Online Learning Centre content and author your own online course materials. It is entirely up to you. You can offer online discussion and message boards that will complement your office hours, and reduce the lines outside your door. Content cartridges are also available for course management systems, such as **WebCT** and **Blackboard**. Ask your *i*Learning Sales Specialist for details.

Acknowledgements

The Sixth Edition is a reflection of the contributions from many dedicated teachers and users of this text. For the Sixth Edition we are particularly grateful for the input of the following reviewers: Joe Campeau, Canadore College; Shari Corrigan, Camosun College; Helen Dakin, Mohawk College of Applied Arts & Technology; Doreen Der, Lakeland College; Tom Fraser, Niagara College; Bruno Fullone, George Brown College; Stephen Hunt, Canadore College; Donald Pelletier, York University; Betty Pratt, Seneca College; Frank Reynolds, University of Waterloo; Terry Smith, Loyalist College.

We also appreciate the work of reviewers and contributors for the Fifth Edition: Richard Brown, York University; Helen Dakin, Mohawk College of Applied Arts & Technology; Josephine Evans, Langara College; Barry Garner, University College of Fraser Valley; Diane Huysmans, Fanshawe College.

We also wish to thank the staff at McGraw-Hill Ryerson. This includes: Lynn Fisher, Publisher; Jennifer Bastarache, Developmental Editor; Margaret Henderson, Senior Supervising Editor; Joy Armitage Taylor, Marketing Manager, and others who we do not know personally, but made important contributions. Throughout the production process, Edie Franks did an excellent job of editing.

Petr Zima
Robert L. Brown
Steve Kopp

Simple Interest and Simple Discount

Learning Objectives

Money is invested or borrowed in thousands of transactions every day. When an investment is cashed in or when borrowed money is repaid, there is a fee that is collected or charged. This fee is called interest.

In this chapter, you will learn how to calculate interest using simple interest. Although most financial transactions use compound interest (introduced in chapter 2), simple interest is still used in many short-term transactions. Many of the concepts introduced in this chapter will be used throughout the rest of this book and are applicable to compound interest.

The chapter starts off with some fundamental relationships for calculating interest and how to determine the future, or accumulated, value of a single sum of money invested today. You will also learn how to calculate the time between dates. Section 1.2 introduces the concept of discounting a future sum of money to determine its value today. This "present value of a future cash flow" is one of the fundamental calculations underlying the mathematics of finance.

Section 1.3 introduces the concept of the time value of money. This section also introduces equations of value, which allow you to accumulate or discount a series of financial transactions and are used to solve many problems in financial mathematics. Section 1.4 introduces two methods that are used to pay off a loan through a series of partial payments. The chapter ends with section 1.5 in which a less common form of simple interest — simple discount — is introduced along with the concept of discounted loans.

Section 1.1 | ## Simple Interest

In any financial transaction, there are two parties involved: an investor, who is lending money to someone, and a debtor, who is borrowing money from the investor. The debtor must pay back the money originally borrowed, and also the fee charged for the use of the money, called **interest**. From the investor's point of view, interest is income from invested capital. The capital originally invested in an interest transaction is called **the principal**. The sum of the principal and interest due is called the **amount** or **accumulated value**. Any interest transaction can be described by the **rate of interest**, which is the ratio of the interest earned in one time unit on the principal.

In early times, the principal lent and the interest paid might be tangible goods (e.g., grain). Now, they are most commonly in the form of money. The practice of charging interest is as old as the earliest written records of humanity. Four thousand years ago, the laws of Babylon referred to interest payments on debts.

At **simple interest**, the interest is computed on the original principal during the whole time, or term of the loan, at the stated annual rate of interest.

We shall use the following notation:

P = the principal, or the present value of S, or the discounted value of S, or the proceeds.

I = simple interest.

S = the amount, or the accumulated value of P, or the future value of P, or the maturity value of P.

r = annual rate of simple interest.

t = time in years.

Simple interest is calculated by means of the formula

$$\boxed{I = Prt} \tag{1}$$

From the definition of the amount S we have

$$S = P + I$$

By substituting for $I = Prt$, we obtain S in terms of P, r, and t:

$$S = P + Prt$$

$$\boxed{S = P(1 + rt)} \tag{2}$$

The factor $(1 + rt)$ in formula **(2)** is called an **accumulation factor at a simple interest rate r** and the process of calculating S from P by formula **(2)** is called **accumulation at a simple interest rate r**.

We can display the relationship between S and P on a time diagram.

$$P \qquad I \text{ earned over } t \text{ years} \qquad S = P + I$$
$$0 \qquad \cdots \qquad t$$

Alternatively,

$$P \qquad \text{accumulated at } r \text{ over } t \text{ years} \qquad S = P(1 + rt)$$
$$0 \qquad \cdots \qquad t$$

The time t must be in years. When the time is given in months, then

$$t = \frac{\text{number of months}}{12}$$

When the time is given in days, there are two different varieties of simple interest in use:

1. **Exact interest**, where $t = \dfrac{\text{number of days}}{365}$

   i.e., the year is taken as 365 days (leap year or not).

2. **Ordinary interest**, where $t = \dfrac{\text{number of days}}{360}$

   i.e., the year is taken as 360 days.

CALCULATION TIP:

The general practice in Canada is to use exact interest, whereas the general practice in the United States and in international business transactions is to use ordinary interest (also referred to as the Banker's Rule). In this textbook, exact interest is used all the time unless specified otherwise. When the time is given by two dates we calculate the exact number of days between the two dates from a table listing the serial number of each day of the year (see the table on the inside back cover). The exact time is obtained as the difference between serial numbers of the given dates. In leap years (years divisible by 4) an extra day is added to February.

OBSERVATION:

When calculating the number of days between two dates, the most common practice in Canada is to count the starting date, but not the ending date. The reason is that financial institutions calculate interest each day on the closing balance of a loan or savings account. On the day a loan is taken out or a deposit is made, there is a non-zero balance at the end of that day, whereas on the day a loan is paid off or the deposit is fully withdrawn, there is a zero balance at the end of that day.

However, it is easier to assume the opposite when using the table on the inside back cover. That is, unless otherwise stated, you should assume that interest is not calculated on the starting date, but is calculated on the ending date. That way, in order to determine the number of days between two dates, all you have to do is subtract the two values you find from the table on the inside back cover. Example 1 will illustrate this.

EXAMPLE 1   A loan of $15 000 is taken out. If the interest rate on the loan is 7%, how much interest is due and what is the amount repaid if
   a) The loan is due in seven months;
   b) The loan was taken out on April 7 and is due in seven months?

Solution a   We have $P = 15\,000$, $r = 0.07$ and since the actual date the loan was taken out is not given, we use $t = \frac{7}{12}$.

Interest due, $I = Prt = \$15\,000 \times 0.07 \times \frac{7}{12} = \$612.50$

Amount repaid = Future or accumulated value,

$$S = P + I = \$15\,000 + \$612.50 = \$15\,612.50$$

Alternatively, we can obtain the above answer in one calculation:

$$S = P(1 + rt) = \$15\,000[1 + 0.07(\tfrac{7}{12})] = \$15\,612.50$$

Solution b Since a date is given when the loan was actually taken out, we must use days. Seven months after April 7 is November 7. Using the table on the inside back cover, we find that April 7 is day 97 and November 7 is day 311. The exact number of days between the two dates is $311 - 97 = 214$. Thus, $t = \frac{214}{365}$.

Interest due, $I = Prt = \$15\,000 \times 0.07 \times \frac{214}{365} = \$615.52$

Future value, $S = P + I = \$15\,000 + \$615.52 = \$15\,615.52$

Alternatively,

$$S = P(1 + rt) = \$15\,000[1 + 0.07(\tfrac{214}{365})] = \$15\,615.52$$

EXAMPLE 2 Determine the exact and ordinary simple interest on a 90-day loan of $8000 at $8\frac{1}{2}\%$.

Solution We have $P = 8000$, $r = 0.085$, numerator of $t = 90$ days.

Exact interest, $I = Prt = \$8000 \times 0.085 \times \frac{90}{365} = \$167.67$

Ordinary Interest, $I = Prt = \$8000 \times 0.085 \times \frac{90}{360} = \$170.00$

OBSERVATION:

Notice that ordinary interest is always greater than the exact interest and thus it brings increased revenue to the lender.

EXAMPLE 3   A loan shark made a loan of $100 to be repaid with $120 at the end of one month. What was the annual interest rate?

Solution   We have $P = 100$, $I = 20$, $t = \frac{1}{12}$, and

$$r = \frac{I}{Pt} = \frac{20}{100 \times \frac{1}{12}} = 240\%$$

EXAMPLE 4   How long will it take $3000 to earn $60 interest at 6%?

Solution   We have $P = 3000$, $I = 60$, $r = 0.06$, and

$$t = \frac{I}{Pr} = \frac{60}{3000 \times 0.06} = \frac{1}{3} = 4 \text{ months}$$

EXAMPLE 5   A deposit of $1500 is made into a fund on March 18. The fund earns simple interest at 5%. On August 5, the interest rate changes to 4.5%. How much is in the fund on October 23?

Solution   Using the table on the inside back cover, we determine the number of days between March 18 and August 5 = 217 − 77 = 140 and the number of days between August 5 and October 23 = 296 − 217 = 79.

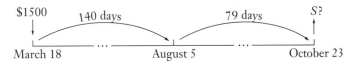

S = original deposit + interest for 140 days + interest for 79 days

$\quad = \$1500 + (\$1500 \times 0.05 \times \frac{140}{365}) + (\$1500 \times 0.045 \times \frac{79}{365})$

$\quad = \$(1500 + 28.77 + 14.61)$

$\quad = \$1543.38$

Demand Loans

On a **demand loan**, the lender may demand full or partial payment of the loan at any time and the borrower may repay all of the loan or any part at any time without notice and without interest penalty. Interest on demand loans is based on the unpaid balance and is usually payable monthly. The interest rate on demand loans is not usually fixed but fluctuates with market conditions.

EXAMPLE 6   Jessica borrowed $1500 from her credit union on a demand loan on August 16. Interest on the loan, calculated on the unpaid balance, is charged to her account on the 1st of each month. Jessica made a payment of $300 on

September 17, a payment of $500 on October 7, a payment of $400 on November 12 and repaid the balance on December 15. The rate of interest on the loan on August 16 was 12% per annum. The rate was changed to 11.5% on September 25 and 12.5% on November 20. Calculate the interest payments required and the total interest paid.

Solution

Interest period	# of days	Balance	Rate	Interest
Aug. 16–Sep. 1	16	$1500	12%	$1500(0.12)(\frac{16}{365}) = \underline{7.89}$ Sep. 1 interest $= \$ 7.89$
Sep. 1–Sep. 17	16	$1500	12%	$1500(0.12)(\frac{16}{365}) = 7.89$
Sep. 17–Sep. 25	8	$1200	12%	$1200(0.12)(\frac{8}{365}) = 3.16$
Sep. 25–Oct. 1	6	$1200	11.5%	$1200(0.115)(\frac{6}{365}) = \underline{2.27}$ Oct. 1 interest $= \$13.32$
Oct. 1–Oct. 7	6	$1200	11.5%	$1200(0.115)(\frac{6}{365}) = 2.27$
Oct. 7–Nov. 1	25	$ 700	11.5%	$700(0.115)(\frac{25}{365}) = \underline{5.51}$ Nov. 1 interest $= \$ 7.78$
Nov. 1–Nov. 12	11	$ 700	11.5%	$700(0.115)(\frac{11}{365}) = 2.43$
Nov. 12–Nov. 20	8	$ 300	11.5%	$300(0.115)(\frac{8}{365}) = 0.76$
Nov. 20–Dec. 1	11	$ 300	12.5%	$300(0.125)(\frac{11}{365}) = \underline{1.13}$ Dec. 1 interest $= \$ 4.32$
Dec. 1–Dec. 15	14	$ 300	12.5%	$300(0.125)(\frac{14}{365}) = \underline{1.44}$ Dec. 15 interest $= \$ 1.44$

Total interest paid $= \$(7.89 + 13.32 + 7.78 + 4.32 + 1.44) = \$34.75$

Invoice Cash Discounts

To encourage prompt payments of invoices many manufacturers and whole-salers offer cash discounts for payments in advance of the final due date. The following typical credit terms may be printed on sales invoices:

2/10, *n*/30 — Goods billed on this basis are subject to a cash discount of 2% if paid within ten days. Otherwise, the full amount must be paid not later than thirty days from the date of the invoice.

A merchant may consider borrowing the money to pay the invoice in time to receive the cash discount. Assuming that the loan would be repaid on the day the invoice is due, the interest the merchant should be willing to pay on the loan should not exceed the cash discount.

EXAMPLE 7   A merchant receives an invoice for a motor boat for $20 000 with terms 4/30, n/100. What is the highest simple interest rate at which he can afford to borrow money in order to take advantage of the discount?

Solution   Suppose the merchant will take advantage of the cash discount of 4% of $20 000 = $800 by paying the bill within 30 days from the date of invoice. He needs to borrow $20 000 = $800 = $19 200. He would borrow this money on day 30 and repay it on day 100 (the day the original invoice is due) resulting in a 70-day loan. The interest he should be willing to pay on borrowed money should not exceed the cash discount $800.

We have $P = 19\,200$, $I = 800$, $t = \frac{70}{365}$, and we calculate

$$r = \frac{I}{Pt} = \frac{800}{19\,200 \times \frac{70}{365}} = 21.73\%$$

The highest simple interest rate at which the merchant can afford to borrow money is 21.73%. This is a break-even rate. If he can borrow money, say at a rate of 15%, he should do so. He would borrow $19 200 for 70 days at 15%. Maturity value of the loan is $19\,200\,[1 + (0.15)(\frac{70}{365})] = \$19\,752.33$. Thus his savings would be $20 000 – $19 752.33 = $247.67.

Exercise 1.1

1. Determine the maturity value of
   a) a $2500 loan for 18 months at 12% simple interest,
   b) a $1200 loan for 120 days at 8.5% ordinary simple interest, and
   c) a $10 000 loan for 64 days at 7% exact simple interest.

2. At what rate of simple interest will
   a) $1000 accumulate to $1420 in $2\frac{1}{2}$ years,
   b) money double itself in 7 years, and
   c) $500 accumulate $10 interest in 2 months?

3. How many days will it take $1000 to accumulate to at least $1200 at 5.5% simple interest?

4. Determine the ordinary and exact simple interest on $5000 for 90 days at $10\frac{1}{2}$%.

5. A student lends his friend $10 for one month. At the end of the month he asks for repayment of the $10 plus purchase of a chocolate bar worth 50¢. What simple interest rate is implied?

6. What principal will accumulate to $5100 in 6 months if the simple interest rate is 9%?

7. What principal will accumulate to $580 in 120 days at 18% simple interest?

8. Determine the accumulated value of $1000 over 65 days at $6\frac{1}{2}$% using both ordinary and exact simple interest.

9. A man borrows $1000 on February 16 at 7.25% simple interest. What amount must he repay in 7 months?

10. A sum of $2000 is invested from May 18, 2006, to April 8, 2007, at 4.5% simple interest. Determine the amount of interest earned.

11. On May 13, 2006, Jacob invested $4000. On February 1, 2007, he intends to pay Fred $4300 for a used car. The bank assured Jacob that his investment would be adequate to cover the purchase. Determine the minimum simple interest rate that Jacob's money must be earning.

12. On January 1, Mustafa borrows $1000 on a demand loan from his bank. Interest is paid at the end of each quarter (March 31, June 30, September 30, December 31) and at the time of the last payment. Interest is calculated at the

rate of 12% on the balance of the loan outstanding. Mustafa repaid the loan with the following payments:

March 1	$ 100
April 17	$ 300
July 12	$ 200
August 20	$ 100
October 18	$ 300
	$1000

Calculate the interest payments required and the total interest paid.

13. On February 3, a company borrowed $50 000 on a demand loan from a bank. Interest on the loan is charged to the company's current account on the 11th of each month. The company repaid the loan with the following payments:

February 20	$10 000
March 20	$10 000
April 20	$15 000
May 20	$15 000
	$50 000

The rate of interest on the loan was originally 6%. The rate was changed to 7% on April 1, and to 6.5% on May 1. Calculate the interest payments required and the total interest paid.

14. A cash discount of 2% is given if a bill is paid 20 days in advance of its due date. At what interest rate could you afford to borrow money to take advantage of this discount?

15. A merchant receives an invoice for $2000 with terms 2/20, n/60. What is the highest simple interest rate at which he can afford to borrow money in order to take advantage of the discount?

16. The ABC general store receives an invoice for goods totalling $500. The terms were 3/10, n/30. If the store were to borrow the money to pay the bill in 10 days, what is the highest interest rate at which the store could afford to borrow?

17. I.C.U. Optical receives an invoice for $2500 with terms 2/5, n/50.
   a) If the company is to take advantage of the discount, what is the highest simple interest rate at which it can afford to borrow money?
   b) If money can be borrowed at 10% simple interest, how much does I.C.U. Optical actually save by using the cash discount?

Section 1.2 **Discounted Value at Simple Interest**

From formula **(2)** we can express P in terms of S, r, and t and obtain

$$P = \frac{S}{1+rt} = S(1+rt)^{-1} \tag{3}$$

> The factor $(1+rt)^{-1}$ in formula **(3)** is called a **discount factor at a simple interest rate r** and the process of calculating P from S is called **discounting at a simple interest rate r**, or simple discount at an interest rate r.

We can display the relationship between P and S on a time diagram.

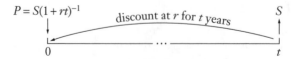

When we calculate P from S, we call P the present value of S or the discounted value of S. The difference $D = S - P$ is called the simple discount on S at an interest rate.

For a given interest rate r, the difference $S - P$ has two interpretations.

1. The interest I on P which when added to P gives S.

2. The discount D on S which when subtracted from S gives P.

EXAMPLE 1 Three months after borrowing money, a person pays back exactly $200. How much was borrowed if the $200 payment includes the principal and simple interest at 9%?

Solution We have $S = 200$, $r = 0.09$, and $t = \frac{3}{12}$. We can display this on a time diagram.

$$P = S(1 + rt)^{-1} = \frac{S}{(1 + rt)} = \frac{\$200}{1 + 0.09(\frac{3}{12})} = \$195.60$$

EXAMPLE 2 Jennifer wishes to have $1000 in eight months time. If she can earn 6%, how much does she need to invest on September 15? What is the simple discount?

Solution Eight months after September 15 (day 258) is May 15 (day 135). The number of days between these two dates $= (365 - 258) + 135 = 242$.

We have $S = 1000$, $r = 0.06$, $t = \frac{242}{365}$

$$P = S(1 + rt)^{-1} = \frac{S}{(1 + rt)} = \frac{\$1000}{1 + 0.06(\frac{242}{365})} = \$961.74$$

The simple discount is

$$D = S - P = \$(1000 - 961.74) = \$38.26$$

Promissory Notes

A **promissory note** is a written promise by a debtor, called the **maker** of the note, to pay to, or to the order of, the creditor, called the **payee** of the note, a sum of money, with or without interest, on a specified date.

The following is an example of an interest-bearing note.

$2000.00   Toronto, September 1, 2006

Sixty days after date, I promise to pay to the order of Mr. A

Two thousand and $\frac{00}{100}$ dollars

for value received with interest at 8% per annum.

(Signed) Mr. B

The **face value** of the note is $2000. The **term** of the note is 60 days. The **due date** is 60 days after September 1, 2006, that is October 31, 2006.

In Canada, *three days of grace** are added to the 60 days to arrive at the **legal due date**, or the **"maturity date,"** that is November 3, 2006. By a **maturity value** of a note we shall understand the value of the note at the maturity date. In our example, the maturity value of the note is the accumulated value of $2000 for 63 days at 8%, i.e., $2000[1 + (0.08)($\frac{63}{365}$)] = $2027.62.

If Mr. B chooses to pay on October 31, he will pay interest for 60 days, not 63 days. However, no legal action can be taken against him until the expiry of the three days of grace. Thus, Mr. B would be within his legal rights to repay as late as November 3, and in that case he would pay interest for 63 days.

A promissory note is similar to a short-term bank loan, but it differs in two important ways:

1. The lender does not have to be a financial institution.

2. A promissory note may be sold one or several times before its maturity. To determine the price a buyer will pay for the note, he/she will take the amount to be received in the future (the maturity value), and discount it to the date of the sale at a rate of interest the buyer wishes to earn on his/her investment. The resulting value is called the proceeds and is paid to the seller. The proceeds are determined by formula **(3)**.

The procedure for discounting of promissory notes can be summarized in 2 steps:

Step 1   Calculate the maturity value, S, of the note.

   The maturity value of a noninterest-bearing note is the face value of the note. The maturity value of an interest-bearing note is the accumulated value of the face value of the note at the maturity date.

Step 2   Calculate the proceeds, P, by discounting the maturity value, S, at a specified simple interest rate from the maturity date back to the date of sale.

Three days of grace. In Canada, "three days of grace" are allowed for the payment of a promissory note. This means that the payment becomes due on the third day after the due date of the note.

If interest is being charged, the three days of grace must be added to the time stated in the note. If the third day of grace falls on a holiday, payment will become due the next day that is itself not a holiday.

If the time is stated in months, these must be calendar months and not months of 30 days. For example, 2 months after July 5 is September 5. Thus the legal due date is September 8, and the number of days to be used in calculating the interest (if any) will be 65 days.

In the month in which the payment falls due, there may be no corresponding date to that from which the time is computed. In such a case, the last day of the month is taken as the corresponding date. For example, two months after December 31 is February 28 (or February 29 in leap years) and March 3 would be the legal due date.

EXAMPLE 3   The promissory note described in the beginning of this section is sold by Mr. A on October 1, 2006 to a bank that discounts notes at a $9\frac{1}{2}\%$ simple interest rate.

    a) How much money would Mr. A receive for the note?

    b) What rate of interest will the bank realize on its investment, if it holds the note till maturity?

    c) What rate of interest will Mr. A realize on his investment, when he sells the note on October 1, 2006?

Solution a   We arrange the dated values on a time diagram below.

Maturity value of the note is $S = \$2000[1 + (0.08)(\frac{63}{365})] = \$2027.62$.

Proceeds on October 1, 2006, are $P = \$2027.62[1 + (0.095)(\frac{33}{365})]^{-1} = \$2010.35$. Thus Mr. A would receive \$2010.35 for the note.

Solution b   The bank will realize a profit of $\$2027.62 - \$2010.35 = \$17.27$ for 33 days. Thus we have $P = \$2010.35$, $I = \$17.27$, and $t = \frac{33}{365}$ and calculate

$$r = \frac{I}{Pt} = \frac{\$17.27}{\$2010.35 \times \frac{33}{365}} = 9.50\%$$

Solution c   Mr. A will realize a profit of $\$2010.35 - \$2000 = \$10.35$ on his investment of \$2000 for the 30 days he held the note. The rate of interest Mr. A will realize is

$$r = \frac{I}{Pt} = \frac{10.35}{2000 \times \frac{30}{365}} = 6.30\%$$

EXAMPLE 4   On April 21, a retailer buys goods amounting to \$5000. If he pays cash he will get a 4% cash discount. To take advantage of this cash discount, he signs a 90-day noninterest-bearing note at his bank that discounts notes at an interest rate of 9%. What should be the face value of this note to give him the exact amount needed to pay cash for the goods?

Solution   The cash discount 4% of \$5000 is \$200. The retailer needs \$4800 in cash. He will sign a noninterest-bearing note with maturity value S calculated by formula **(2)**, given $P = 4800$, $r = 9\%$, and $t = \frac{93}{365}$. Thus

$$S = P(1 + rt) = \$4800[1 + (0.09)(\tfrac{93}{365})] = \$4910.07$$

The face value of the noninterest-bearing note should be $4910.07.

Note: The retailer could also sign a 90-day 9% interest-bearing note with a face value of $4800 and a maturity value of $4910.07 in 93 days. He would receive cash of $4800 immediately as the proceeds $P = \$4910.07[1 + (0.09)(\frac{93}{365})]^{-1} = \$4800$.

Treasury Bills (or T-bills)

Treasury bills are popular short-term and low-risk securities issued by the Federal Government of Canada every other Tuesday with maturities of 13, 26, or 52 weeks (91, 182, or 364 days). They are basically promissory notes issued by the government to meet their short-term financing needs.

Treasury bills are issued in denominations, or face values, of $1000, $5000, $25 000, $100 000 and $1 000 000. The face value of a T-bill is the amount the government guarantees it will pay on the maturity date. There is no interest rate stated on a T-bill. Instead, to determine the purchase price of a T-bill, you need to discount the face value to the date of sale at an interest rate that is determined by market conditions. Since all T-bills have a term of less than one year, you would use simple interest formulas.

EXAMPLE 5   A 182-day T-bill with a face value of $25 000 is purchased by an investor who wishes to yield 3.80%. What price is paid?

Solution   We have $S = 25\,000$, $r = 0.038$, $t = \frac{182}{365}$.

$$P = S[1 + rt]^{-1} = \$25\,000\,[1 + 0.038(\tfrac{182}{365})]^{-1}$$
$$= \$24\,535.11$$

The investor will pay $24 535.11 for the T-bill and receive $25 000 in 182 days' time.

EXAMPLE 6   A 91-day T-bill with a face value of $100 000 is purchased for $97 250. What rate of interest is assumed?

Solution   We have $S = 100\,000$, $P = 97\,250$, $t = \frac{91}{365}$ and we calculate

$$r = \frac{I}{Pt} = \frac{2750}{97\,250(\frac{91}{365})} = 0.113421283 = 11.34\%$$

Exercise 1.2

For each promissory note in problems 1 to 4 determine the maturity date, maturity value, discount period, and the proceeds:

No.	Date of Note	Face Value	Interest Rate on Note	Term	Date of Discount	Interest Rate for Discounting
1.	Nov. 3	$3000	None	3 months	Dec. 1	10.25%
2.	Sept. 1	$1200	5.5%	60 days	Oct. 7	4.75%
3.	Dec. 14	$ 500	7.0%	192 days	Dec. 24	7.00%
4.	Feb. 4	$4000	None	2 months	Mar. 1	8.50%

5. A 90-day note promises to pay Ms. Chiu $2000 plus simple interest at 13%. After 51 days it is sold to a bank that discounts notes at a 12% simple interest rate.
   a) How much money does Ms. Chiu receive?
   b) What rate of interest does Ms. Chiu realize on her investment?
   c) What rate of interest will the bank realize if the note is paid in full in exactly 90 days?

6. An investor lends $5000 and receives a promissory note promising repayment of the loan in 90 days with 8.5% simple interest. This note is immediately sold to a bank that charges 8% simple interest. How much does the bank pay for the note? What is the investor's profit? What is the bank's profit on this investment when the note matures?

7. A 90-day note for $800 bears interest at 6% and is sold 60 days before maturity to a bank that uses a 8% simple interest rate. What are the proceeds?

8. Jacob owes Kieran $1000. Kieran agrees to accept as payment a noninterest-bearing note for 90 days that can be discounted immediately at a local bank that charges a simple interest rate of 10%. What should be the face value of the note so that Kieran will receive $1000 as proceeds?

9. Justin has a note for $5000 dated October 17, 2006. The note is due in 120 days with interest at 7.5%. If Justin discounts the note on January 15, 2007, at a bank charging a simple interest rate of 7%, what will be the proceeds?

10. A merchant buys goods worth $2000 and signs a 90-day noninterest-bearing promissory note. Determine the proceeds if the supplier sells the note to a bank that uses a 13% simple interest rate. How much profit did the supplier make if the goods cost $1500?

11. On August 16 a retailer buys goods worth $2000. If he pays cash he will get a 3% cash discount. To take advantage of this he signs a 60-day noninterest-bearing note at a bank that discounts notes at a 6% simple interest rate. What should be the face value of this note to give the retailer the exact amount needed to pay cash for the goods?

12. Monique has a note for $1500 dated June 8, 2006. The note is due in 120 days with interest at 6.5%.
   a) If Monique discounts the note on August 1, 2006, at a bank charging an interest rate of 8.5%, what will the proceeds be?
   b) What rate of interest will Monique realize on her investment?
   c) What rate of interest will the bank realize if the note is paid off in full in exactly 120 days?

13. Yufeng needs to have $3500 in 10 months time. If she can earn 6% simple interest,
   a) how much does she need to invest today?
   b) how much does she need to invest today if the $3500 is needed on July 31? What is the simple discount?

14. An investor bought a 91-day treasury bill to yield 3.45%.
   a) What was the price paid by the investor if the face value was $5000?
   b) The investor sold the T-bill 40 days later to another investor who wishes to yield 3.10%. What price did the T-bill sell for?
   c) What rate of return did the original investor earn on his investment?

15. An investment dealer bought a $25 000 364-day treasury bill for $23 892.06.
   a) What yield rate is implied?
   b) The treasury bill was purchased on September 7, 2006. The dealer sold it to another investor on January 25, 2007 for $24 102.25. What yield rate did the other investor wish to earn? What rate of return did the dealer end up earning?

Equations of Value

All financial decisions must take into account the basic idea that **money has time value**. In other words, receiving $100 today is not the same as receiving $100 one year ago, nor receiving $100 one year from now if there is a positive interest rate. In a financial transaction involving money due on different dates, every sum of money should have an attached date, the date on which it falls due. That is, the mathematics of finance deals with **dated values**. This is one of the most important facts in the mathematics of finance.

Illustration: At a simple interest rate of 8%, $100 due in 1 year is considered to be equivalent to $108 in 2 years since $100 would accumulate to $108 in 1 year. In the same way

$$\$100(1 + 0.08)^{-1} = \$92.59$$

would be considered an equivalent sum today.

Another way to look at this is to suppose you were offered $92.59 today, or $100 one year from now, or $108 two years from now. Which one would you choose? Most people would probably take the $92.59 today because it is money in their hands. However, from a financial point of view, all three values are the same, or are equivalent, since you could take the $92.59 and invest it for one year at 8%, after which you would have $100. This $100 could then be invested for one more year at 8% after which it would have accumulated to $108. Note that the three dated values are not equivalent at some other rate of interest.

In general, we compare dated values by the following **definition of equivalence:**

> X due on a given date is equivalent at a given simple interest rate r to Y due t years later if
>
> $$Y = X(1 + rt) \quad \text{or} \quad X = \frac{Y}{1 + rt} = Y(1 + rt)^{-1}$$

The following time diagram illustrates dated values equivalent to a given dated value X.

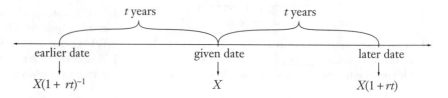

Based on the time diagram above we can state the following simple rules:

> **1.** When we move money forward in time, we accumulate, i.e., multiply the sum by an accumulation factor $(1 + rt)$.
>
> **2.** When we move money backward in time, we discount, i.e., multiply the sum by a discount factor $(1 + rt)^{-1}$.

EXAMPLE 1   A debt of \$1000 is due at the end of 9 months. Determine an equivalent debt at a simple interest rate of 9% at the end of 4 months and at the end of 1 year.

Solution   Let us arrange the data on a time diagram below.

According to the definition of equivalence

$$X = 1000[1 + rt]^{-1} = \$1000[1 + (0.09)(\tfrac{5}{12})]^{-1} = \$963.86$$
$$Y = 1000[1 + rt] = \$1000[1 + (0.09)(\tfrac{3}{12})] = \$1022.50$$

The sum of a set of dated values, due on different dates, has no meaning. We must take into account the time value of money, which means we have to replace all the dated values by **equivalent dated values**, due on the same date. The sum of the equivalent values is called the **dated value of the set**.

EXAMPLE 2   A person owes \$300 due in 3 months and \$500 due in 8 months. The lender agrees to allow the person to pay off these two debts with a single payment. What single payment a) now; b) in 6 months; c) in 1 year, will liquidate these obligations if money is worth 8%?

Solution

We calculate equivalent dated values of both obligations at the three different times and arrange them in the table below.

Obligations	Now	In 6 Months	In 1 Year
First	$300[1 + (0.08)(\tfrac{3}{12})]^{-1} = 294.12$	$300[1 + (0.08)(\tfrac{3}{12})] = 306.00$	$300[1 + (0.08)(\tfrac{9}{12})] = 318.00$
Second	$500[1 + (0.08)(\tfrac{8}{12})]^{-1} = 474.68$	$500[1 + (0.08)(\tfrac{2}{12})]^{-1} = 493.42$	$500[1 + (0.08)(\tfrac{4}{12})] = 513.33$
Sum	$X_1 = 768.80$	$X_2 = 799.42$	$X_3 = 831.33$

Equation of Value

One of the most important problems in the mathematics of finance is the replacing of a given set of payments by an equivalent set.

We say that two sets of payments are equivalent at a given simple interest rate if the dated values of the sets, on any common date, are equal. An equation stating that the dated values, on a common date, of two sets of payments are equal is called an **equation of value** or an **equation of equivalence**. The date used is called the **focal date** or the **comparison date** or the **valuation date**.

A very effective way to solve many problems in mathematics of finance is to use the equation of value. The procedure is carried out in the following steps:

Step 1 Make a good time diagram showing the dated values of original debts on one side of the time line and the dated values of replacement payments on the other side. A good time diagram is of great help in the analysis and solution of problems.

Step 2 Select a focal date and bring all the dated values to the focal date using the specified interest rate.

Step 3 Set up an equation of value at the focal date.
  dated value of payments = dated value of debts

Step 4 Solve the equation of value using methods of algebra.

EXAMPLE 3 Debts of $500 due 20 days ago and $400 due in 50 days are to be settled by a payment of $600 now and a final payment 90 days from now. Determine the value of the final payment at a simple interest rate of 11% with a focal date at the present.

Solution We arrange the dated values on a time diagram.

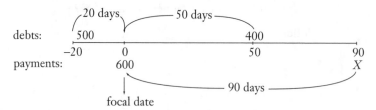

Equation of value at the present time:

dated value of payments = dated value of debts

$$X[1 + (0.11)(\tfrac{90}{365})]^{-1} + 600 = 500[1 + (0.11)(\tfrac{20}{365})] + 400[1 + (0.11)(\tfrac{50}{365})]^{-1}$$
$$0.973592958X + 600 = 503.01 + 394.06$$
$$0.973592958X = 297.07$$
$$X \doteq 305.13$$

The final payment to be made in 90 days is $305.13.

EXAMPLE 4 Dated payments X, Y, and Z are as follows: X is \$8557.92 on January 12, 2007; Y is \$8739.86 on April 19, 2007; and Z is \$9159.37 on November 24, 2007. If the annual rate of simple interest is 8%, show that X is equivalent to Y and Y is equivalent to Z but that X is not equivalent to Z.

Solution We arrange the dated values X, Y, and Z on a time diagram, listing for each date the day number from the table on the inside back cover.

$X = \$8557.92$	$Y = \$8739.86$	$Z = \$9159.37$
Jan. 12	Apr. 19	Nov. 24
2007	2007	2007
(12)	(109)	(328)

97 days   219 days

At a simple rate of interest $r = 0.08$

X is equivalent to Y since $Y = \$8557.92[1 + (0.08)(\frac{97}{365})] = \$8739.86$

and Y is equivalent to Z since $Z = \$8739.86[1 + (0.08)(\frac{219}{365})] = \$9159.37$

but X **is not** equivalent to Z since $Z \neq \$8557.92[1 + (0.08)(\frac{97+219}{365})] = \$9150.64$

In mathematics, an equivalence relationship must satisfy the so-called **property of transitivity,** that is, if X is equivalent to Y and Y is equivalent to Z, then X is equivalent to Z.

OBSERVATION:

> Example 4 illustrates that the definition of equivalence of dated values at simple interest r does not satisfy the property of transitivity. As a result, the solutions to the problems of equations of value at simple interest do depend on the selection of the focal date. The following Example 5 illustrates that in problems involving equations of value at simple interest the answer will vary slightly with the location of the focal date. It is therefore important that the parties involved in the financial transaction agree on the location of the focal date.

EXAMPLE 5 A person borrows \$1000 at 6% simple interest. She is to repay the debt with 3 equal payments, the first at the end of 3 months, the second at the end of 6 months, and the third at the end of 9 months. Determine the size of the payments. Put the focal date a) at the present time; b) at the end of 9 months.

Solution a Arrange all the dated values on a time diagram.

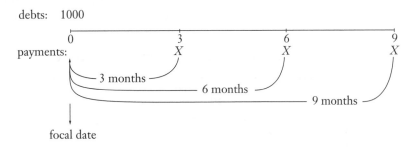

Equation of value at the present time:

$$X[1 + (0.06)(\tfrac{3}{12})]^{-1} + X[1 + (0.06)(\tfrac{6}{12})]^{-1} + X[1 + (0.06)(\tfrac{9}{12})]^{-1} = 1000.00$$
$$0.98522167X + 0.97087379X + 0.95693780X = 1000.00$$
$$2.91303326X = 1000.00$$
$$X \doteq 343.28$$

Solution b   Equation of value at the end of 9 months:

$$X[1 + (0.06)(\tfrac{6}{12})] + X[1 + (0.06)(\tfrac{3}{12})] + X = 1000[1 + (0.06)(\tfrac{9}{12})]$$
$$1.03X + 1.015X + X = 1045.00$$
$$3.045X = 1045.00$$
$$X = 343.19$$

Notice the slight difference in the answer for the different focal dates.

EXAMPLE 6   A woman owes \$3000 in 4 months with interest at 8% and another \$4000 is due in 10 months with interest at 7%. These two debts are to be replaced with a single payment due in 8 months. Determine the value of the single payment if money is worth 6.5%, using the end of 8 months as the focal date.

Solution   Since the two original debts are due with interest, we first must determine the maturity value of each of them.

$$\text{First debt:}\quad S_1 = P_1[1 + r_1 t_1] = 3000[1 + 0.08(\tfrac{4}{12})] = 3080.00$$
$$\text{Second debt:}\quad S_2 = P_2[1 + r_2 t_2] = 4000[1 + 0.07(\tfrac{10}{12})] = 4233.33$$

Now arrange all the dated values on a time diagram.

Equation of value at end of 8 months, using $r_3 = 6.5\%$:

$$X = 3080.00[1 + 0.065(\tfrac{4}{12})] + 4233.33[1 + 0.065(\tfrac{2}{12})]^{-1}$$
$$= 3146.7333 \qquad\qquad + 4187.9604$$
$$\doteq 7334.69$$

The size of the single payment needed in 8 months is \$7334.69.

Exercise 1.3

For problems 1 to 6 make use of the following table. In each case determine the equivalent payments for each of the debts.

No.	Debts	Equivalent Payments	Focal Date	Rate
1.	$1200 due in 80 days	In full	Today	12%
2.	$100 due in 6 months, $150 due in 1 year	In full	Today	6%
3.	$200 due in 3 months, $800 due in 9 months	In full	6 months hence	8%
4.	$600 due 2 months ago, $400 due in 3 months	$500 today and the balance in 6 months	Today	13%
5.	$800 due today	Two equal payments due in 4 and 7 months	7 months hence	5%
6.	$2000 due 300 days ago	Three equal payments due today, in 60 days and in 120 days	Today	11%

7. Thérèse owes $500 due in 4 months and $700 due in 9 months. If money is worth 7%, what single payment a) now; b) in 6 months; c) in 1 year, will liquidate these obligations?

8. Andrew owes Nicola $500 in 3 months and $200 in 6 months both due with interest at 6%. If Nicola accepts $300 now, how much will Andrew be required to repay at the end of 1 year, provided they agree to use an interest rate of 8% and a focal date at the end of 1 year?

9. A person borrows $1000 to be repaid with two equal instalments, one in six months, the other at the end of 1 year. What will be the size of these payments if the interest rate is 8% and the focal date is 1 year hence? What if the focal date is today?

10. Frank borrows $5000 on January 8, 2007. He pays $2000 on April 30, 2007, and $2000 on August 31, 2007. The last payment is to be on January 2, 2008. If interest is at 6% and the focal date is January 2, 2008, determine the size of the final payment.

11. Mrs. Adams has two options available in repaying a loan. She can pay $200 at the end of 5 months and $300 at the end of 10 months, or she can pay $X at the end of 3 months and $2X at the end of 6 months. Determine X if interest is at 12% and the focal date is 6 months hence and the options are equivalent. What is the answer if the focal date is 3 months hence and the options are equivalent?

12. Mr. A will pay Mr. B $2000 at the end of 5 years and $8000 at the end of 10 years if Mr. B will give him $3000 today plus an additional sum of money $X at the end of 2 years. Determine X if interest is at 8% and the comparison date is today. Determine X if the comparison date is 2 years hence (i.e., at the time $X is paid).

13. Mr. Malczyk borrows $2000 at 14%. He is to repay the debt with 4 equal payments, one at the end of each 3-month period for 1 year. Determine the size of the payments given a focal date a) at the present time; b) at the end of 1 year.

14. A person borrows $800 at 10%. He agrees to pay off the debt with payments of size $X, $2X, and $4X in 3 months, 6 months, and 9 months respectively. Determine X using all four transaction dates as possible focal dates.

Section 1.4   Partial Payments

Financial obligations are sometimes liquidated by a series of partial payments during the term of obligation. Then it is necessary to determine the balance due on the final due date. There are two common ways to allow interest credit on short-term transactions.

Method 1 (also known as **Declining Balance Method**) This is the method most commonly used in practice. The interest on the unpaid balance of the debt is computed each time a partial payment is made. If the payment is greater than the interest due, the difference is used to reduce the debt. If the payment is less than the interest due, it is held without interest until other partial payments are made whose sum exceeds the interest due at the time of the last of these partial payments. (This point is illustrated in Example 3.) The balance due on the final date is the outstanding balance after the last partial payment carried to the final due date.

EXAMPLE 1   On February 4, David borrowed $3000 at a simple interest rate of 11%. He paid $1000 on April 21, $600 on May 12, and $700 on June 11. What is the balance due on August 15 using the declining balance method?

Solution   We arrange all dated values on a time diagram.

	76 days	21 days	30 days	65 days
debts:	3000			
	Feb. 4	April 21	May 12	June 11	Aug. 15
payments:		1000	600	700	X

Instead of having one comparison date we have 4 comparison dates. Each time a payment is made, the preceding balance is accumulated at a simple interest rate of 11% to this point and a new balance is obtained.

The calculations are given below.

Original debt	$3000.00
Interest for 76 days	68.71
Amount due on April 21	3068.71
First partial payment	1000.00
Balance due on April 21	2068.71
Interest for 21 days	13.09
Amount due on May 12	2081.80
Second partial payment	600.00
Balance due on May 12	1481.80
Interest for 30 days	13.40
Amount due on June 11	1495.20
Third partial payment	700.00
Balance due on June 11	795.20
Interest for 65 days	15.58
Balance due on August 15	$ 810.78

The above calculations also may be carried out in a shorter form, as shown below.

Balance due on April 21	$3000[1 + (0.11)(\frac{76}{365})] - $1000 = $2068.71
Balance due on May 12	$2068.71[1 + (0.11)(\frac{21}{365})] - $600 = $1481.80
Balance due on June 11	$1481.80[1 + (0.11)(\frac{30}{365})] - $700 = $795.20
Balance due on August 15	$795.20[1 + (0.11)(\frac{65}{365})] = $810.78

Method 2 (also known as **Merchant's Rule**) The entire debt and each partial payment earn interest to the final settlement date. The balance due on the final due date is simply the difference between the accumulated value of the debt and the accumulated value of the partial payments.

EXAMPLE 2   Solve Example 1 using the Merchant's Rule.

Solution   We arrange all dated values on a time diagram.

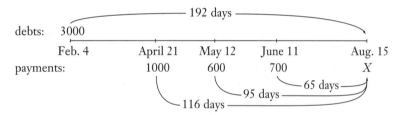

Simple interest is computed at 11% on the original debt of $3000 for 192 days, on the first partial payment of $1000 for 116 days, on the second partial payment of $600 for 95 days, and on the third partial payment of $700 for 65 days.

Calculations are given below:

Original debt	$3000.00	1st partial payment	$1000.00
Interest for 192 days	173.59	Interest for 116 days	34.96
Accumulated value	$3173.59	2nd partial payment	600.00
of the debt		Interest for 95 days	17.18
		3rd partial payment	700.00
		Interest for 65 days	13.71
		Accumulated value	$2365.85
		of the partial	
		payments	

Balance due on August 15: $(3173.59 - 2365.85) = $807.74

Alternative Solution   We can write an equation of value with August 15 as the focal date.

On August 15: dated value of payments = dated value of debts

$$X + 1000[1 + (0.11)(\tfrac{116}{365})] + 600[1 + (0.11)(\tfrac{95}{365})] + 700[1 + (0.11)(\tfrac{65}{365})] = 3000[1 + (0.11)(\tfrac{192}{365})]$$

$$X + 1034.96 + 617.18 + 713.71 \doteq 3173.59$$

$$X = 807.74$$

Note: The methods result in two different concluding payments. It is important that the two parties to a business transaction agree on the method to be used. Common business practice is the Declining Balance Method.

EXAMPLE 3 Suzanne borrowed $10 000 at 8%. She pays $1000 in 2 months, $150 in 5 months, and $1500 in 7 months. What is the balance due in 11 months under the a) Declining Balance Method, b) Merchant's Rule?

Solution a We arrange all dated values on a time diagram.

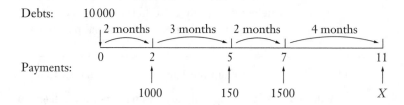

Balance due in two months = $10 000[1 + 0.08($\frac{2}{12}$)] − $1000 = $9133.33

Interest due in three months = Prt = $9133.33(0.08)($\frac{3}{12}$) = $182.67 > $150

Thus, the $150 payment is not applied towards reducing the loan, but instead is carried forward, without interest, to the next payment date.

Balance due in five months = $9133.33[1 + 0.08($\frac{3+2}{12}$)] − $(150 + 1500)

$$= \$7787.77$$

Balance due in four months, X = $7787.77[1 + 0.08($\frac{4}{12}$)] = $7995.44

Solution b We arrange all dated values on a time diagram.

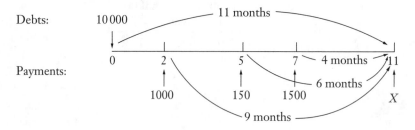

Setting up an equation of value, with the end of 11 months as the focal date,

$$1000[1 + 0.08(\tfrac{9}{12})] + 150[1 + 0.08(\tfrac{6}{12})] + 1500[1 + 0.08(\tfrac{4}{12})] + X = 10\,000[1 + 0.08(\tfrac{11}{12})]$$
$$1060.00 + 156.00 + 1540.00 + X = 10\,733.33$$
$$X = 7977.33$$

Again, note that the declining balance method leads to a higher final balance.

Exercise 1.4

1. Jean-Luc borrowed $1000, repayable in one year, with interest at 9%. He pays $200 in 3 months and $400 in 7 months. Determine the balance in one year using the Declining Balance Method and the Merchant's Rule.

2. On June 1, 2006, Sheila borrows $2000 at 7%. She pays $800 on August 17, 2006; $400 on November 20, 2006; and $500 on February 2, 2007. What is the balance due on April 18, 2007, by the Declining Balance Method? By the Merchant's Rule?

3. A debt of $5000 is due in six months with interest at 5%. Partial payments of $3000 and $1000 are made in 2 and 4 months respectively. What is the balance due on the final statement date by the Declining Balance Method? By the Merchant's Rule?

4. Alexandra borrows $1000 on January 8 at 16%. She pays $350 on April 12, $20 on August 10, and $400 on October 3. What is the balance due on December 15 using the Declining Balance Method? The Merchant's Rule?

5. A loan of $1400 is due in one year with simple interest at 12%. Partial payments of $400 in 2 months, $30 in 6 months, and $600 in 8 months are made. Determine the balance due in one year using the Declining Balance Method.

6. A loan of $2500 is taken out on May 12. It is to be paid back within a one-year period with partial payments of $1000 on August 26, $40 on November 19, and $350 on January 9. If the rate of interest is 8%, what is the final balance due on March 20 by the Declining Balance Method? By the Merchant's Rule?

Section 1.5 ## Simple Discount at a Discount Rate

The calculation of present (or discounted) value over durations of less than one year is sometimes based on a simple discount rate. The **annual simple discount rate** d is the ratio of the discount D for the year to the amount S on which the discount is given. The simple discount D on an amount S for t years at the discount rate d is calculated by means of the formula:

$$\boxed{D = Sdt} \tag{4}$$

and the discounted value P of S, or the proceeds P, is given by

$$P = S - D$$

By substituting for $D = Sdt$ we obtain P in terms of S, d, and t

$$P = S - Sdt$$

$$\boxed{P = S(1 - dt)} \tag{5}$$

> The factor $(1 - dt)$ in formula **(5)** is called **a discount factor at a simple discount rate d**.

Simple discount is not very common. However, it should not be ignored. Some financial institutions offer what are referred to as **discounted loans.** For these types of loans, the interest charge is based on the final amount, S, rather than on the present value. The lender calculates the interest (which is called discount) D, using formula **(4)** and deducts this amount from S. The difference, P, is the amount the borrower actually receives, even though the actual loan amount is considered to be S. The borrower pays back S on the due date. For this reason the interest charge on discounted loans is sometimes referred to as **interest in advance**, as the interest is paid up front, at the time of the loan, instead of the more common practice of paying interest on the final due date.

In theory, we can also accumulate a sum of money using simple discount, although it is not commonly done in practice. From formula **(5)**, we can express S in terms of P, d, and t and obtain

$$S = \frac{P}{1 - dt} = P(1 - dt)^{-1} \tag{6}$$

> The factor $(1 - dt)^{-1}$ in formula **(6)** is called **an accumulation factor at a simple discount rate d.**

Formula **(6)** can be used to calculate the maturity value of a loan for a specified proceeds.

EXAMPLE 1   A person takes out a discounted loan with a face value of $500 for 6 months from a lender who charges a $9\frac{1}{2}\%$ discount rate. a) What is the discount, and how much money does the borrower receive? b) What size loan should the borrower ask for if he wants to receive $500 cash?

Solution a   We have $S = 500$, $d = 9\frac{1}{2}\%$, $t = \frac{1}{2}$ and calculate

$$\text{discount } D = Sdt = \$500 \times 0.095 \times \tfrac{1}{2} = \$23.75$$
$$\text{proceeds } P = S - D = \$(500 - 23.75) = \$476.25$$

Alternatively, we could calculate the proceeds by formula **(5)**

$$P = S(1 - dt) = \$500[1 - (0.095)(\tfrac{1}{2})] = \$476.25$$

What is happening in this situation is that the borrower receives a loan of $500, but he must pay $23.75 in interest charges today. He ends up with a net of $476.25 in his pocket. Six months later, he repays the original loan amount, $500, but does not pay any interest at that time, as he has already paid the interest up front.

Solution b   We have $P = 500$, $d = 9\frac{1}{2}\%$, $t = \frac{1}{2}$ and calculate the maturity value of the loan

$$S = \frac{P}{1 - dt} = \frac{\$500}{1 - (0.095)(\tfrac{1}{2})} = \$524.93$$

The borrower should ask for a loan of $524.93 to receive proceeds of $500.

EXAMPLE 2 Calculate the discounted value of $1000 due in 1 year: a) at a simple interest rate of 7%; b) at a simple discount rate of 7%.

Solution a We have $S = 1000$, $r = 7\%$, $t = 1$ and calculate the discounted value P by formula **(2)**

$$P = \frac{S}{1 + rt} = \frac{\$1000}{1 + (0.07)(1)} = \$934.58$$

Solution b We have $S = 1000$, $d = 7\%$, $t = 1$ and calculate the discounted value P by formula **(5)**

$$P = S(1 - dt) = \$1000[1 - (0.07)(1)] = \$1000(0.93) = \$930.00$$

Note the difference of $4.58 between the discounted value at a simple interest rate and the discounted value at a simple discount rate. We can conclude that a given simple discount rate results in a larger money return to a lender than the same simple interest rate. Note also that in **a)**, the borrower is taking out a loan for $934.58. At the end of 1 year, he/she pays back the original principal of $934.58 plus interest of $65.42 for a total of $1000. In **b)**, the borrower is taking out a loan for $1000. He/she pays $70 in interest up front, receives $930 and repays the original principal of $1000 at the end of 1 year.

EXAMPLE 3 If $1200 is the present value of $1260 due at the end of 9 months, determine a) the annual simple interest rate, and b) the annual simple discount rate.

Solution a We have $P = 1200$, $I = 60$, $t = \frac{9}{12}$, and calculate

$$r = \frac{I}{Pt} = \frac{60}{1200(\frac{9}{12})} \doteq 6.67\%$$

Solution b We have $S = 1260$, $D = 60$, $t = \frac{9}{12}$, and calculate

$$d = \frac{D}{St} = \frac{60}{1260(\frac{9}{12})} \doteq 6.35\%$$

In general, we can calculate **equivalent rates** of interest or discount by using the following definition:

> Two rates are equivalent if they have the same effect on money over the same period of time.

The above definition can be used to determine simple (or compound) equivalent rates of interest or discount.

EXAMPLE 4 What simple rate of discount d is equivalent to a simple rate of interest $r = 6\%$ if money is invested for a) 1 year; b) 2 years?

Solution a Compare the discounted values of $1 due at the end of 1 year under simple discount and simple interest:

$$[1 - d(1)] = [1 + (0.06)(1)]^{-1}$$
$$1 - d = (1.06)^{-1}$$
$$d \doteq 5.66\%$$

Solution b Compare the discounted values of $1 due at the end of 2 years under simple discount and simple interest:

$$[1 - d(2)] = [1 + (0.06)(2)]^{-1}$$
$$1 - 2d = (1.12)^{-1}$$
$$d \doteq 5.36\%$$

OBSERVATION:

Notice that for simple rates of interest and discount, the equivalent rates are dependent on the period of time.

Application of Simple Discount — Promissory Notes

Promissory notes are occasionally sold based on simple discount from the maturity value, as illustrated in the following example.

EXAMPLE 5 On August 10 Smith borrows $4000 from Jones and gives Jones a promissory note at a simple interest rate of 10% with a maturity date of February 4 in the following year. Brown buys the note from Jones on November 3, based on a simple discount rate of 11%. Determine Brown's purchase price.

Solution We arrange the dated values on a time diagram.

Maturity value of the note, $S = \$4000[1 + 0.10(\frac{178}{365})] = \$4195.07$

Since Brown is buying the note using a simple discount rate, the proceeds are determined using formula **(5)**:

Proceeds on November 3, $P = S[1 - dt] = \$4195.07[1 - 0.11(\frac{93}{365})] = \$4077.49$

The amount paid by Brown to Jones is $4077.49.

Exercise 1.5

1. Determine the discounted value of $2000 due in 130 days
   a) at a simple interest rate of 8.5%;
   b) at a simple discount rate of 8.5%.

2. A bank offers a 272-day discounted loan at a simple discount rate of 12%.
   a) How much money would a borrower receive if he asked for a $5000 loan?
   b) What size loan should the borrower ask for in order to actually receive $5000?
   c) What is the equivalent simple interest rate that is being charged on the loan?

3. A note with a maturity value of $700 is sold at a discount rate of 8%, 45 days before maturity. Determine the discount and the proceeds.

4. A promissory note with face value $2000 is due in 175 days and bears 7% simple interest. After 60 days it is sold for $2030. What simple discount rate can the purchaser expect to earn?

5. A storekeeper buys goods costing $800. He asks his creditor to accept a 60-day noninterest-bearing note, which, if his creditor discounts immediately at a 10% discount rate, will result in proceeds of $800. For what amount should he make the note?

6. A company borrowed $50 000 on May 1, 2007, and signed a promissory note bearing interest at 11% for 3 months. On the maturity date, the company paid the interest in full and gave a second note for 3 months without interest and for such an amount that when it was discounted at a 12% discount rate on the day it was signed, the proceeds were just sufficient to pay the debt. Determine the amount of interest paid on the first note and the face value of the second note.

7. A discounted loan of $3000 at a simple discount rate of 6.5% is offered to Mr. Jones. If the actual amount of money that Mr. Jones receives is $2869.11, when is the $3000 due to be paid back?

8. A borrower receives $1500 today and must pay back $1580 in 200 days. If this is a discounted loan, what rate of simple discount is assumed?

9. If a borrower actually wanted to receive $1800 today, what size discounted loan should they ask for if $d = 8.7\%$ and the loan is due in 1 year?

Section 1.6   ## Summary and Review Exercises

- Accumulated value of P at the end of t years at a simple interest rate r is given by $P(1 + rt)$ where $(1 + rt)$ is called an accumulation factor at simple interest rate r.

- Discounted value of S due in t years at a simple interest rate r is given by $S(1 + rt)^{-1}$ where $(1 + rt)^{-1}$ is called a discount factor at a simple interest rate r.

- Discounted value of S due in t years at a simple discount rate d is given by $S(1 - dt)$ where $(1 - dt)$ is called a discount factor at a simple discount rate d.

- Accumulated value of P at the end of t years at a simple discount rate d is given by $P(1 - dt)^{-1}$ where $(1 - dt)^{-1}$ is called an accumulation factor at a simple discount rate d.

- Equivalence of dated values at a simple interest rate r:
  X due on a given date is equivalent to Y due t years later,
  if $Y = X(1 + rt)$ or $X = Y(1 + rt)^{-1}$.

Note: The above definition of equivalence of dated values at a simple interest rate r does not satisfy the property of transitivity. The lack of transitivity leads to different answers when different comparison dates are used for equations of value.

● Equivalent rates:
Two rates are equivalent if they have the same effect on money over the same period of time.

Note: At simple rates of interest and discount, the equivalent rates are dependent on the period of time.

Review Exercises 1.6

1. How long will it take $1000
   a) to earn $100 at 6% simple interest?
   b) to accumulate to $1200 at $13\frac{1}{2}$% simple interest?

2. Determine the accumulated and the discounted value of $1000 over 55 days at 7% using both ordinary and exact simple interest.

3. A taxpayer expects an income tax refund of $380 on May 1. On March 10, a tax discounter offers 85% of the full refund in cash. What rate of simple interest will the tax discounter earn?

4. A retailer receives an invoice for $8000 for a shipment of furniture with terms 3/10, *n*/40.
   a) What is the highest simple interest rate at which he can afford to borrow money in order to take advantage of the cash discount?
   b) If the retailer can borrow at a simple interest rate of 12%, calculate his savings resulting from the cash discount, when he pays the invoice within 10 days.

5. A cash discount of 3% is given if a bill is paid 40 days in advance of its due date.
   a) What is the highest simple interest rate at which you can afford to borrow money if you wanted to take advantage of this discount?
   b) If you can borrow money at a simple interest rate 8%, how much can you save by paying an invoice for $5000 forty days in advance of its due date?

6. A loan of $2500 taken out on April 2 requires equal payments on May 25, July 20, September 10, and a final payment of $500 on October 15. If the focal date is October 15, what is the size of the equal payments at 9% simple interest?

7. Last night Marion won $5000 in a lottery. She was given two options. She can take $5000 today or $X every six months (beginning six months from now) for 2 years. If the options are equivalent and the simple interest rate is 10%, determine X using a focal date of 2 years.

8. Today Mr. Mueller borrowed $2400 and arranged to repay the loan with three equal payments of $X at the end of 4, 8, and 12 months respectively. If the lender charges a simple interest rate of 6%, find X using today as a focal date.

9. Roger borrows $4500 at 9% simple interest on July 3, 2006. He pays $1250 on October 27, 2006, and $2500 on January 7, 2007. Determine the balance due on May 1, 2007, using the Declining Balance Method and the Merchant's Rule.

10. Paul borrows $4000 at a 7.5% simple interest rate. He is to repay the loan by paying $1000 at the end of 3 months and two equal payments at the end of 6 months and 9 months. Determine the size of the equal payments using
    a) the end of 6 months as a focal date.
    b) the present time as a focal date.

11. Melissa borrows $1000 on May 8, 2006 at an 8% simple interest rate. She pays $500 on July 17, 2006 and $400 on September 29, 2006. What is the balance due on October 31, 2006 using the Declining Balance Method and the Merchant's Rule?

12. Robert borrows $1000 for 8 months from a lender who charges an 11% discount rate.
    a) How much money does Robert receive?
    b) What size loan should Robert ask for in order to receive $1000 cash?

13. Consider the following promissory note:

> $1500.00   Vancouver, May 11, 2006
>
> Ninety days after date, I promise to pay to the order of J.D. Prasad
>
>   Fifteen hundred and $\frac{00}{100}$ dollars
>
> for value received with interest at 12% per annum.
>
>   (Signed) J.B. Lau

Mr. Prasad sells the note on July 2, 2006, to a bank that discounts notes at a 13% discount rate.
a) How much money does Mr. Prasad receive?
b) What rate of interest does Mr. Prasad realize on his investment?
c) What rate of interest does the bank realize on its investment if it holds the note until maturity?
d) What rate of interest does the bank realize if Mr. Lau pays off the loan as due in exactly 90 days?

14. A 180-day promissory note for $2000 bears 7% simple interest. After 60 days it is sold to a bank that charges a discount rate of 7%.
a) Calculate the price paid by the bank for the note.
b) What simple interest rate did the original owner of the note actually earn?
c) If the note is actually paid on the **due** date, what discount rate will the bank have realized?

15. A note for $800 is due in 90 days with simple interest at 6%. On the maturity date, the maker of the note paid the interest in full and gave a second note for 60 days without interest and for such an amount that when it was discounted at a 7% discount rate on the day it was signed, the proceeds were just sufficient to pay the debt. Determine the interest paid on the first note and the face value of the second note.

16. A debt of $1200 is to be paid off by payments of $500 in 45 days, $300 in 100 days, and a final payment of $436.92. Interest is at $r = 11\%$ and the Merchant's Rule was used to calculate the final payment. In how many days should the final payment be made?

17. Determine the difference in simple interest on a $20 000 loan at a simple interest rate of 9% from April 15 to the next February 4, using the Banker's Rule and Canadian practice.

18. A person borrows $3000 at a 14% simple interest rate. He is to repay the debt with 3 equal payments, the first at the end of 3 months, the second at the end of 7 months, and the third at the end of 12 months. Determine the difference between payments resulting from the selection of the focal date at the present time and at the end of 12 months.

19. A promissory note for $1500 is due in 170 days with simple interest at 9.5%. After 40 days it is sold to a finance company that charges a simple discount rate of 14%. How much does the finance company pay for the note?

20. You borrow $1000 now and $2000 in 4 months. You agree to pay $X in 6 months and $2X in 8 months (from now). Determine X using a focal date 8 months from now
a) at simple interest rate $r = 8\%$;
b) at simple discount rate $d = 8\%$.

CHAPTER 2

Compound Interest

Learning Objectives

In chapter 1, we learned how to perform financial calculations using simple interest. However, most financial transactions involve compound interest rates. Beginning with this chapter, the rest of this textbook is devoted to financial calculations using compound interest. And, once you understand how compound interest works, you will have a powerful tool at your disposal that will allow you to do many financial calculations yourself which will help you in making more informed financial decisions without having to rely on others.

Section 2.1 begins with the concept of interest earned in a given period being added to your principal and thereafter earning interest. This leads to the fundamental formula for accumulating with compound interest. Section 2.2 discusses how interest rates with different compounding periods are related. Section 2.3 shows how to calculate discounted or present values under compound interest. Long-term promissory notes are shown as an application.

Section 2.4 deals with accumulating or discounting over fractional periods of time. Simple interest reappears in this section. Section 2.5 shows how to determine the rate of return on an investment and how to determine the term of an investment needed to obtain a desired rate of interest. Section 2.6 re-introduces the valuable concept of equations of value which was first introduced in section 1.3.

In many loans and investments, the interest rate changes over time and section 2.7 discusses how to handle situations like these. Section 2.8 talks about how the principles of compound interest can be used to solve nonfinancial problems that involve geometric growth. And finally, section 2.9 extends the concept of compound interest to the case of interest being compounded every second of every day.

Fundamental Compound Interest Formula

If the interest due is added to the principal at the end of each interest period and thereafter earns interest, the interest is said to be **compounded**. The sum of the original principal and total interest is called the **compound amount** or **accumulated value**. The difference between the accumulated value and the original principal is called the **compound interest**. The time between two successive interest computations is called the **interest period, compounding period,** or **conversion period**. This time unit need not be a year. Most of you will already be familiar with situations where interest is "payable quarterly," or "compounded semi-annually" or "convertible monthly."

EXAMPLE 1	Determine the compound interest earned on $1000 for 2 years at 6% compounded semi-annually and compare it with the simple interest earned on $1000 for 2 years at 6% per annum.
Solution	Since the compounding period is 6 months, interest is earned at the rate of 3% per period, and there are 4 interest periods in 2 years.

At the End of	Compound Interest	Accumulated Value
the 1st interest period	$1000 × 0.03 = $30	$1030.00
the 2nd interest period	$1030 × 0.03 = $30.90	$1060.90
the 3rd interest period	$1060.92 × 0.03 = $31.83	$1092.73
the 4th interest period	$1092.73 × 0.03 = $32.78	$1125.51

The compound interest earned on $1000 for 2 years at 6% compounded semi-annually is $125.51; whereas the simple interest on $1000 for 2 years at 6% is $I = \$1000 \times 0.06 \times 2 = \$120$.

In this section we shall develop quicker methods for calculating the compound interest.

The following notation will be used:

P = the original principal, or the present value of S, or the discounted value of S.

S = the future value of P, or the accumulated value of P.

n = the term of the investment in interest (or compounding) periods.

m = the number of interest periods per year, or the frequency of compounding.

j_m = the nominal (yearly) interest rate that is compounded (payable, convertible) m times per year.*

i = the interest rate per compounding period.

Note 1: Commonly used frequencies of compounding are $m = 1$ for annual compounding, $m = 2$ for semi-annual compounding, $m = 4$ for quarterly compounding, $m = 12$ for monthly compounding, $m = 52$ for weekly compounding, and $m = 365$ for daily compounding (leap year or not). Continuous compounding that uses compounding intervals shorter than one day is covered in section 2.9.

Note 2: The rate i equals $\frac{j_m}{m}$ and is always used in the compound interest calculation. For example, $j_{12} = 9\%$ means that a yearly rate of 9% is compounded (converted, payable) 12 times per year and that $i = \frac{9}{12}\% = \frac{3}{4}\% = 0.0075$ is the interest rate per month.

---

*Actuaries use the symbol $i^{(m)}$ instead of j_m.

Let P represent the principal at the beginning of the first interest period and i the interest rate per compounding period. We shall calculate the accumulated values at the ends of the successive interest periods for n periods.

At the end of the 1st period:
the interest due $\qquad Pi$
the accumulated value $\qquad P + Pi = P(1+i)$

At the end of the 2nd period:
the interest due $\qquad [P(1+i)]i$
the accumulated value $\qquad P(1+i) + [P(1+i)]i$
$= P(1+i)(1+i) = P(1+i)^2$

At the end of the 3rd period:
the interest due $\qquad [P(1+i)^2]i$
the accumulated value $\qquad P(1+i)^2 + [P(1+i)^2]i$
$= P(1+i)^2(1+i) = P(1+i)^3$

Continuing in this manner for n periods the accumulated value S at the end of n periods is given by the **fundamental compound interest formula**

$$S = P(1 + i)^n \qquad (7)$$

The factor $(1+i)^n$ is called the **accumulation factor** or the **accumulated value of \$1**. The process of calculating S from P is called **accumulation**. To obtain the accumulated value S of P for n periods at rate i, we multiply P by the corresponding accumulation factor $(1 + i)^n$.

EXAMPLE 2   Accumulate \$10 000 at $j_{12} = 6\%$ for a) 5 years; b) 25 years.

Solution a   We have $P = 10\,000$, $i = 0.06/12 = 0.005$ per month, $n = 5$ years $\times 12 = 60$ months, and calculate:

$$S = P(1+i)^n = \$10\,000(1.005)^{60} = \$13\,488.50$$

The compound interest on \$10 000 at $j_{12} = 6\%$ for 5 years is \$3488.50.

Solution b   We have $P = 10\,000$, $i = 0.005$ per month, $n = 25 \times 12 = 300$ months, and calculate:

$$S = \$10\,000(1.005)^{300} = \$44\,649.70$$

The compound interest on \$10 000 at $j_{12} = 12\%$ for 25 years is \$34 649.70, which is almost 3.5 times the original investment. If the \$10 000 had been invested at 6% simple interest ($r = 0.06$ and $t = 25$ years), the interest earned would have been only \$10 000(0.06)(25) = \$15 000. This illustrates the power of compound interest over a long period of time.

The table and graph below show the effect of time and rate on the growth of money at compound interest.

	Growth of $10 000 at Compound Interest Rate j_{12}			
Years	**6%**	**8%**	**10%**	**12%**
5	13 488.50	14 898.46	16 453.09	18 166.97
10	18 193.97	22 196.40	27 070.41	33 003.87
15	24 540.94	22 069.21	44 539.20	59 958.02
20	33 102.04	49 268.03	73 280.74	108 925.54
25	44 649.70	73 401.76	120 569.45	197 884.66
30	60 225.75	109 357.30	198 373.99	359 496.41
35	81 235.51	162 925.50	326 386.50	653 095.95
40	109 564.54	242 733.86	537 006.63	1 186 477.25

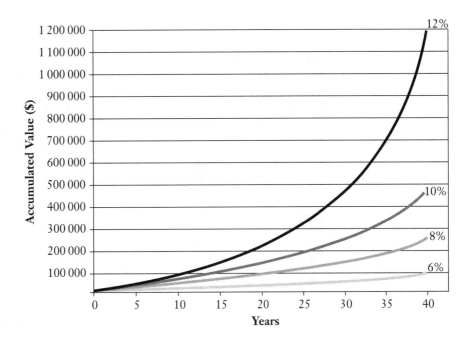

Using a Computer Spreadsheet

A computer spreadsheet is tailor made for many of the financial calculations that will be studied in this textbook. There are several spreadsheets available (such as EXCEL, LOTUS, QUATTRO PRO) and all can generate the required calculations very well. In this text, we will present Excel spreadsheets.

We will illustrate the formulas needed to perform the calculations of Example 2 on a spreadsheet. The entries in an Excel spreadsheet are summarized below. It is assumed that the initial investment, $10 000, is entered in cell B11 (typed in as 10000, no commas or dollar sign).

CELL	ENTER	INTERPRETATION
A1	'Years'	'End of Year'
B1	0.06	Should format so that it appears as 6%
C1	0.08	Should format so that it appears as 8%
D1	0.10	Should format so that it appears as 10%
E1	0.12	Should format so that it appears as 12%

In A2 to A9, type 5, 10, 15, 20, 25, 30, 35, and 40. In B2, we need to type the formula that will accumulate the initial investment (given in B11) to the end of 5 years at the given interest rate. Remember that the given interest rate needs to be divided by 12 (to obtain the monthly rate) and the exponent must be multiplied by 12 (to give the term in months). In B2 we type,

$$= \$B\$11*(1 + B\$1/12)^\wedge(\$A2*12)$$

To generate the rest of the values, copy B2 into C2 to E2 and then copy into B3 to E9.

Note that dollar signs before and after a letter ($B$11) means the value in that cell will not change when you copy the formula. A dollar sign after the letter (B$1) means the value in that cell will change when you copy across a row, but not when you copy down a column. A dollar sign before the letter ($A2) means the value in that cell will change when you copy down a column, but not when you copy across a row.

A copy of the resulting spreadsheet is given below.

	A	B	C	D	E
1	Years	6%	8%	10%	12%
2	5	13,488.50	14,898.46	16,453.09	18,166.97
3	10	18,193.97	22,196.40	27,070.41	33,003.87
4	15	24,540.94	33,069.21	44,539.20	59,958.02
5	20	33,102.04	49,268.03	73,280.74	108,925.54
6	25	44,649.70	73,401.76	120,569.45	197,884.66
7	30	60,225.75	109,357.30	198,373.99	359,496.41
8	35	81,235.51	162,925.50	326,386.50	653,095.95
9	40	109,574.54	242,733.86	537,006.63	1,186,477.25
10					
11	Principal= $	10,000			

EXAMPLE 3   A person deposits $1000 into a savings account that earns interest at 4.25% compounded semi-annually. How much interest will be earned: a) during the first year? b) during the second year?

Solution a   We have, $P = 1000$, $i = \frac{0.0425}{2} = 0.02125$ per half year, $n = 2$ and calculate the accumulated value at the end of 1 year

$$S = P(1 + i)^n = \$1000(1.02125)^2 = \$1042.95$$

The compound interest earned during the first year is $42.95.

Solution b   We calculate the accumulated value at the end of 2 years

$$S = \$1000(1.02125)^4 = \$1087.75$$

The compound interest earned during the second year is

$$\$1087.75 - \$1042.95 = \$44.80$$

CALCULATION TIP:

When using the fundamental compound interest formula **(7)** in calculations, do not round off the value of i. Use all digits provided by your calculator.

EXAMPLE 4   Ying invests $3500 in a fund that pays interest at $j_4 = 5\%$. How much has been accumulated in the fund a) at the end of 33 months; b) at the end of six and a half years?

Solution a   We have $P = 3500$, $i = 0.05/4 = 0.0125$ per quarter year. To calculate n, we observe that 33 months is equal to 2.75 years. Thus, $n = 2.75 \times 4 = 11$ quarterly interest periods. We then calculate:

$$S = P(1 + i)^n = \$3500(1.0125)^{11} = \$4012.48$$

Solution b   We have $P = 3500$, $i = 0.0125$, $n = 6.5 \times 4 = 26$ and we calculate

$$S = \$3500(1.0125)^{26} = \$4834.36$$

OBSERVATION:

For interest rates that are compounded quarterly, $m = 4$. Sometimes $m = 3$ is mistakenly used, because one quarter of a year equals 3 months. But m represents the *number of interest periods* per year (which is 4), not the *number of months* in the interest period.

EXAMPLE 5   Gustav opens a savings account by depositing $5000 on May 17. The account pays interest at 4% per annum. How much is in the account on December 31 if
   a) the interest is compounded daily?
   b) the interest is calculated daily and paid into the account at the end of each month?

Solution a We have $P = 5000$, $i = 0.04/365$ per day, $n = 365 - 137 = 228$ days (note: Gustav would not earn any interest on his $5000 on the first day, May 17, but would earn one day's worth of interest on December 31) and we calculate:

$$S = \$5000(1.000109589)^{228} = \$5126.50$$

Total interest earned during the year is

$$I = \$5126.50 - \$5000 = \$126.50$$

Solution b Most daily interest savings accounts calculate interest on the minimum daily balance using simple interest (in this case, $r = 0.04$), with the interest added to the account at the end of each month.

Period	Days	Interest
May	14	$\$5000.00 \times 0.04 \times 14/365 = \$\ 7.67$
June	30	$\$5007.67 \times 0.04 \times 30/365 = \$16.46$
July	31	$\$5024.13 \times 0.04 \times 31/365 = \$17.07$
August	31	$\$5041.20 \times 0.04 \times 31/365 = \$17.13$
September	30	$\$5058.33 \times 0.04 \times 30/365 = \$16.63$
October	31	$\$5074.96 \times 0.04 \times 31/365 = \$17.24$
November	30	$\$5092.20 \times 0.04 \times 30/365 = \$16.74$
December	31	$\$5108.94 \times 0.04 \times 31/365 = \$17.36$

Balance at the end of the day on December 31 = $\$5108.94 + \$17.36 = \$5126.30$. Total interest earned during the year = $\$126.30$.

Note how the account with interest compounded daily earns more interest during the year than the account with interest calculated daily.

Exercise 2.1

Part A

Problems 1 to 8 make use of the following table. In each case find the accumulated value and the compound interest earned.

No.	Principal	Nominal Rate	Conversion Frequency	Time
1.	$ 100	$5\frac{1}{2}\%$	annually	5 years
2.	$ 500	$11\frac{1}{4}\%$	monthly	2 years
3.	$ 220	8.8%	quarterly	3 years
4.	$1000	9%	semi-annually	6 years
5.	$ 50	6%	monthly	4 years
6.	$ 800	$7\frac{3}{4}\%$	annually	10 years
7.	$ 300	8%	weekly	3 years
8.	$1000	10%	daily	2 years

9. Accumulate $500 for one year at a) $j_{12} = 4\%$, b) $j_{12} = 8\%$, c) $j_{12} = 12\%$.

10. How much money will be required on December 31, 2009, to repay a loan of $2000 made December 31, 2006, if $j_4 = 7\%$?

11. Determine the accumulated value of $100 over 5 years at an 8% nominal rate compounded: a) annually; b) semi-annually; c) quarterly; d) monthly; e) daily.

12. Parents put $1000 into a savings account at the birth of their daughter. If the account earns interest at 6% compounded monthly, how much money will be in the account when their daughter is 18 years old?

13. In 1492, Queen Isabella sponsored Christopher Columbus' journey by giving him $10 000. If she had placed this money in a bank account at $j_1 = 3\%$, how much money would be in the account in 2006? If the bank account earned a simple interest rate of 3%, how much money would be in the account in 2006?

14. Determine the accumulated value of $1000 at the end of 1 year at a) $j_1 = 6.136\%$; b) $j_2 = 6.045\%$; c) $j_4 = 6\%$; d) $j_{12} = 5.970\%$.

Part B

1. Melinda has a savings account that earns interest at 6% per annum. She opened her account with $1000 on December 31. How much interest will she earn during the first year if

a) the interest is compounded daily;
b) the interest is calculated daily and paid into the account on June 30 and December 31;
c) the interest is calculated daily and paid into the account at the end of each month?

2. Prove the fundamental compound interest formula $S = P(1 + i)^n$ using mathematical induction.

3. Set up a table and plot the graph showing the growth of $100 at compound interest rates $j_{365} = 8\%$, 12%, 16% and time = 5, 10, 15, 20, and 25 years.

4. Determine the compound interest earned on an investment of $10 000 for 10 years at a nominal rate of 5.4% compounded with frequencies $m = 1$, 2, 4, 12, 52, and 365.

Section 2.2 **Equivalent Compound Interest Rates**

The yearly nominal rate is meaningless until we specify the frequency of conversion m. The table below illustrates the effect of the frequency of conversion on the amount to which $10 000 will accumulate in 10 years at a nominal rate of 8% compounded with frequencies $m = 1, 2, 4, 12,$ and 365.

Frequency of Conversion	Rate per Period	Number of Periods	Amount
$m = 1$	$i = 8\%$	10	$21 589.25
$m = 2$	$i = 4\%$	20	$21 911.23
$m = 4$	$i = 2\%$	40	$22 080.40
$m = 12$	$i = \frac{2}{3}\%$	120	$22 196.40
$m = 365$	$i = \frac{8}{365}\%$	3650	$22 253.41

At the same nominal rate the accumulated value depends on the frequency of conversion; it increases with the increased frequency of conversion.

For a given nominal rate j_m compounded m times per year, we define the corresponding **annual effective rate** to be that rate j which, if compounded annually, will produce the same amount of interest per year. To determine the yearly effective rate j corresponding to a given nominal rate j_m we compare the accumulated values of $1 at the end of 1 year. At the rate j, $1 will accumulate at the end of 1 year to $1 + j$. At the rate $i = j_m/m$, $1 will accumulate at the end of 1 year to $(1 + i)^m$.

Thus

$$1 + j = (1 + i)^m$$

$$\boxed{j = (1 + i)^m - 1} \tag{8}$$

EXAMPLE 1   Determine the annual effective rate j corresponding to a) $j_2 = 10\%$; b) $j_{12} = 18\%$; c) $j_{365} = 5\frac{1}{4}\%$.

Solution a $1 at rate j for 1 year will accumulate to $1 + j$.
$1 at rate $j_2 = 10\%$ for 1 year will accumulate to $(1.05)^2$.
Comparing the accumulated values we obtain:
$1 + j = (1.05)^2 = 1.1025$, hence $j = 0.1025 = 10.25\%$.

Solution b   We have $i = 0.18/12 = 0.015$ per month and applying equation **(8)**

$$j = (1.015)^{12} - 1 = 0.195618171\% \doteq 19.56\%$$

Note that 18% compounded monthly is a typical interest rate charged on overdue payments on a credit card. When your credit card company says they are charging you 18%, they are really charging you 19.56% per year.

Solution c   Applying equation **(8)** we have

$$j = (1 + \tfrac{0.0525}{365})^{365} - 1 = 0.0538986 \doteq 5.39\%.$$

Calculating equivalent interest rates and, in particular, the annual effective rate is very useful when you need to compare investments that have interest rates with different compounding periods. The following example illustrates this point.

EXAMPLE 2   You wish to invest a sum of money for a number of years and have narrowed your choices to the following three interest rates:

Investment A: $j_2 = 10.35\%$
Investment B: $j_{12} = 10.15\%$
Investment C: $j_4 = 10.25\%$

Which investment should you choose?

Solution   On the surface it looks like investment A is best, as it has the highest nominal rate of interest. However, it pays interest only twice a year. What about investment B? It pays interest 12 times a year, but it has the lowest nominal rate of interest. To choose which investment is best we need to calculate the equivalent rate of interest, compounded with the same frequency, for each investment.

Investment A: $j = \left(1 + \frac{0.1035}{2}\right)^2 - 1 = 0.106178063 \doteq 10.6178\%$

Investment B: $j = \left(1 + \frac{0.1015}{12}\right)^{12} - 1 = 0.106357563 \doteq 10.6358\%$

Investment C: $j = \left(1 + \frac{0.1025}{4}\right)^4 - 1 = 0.106507581 \doteq 10.6508\%$

It turns out that investment C has the highest annual effective rate and should be the investment that is chosen.

In Chapter 1 we defined equivalent rates as the rates that have the same effect on money over the same period of time. (See p. 25.)

Applying the general definition specifically for compound interest rates we say:

> Two nominal compound interest rates are **equivalent** if they yield the same accumulated values at the end of one year, and hence at the end of any number of years.

EXAMPLE 3   Determine the rate j_4 equivalent to a) $j_{12} = 12\%$; b) $j_2 = 5.5\%$.

Solution   We shall compare the accumulated values of $1 at the end of 1 year.

Solution a $1 at the rate j_4 will accumulate at the end of 1 year to $(1 + i)^4$. $1 at the rate $j_{12} = 12\%$ will accumulate at the end of 1 year to $(1.01)^{12}$. Thus

$$(1+i)^4 = (1.01)^{12}$$
$$1+i = (1.01)^3$$
$$i = (1.01)^3 - 1$$
$$i = 0.030301$$

and

$$j_4 = 4i = 0.121204 \doteq 12.12\%$$

Solution b $1 at the rate j_4 will accumulate at the end of 1 year to $(1 + i)^4$. $1 at the rate $j_2 = 5.5\%$ will accumulate at the end of 1 year to $(1.0275)^2$. Thus

$$(1+i)^4 = (1.0275)^2$$
$$1+i = (1.0275)^{1/2}$$
$$i = (1.0275)^{1/2} - 1$$
$$i = 0.013656746$$

and

$$j_4 = 4i = 0.0546270 \doteq 5.46\%$$

EXAMPLE 4   What simple interest rate is equivalent to $j_2 = 9\%$ if money is invested for 3 years?

Solution   Let r be the unknown simple interest rate. $1 invested at rate r will accumulate at the end of 3 years to $1 + 3r$. $1 invested at $j_2 = 9\%$ will accumulate at the end of 3 years to $(1.045)^6$.

Thus

$$1 + 3r = (1.045)^6$$
$$1 + 3r = 1.3022601$$
$$r = 0.10075338$$
$$r \doteq 10.08\%$$

CALCULATION TIP:

When calculating unknown yearly rates of interest, carry all decimal digits and then round off your final answer to the nearest hundredth of a percent.

Exercise 2.2

Part A

1. Determine the annual effective rate (two decimals) equivalent to the following rates:
   a) $j_2 = 7\%$;   b) $j_4 = 16\%$;   c) $j_4 = 8\%$;
   d) $j_{365} = 12\%$;   e) $j_{12} = 9\%$.

2. Determine the nominal rate (two decimals) equivalent to the given annual effective rate:
   a) $j = 6\%$ determine j_2;
   b) $j = 9\%$ determine j_4;
   c) $j = 10\%$ determine j_{12};
   d) $j = 17\%$ determine j_{365};
   e) $j = 4.5\%$ determine j_{52}.

3. Determine the nominal rate (two decimals) equivalent to the given nominal rate:
   a) $j_2 = 8\%$ determine j_4;
   b) $j_4 = 6\%$ determine j_2;
   c) $j_{12} = 18\%$ determine j_4;
   d) $j_6 = 10\%$ determine j_{12};
   e) $j_4 = 8\%$ determine j_2;
   f) $j_{52} = 4\%$ determine j_2;
   g) $j_2 = 5\frac{1}{4}\%$ determine j_{12};
   h) $j_4 = 12.79\%$ determine j_{365}.

4. What simple interest rate is equivalent to $j_{12} = 5.7\%$ if money is invested for 2 years?

5. What simple interest rate is equivalent to $j_{365} = 8\%$ if money is invested for 3 years?

6. If the interest on the outstanding balance of a credit card account is charged at $1\frac{3}{4}\%$ per month, what is the annual effective rate of interest?

7. A trust company offers guaranteed investment certificates paying $j_2 = 8.9\%$ and $j_1 = 9\%$. Which option yields the higher annual effective rate of interest?

8. Which rate gives the best and the worst rate of return on your investment?
   a) $j_{12} = 15\%$, $j_2 = 15\frac{1}{2}\%$, $j_{365} = 14.9\%$
   b) $j_{12} = 6\%$, $j_2 = 6\frac{1}{2}\%$, $j_{365} = 5.9\%$.

9. Bank A has an annual effective interest rate of 10%. Bank B has a nominal interest rate of $9\frac{3}{4}\%$. What is the minimum frequency of compounding for bank B in order that the rate at bank B be at least as attractive as that at bank A?

Part B

1. Determine what is the current best and worst interest rate available on 5-year guaranteed investment certificates by checking three different financial institutions. Calculate the difference in compound interest earned using the best and the worst rate available if you buy a $2000, 5-year certificate.

2. Determine the annual effective rate of interest on the major credit cards and charge-accounts in major department stores.

3. For a given nominal rate, $j_2 = 2i$, develop equations for equivalent nominal rates j_1, j_4, j_{12}, and j_{365}.

4. For a given nominal rate $j_{12} = 12i$, develop equations for equivalent nominal rates j_1, j_2, j_4, j_{52}, and j_{365}.

5. Twenty thousand dollars is invested for 5 years at a nominal rate of 6%. Determine the accumulated value of the investment if the rate is compounded with frequencies $m = 1, 2, 4, 12,$ and 365 using
   a) the fundamental compound interest formula;
   b) equivalent annual effective rates;
   c) equivalent nominal rates compounded monthly.
   Compare your answers in a), b), and c).

6. A bank pays 6% per annum on its savings accounts. At the end of every 3 years a 2% bonus is paid on the balance. Determine the annual effective rate of interest, j_1, earned by an investor if the deposit is withdrawn:
   a) in 2 years,
   b) in 3 years,
   c) in 4 years.

7. A fund earns interest at the nominal rate of 8.04% compounded quarterly. At the end of each quarter, just after interest is credited, an expense charge equal to 0.50% of the fund is withdrawn. Determine the annual effective yield realized by the fund.

8. An insurance company says you can pay for your life insurance by paying $100 at the beginning of each year or $51.50 at the beginning of each half-year. They say the rate of interest underlying this calculation is $j_2 = 3\%$. What is the true value of j_2?

9. In general, the *annual effective rate of interest* is the ratio of the amount of interest earned during the year to the amount of principal invested at the beginning of the year.

   a) Show that, at a simple interest rate r, the annual effective rate of interest for the nth year is $\dfrac{r}{1 + r(n-1)}$, which is a decreasing function of n. Thus a constant rate of simple interest implies a decreasing annual effective rate of interest.

   b) Show that, at a compound interest rate i per year, the annual effective rate of interest for the nth year is i, which is independent of n. Thus a constant rate of compound interest implies a constant annual effective rate of interest.

Section 2.3   Discounted Value at Compound Interest

In business transactions it is frequently necessary to determine what principal P now will accumulate at a given interest rate to a specified amount S at a specified future date. From fundamental formula (7) we can obtain

$$P = \frac{S}{(1 + i)^n} = S(1 + i)^{-n} \tag{9}$$

P is called the **discounted value** of S, or the **present value** of S, or the **proceeds**. The process of determining P from S is called **discounting**. The difference $S - P$ is called **compound discount** on S. It is *compound discount at an interest rate* and it is the prevailing practice in compound discount problems.

> The factor $(1 + i)^{-n}$ in (9) is called the **discount factor** or the **discounted value of \$1**. To obtain a discounted value P of S for n periods at rate i, we multiply S by the corresponding discount factor $(1 + i)^{-n}$. Values of $(1 + i)^{-n}$ will be calculated by using the function y^x of your calculator.

EXAMPLE 1   Calculate the discounted value of $100\,000 due in a) 10 years, b) 25 years, if money is worth $j_{12} = 6\%$.

Solution a   We have $S = 100\,000$, $i = 0.005$ per month, $n = 10 \times 12 = 120$ and calculate

$$P = S(1 + i)^{-n} = \$100\,000(1.005)^{-120} = \$54\,963.27$$

Solution b   We have $S = 100\,000$, $i = 0.005$, $n = 25 \times 12 = 300$ and calculate

$$P = \$100\,000(1.005)^{-300} = \$22\,396.57.$$

Application of Discounted Values — Business Decision Making

Calculating the discounted, or present, value of sums of money that are expected in the future (often referred to as future cash flows) is a useful method in comparing different financial options. It is also very useful in attaching a value to a company when preparing for an initial public offering (IPO) of shares.

EXAMPLE 2   Let us suppose you can buy a lot for $84 000 cash or for payments of $50 000 now, $20 000 in 1 year and $20 000 in 2 years. If money is worth $j_{12} = 9\%$, which option is better for you?

Solution   We arrange the data on a time diagram below. Notice that time is in terms of interest compounding periods.

Option 1: $84 000

```
|----------------------------|----------------------------|
0                            12                           24
                          (1 year)                    (2 years)
```

Option 2: $50 000 $20 000 $20 000

Discounted value of option 1 is $84 000.
Discounted value of option 2 is

$$\$50\,000 + \$20\,000\left(1 + \tfrac{0.09}{12}\right)^{-12} + \$20\,000\left(1 + \tfrac{0.09}{12}\right)^{-24}$$

$$= \$50\,000 + \$18\,284.76 + \$16\,716.63$$
$$= \$85\,001.39$$

You should take option 1 and save $85 001.39 – $84 000 = $1001.39 at the present time.

A different rate of interest could lead to a different decision. If money were worth $j_{12} = 12\%$, the discounted value of option 2 would be

$$\$50\,000 + \$20\,000(1.01)^{-12} + \$20\,000(1.01)^{-24}$$
$$= \$50\,000 + \$17\,748.98 + \$15\,751.32$$
$$= \$83\,500.30$$

and you should take option 2 and save $84 000 – $83 500.30 = $499.70 at the present time.

Application of Discounted Values — Long-Term Promissory Notes

Long-term promissory notes have a term greater than one year and are usually subject to compound interest. For interest-bearing notes, the proceeds are determined by discounting the maturity value of the note from the maturity date back to the date of sale using equation **(9)** (if it is a noninterest-bearing note, you would discount the face value since it is equal to the maturity value). It should be noted there is no requirement to add three days of grace in determining the legal due date (maturity date) of a long-term promissory note.

EXAMPLE 3   A note for $2000 dated September 1, 2006, is due with compound interest at $j_{12} = 7.2\%$, 3 years after the date. On December 1, 2007, the holder of the note has it discounted by a lender who charges $j_4 = 8\%$. Determine the proceeds and the compound discount.

Solution   We arrange the data on a time diagram below.

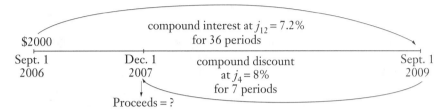

The time between September 1, 2006 and September 1, 2009 is exactly 3 years and $n = 3 \times 12 = 36$ months. The time between December 1, 2007 and September 1, 2009 is 21 months or 1.75 years and $n = 1.75 \times 4 = 7$ quarters.

The maturity value of the note is $S = \$2000 \left(1 + \frac{0.072}{12}\right)^{36} = \$2480.60$.

The proceeds are $P = S(1 + i)^{-n} = \$2480.60 \left(1 + \frac{0.08}{4}\right)^{-7} = \$2159.51$.

The compound discount equals $\$2480.60 - \$2159.51 = \$321.09$.

Exercise 2.3

Part A

Calcuate the discounted value in problems 1 to 5.

No.	Amount	Nominal Rate	Conversion	Time
1.	$ 100	6%	quarterly	3 years
2.	$ 50	$8\frac{1}{2}\%$	monthly	2 years
3.	$2000	11.8%	yearly	10 years
4.	$ 500	10%	semi-annually	5 years
5.	$ 800	5%	daily	3 years

6. What amount of money invested today will grow to $1000 at the end of 5 years if $j_4 = 8\%$?

7. How much would have to be deposited today in an investment fund paying $j_{12} = 10.4\%$ to have $2000 in three years' time?

8. What is the discounted value of $2500 due in 10 years if $j_2 = 9.6\%$?

9. On her 20th birthday a woman receives $1000 as a result of a deposit her parents made on the day she was born. How large was that deposit if it earn interest at $j_2 = 6\%$?

10. An obligation of $2000 is due December 31, 2011. What is the value of this obligation on June 30, 2007, at $j_4 = 5.5\%$?

11. A note dated October 1, 2007, calls for the payment of $800 in 7 years. On October 1, 2008, it is sold at a price that will yield the investor $j_4 = 12\%$. How much is paid for the note?

12. A note for $250 dated August 1, 2006, is due with compound interest at $j_{12} = 9\%$ 4 years after date. On November 1, 2007, the holder of the note has it discounted by a lender who charges $j_4 = 7.5\%$. What are the proceeds?

13. A note for $1000 dated January 1, 2006, is due with interest at 6% compounded semi-annually 5 years after date. On July 1, 2007, the holder of the note has it discounted by a lender who charges 7% compounded quarterly. Determine the proceeds.

14. A man can buy a piece of land for $170 000 cash or payments of $120 000 down and $100 000 in 5 years. If he can earn $j_{365} = 10\%$, which plan is better?

15. Calculate the total value on July 1, 2007, of payments of $1000 on July 1, 1997, and $600 on July 1, 2014, if $j_2 = 9\%$.

16. If money is worth $j_1 = 10\%$, determine the present value of a debt of $3000 with interest at $11\frac{1}{2}\%$ compounded semi-annually due in 5 years.

Part B

1. A note for $2500 dated January 1, 2007, is due with interest at $j_{12} = 12\%$ 40 months later. On May 1, 2007, the holder of the note has it discounted by Financial Consultants Inc. at $j_4 = 13\frac{1}{4}\%$. The same day the note is sold by Financial Consultants Inc. to a bank that discounts notes at $j_1 = 13\%$. What is the profit made by Financial Consultants Inc.?

2. Determine the compound discount if $1000, due in 5 years with interest at $j_1 = 7\frac{1}{2}\%$, is discounted at a nominal rate of 6% compounded with frequencies $m = 1, 2, 4, 12, 52,$ and 365.

3. The management of a company must decide between two proposals. The following information is available:

Proposal	Investment Now	Net Cash Inflow at the End of		
		Year 1	Year 2	Year 3
A	80 000	95 400	39 000	12 000
B	100 000	35 000	58 000	80 000

Advise management regarding the proposal that should be selected, assuming that on projects of this type the company can earn $j_1 = 14\%$.

| Section 2.4 | **Accumulated and Discounted Value for a Fractional Period of Time** |

Formulas **(7)** and **(9)** were developed under the assumption that n is an integer. Theoretically, formulas **(7)** and **(9)** can be used when n is a fraction. When we calculate the accumulated or the discounted value using formulas **(7)** or **(9)** for a fractional part of an interest compounding period, we call it the **exact** or **theoretical method** of accumulating or discounting.

EXAMPLE 1   Calculate the accumulated value of $1500 for 16 months at $j_4 = 7\%$, using the exact method.

Solution   We have $P = 1500$ and $i = \frac{0.07}{4} = 0.0175$ per quarter year. To calculate n, we note that 16 months is $1\frac{1}{3}$ years. Thus, $n = 1\frac{1}{3} \times 4 = 5\frac{1}{3} = 5.333333$ quarters. We obtain,

$$S = P(1 + i)^n = \$1500(1.0175)^{5.33333} = \$1645.41.$$

EXAMPLE 2   Jennifer wants to have $5000 in 29 months time. How much does she have to invest today at $j_2 = 5\%$ using the exact method?

Solution   We have $S = 5000$, $i = \frac{0.05}{2} = 0.025$ per half year. To calculate n, we note that 29 months is $2\frac{5}{12}$ years. Thus, $n = 2\frac{5}{12} \times 2 = 4\frac{10}{12} = 4.833333$ half-years. The amount Jennifer needs to invest today is

$$P = S(1 + i)^{-n} = \$5000(1.025)^{-4.83333} = \$4437.50.$$

In practice, compound interest for the full number of interest periods and simple interest for the fractional part of an interest period are often used. This method is called an **approximate or practical** method of accumulating or discounting and is illustrated in the following example. The use of simple interest for the fraction of a period is equivalent to linear interpolation as will be shown in problem 2 of Part B of Exercise 2.4. Linear interpolation is explained, in detail, in Appendix 3.

EXAMPLE 3   Calculate the accumulated value of $1500 for 16 months at $j_4 = 7\%$, using the approximate method, and compare the results with those of Example 1.

Solution   From example 1, we have $n = 5$ quarters $+ \frac{1}{3}$ of a quarter ($= 1$ month). Thus we first accumulate $1500 for 5 periods at $j_4 = 7\%$ ($i = 0.0175$ per quarter) and then accumulate this value for an additional 1 month at a simple interest rate of 7%. (See diagram.)

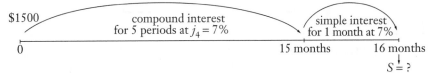

Numerically, we can combine the two accumulations and obtain

$$S = \$1500(1.0175)^5 [1 + (0.07)(\tfrac{1}{12})] = \$1645.47$$

Note that in the simple interest accumulation we multiply by an accumulation factor $(1 + rt)$ where r is the nominal rate j_4 and t is time in years.

EXAMPLE 4   Calculate the discounted value of $5000 due in 29 months time at $j_2 = 5\%$ using the approximate method, and compare the results to Example 2.

Solution   Things are slightly different when discounting using the approximate method. We are required to discount past time 0 using compound interest, followed by accumulating to time 0 using simple interest. Since $n = 4\frac{10}{12}$, we round up to the next integer, and discount for $n = 5$ periods. This is $\frac{1}{6}$ of a half year, or 1 month before time 0. Thus, we first discount $5000 for 5 periods at $j_2 = 5\%$ and then **accumulate** this value for 1 month at a simple interest rate of 5%. (See diagram.)

Numerically, we can combine the compound discount and simple interest calculations and obtain:

$$P = \$5000(1.025)^{-5}[1 + (0.05)\tfrac{1}{12}] = \$4437.69.$$

OBSERVATION:

Comparing the result of Example 3 with that of Example 1 we can conclude that the approximate accumulated value is slightly greater than the exact accumulated value.

Comparing the result of Example 4 with that of Example 2, we can make a similar conclusion. That is, the approximate discounted value is slightly greater than the exact discounted value.

The proof that the approximate accumulated and discounted values are always greater than the exact accumulated and discounted values is left as an exercise. See problem 1 of Part B of Exercise 2.4.

CALCULATION TIP:

Unless stated otherwise, it will be understood that the **approximate** or **practical** method is to be used throughout this textbook.

EXAMPLE 5   A note for $3000 without interest is due on August 18, 2008. On June 11, 2007, the holder of the note has it discounted by a lender who charges $j_{12} = 12\%$. What are the proceeds?

Solution   The due date is August 18, 2008. We arrange the data on the diagram below.

From June 11, 2007 to August 11, 2008 is 14 months. From August 11 to August 18 is 7 days. Thus, $n = 14\frac{7}{31}$ (note: this would be the value of n to use under the exact method). Under the practical method, we must discount using compound interest past time 0. We round up to $n = 15$ months, and discount the $3000 at $j_{12} = 12\%$ back to May 18, 2007. Then we accumulate this value using simple interest at 12% from May 18 to June 11, which is 24 days. Numerically,

$$P = \$3000(1.01)^{-15}[1 + (0.12)(\tfrac{24}{365})] = \$2604.44$$

The proceeds are $2604.44.

Exercise 2.4

Part A

For each of problems 1 to 4 determine the answer first using the exact method and then the practical method. Compare your answers in each case. In problems 5 to 9 use the practical method.

1. Determine the accumulated value of $100 over 5 years 7 months if $j_2 = 6\frac{1}{2}\%$.

2. Determine the accumulated value of $800 over 4 years 7 months if $j_4 = 8\%$.

3. Determine the discounted value of $5000 due in 8 years 10 months if interest is at rate $j_2 = 7.4\%$.

4. Determine the discounted value of $280 due in 3 years 7 months if interest is at rate $j_1 = 10\%$.

5. A note of $2000 face value is due without interest on October 20, 2012. On April 28, 2007, the holder of the note has it discounted at a bank that charges $j_4 = 12\%$. What are the proceeds?

6. On July 7, 2006, Mrs. Smith borrowed $1200 at $j_{12} = 6.3\%$. How much would she have to repay on September 18, 2009?

7. On April 7, 2002, a debt of $4000 was incurred at rate $j_2 = 10\%$. What amount will be required to settle the debt on September 19, 2007?

8. A noninterest-bearing note for $850 is due December 8, 2009. On August 7, 2006, the holder of the note has it discounted by a lender who charges $j_2 = 9\frac{1}{4}\%$. What are the proceeds?

9. A note for $1200 dated August 24, 2005, is due with interest at $j_{12} = 8\frac{3}{4}\%$ in 2 years. On June 18, 2006, the holder of the note has it discounted by a lender who charges 9.5% compounded quarterly. Calculate the proceeds and the compound discount.

Part B

1. a) Assuming that $0 < i < 1$, prove that
   i) $(1 + i)^t < 1 + it$ if $0 < t < 1$
   ii) $(1 + i)^t > 1 + it$ if $t > 1$
   [Hint: Use the binomial theorem.]

b) Give a geometric illustration of the relationships in a) by graphing $(1 + i)^t$ and $1 + it$.

c) Show that the approximate accumulated and discounted values are greater than the exact accumulated and discounted values when fractional parts of interest periods are involved.

2. A common method for calculating an unknown value between two known values is called linear interpolation. It is based on the following formula:

$$f(n + k) = (1 - k)f(n) + kf(n + 1) \quad 0 < k < 1$$

e.g.,

$$f\left(2\tfrac{2}{3}\right) = \tfrac{1}{3}f(2) + \tfrac{2}{3}f(3)$$

Applying this to the compound interest formula where $f(n) = (1 + i)^n$ we get:

$$(1 + i)^{n+k} = (1 - k)(1 + i)^n + k(1 + i)^{n+1} \quad 0 < k < 1$$

Prove that using linear interpolation is equivalent to assuming simple interest in the final fractional period, i.e., prove

$$(1 - k)(1 + i)^n + k(1 + i)^{n+1} = (1 + i)^n(1 + ki)$$

Students not familiar with linear interpolation should read Appendix 3.

3. A promissory note for $2000 dated April 5, 2006, is due on October 4, 2010, with interest at $j_1 = 12\%$. On June 7, 2007, the holder of the note has it discounted at a bank that charges $j_4 = 14\%$. Calculate the proceeds and the compound discount.

Section 2.5 ## Determining the Rate and the Time

Determining the Rate: When S, P, and n are given, we can substitute the given values into the fundamental compound interest formula $S = P(1 + i)^n$ and solve it for the unknown interest rate i.

$$S = P(1 + i)^n$$
$$(1 + i)^n = \frac{S}{P}$$
$$1 + i = \left(\frac{S}{P}\right)^{1/n}$$

$$\boxed{i = \left(\frac{S}{P}\right)^{1/n} - 1}$$

CALCULATION TIP:

Using the power key of our calculator, we calculate the exact value of i. The nominal annual rate of interest is determined by multiplying the effective rate i by the number of compounding periods per year, $j_m = mi$, and then rounding off to the nearest hundredth of a percent.

EXAMPLE 1   At what nominal rate j_{12} will money triple itself in 12 years?

Solution   We can use any sum of money as the principal. Let $P = x$, then $S = 3x$, and $n = 12 \times 12 = 144$.

Substituting in $S = P(1 + i)^n$ we obtain an equation for the unknown interest rate i per month

$$3x = x(1 + i)^{144}$$
$$(1 + i)^{144} = 3$$

Solving the exponential equation $(1 + i)^{144} = 3$ directly for i and then using a pocket calculator we have

$$(1 + i)^{144} = 3$$
$$1 + i = 3^{1/144}$$
$$i = 3^{1/144} - 1$$
$$i = 0.007658429$$
$$j_{12} = 12i = 0.091901147$$
$$j_{12} \doteq 9.19\%$$

Using a Financial Calculator

Many of the calculations that have been presented so far in this textbook can be performed using a financial calculator. However, for most of the exercises, it is easiest to set up an equation of value and solve for the answer using the symbols and formulas presented in this text, using a calculator to do only the basic math. There has been no real need for a financial calculator.

However, there are situations where a financial calculator can lead to quicker answers and calculating the value of i is one such situation.

There are many different financial calculators on the market. Four good ones are: Sharp EL-733A, Hewlett Packard 10B, Texas Instruments BA-35, and Texas Instruments BA-II Plus. We will illustrate the calculations using the notation from the Texas Instruments BA-35 calculator.

In Example 1, we have $PV = -1$ (note that you need a negative sign in front of the present value), $FV = S = 3$, and $n = 144$ (the term is always entered as the number of interest periods). The steps are as follows (make sure your calculator has been set to the FIN mode):

-1 $\boxed{PV}$ 3 $\boxed{FV}$ 144 $\boxed{N}$ $\boxed{CPT}$ $\boxed{I/Y}$

0.765842888 (per month)

Note that the answer is given as a percentage. That is, the monthly rate is 0.765842888%. To obtain the nominal rate, we need to multiply by 12:

$$j_{12} = 12(0.76584288)\% = 9.190114656\% \doteq 9.19\%$$

EXAMPLE 2   Suppose you would like to earn \$600 of interest over 21 months on an initial investment of \$2500. What nominal rate of interest, j_4, is needed?

Solution   We have $P = 2500$, $S = 2500 + 600 = 3100$, $n = 1.75 \times 4 = 7$ quarters, and $i = j_4/4$. Setting up the equation and solving, we get

$$3100 = 2500(1 + i)^7$$
$$1 + i = (1.24)^{1/7}$$
$$i = (1.24)^{1/7} - 1$$
$$i = 0.031207243$$
$$j_4 = 4i = 0.124828974$$
$$j_4 \doteq 12.48$$

Using the BA-35 calculator:

−2500 $\boxed{PV}$ 3100 $\boxed{FV}$ 7 $\boxed{N}$ $\boxed{CPT}$ $\boxed{I/Y}$

3.120724362 (per quarter)

To obtain the nominal rate,

$$j_4 = 4(3.120724362)\% = 12.482897\% \doteq 12.48\%$$

Determining the Time: When S, P, and i are given, we can substitute the given values into the fundamental compound amount formula $S = P(1 + i)^n$ and solve it for the unknown n using one of the following methods:

a) Logarithms may be used to solve the exponential equation $P(1 + i)^n = S$ for the unknown exponent n. If the exact method of accumulation is used, i.e., compound interest is allowed for the fractional part of the conversion period, a logarithmic solution gives the correct value of n. An explanation of common logarithms together with applications to compound interest problems will be found in Appendix 1. In this textbook we assume that students have pocket calculators with a built-in common logarithmic function $\log x$ and its inverse function 10^x.

Solving the formula $S = P(1 + i)^n$ for n we obtain:

$$(1 + i)^n = \frac{S}{P}$$
$$n \log(1 + i) = \log\left(\frac{S}{P}\right)$$

$$\boxed{n = \frac{\log\left(\frac{S}{P}\right)}{\log(1 + i)}}$$

b) Method of interpolation. Linear interpolation is explained in Appendix 3. If the practical method of accumulation is used, i.e., simple interest is allowed for the fractional part of the conversion period, interpolation gives the correct value of n.

The actual accuracy of the solution depends on the number of decimal places in the accumulation factors used in the interpolation. In our examples we shall round off the factors to 4 decimal places, since additional places do not significantly increase the accuracy.

EXAMPLE 3   How long will it take $500 to accumulate to $850 at $j_{12} = 12\%$? Assume that a) the exact method of accumulation is in effect; b) the practical method of accumulation is in effect.

Solution   Let n represent the number of months, then we have

$$500(1.01)^n = 850$$
$$(1.01)^n = \tfrac{850}{500}$$
$$(1.01)^n = 1.7$$

a) If compound interest is allowed for the fractional part of the interest conversion period, we can solve the equation $(1.01)^n = 1.7$ by logarithms. We have

$$n \log 1.01 = \log 1.7$$
$$n = \frac{\log 1.7}{\log 1.01}$$
$$n = 53.3277 \text{ months}$$
$$n = 4.4440 \text{ years}$$
$$= 4 \text{ years,} \quad \underbrace{5 \text{ months,}}_{\substack{0.4440 \times 12 \\ = 5.328}} \quad \underbrace{10 \text{ days}}_{\substack{0.328 \times 30 \\ = 9.84 \doteq 10}}$$

b) If simple interest is allowed for the fractional part of the interest conversion period, then we determine n by interpolation. Arranging the data in an interpolation table we have:

	$(1.01)^n$	n	
	1.6945	53	
0.0169 { 0.0055 { 1.7000		n } d } 1	
	1.7114	54	

$$\frac{d}{1} = \frac{0.0055}{0.0169}$$
$$d = 0.3333$$
and $n = 53.3333$ months
$$n = 4.4444 \text{ years}$$
$$= 4 \text{ years,} \quad \underbrace{5 \text{ months,}}_{\substack{0.4444 \times 12 \\ = 5.3328}} \quad \underbrace{10 \text{ days}}_{\substack{0.3328 \times 30 \\ = 9.984 \doteq 10}}$$

Alternative Solution   The accumulated value of $500 for 53 periods at $j_{12} = 12\%$ is $500(1.01)^{53} = \$847.23$. Now we calculate how long it will take $847.23 to accumulate $2.77 simple interest at rate 12%.

$$t = \frac{I}{Pr} = \frac{2.77}{847.23 \times 0.12} = 0.027245652 \text{ years} \doteq 10 \text{ days}$$

Thus the time is 4 years, 5 months, and 10 days.

In this example both methods, exact and practical, give the same answer, when the time is expressed in days. The actual difference in time between the two solutions is less than $\frac{3}{100}$ of a day.

Using a Financial Calculator

To calculate n using the BA-35 calculator, we have $PV = -500$, $FV = 850$, and $i\% = 1$ (the interest rate is the effective rate per compounding period, entered as a number, not a decimal). The steps are as follows:

-500 | PV | 850 | FV | 1 | I/Y | CPT | N
53.32769924 (months)

CALCULATION TIP:

When calculating unknown n from the fundamental compound interest formula **(7)**, use logarithms (that is, the exact method) in all exercises. The difference between the answers by the exact and the practical method is negligible.

EXAMPLE 4   Jerry invests \$1000 today in a fund earning $j_2 = 5\%$. How long will it take for his money to double?

Solution   We have $P = 1000$, $S = 2000$, $i = 0.025$ and will let n represent the number of half-years. Setting up the equation, we obtain

$$1000(1.025)^n = 2000$$
$$(1.025)^n = 2$$
$$n \log 1.025 = \log 2$$
$$n = \frac{\log 2}{\log 1.025}$$
$$n = 28.0710 \text{ half years}$$
$$= 14.0355 \text{ years}$$
$$= 14 \text{ years,} \quad \overbrace{0 \text{ months,}}^{0.0355 \times 12} \quad \overbrace{13 \text{ days}}^{0.4260 \times 30}$$
$$= 0.426 \qquad = 12.78 \doteq 13$$

Note: If the interest rate had been $j_2 = 10\%$, $n = 7$ years, 1 month, 8 days.

Using the BA-35 calculator and $i = 0.05/2 = 0.025$ per half year,

-1000 | PV | 2000 | FV | 2.5 | I/Y | CPT | N
28.07103453 (half years)

Using $i = 0.10/2 = 0.05$ per half year,

-1000 | PV | 2000 | FV | 5 | I/Y | | CPT | | N

14.20669908 (half years)

Rule of 70

A quick estimate for the amount of time needed for money to double in value can be obtained using the "Rule of 70". According to this rule, the number of interest periods needed for money to double in value is approximately equal to 70 divided by the effective rate of interest per period.

Using this rule in Example 4, we obtain,

i)   If $j_2 = 5\%$, then $i = 0.025$ and $n \doteq 70/2.5 = 28.0$ half years. Compare this to the correct answer of 28.0710.

ii) If $j_2 = 10\%$, then $i = 0.05$ and $n \doteq 70/5 = 14.0$ half years. Compare this to the correct answer of 14.2067.

Exercise 2.5

Part A

In problems 1 to 4 calculate the nominal rate of interest.

No.	Principal	Amount	Time	Conversion
1.	$2000	$3000.00	3 years 9 months	quarterly
2.	$ 100	$ 150.00	4 years 7 months	monthly
3.	$ 200	$ 600.00	15 years	annually
4.	$1000	$1581.72	3 years 6 months	semi-annually

In problems 5 to 8 determine the time.

No.	Principal	Amount	Interest Rate	Conversion
5.	$2000	$2800	10%	quarterly
6.	$ 100	$ 130	9%	semi-annually
7.	$ 500	$ 800	6%	monthly
8.	$1800	$2200	8%	quarterly

9. An investment fund advertises that it will guarantee to double your money in 10 years. What rate of interest j_1 is implied?

10. If an investment grows 50% in 4 years, what rate of interest j_4 is being earned?

11. From 2002 to 2007, the earnings per share of common stock of a company increased from $4.71 to $9.38. What was the compounded annual rate of increase?

12. At what rate j_{365} will an investment of $4000 grow to $6000 in 3 years?

13. How long will it take to double your deposit in a savings account that accumulates at
a) $j_1 = 4.56\%$?
b) $j_{365} = 7\%$?
c) Redo a) and b) using the "Rule of 70".

14. How long will it take for $800 to grow to $1500 in a fund earning interest at rate 9.8% compounded semi-annually?

15. How long will it take to increase your investment by 50% at rate 5% compounded daily?

Part B

1. At a given rate of interest, j_2, money will double in value in 8 years. If you invest $1000 at this rate of interest, how much money will you have
a) in 5 years?
b) in 10 years?

2. If money doubles at a certain rate of interest compounded daily in 6 years, how long will it take for the same amount of money to triple in value?

3. Draw a graph showing the time needed to double your money at rate j_1 for the rates 2%, 4%, 6%, ... , 20%. Calculate the exact answers and the answers using the "Rule of 70".

4. Determine how long $1 must be left to accumulate at $j_{12} = 18\%$ for it to amount to twice the accumulated value of another $1 deposited at the same time at $j_2 = 10\%$.

5. Money doubles in t years at rate of interest j_1. At what rate of interest, j_1^*, will money double in $\frac{t}{2}$ years?

6. You deposit $800 in an account paying $j_2 = 9\%$, and $600 in a second account paying $j_2 = 7\%$. When will the first account have twice the accumulated value of the second account?

7. Account A starts now with $100 and pays $j_1 = 4\%$. After 2 years an additional $25 is deposited in account A. Account B is opened 1 year from now with a deposit of $95 and pays $j_1 = 8\%$. When (in years and days) will account B have $1\frac{1}{2}$ times the accumulated value in Account A if simple interest is allowed for part of a year?

8. In how many years and days should a single payment of $2000 be made in order to be equivalent to payments of $500 now and $800 in 3 years if interest is $j_1 = 8\%$ and simple interest is allowed for part of a year?

Section 2.6

Equations of Value

In chapter 1, we discussed the concept of the time value of money, where sums of money coming due at different times (dated values) are not directly comparable. Instead we must discount or accumulate each dated value to a common date, called the focal date, in order to compare sums of money. In section 1.3 we dealt with equations of value at a simple interest rate. We suggest that the student read over section 1.3 before studying this section, since most of the principles and procedures from section 1.3 will apply here as well.

In general, we compare dated values by the following **definition of equivalence:**

> X due on a given date is equivalent at a given compound interest rate i to Y due n periods later, if
> $$Y = X(1 + i)^n \quad \text{or} \quad X = Y(1 + i)^{-n}$$

The following diagram illustrates dated values equivalent to a given dated value X.

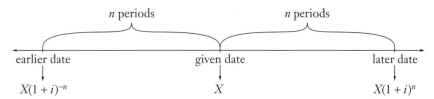

Based on the time diagram above we can state the following simple rules:

> **1.** When we move money forward in time, we accumulate, i.e., we multiply the sum by an accumulation factor $(1 + i)^n$.
>
> **2.** When we move backward in time, we discount, i.e., we multiply the sum by a discount factor $(1 + i)^{-n}$.

The following property of equivalent dated values, called the property of transitivity, holds at compound interest:

At a given compound interest rate, if X is equivalent to Y, and Y is equivalent to Z, then X is equivalent to Z.

To prove this property we arrange our data on a time diagram.

$$\begin{array}{ccccc} & X & & Y & & Z \\ \hline 0 & n_1 & & n_2 & & n_3 \end{array}$$

If X is equivalent to Y, then $Y = X(1+i)^{n_2-n_1}$
If Y is equivalent to Z, then $Z = Y(1+i)^{n_3-n_2}$

Eliminating Y from the second equation we obtain

$$Z = X(1+i)^{n_2-n_1}(1+i)^{n_3-n_2} = X(1+i)^{n_3-n_1}$$

Thus Z is equivalent to X.

As a result, the solutions to the problems by equations of value at compound interest do not depend on the selection of the focal date.

OBSERVATION:

In mathematics, an equivalence relation must satisfy the property of transitivity. Thus, strictly speaking, the equivalence of dated values at a simple interest rate is not an equivalence relation. The equivalence of dated values at a compound interest rate is an equivalence relation.

EXAMPLE 1 A debt of $5000 is due at the end of 3 years. Determine an equivalent debt due at the end of a) 3 months; b) 3 years 9 months, if $j_4 = 12\%$.

Solution We arrange the data on a time diagram below.

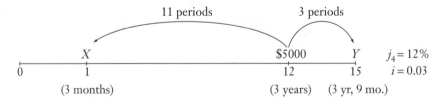

By definition of equivalence

$$X = \$5000(1.03)^{-11} = \$3612.11$$
$$Y = \$5000(1.03)^3 = \$5463.64$$

Note that X and Y are equivalent by verifying

$$Y = X(1.03)^{14} \quad \text{or} \quad \$5463.34 = \$3612.11(1.03)^{14}$$

The sum of a set of dated values, due on different dates, has no meaning. We have to replace all the dated values by equivalent dated values, due on the same date. The sum of the equivalent values is called the **dated value of the set**.

At compound interest the following property is true: *The various dated values of the same set are equivalent*. The proof is left as an exercise. See problem 1 of Part B of Exercise 2.6.

EXAMPLE 2   A person owes $200 due in 6 months and $300 due in 15 months. What single payment a) now, b) in 12 months, will liquidate these obligations if money is worth $j_{12} = 6\%$?

Solution   We arrange the data on the diagram below. Let X be the single payment due now and Y be the single payment due in 12 months.

To calculate the equivalent dated value X, we must discount the $200 debt for 6 months and discount the $300 debt for 15 months.

$$X = \$200(1.005)^{-6} + \$300(1.005)^{-15} = \$194.10 + \$278.38 = \$472.48$$

To calculate the equivalent dated value Y, we must accumulate the $200 debt from time 6 to time 12, or 6 periods and discount the $300 debt from time 15 to time 12, or 3 periods.

$$Y = \$200(1.005)^6 + \$300(1.005)^{-3} = \$206.08 + \$295.54 = \$501.62$$

We can verify the property of equivalence of X and Y by showing that

$$Y = X(1.005)^{12} = \$472.48(1.005)^{12} = \$501.62$$
$$\text{or} \quad X = Y(1.005)^{-12} = \$501.62(1.005)^{-12} = \$472.48$$

As stated in section 1.3, one of the most important problems in the mathematics of finance is the replacing of a given set of payments by an equivalent set. Two sets of payments are equivalent at a given compound interest rate if the dated values of the sets, on any common date, are equal. An equation stating that the dated values, on a common date, of two sets of payments are equal is called an **equation of value** or an **equation of equivalence**. The date used is called the **focal date** or the **comparison date** or the **valuation date**.

The procedure described in section 1.3 for solving problems in the mathematics of finance by equations of value applies the same way when compound interest is used. The answers, however, will not depend on the location of the focal date.

For your convenience, the procedure is re-stated below.

> **Step 1**   Draw a good time diagram showing the dated values of debts on one side of the time line and the dated values of payments on the other side. The times on the line should be stated in terms of interest compounding periods.
>
> **Step 2**   Select one, and only one, focal date and accumulate/discount all dated values to the focal date using the specified compound interest rate.
>
> **Step 3**   Set up an equation of value at the focal date:
>   dated value of payments = dated value of debts.
>
> **Step 4**   Solve the equation of value using methods of algebra.

The following examples illustrate the use of equations of value in the mathematics of finance.

EXAMPLE 3   A debt of $1000 with interest at $j_4 = 10\%$ will be repaid by a payment of $200 at the end of 3 months and 3 equal payments at the ends of 6, 9, and 12 months. What will these payments be?

Solution   We arrange all the dated values on a time diagram.

Any date can be selected as a focal date. We show the calculation using the end of 12 months and the present time.

Equation of value at the end of 12 months:

$$\text{dated value of the payments} = \text{dated value of the debts}$$
$$200(1.025)^3 + X(1.025)^2 + X(1.025)^1 + X = 1000(1.025)^4$$
$$215.38 + 1.050625X + 1.025X + X = 1103.81$$
$$3.075625X = 888.43$$
$$X \doteq 288.86$$

Equation of value at the present time:

$$200(1.025)^{-1} + X(1.025)^{-2} + X(1.025)^{-3} + X(1.025)^{-4} = 1000.00$$
$$195.12 + 0.951814396X + 0.928599411X + 0.905950645X = 1000.00$$
$$2.786364452X = 804.88$$
$$X \doteq 288.86$$

CALCULATION TIP:

Choose a convenient focal date, one that simplifies your calculations, when using equations of value at compound interest.

EXAMPLE 4 A man leaves an estate of $50 000 that is invested at $j_{12} = 9\%$. At the time of his death, he has two children aged 13 and 18. Each child is to receive an equal amount from the estate when they reach age 21. How much does each child get?

Solution The older child will get X in 3 years (36 months); the younger child will get X in 8 years (96 months). We arrange the dated values on a time diagram.

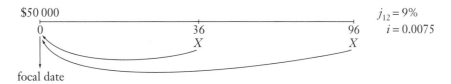

Equation of value at present:

$$X(1.0075)^{-36} + X(1.0075)^{-96} = 50\ 000$$
$$0.764148961X + 0.488061711X = 50\ 000$$
$$1.252210671X = 50\ 000$$
$$X \doteq 39\ 929.38$$

Each child will receive $39 929.38.

The following calculation checks the correctness of the answer:

Amount in fund at the end of 3 years = $50 000(1.0075)^{36}$ = \$65 432.27
Payment to the older child = <u>\$39 929.38</u>
Balance in the fund = \$25 502.89
Amount in fund after 5 more years = $25 502.88(1.0075)^{60}$ = \$39 929.39

The 1-cent difference is due to rounding.

EXAMPLE 5 Stephanie owes $8000 due at the end of 3 years with interest at $j_2 = 8\%$. The lender agrees to allow her to pay back the loan early with a payment of $3000 at the end of 9 months and X at the end of 27 months. If the lender can reinvest any payments at $j_4 = 5\%$, what is X?

Solution In this example, there are two interest rates: 8% is the interest rate on the original loan, while 5% is the rate that will be used in the equation of value.

First we need to calculate the maturity value of the loan, which is due in 3 years (6 half years).

$$S = 8000(1.04)^6 = 10\ 122.55$$

We now set up our time diagram, with $10 122.55 as the original debt and using quarter years as the times.

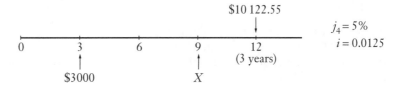

Equation of value at time 9:

$$3000(1.0125)^6 + X = 10\ 122.55(1.0125)^{-3}$$
$$3232.149542 + X = 9752.250203$$
$$X \doteq 6520.10$$

A payment of $3000 at the end of 9 months and $6520.10 at the end of 27 months is equivalent to a debt of $10 122.55 at the end of 3 years.

To check this is the correct answer:

Payment at end of 9 months, invested at $j_4 = 5\%$, $3000(1.0125)^6 = \$3232.15$

Payment at end of 27 months = $6520.10

Balance $9752.25

Balance invested at $j_4 = 5\%$ to end of 3 years = $9752.25(1.0125)^3 = \$10\ 122.55$ which is equal to the original debt owed at the end of 3 years.

Exercise 2.6

Part A

1. If money is worth $j_4 = 6\%$ determine the sum of money due at the end of 15 years equivalent to $1000 due at the end of 6 years.

2. What sum of money, due at the end of 5 years, is equivalent to $1800 due at the end of 12 years if money is worth $j_2 = 11\frac{3}{4}\%$?

3. An obligation of $2500 falls due at the end of 7 years. Determine an equivalent debt at the end of a) 3 years and b) 10 years, if $j_{12} = 10\%$.

4. One thousand dollars is due at the end of 2 years and $1500 at the end of 4 years. If money is worth $j_4 = 8\%$, calculate an equivalent single amount at the end of 3 years.

5. Eight hundred dollars is due at the end of 4 years and $700 at the end of 8 years. If money is worth $j_{12} = 12\%$, determine an equivalent single amount at a) the end of 2 years; b) the end of 6 years; c) the end of 10 years. Show your answers are equivalent.

6. A debt of $2000 is due at the end of 8 years. If $1000 is paid at the end of 3 years, what single payment at the end of 7 years would liquidate the debt if money is worth $j_2 = 7\%$?

7. A person borrows $4000 at $j_4 = 6\%$. He promises to pay $1000 at the end of one year, $2000 at the end of 2 years and the balance at the end of 3 years. What will the final payment be?

8. A consumer buys goods worth $1500. She pays $300 down and will pay $500 at the end of 6 months. If the store charges $j_{12} = 18\%$ on the unpaid balance, what final payment will be necessary at the end of one year?

9. A debt of $1000 is due at the end of 4 years. If money is worth $j_{12} = 8\%$, and $375 is paid at the end of 1 year, what equal payments at the end of 2 and 3 years respectively would liquidate the debt?

10. On September 1, 2005, Paul borrowed $3000, agreeing to pay interest at 12% compounded quarterly. He paid $900 on March 1, 2006, and $1200 on December 1, 2006.
    a) What equal payments on June 1, 2007, and December 1, 2007, will be needed to settle the debt?
    b) If Paul paid $900 on March 1, 2006, $1200 on December 1, 2006, and $900 on March 1, 2007, what would be his outstanding balance on September 1, 2007?

11. A woman's bank account showed the following deposits and withdrawals:

	Deposits	Withdrawals
January 1, 2006	$200	
July 1, 2006	$150	
January 1, 2007		$250
July 1, 2007	$100	

If the account earns $j_2 = 6\%$, determine the balance in the account on January 1, 2008.

12. Instead of paying $400 at the end of 5 years and $300 at the end of 10 years, a man agrees to pay X at the end of 3 years and $2X$ at the end of 6 years. Determine X if $j_1 = 10\%$.

13. A man stipulates in his will that $50 000 from his estate is to be placed in a fund from which his three children are to each receive an equal amount when they reach age 21. When the man dies, the children are ages 19, 15, and 13. If this fund earns interest at $j_2 = 6\%$, how much does each receive?

14. To pay off a loan of $4000 at $j_{12} = 7.2\%$, Ms. Fil agrees to make three payments in three, seven, and twelve months respectively. The second and third payment are to be double the first. What is the size of the first payment?

15. Mrs. Singh borrows $3000, due with interest at $j_{12} = 9\%$ in 2 years. The lender agrees to let Mrs. Singh repay the loan with a payment of $1000 in 6 months, $1500 in 12 months, and X in 30 months. If money is worth $j_2 = 6\%$, what is the value of X?

Part B

1. a) Prove the following property in the case of a set of two dated values: The various dated values of the same set are equivalent at compound interest.
   b) Show, algebraically, why this is not true for simple interest.

2. If money is worth $j_1 = 8\%$, what single sum of money payable at the end of 2 years will equitably replace $1000 due today plus a $2000 debt due at the end of 4 years with interest at $12\frac{1}{2}\%$ per annum compounded semi-annually?

3. On January 1, 2006, Mr. Planz borrowed $5000 to be repaid in a lump-sum payment with interest at $j_4 = 9\%$ on January 1, 2012. It is now January 1, 2008. Mr. Planz would like to pay $500 today and complete the liquidation with equal payments on January 1, 2010, and January 1, 2012. If money is now worth $j_4 = 8\%$, what will these payments be?

4. You are given two loans, with each loan to be repaid by a single payment in the future. Each payment will include both principal and interest. The first loan is repaid by a $3000 payment at the end of 4 years. The interest is accrued at 10% per annum compounded semi-annually. The second loan is repaid by a $4000 payment at the end of 5 years. The interest is accrued at 8% per annum compounded semi-annually. These two loans are to be consolidated. The consolidated loan is to be repaid by two equal instalments of X, with interest at 12% per annum compounded semi-annually. The first payment is due immediately and the second payment is due one year from now. Calculate X.

5. You are given the following data on three series of payments:

	Payment at End of Year			Accumulated Value at End of Year 18
	6	12	18	
Series A	240	200	300	X
Series B	0	360	700	$X + 100$
Series C	Y	600	0	X

Assume interest is compounded annually. Calculate Y.

Section 2.7	**Compound Interest at Changing Interest Rates**

The previous sections have assumed that the rate of compound interest relevant to any particular problem remains unchanged throughout the term of the problem. However, this need not be the case and, in practice, interest rates vary with considerable frequency. For instance, banks, trust companies, and credit unions vary their deposit rates with changes in market conditions.

In situations like this, an investor is most often interested in two things: how much will their investment accumulate to and what was the return on investment (ROI).

This complication of changing interest rates is not really a difficulty as the problems may be solved by completing the appropriate compound interest calculations in stages. As shown in the following examples, intermediate values are found at each date that has an interest rate change. No new compound interest techniques are required and these problems may be considered to be two or more compound interest problems, simply expressed in one question.

EXAMPLE 1   Marc invested $1000 in a savings account. The account paid interest at $j_1 = 6\%$ for 6 years followed by $j_1 = 4\%$ thereafter. How much did Marc have in the account after 8 years? What annual effective rate of return, j, did he earn each year over the 8 years?

Solution   The time diagram below sets out the 2 stages in the calculation and the 2 interest rates.

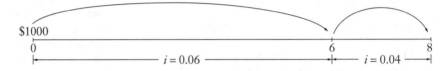

$1000
0   6   8
$|\!\!-\!\!\!-\!\!\!-\!\!\!-\!\!\!-\!\!\!-\!\!\!-\!\!\!-\!\!\!-\ i = 0.06\ -\!\!\!-\!\!\!-\!\!\!-\!\!\!-\!\!\!-\!\!\!-\!\!\!-\!\!|\!\!-\ i = 0.04\ -\!\!|$

$$\text{Accumulated value after 6 years} = 1000(1.06)^6$$
$$\doteq 1418.52$$
$$\text{Accumulated value after 8 years} = 1418.52(1.04)^2$$
$$\doteq 1534.27$$
$$\text{or}\quad \text{Accumulated value after 8 years} = 1000(1.06)^6(1.04)^2$$
$$\doteq 1534.27$$

To calculate Marc's annual effective rate of return over 8 years, we use the principles of section 2.2. The accumulated value of $1 over 8 years at j is $(1 + j)^8$. The accumulated value of $1 over 8 years at the given interest rates is $(1.06)^6(1.04)^2$. Thus,

$$(1 + j)^8 = (1.06)^6(1.04)^2 = 1.534270272$$
$$j = (1.534270272)^{1/8} - 1$$
$$j = 0.054964228$$
$$j \doteq 5.50\%$$

OBSERVATION:

When compound interest rates vary, an average interest rate must *never* be calculated. Each compound interest rate must be allowed to have its full effect.

EXAMPLE 2   Cheryl took out a loan and must repay $10 000 in 10 years. The interest rates on the loan were $j_4 = 8\%$ for the first 3 years, $j_2 = 10\%$ for the next 5 years, and $j_1 = 9\%$ for the last 2 years. What was the original amount of the loan? What annual effective rate of interest was Cheryl charged over the 10-year period?

Solution   This problem should be tackled in three stages, moving from the value in 10 years' time towards the present value, stopping at each date that has an interest rate change. The following time diagram illustrates the problem:

The three stages in this solution are:

> *Step* 1   Value in 8 years' time $= 10\,000(1.09)^{-2}$
> $\doteq 8416.80$
>
> *Step* 2   Value in 3 years' time $= 8416.80(1.05)^{-10}$
> $\doteq 5167.19$
>
> *Step* 3   Value now $= 5167.19(1.02)^{-12}$
> $\doteq 4074.29$

This solution may also be expressed as:

$$\text{Present value} = \$10\,000(1.02)^{-12}(1.05)^{-10}(1.09)^{-2}$$
$$= \$4074.29$$

There are two ways to determine the annual effective rate of interest, j.

$$\$4074.29 = \$10\,000(1+j)^{-10}, \quad \text{which solves for } j = j_1 \doteq 9.39\%$$

OR

Accumulate \$1 for 10 years at j and set equal to the accumulated value of \$1 at the given interest rates.

$$(1+j)^{10} = (1.02)^{12}(1.05)^{10}(1.09)^2$$
$$j = (2.45441529)^{1/10} - 1 = 0.09394328 \doteq 9.39\%$$

Equations of value may also involve more than one interest rate. The above methods are appropriate for these problems such that when there is a change of interest rate, intermediate values should be calculated.

EXAMPLE 3   A student owes \$200 in 6 months and \$300 in 15 months. What single payment now will repay these debts if the interest rate is $j_4 = 12\%$ for 9 months and $j_4 = 8\%$ thereafter?

Solution   We arrange the data as set out in the following time diagram, where X is the single payment and time is expressed in quarters.

The present value of the \$200 debt $= 200(1.03)^{-2}$
$$\doteq 188.52$$
The value at time 3 of the \$300 debt $= 300(1.02)^{-2}$
$$\doteq 288.35$$
The present value of the \$300 debt $= 288.35(1.03)^{-3}$
$$\doteq 263.88$$
Hence the present value of both debts $= \$188.52 + \$263.88$
$$= \$452.40$$

This solution may also be expressed as

$$X = 200(1.03)^{-2} + 300(1.02)^{-2}(1.03)^{-3}$$
$$\doteq 188.52 + 263.88$$
$$= 452.40$$

Exercise 2.7

Part A

1. How much will \$2000 accumulate to in 12 years' time if the interest rate is $j_1 = 11\%$ for the first 6 years and $j_1 = 9\%$ for the next 6 years?

2. What is the present value of \$1000 in 6 years if $j_1 = 8\%$ for 2 years and $j_1 = 7\%$ thereafter?

3. Carol deposited \$500 into her credit union account on January 1, 2003. What will be in the account on January 1, 2008, if $j_2 = 5\%$ for 2003, $j_2 = 6\%$ for 2004 and 2005, and $j_2 = 4.5\%$ for 2006 and 2007? What effective rate of return did Carol earn over the 5-year period?

4. Two thousand dollars are invested for 10 years at the following interest rates:
$j_2 = 5\%$ for years 1, 2, and 3;
$j_4 = 8\%$ for years 4, 5, 6, and 7; and
$j_{12} = 6\%$ for years 8, 9, and 10.
Determine the accumulated value and the compound interest earned. What equivalent nominal rate, j_2, was earned over the 10-year period?

5. What sum of money due on July 1, 2007, is equivalent to \$2000 due on January 1, 2001, if $j_2 = 10\%$ for 2001 and 2002, and $j_2 = 9\%$ thereafter?

6. A debt of \$5000 is due at the end of 5 years. It is proposed that \$X be paid now with another \$X paid in 10 years' time to liquidate the debt.

Calculate the value of X if the effective interest rate is 12% for the first 6 years and 8% for the next 4 years.

7. A company wishes to replace the following three debts:
\$20 000 due on July 1, 2004
\$30 000 due on January 1, 2007 and
\$35 000 due on July 1, 2010
with a single debt of \$Y payable on January 1, 2007. Calculate the value of Y if $j_2 = 12\%$ prior to January 1, 2007 and $j_2 = 10\%$ after January 1, 2007.

8. A young couple owns a block of land worth \$29 000. They are offered a 20% deposit and 2 equal payments of \$15 000 each at the end of years 2 and 4. If money is worth $j_2 = 8\%$ for the first 2 years and $j_4 = 12\%$ for the next 2 years, should they accept the offer?

9. A person can buy a lot for \$15 000 cash outright or \$6000 down, \$6000 in 2 years, and \$6000 in 5 years. Which option is better if money can be invested at
a) $j_{12} = 18\%$?
b) $j_4 = 7.5\%$ for the first 3 years and $j_4 = 6\%$ for the next 2 years?

10. Determine the annual effective rate of interest that is equivalent to $j_4 = 6\%$ for 2 years followed by $j_{12} = 8\%$ for 4 years.

Part B

1. Show algebraically that

$$(1 + i)^n \times (1 + j)^n \neq \left(1 + \frac{i + j}{2}\right)^{2n}$$

and hence conclude that compound interest rates should not be averaged.

2. Gus invests $500 for 4 years. The nominal interest rate remains 8% each year although in the first year it is compounded semi-annually, in the second year compounded quarterly, in the third year compounded monthly, and in the fourth year compounded daily. What is the accumulated value? How much greater is this value than the corresponding value assuming that the first rate had remained unchanged for the 4 years?

3. Calculate the payment due on July 1, 2007, that is equivalent to $1000 due on January 1, 2004, plus $2000 due on March 1, 2009, if $j_4 = 8\%$ prior to July 1, 2007, and $j_{12} = 12\%$ thereafter.

4. Determine the lump sum that is needed to be invested today in order to receive $20 000 in 8 years and another $30 000 in 15 years if

$j_1 = 12\%$ for years 1, 2, and 3;
$j_2 = 10\%$ for years 4, 5, 6, 7, 8, and 9;
$j_4 = 8\%$ for years 10, 11, and 12; and
$j_{12} = 9\%$ for years 13, 14, and 15.

5. $1000 was deposited on January 1, 2002, and $2000 was deposited in an account on July 1, 2004. Interest was paid on the account at $j_4 = 7\%$ from January 1, 2002, to October 1, 2004, and at $j_2 = 5\%$ from October 1, 2004, until April 1, 2006. Determine the amount in the account on April 1, 2006, and determine the equivalent nominal interest rate compounded monthly actually earned on the investment over the period.

6. A sum of money is left invested for 3 years. In the first year, it earns interest at $j_{12} = 4\%$. In the second year, the rate of interest earned is $j_4 = 8\%$, and in the third year the rate of interest changes to $j_{365} = 5.5\%$. Calculate the level rate of interest, j_1, that would give the same accumulated value at the end of three years.

7. What compound interest rate, j_4, is equivalent over a 3-year period to a simple interest rate of 6% the first year, followed by a simple discount rate of 8% for the next 2 years?

| Section 2.8 | **Other Applications of Compound Interest Theory, Inflation, and the "Real" Rate of Interest** |

We know that the more money you invest at some given interest rate, i, the more dollars of interest you will earn. Further, once you earn a dollar's worth of interest, it becomes a part of the invested money and earns interest itself. The latter characteristic is referred to as multiplicative or geometric growth and is what differentiates compound interest from simple interest.

In any problem where there is geometric growth, even in nonfinancial situations, we can use the theory of compound interest.

EXAMPLE 1   A tree, measured in 2003, contains an estimated 150 cubic metres of wood. If the tree grows at a rate of 3% per annum, how much wood would it contain in 2013?

Solution   This is just geometric growth, so we can use compound interest theory. We have $P = 150$, $i = 0.03$, and $n = 10$. Thus, in 2013,

$$\text{Amount of wood,} \quad S = 150(1.03)^{10}$$
$$\doteq 202 \text{ cubic metres}$$

EXAMPLE 2 The population of Canada in July 1987 was 26.5 million people. In July 1997 it was 30.3 million people.
a) What was the annual growth rate from July 1987 to July 1997?
b) At this rate of growth, when will the population reach 40 million people?

Solution a We have $P = 26.5$, $S = 30.3$, $n = 10$, and we wish to determine $i = j_1$. Hence,

$$26.5(1 + i)^{10} = 30.3$$
$$(1 + i)^{10} = \frac{30.3}{26.5}$$
$$1 + i = \left(\frac{30.3}{26.5}\right)^{1/10}$$
$$1 + i = 1.013490484$$
$$i \doteq 1.35\%$$

Solution b We have $i = 0.0135$ from a), $P = 30.3$, $S = 40$, and we wish to determine n. Therefore,

$$30.3(1.0135)^n = 40$$
$$(1.0135)^n = \frac{40}{30.3}$$
$$n \log(1.0135) = \log \frac{40}{30.3}$$
$$n \doteq 20.71 \text{ years}$$
$$\doteq 20 \text{ years } 9 \text{ months}$$

Therefore our population will reach 40 million sometime in March 2018 assuming the same rate of growth.

EXAMPLE 3 In 1980, Nolan Ryan, a pitcher for the Houston Astros, became the first million-dollar-a-year major league baseball player. In 2001, Alex Rodriquez signed a contract with the Texas Rangers that paid him an average of $25.2 million per season. What is the annual rate of salary inflation from 1980 to 2001? If this salary increase continues, what is the expected highest annual salary in the 2010 season?

Solution We have $P = 1\,000\,000$, $S = 25\,200\,000$, $n = 2001 - 1980 = 21$ years. Thus,

$$1\,000\,000\,(1 + i)^{21} = 25\,200\,000$$
$$(1 + i)^{21} = 25.2$$
$$1 + i = (25.2)^{1/21}$$
$$1 + i = 1.166093459$$
$$i = j_1 \doteq 16.61\%$$

In the 2010 season, we expect the highest annual salary to grow to

$$S = \$25\,200\,000(1.166093459)^9 \doteq \$100\,461\,758$$

This appears to be unlikely to happen; thankfully, baseball owners have regained some sense of economic responsibility since 2001.

Inflation and the "Real" Rate of Interest

One very valuable use of compound interest theory is the analysis of rates of inflation. A widely used measure of inflation is the annual change in the Consumer Price Index. It measures the annual effective rate of change in the cost of a specified "basket" of consumer items.*

EXAMPLE 4   In June 1992 the Canadian Consumer Price Index was set at 100. In June 2005 the index was 125.95. That means that if goods cost an average of $100 in June 1992, they cost $125.95 in June 2005.
   a) Over that 13-year period, what was the average annual compound percentage rate of change?
   b) If that rate of inflation were to continue, how long would it take before the purchasing power of a June 1992 Canadian dollar was only 80¢?

Solution a   We have $P = 100$, $S = 125.95$, $n = 13$ and we wish to determine $i = j_1 =$ rate of inflation. Hence,

$$100(1 + i)^{13} = 125.95$$
$$(1 + i)^{13} = 1.2595$$
$$i = (1.2595)^{1/13} - 1$$
$$i \doteq 1.79\%$$

Solution b   In order to use the fundamental compound interest formula, we set $P = 0.80$, $S = 1$, $i = 0.0179$ and solve for n.

$$0.80(1.0179)^n = 1$$
$$(1.0179)^n = \tfrac{1}{0.80}$$
$$n \log 1.0179 = -\log 0.8$$
$$n \doteq 12.58 \text{ years}$$

The last example illustrated the effect of the rate of inflation as measured by the Consumer Price Index (CPI). Inflation rates vary from country to country and from time to time and can be relatively difficult to predict very far into the future. It is also possible to experience a period of time where prices drop and the CPI decreases. This is called deflation.

There is often a relationship between interest rates and rates of inflation. To illustrate this point, let's suppose that today you have $100 and you could buy a basket of goods with that $100. Suppose there is an inflation rate of 5%. This same basket of goods will now cost $105 at the end of the year. If you have not invested your $100, then at the end of the year it would only be worth $100/(1.05) = $95.24. In other words, if you wanted to buy that same basket of goods, you would be able to afford only 95.24% of the goods in the basket and would have to throw out 4.76% of them.

Had you invested your $100 at $i = 5\%$, you would have had $105 at the end of the year and would have been able to buy the exact same basket of goods. And

*The following Web site describes the CPI and also includes an inflation calculator. **http://www.bankofcanada.ca/en/rates/inflation_calc.html**

if you had earned more than 5%, you would have been ahead of the game at the end of the year. (For example, if you earned 8%, you would have had $108 at the end of the year and it would have bought $108/1.05 = $102.86 worth of goods, an increase of 2.86%.)

Investors need to take into account the rate of inflation when calculating the rate of return they have earned on an investment. When doing so, investors are calculating what is referred to as the "real" rate of return.

If i is the annual rate of interest being paid in the marketplace and r is the annual rate of inflation, then $1 invested at the beginning of the year will grow to $(1 + i)$ at the end of the year. However, its purchasing power is only equal to $\$\left(\dfrac{1+i}{1+r}\right)$. Hence, the real rate of return is

$$i_{real} = \frac{1+i}{1+r} - 1 = \frac{i-r}{1+r}.$$

To make a meaningful comparison of interest and inflation, both rates should refer to the same one-year period.

EXAMPLE 5   Jack invested $1000 for one year at $j_1 = 8\%$. The annual inflation rate for that year was 2%.

a) What was the annual real rate of return on Jack's investment?
b) What was Jack's annual real after-tax rate of return, if he paid tax at a 40% rate?
c) Repeat part b) for a 50% tax rate.

Solution a
$$i_{real} = \frac{0.08 - 0.02}{1 + 0.02} = 0.058823529 \doteq 5.88\%$$

What is happening is that Jack has $1080 at the end of the year. However, he cannot buy an additional $80 worth of goods because the price of those goods has increased by 2%. Jack can now buy $1080/1.02 = $1058.82 worth of goods at the end of the year in real terms, or an extra $58.82 worth of goods.

Solution b   Jack's annual real after-tax rate of return was

$$i_{real\ after\text{-}tax} = \frac{0.08(0.6) - 0.02}{1 + 0.02} = 0.02745098 \doteq 2.75\%$$

At the end of the year, Jack has an extra $80 in interest. However, 40% of this is taxed as income, so he gets to keep only 60% or $48. Since prices have increased by 2%, Jack can buy only $1048/1.02 = $1027.45 worth of goods at the end of the year. He is still ahead of the game, but both the government and the economy have conspired to eat away at his $80 of extra income.

Solution c   Jack's annual real after-tax rate of return was

$$i_{real\ after\text{-}tax} = \frac{0.08(0.5) - 0.02}{1 + 0.02} = 0.019607843 \doteq 1.96\%.$$

EXAMPLE 6   a) Suppose that the forecast for next year's annual inflation rate is $r = 5\%$, and for the annual interest rate it is $i = 4\%$. What will be the corresponding real rate of interest for the next year?

b) Using the values of r and i in part a), suppose you borrow $10 000 for a year at $i = 4\%$ and buy 5000 units of a certain item that has a current cost of $2 per unit. If the price of this item is tied to a rate of inflation $r = 5\%$ and you sell the items one year from now at the inflated price, what will be your net gain on this transaction?

Solution a

$$i_{real} = \frac{0.04 - 0.05}{1.05} \doteq -0.00952381 \doteq -0.95\%$$

Solution b

$$\text{Sell goods} = \$5000(2)(1.05) = \$10\ 500$$
$$\text{Pay back loan} = \$10\ 000(1.04) = \underline{\$10\ 400}$$
$$\text{Net gain} = \qquad \$100$$

OBSERVATION:

Example 6 illustrates that during times when inflation rates exceed interest rates there is an incentive to borrow at the negative real rate of interest. Similarly, it can be shown that at low real rates of interest there is an incentive to consume rather than to save.

Exercise 2.8

Part A

1. A city increased in population 4% a year during the period 1995 to 2005. If the population was 40 000 in 1995, what is the estimated population in 2015, assuming the rate of growth remains the same?

2. The population of Happy Town on December 31, 2002, was 15 000. The town is growing at a rate of 2% per annum. What would be the increase in population in the calendar year 2010?

3. At what annual growth rate will the population of a city double in 11 years?

4. If the cost of living rises 8% a year, how long will it take for the purchasing power of $1 to fall to 60¢?

5. The cost of living rises 2.1% a year for 5 years. Over that period of time, what would be the increase in value of a $160 000 house due to inflation only?

6. A university graduate starts his new job on his 22nd birthday at an annual salary of $28 000. If his salary goes up 5% a year (on his birthday), how much will he be making when he retires one day before his 65th birthday?

7. Calculate the real annual rate of return for the following pairs of annual interest rates i and annual inflation rates r:
   a) $i = 6\%$ $r = 2\%$
   b) $i = 8\%$ $r = 4\%$
   c) $i = 10\%$ $r = 6\%$

   For a), b), and c), calculate the real after-tax rate of return if the tax rate is 26%.

8. A potentially dangerous oil spill has occurred. It initially covered 0.25 square kilometres, but it is spreading at a rate of 10% per hour. If nothing is done to stop it, how long will it take before it covers an area of 10 square kilometres?

Part B

1. a) The number of fruit-flies in a certain lab increases at the compound rate of 4% every 40 minutes. If there are 100 000 flies at 1 p.m. today, what will be the increase in the number of flies between 7 a.m. and 11 a.m. tomorrow?

   b) At what time will there be 200 000 flies in the lab?

2. The population of a county was 200 000 in 1985 and 250 000 in 1995. Estimate the change in population of the county between 2005 and 2010.

3. You will need $X U.S. one year from now and can invest funds in a U.S. dollar account for the next year at $j_1 = 3\%$. Alternatively, you can invest in a Canadian dollar account for the next year at $j_1 = 6\%$. If the current exchange rate* is $0.82 U.S. = $1 Cdn., what is the implied exchange rate one year from now? Assume that both alternatives require the same amount of currency today.

4. Let i be the annual effective interest rate and r be the annual effective inflation rate. Show that the present value of $(1 + r)^n$ due in n years at an annual effective rate i is equal to the present value of 1 due in n years at an annual effective rate $\frac{i - r}{1 + r}$.

| Section 2.9 | **Continuous Compounding** |

In any text on calculus one will find the equation

$$\lim_{m \to \infty} \left(1 + \frac{x}{m}\right)^m = e^x$$

where the number $e \doteq 2.718$ has an infinite expansion and is the base of the natural logarithms.

This equation will be useful in compound interest problems where a nominal rate of interest is compounded continuously. Continuous compounding is an important topic for actuaries to develop theoretical models in actuarial science.

We have already dealt with problems where the nominal rate j has been compounded as often as daily. For example, consider the nominal rate of interest $j_m = 12\%$ compounded at different frequencies and compare the accumulated value of $1 over a 1-year period (so-called annual accumulation factors). The results can be summarized in the following table.

$$j_m = 12\%$$

m	**Annual Accumulation Factor**
1	$(1.12)^1$ $= 1.12$
2	$(1 + \frac{0.12}{2})^2$ $= 1.1236$
4	$(1 + \frac{0.12}{4})^4$ $= 1.12550881$
12	$(1 + \frac{0.12}{12})^{12}$ $= 1.12682503$
52	$(1 + \frac{0.12}{52})^{52}$ $= 1.127340987$
365	$(1 + \frac{0.12}{365})^{365}$ $= 1.127474614$

*For a current exchange rate, see **www.bankofcanada.ca/en/rates/exchform.htm***

From the above table we can see that as the frequency m of compounding increases, the annual accumulation factor also increases and approaches an upper bound as m is increased without limit, i.e., $m \to \infty$. To determine this upper bound that represents the annual accumulation factor at nominal rate 12% compounded continuously (i.e., $j_\infty = 12\%$), we wish to calculate:

$$\lim_{m \to \infty} \left(1 + \frac{0.12}{m}\right)^m$$

Using the equation

$$\lim_{m \to \infty} \left(1 + \frac{x}{m}\right)^m = e^x$$

we obtain

$$\lim_{m \to \infty} \left(1 + \frac{0.12}{m}\right)^m = e^{0.12} = 1.127496852$$

EXAMPLE 1   Determine

a) The rates j_2 and j_4 that are equivalent to $j_\infty = 6\%$.

b) The rate j_∞ that is equivalent to $j_1 = 9\%$ and $j_{12} = 9\%$.

Solution a   Using the principles of section 2.2, we equate the annual accumulation factors at each interest rate and obtain:

$$(1 + i)^2 = e^{0.06}$$
$$i = e^{0.06/2} - 1$$
$$i = 0.030454533$$
$$j_2 = 2i = 0.060909067$$
$$j_2 \doteq 6.09\%$$

$$(1 + i)^4 = e^{0.06}$$
$$i = e^{0.06/4} - 1$$
$$i = 0.015113064$$
$$j_4 = 4i = 0.060452258$$
$$j_4 \doteq 6.05\%$$

Solution b   Again using the principles of accumulating \$1 for 1 year under each interest rate, we obtain (note: ln = natural log):

$$(1.09) = e^{j_\infty}$$
$$j_\infty = \ln(1.09) = 0.086177696 \doteq 8.62\%$$
$$(1.0075)^{12} = e^{j_\infty}$$
$$j_\infty = 12 \ln(1.0075) = 0.089664178 \doteq 8.97\%.$$

OBSERVATION:

We can generalize the results of Example 1a) and state that for rates of interest that are equivalent,

$$j_1 > j_2 > j_4 > j_{12} > j_{365} > j_\infty.$$

The accumulated value S of principal P at rate j_m for t years is given by the fundamental compound interest formula **(7)**

$$S = P(1 + i)^n = P\left(1 + \frac{j_m}{m}\right)^{mt} = P\left[\left(1 + \frac{j_m}{m}\right)^m\right]^t$$

If interest is compounded continuously

$$S = \lim_{m \to \infty} P\left[\left(1 + \frac{j_m}{m}\right)^m\right]^t = Pe^{j_\infty t}$$

Similarly we can develop the formula for the discounted value P, given S, j_∞, and t.

$$P = Se^{-j_\infty t}$$

The following examples illustrate how the formula $S = Pe^{j_\infty t}$ can be used to determine the accumulated value S, the discounted value P, the rate j_∞, the effective rate j, and time in years t.

EXAMPLE 2   Determine the accumulated and the discounted value of $5000 over 15 months at a nominal rate of 8% compounded continuously.

Solution   We have $j_\infty = 0.08$, $t = \frac{15}{12} = 1.25$, and so can calculate the accumulated value S of $5000:

$$S = \$5000 \ e^{(0.08)(1.25)} = \$5525.85$$

and then the discounted value P of $5000

$$P = \$5000 \ e^{-(0.08)(1.25)} = \$4524.19$$

EXAMPLE 3   A mutual fund deposit of $1000 increased in value by $560 over 30 months. Determine

  a) the continuous rate of increase;

  b) the annual effective rate of increase.

Solution a   We have $P = 1000$, $S = 1560$, $t = \frac{30}{12} = 2.5$, and can solve the equation for j_∞.

$$1000 \ e^{j_\infty(2.5)} = 1560$$
$$e^{2.5j_\infty} = 1.560$$
$$2.5j_\infty = \ln 1.560$$
$$j_\infty = \frac{\ln 1.560}{2.5}$$
$$j_\infty = 0.177874329$$
$$j_\infty \doteq 17.79\%$$

Solution b We want to determine the equivalent annual effective rate j for a given rate $j_\infty = 0.177874329$ by comparing the accumulated value of $1 at the end of 1 year

$1 at j will accumulate to $1 + j$

$1 at $j_\infty = 0.177874329$ will accumulate to $e^{0.177874329}$

Thus

$$1 + j = e^{0.177874329}$$
$$j = e^{0.177874329} - 1$$
$$j = 0.194675175$$
$$j \doteq 19.47\%$$

We can also determine j by solving the equation

$$1000(1 + j)^{2.5} = 1560$$
$$(1 + j)^{2.5} = 1.560$$
$$1 + j = (1.560)^{1/2.5}$$
$$j = (1.560)^{1/2.5} - 1$$
$$j = 0.194675175$$
$$j \doteq 19.47\%$$

EXAMPLE 4 How long will it take to triple your investment at 6.25% compounded continuously?

Solution We have $P = x$, $S = 3x$, $j_\infty = 0.0625$ and can solve the equation below for time t in years.

$$x\, e^{0.0625t} = 3x$$
$$e^{0.0625t} = 3$$
$$0.0625t = \ln 3$$
$$t = \frac{\ln 3}{0.0625}$$
$$t = 17.5777966 \text{ years}$$
$$t \doteq 17 \text{ years, 6 months, 28 days}$$

Exercise 2.9

Part A

1. Fifteen hundred dollars is invested for 18 months at a nominal rate of 9%. Determine the accumulated value if interest is compounded a) annually; b) monthly; c) continuously.

2. A debt of $8000 is due in 5 years. Determine the original loan amount if the interest rate is 8% compounded a) quarterly; b) daily; c) continuously.

3. At what nominal rate compounded continuously will your investment increase 50% in value in 3 years? Determine also the equivalent annual effective rate.

4. By what date will $800 deposited on February 4, 2005, be worth at least $1200
   a) at 6% compounded daily;
   b) at 6% compounded continuously?

5. If money doubles at a certain rate of interest compounded continuously in 5 years, how long will it take for the same amount of money to triple in value?

6. Shirley must borrow $1000 for 2 years. She is offered the money at
   a) 8% compounded continuously;
   b) $8\frac{1}{4}$% compounded semi-annually;
   c) $8\frac{1}{2}$% simple interest.

   Which offer should she accept?

Part B

Actuaries use the notation δ for $j_\infty = i^{(\infty)}$ and call it the "force of interest."

1. What simple interest rate is equivalent to the force of interest $\delta = 7\%$ if money is invested for 5 years?

2. If the population of the world doubles every 25 years, how long does it take to increase by 50%? Assume population growth takes place continuously at a uniform rate.

3. The force of interest is $\delta = 10\%$. At what time should a single payment of $2500 be made so as to be equivalent to payments of $1000 in 1.25 years and $1500 in 6.5 years?

4. How long will it take $250 to accumulate to $400, if the force of interest is $\delta = 7\%$ for the first 2 years and $\delta = 8\%$ thereafter?

5. Jill borrowed $1000 and wants to pay off the debt by payments of $400 at the end of 3 months and 2 equal payments at the end of 6 months and 12 months. What will these payments be, if the force of interest is $\delta = 10\%$?

6. What simple discount rate is equivalent to 8% compounded continuously if money is invested for 4 years?

Section 2.10   **Summary and Review Exercises**

● Accumulated value of X at the end of n periods at the interest rate $i = \frac{j_m}{m}$ per interest period is given by $X(1 + i)^n$ where $(1 + i)^n$ is called an accumulation factor at compound interest.

● Discounted value of X due at the end of n periods at the interest rate $i = \frac{j_m}{m}$ per interest period is given by $X(1 + i)^{-n}$ where $(1 + i)^{-n}$ is called a discount factor at compound interest.

● Exact (theoretical) method of accumulating or discounting uses compound interest for the fractional part of an interest period.

  Approximate (practical) method of accumulating or discounting uses simple interest for the fractional part of an interest period.

● Equivalence of dated values at compound interest rate $i = \frac{j_m}{m}$:
  X is due on a given date is equivalent to Y due n periods later,
  $$\text{if} \quad Y = X(1 + i)^n \quad \text{or} \quad X = Y(1 + i)^{-n}.$$

Note: The above definition of equivalence of dated values at compound interest rate i satisfies the property of transitivity. At compound interest rate i, any choice of a comparison date to set up an equation of value will result in the same answer.

● Accumulated value of X at the end of t years at force of interest $\delta \equiv j_\infty$ is given by $Xe^{\delta t}$ where $e^{\delta t}$ is called an accumulation factor at continuous compounding.

● Discounted value of X due in t years at force of interest $\delta \equiv j_\infty$ is given by $Xe^{-\delta t}$ where $e^{-\delta t}$ is called a discount factor at continuous compounding.

Review Exercise 2.10

1. Determine the total value on June 1, 2007, of $1000 due on December 1, 2002, and $800 due on December 1, 2012, at $j_2 = 6.38\%$.

2. A person deposits $1500 into a mutual fund. If the fund earns 9.8% a year compounded daily for 10 years, what will be the accumulated value of the initial deposit?

3. On the birth of their first grandchild, the Guimonds bought a $100 savings bond that paid interest at $j_1 = 8\%$. How much money did their grandchild receive upon cashing this bond on her 20th birthday?

4. Determine a) the accumulated value; b) the discounted value of $2000 for 14 months at $j_2 = 8\%$ using both the theoretical and practical method.

5. The XYZ company has had an increase in sales of 4% per annum. If sales in 2006 are $680 000, what would be the estimated sales for 2011?

6. Calculate the amount of interest earned between 5 and 10 years after the date of an investment of $100 if interest is paid semi-annually at $j_2 = 7\%$.

7. Ahmed buys goods worth $1500. He wants to pay $500 at the end of 3 months, $600 at the end of 6 months, and $300 at the end of 9 months. If the store charges $j_{12} = 21\%$ on the unpaid balance, what down payment will be necessary?

8. A trust company offers guaranteed investment certificates paying $j_2 = 6\frac{3}{4}\%$, $j_4 = 6\frac{1}{4}\%$, or $j_{12} = 6\frac{1}{8}\%$ Rate the options from best to worst.

9. A note with face value $3000 is due without interest on November 21, 2010. On April 3, 2006 the holder of the note has it discounted at a bank charging $j_4 = 6\%$. What are the proceeds?

10. How long will it take $1000 to accumulate to $2500 at $j_{365} = 6\%$?

11. An investment fund advertises that it will triple your money in 10 years. What rate of interest, j_4, is implied?

12. A loan of $10 000, taken on January 1, 2005, is to be repaid with interest at $j_2 = 12\%$ on January 1, 2011. The debtor would like to pay $2000 on January 1, 2008, and make equal payments on January 1, 2010, and January 1, 2011. What will the size of these payments be if money is worth $j_4 = 8\%$?

13. By what date will $1000 deposited on November 20, 2006, at $j_{365} = 12\frac{1}{2}\%$ be worth at least $1250?

14. To pay off a loan of $5000 at $j_{12} = 9\%$, Mrs. Leung agrees to make three payments in two, five, and ten months respectively. The second payment is to be double the first, and the third payment is to be triple the first. What is the size of the first payment?

15. At what nominal rate compounded a) monthly, b) daily, c) continuously will money triple in value in 10 years?

16. Paul has deposited $1000 in a savings account paying interest at $j_1 = 4.5\%$ and now finds that his deposits have accumulated to $1246.18. If he had been able to invest the $1000 over the same period in a guaranteed investment certificate paying interest at $j_1 = 6\%$, to what sum would his $1000 now have accumulated?

17. A piece of land can be purchased by paying $50 000 cash or $20 000 down and equal payments of $20 000 at the end of two and four years respectively. To pay cash, the buyer would have to withdraw money from an investment earning interest at rate $j_2 = 8\%$. Which option is better and by how much?

18. A note for $2000 dated October 6, 2005 is due with compound interest at $j_{12} = 8\%$, two years after the date. On January 16, 2007, the holder of the note has it discounted by a lender who charges $j_4 = 9\%$. Determine the proceeds and the compound discount.

19. Jackie invested $500 in an investment fund. Determine the accumulated value of her investment at the end of 6 years, if the interest rate was $j_2 = 5.3\%$ for the first two years, $j_{12} = 7\%$ for the next three years, and $j_{365} = 4.5\%$ for the last year. What effective rate, j, did she earn over the 6 years?

20. Calculate the present value of $2000 due in $5\frac{1}{2}$ years if $j_4 = 8\%$ for the first 2 years and $j_2 = 10\%$ thereafter.

21. Calculate the accumulated value of $1000 at the end of 5 years using:
    a) annual effective interest rate of 6%;
    b) nominal interest rate of 6% compounded monthly;
    c) force of interest of 6% per annum.

22. Julie bought $2000 in Canada Savings Bonds that paid interest at $j_1 = 5\%$ with interest accruing at a simple interest rate for each month before November 1 (i.e., for any partial year). How much will she receive for the bonds if they are cashed in 5 years and 3 months after the date of issue?

23. $5000 is invested at $j_{12} = 11.8\%$ on May 10, 2006. What is the accumulated value on April 5, 2008, if the contract states that a) simple interest is calculated for a fraction of a month and b) compound interest is calculated for a fraction of a month?

24. An obligation of $2000 is due on February 4, 2009. Determine the value of this obligation on December 13, 2006, at 10% compounded quarterly, if simple interest is used for part of an interest period.

25. You borrow $4000 now and agree to pay $X in 3 months, $2X in 7 months, and $2X in 12 months. Determine X, if interest is at 9% compounded a) monthly; b) continuously.

26. How long will it take to double your money at a nominal interest rate of 10% compounded a) daily, b) continuously, c) quarterly, d) semi-annually? Calculate both the exact answers and the answers using the "Rule of 70" for a), c), and d).

CHAPTER 3

Simple Annuities

Learning Objectives

There are many situations where people make regular deposits into an account, or regular payments on a loan, or regular withdrawals from a fund. If the deposits, payments, or withdrawals are made at equal intervals of time and are the same amount each period, we end up with what is referred to as an annuity.

There are many examples of annuities in the financial world. Mortgage payments on a home, car loan payments, monthly retirement income, interest payments on bonds, payments of rent, deposits to and withdrawals from mutual fund accounts, dividends, payments on instalment purchases, and premiums on insurance policies are but a few examples of annuities.

In this chapter we introduce simple annuities. These are annuities where the frequency of payments matches the frequency at which interest on the annuity is compounded. Basic terminology is introduced in section 3.1, along with typical symbols that you would find on a financial calculator.

In section 3.2, the methods and symbols for determining the accumulated value of a series of payments made at the end of each period is developed, while section 3.3 deals with the discounted value of these payments. Section 3.4 begins by showing how to calculate the accumulated and discounted value of annuities where the payments are made at the beginning, as opposed to the end, of each period. These are called annuities-due. The section finishes by showing how to calculate the discounted value of a series of payments where the first payment is due sometime in the future. These are called deferred annuities.

Section 3.5 illustrates how to determine the number of payments needed if you wish to accumulate a certain sum of money, or if you invest a certain lump sum of money today. It also introduces two methods for determining the size of the final payment. The chapter ends with section 3.6, an important section that will show you how to determine the rate of return on an annuity. Both sections 3.5 and 3.6 also provide instructions on how to perform the various calculations using either a financial calculator or a computer spreadsheet program.

Section 3.1   Definitions

An **annuity** is a sequence of periodic payments, usually equal, made at equal intervals of time. The time between successive payments of an annuity is called the **payment interval.** The time from the beginning of the first payment interval to the end of the last payment interval is called the **term** of an annuity. When the term of an annuity is fixed, i.e., the dates of the first and the last payments are fixed, the annuity is called an **annuity certain.** When the term of the annuity depends on some uncertain event, the annuity is called a **contingent annuity.** Bond interest payments form an annuity certain; life-insurance premiums form a contingent annuity (they cease with the death of the insured). Unless otherwise specified, the word annuity will refer to an annuity certain.

When the payments are made at the ends of the payment intervals, the annuity is called an **ordinary annuity** (or **immediate annuity**). When the payments are made at the beginning of the payment intervals, the annuity is called an **annuity due**. A **deferred annuity** is an annuity whose first payment is due at some later date.

When the payment interval and interest compounding period coincide, the annuity is called a **simple annuity**, otherwise, it is a **general annuity** (see section 4.1).

We define the **accumulated value** of an annuity as the equivalent dated value of the set of payments due at the end of the term. Similarly, the **discounted value** of an annuity is defined as the equivalent dated value of the set of payments due at the beginning of the term.

We shall use the following notation (in parentheses are typical symbols used on a financial calculator):

R = the periodic payment of the annuity (PMT).

n = the number of interest compounding periods during the term of an annuity (in the case of a simple annuity, n equals the total number of payments) (N or n).

i = interest rate per conversion period (assume $i > 0$). (I/Y, $\%i$, or i).

S = the accumulated value, or the amount of an annuity (FV).

A = the discounted value, or the present value of an annuity (PV).

Section 3.2

Accumulated Value of an Ordinary Simple Annuity

The accumulated value S of an ordinary simple annuity is defined as the equivalent dated value of the set of payments due at the end of the term, i.e., **on the date of the last payment**. Below we display an ordinary simple annuity on a time diagram with the interest period as the unit of measure.

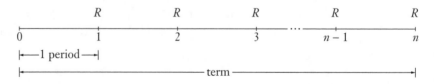

We can calculate the accumulated value S by repeated application of the compound interest formula as shown in the following example.

EXAMPLE 1   Calculate the accumulated value of an ordinary simple annuity consisting of 4 quarterly payments of $250 each if money is worth 6% per annum compounded quarterly.

Solution   We arrange the data on a time diagram below.

$j_4 = 6\%;\ i = \frac{0.06}{4} = 0.015$ per quarter

To obtain S we need to recognize the time value of money. That is, $250 paid at time 4 is not the same as $250 paid at time 1. We must write an equation of value using the end of the term (date of the last payment) as the focal date. This gives

S = sum of the accumulated value of each $250 payment
$= 250 + 250(1.015)^1 + 250(1.015)^2 + 250(1.015)^3$
$= 250 + 253.75 + 257.56 + 261.42$
$= \$1022.73$

Now we develop a formula for the accumulated value S of an ordinary simple annuity using the sum of a geometric progression. Geometric progressions are dealt with in Appendix 2.

Let us consider an ordinary simple annuity of n payments of $1 each as shown on a time diagram below.

Let us denote the accumulated value of this annuity $s_{\overline{n}|i}$ (read "s angle n at i"). Note that the symbol $s_{\overline{n}|i}$ is the accumulated value of the n-payments of $1 using the date of the nth payment as the focal date. To obtain $s_{\overline{n}|i}$ we write an equation of value at the end of the term, accumulating each $1 payment to the date of the last payment.

$$s_{\overline{n}|i} = 1 + 1(1+i)^1 + 1(1+i)^2 + 1(1+i)^3 + \cdots + 1(1+i)^{n-1}$$

The expression on the right side of the equal sign in the above equation is a geometric progression of n terms whose first term is $t_1 = 1$ and whose common ratio is $r = (1+i) > 1$. Then, applying the formula for the sum of a geometric progression, we obtain

$$s_{\overline{n}|i} = t_1 \frac{r^n - 1}{r - 1} = 1\frac{(1+i)^n - 1}{(1+i) - 1} = \frac{(1+i)^n - 1}{i}$$

> The factor $s_{\overline{n}|i} = \frac{(1+i)^n - 1}{i}$ is called an **accumulation factor for n payments**, or the **accumulated value of \$1 per period**.

To obtain the accumulated value S of an ordinary simple annuity of n payments of $\$R$ each, we simply multiply R by $s_{\overline{n}|i}$. Thus the basic formula for the accumulated value S of an ordinary simple annuity is

$$S = Rs_{\overline{n}|i} = R\frac{(1+i)^n - 1}{i} \tag{10}$$

Applying **(10)** in Example 1 above, we calculate

$$S = 250s_{\overline{4}|0.015} = 250\frac{(1.015)^4 - 1}{0.015} = \$1045.91$$

CALCULATION TIP:

In this textbook we calculate the factor $s_{\overline{n}|i} = \frac{(1+i)^n - 1}{i}$ directly on a calculator using all the digits of the display of the calculator to achieve the highest possible accuracy in our results.

EXAMPLE 2   A couple deposits \$500 every 3 months into a savings account that pays interest at $j_4 = 4\%$. They made the first deposit on March 1, 2006. How much money will they have in the account just after they make their deposit on September 1, 2010?

Solution   We arrange the data on a time diagram below, noting that the first deposit is made on March 1, 2006 (designated as time 1). To assist in calculating the correct value of n, we determine the date that represents time 0, which is one interest period (one quarter year) before the first deposit, or December 1, 2005.

	500	500	500		500	500
0	1	2	3	$\cdots$	18	19
Dec. 1	March 1	June 1	Sept. 1		June 1	Sept. 1
2005	2006	2006	2006		2010	2010

The time elapsed from December 1, 2005, to September 1, 2010, is exactly 4 years 9 months, or $n = 4.75 \times 4 = 19$ quarters of a year. Thus we calculate the accumulated value S of an ordinary simple annuity of 19 payments of \$500 each at $j_4 = 4\%$ or $i = 0.01$ per quarter as

$$S = 500s_{\overline{19}|0.01} = 500\frac{(1.01)^{19} - 1}{0.01} = \$10\,405.45$$

EXAMPLE 3   You make deposits of $1500 every six months starting today into a fund that pays interest at $j_2 = 7\%$. How much do you have in your fund immediately after the 30th deposit?

Solution   We have $R = 1500$, $n = 30$, and $i = 0.07/2 = 0.035$ per half year. Even though your first deposit is made today, you have been asked to determine the accumulated value on the date of your 30th deposit, which makes this an ordinary annuity. Thus,

$$S = 1500 s_{\overline{30}|0.035} = 1500 \frac{(1.035)^{30} - 1}{0.035} = \$77\,434.02$$

Calculating the Periodic Payment

When equation **(10)** is solved for R, we obtain

$$\boxed{R = \frac{S}{s_{\overline{n}|i}} = \frac{S}{\frac{(1+i)^n - 1}{i}}}$$

as the periodic payment of an ordinary simple annuity whose accumulated value S is given. This result is particularly useful for determining the deposit needed to achieve a future financial goal as the next example illustrates.

EXAMPLE 4   A man wants to accumulate a $200\,000$ retirement fund. He made the first deposit on March 1, 1994, and his plan calls for the last deposit to be made on September 1, 2015. Determine the size of each deposit needed if
   a) he makes the deposits semi-annually in a fund that pays 5% per annum compounded semi-annually.
   b) he makes the deposits monthly in a fund that pays 5% per annum compounded monthly.

Solution a   We have $S = 200\,000$ and $i = 0.05/2 = 0.025$ per half year. We wish to determine R.
   The first deposit is made on March 1, 1994 (designated as time 1). We need a date to represent time 0. It would be one interest period (in this case 6 months) earlier, which is September 1, 1993. We then note September 1, 1993 to September 1, 2015 (date of final deposit) is exactly 22 years or $n = 44$ half years.

We calculate $R = \dfrac{200\,000}{s_{\overline{44}|0.025}} = \dfrac{200\,000}{\frac{(1.025)^{44}-1}{0.025}} = \$2546.07.$

Semi-annual deposits of \$2546.07 will accumulate at $j_2 = 5\%$ to \$200 000 by September 1, 2015.

Solution b   We have $S = 200\,000$ and $i = 0.05/12 = 0.00416666$ per month.

The date that would represent time 0 is one interest period (in this case 1 month) before March 1, 1994, which is February 1, 1994. We then note February 1, 1994 to September 1, 2015 is exactly 21 years 7 months. Thus $n = 259$ months.

We calculate $R = \dfrac{200\,000}{s_{\overline{259}|i}} = \dfrac{200\,000}{\frac{(1+i)^{259}-1}{i}} = \$430.52.$

Monthly deposits of \$430.52 will accumulate at $j_{12} = 5\%$ to \$200 000 by September 1, 2015.

For some annuities, the interest rate may change over time. In other annuities, the periodic payment may change after a certain period of time.

To calculate the accumulated value for these types of annuities, we can use the "blocking technique". Every time the interest rate changes, or every time the periodic payment changes, we can consider that to be a "block". We then accumulate that "block" of payments to the focal date. The final equation of value will be the sum of the accumulated values of each "block" of payments.

Example 5 illustrates this method in a situation where the interest rate changes over time.

EXAMPLE 5   Mrs. Simpson has deposited \$1000 at the end of each year into her Registered Retirement Savings Plan for the last 10 years. Her investments earned $j_1 = 9\%$ for the first 4 years and $j_1 = 9\frac{1}{2}\%$ for the last 6 years. What is the value of her RRSP 5 years after the last deposit, assuming that her RRSP earns $j_1 = 9\frac{1}{2}\%$ for the 5-year period after the last deposit?

Solution   We arrange the data on a time diagram below.

In this example, there are two "blocks". The first block consists of the 4 deposits of $1000 while the interest rate is $i = 9\%$. The second block consists of the 6 deposits made while the interest rate is $i = 9.5\%$.

We need to accumulate each block to the focal date, which in this case is the end of 15 years (time 15). Don't forget that the first block of payments is first accumulated to the date of the last payment (time 4) at $i = 9\%$, and then that accumulated value is accumulated to time 15 at $i = 9.5\%$, which is the interest rate in effect for the 11 years from time 4 to time 15.

$$S = \text{accumulated value of block 1} + \text{accumulated value of block 2}$$

$$= 1000 s_{\overline{4}|0.09}(1.095)^{11} + 1000 s_{\overline{6}|0.095}(1.095)^5$$

$$= 1000 \frac{(1.09)^4 - 1}{0.09}(1.095)^{11} + 1000 \frac{(1.095)^6 - 1}{0.095}(1.095)^5$$

$$= 12\,409.91 + 11\,993.90 = 24\,403.81$$

The value of the RRSP 5 years after the last deposit is $24 403.81.

Using a Financial Calculator to Calculate Accumulated Values

We will illustrate the process using the Texas Instruments BA-35 calculator. Make sure the calculator is in FIN mode but is not in BGN mode (that will be needed for section 3.4).

To calculate the accumulated value of an ordinary simple annuity, you will need to enter the term in interest periods (N key), the periodic interest rate as a number not a percentage (I/Y key), the periodic payment entered as a negative value (PMT key) and a value of 0 for the present value (PV key). The latter value is entered as a precaution to avoid incorrect answers. To obtain the accumulated value, hit the CPT key followed by the FV key.

To calculate the periodic payment of an ordinary simple annuity, you will need to enter the accumulated value as a negative number (FV key). Then hit the CPT key followed by the PMT key.

The following illustrates the proper calculator entries for calculating the accumulated value of the annuity in Example 3 (Note: the values can be entered in any order):

30 $\boxed{N}$ 3.5 $\boxed{I/Y}$ −1500 $\boxed{PMT}$ 0 $\boxed{PV}$ $\boxed{CPT}$ $\boxed{FV}$
77 434.01591

The following illustrates the proper calculator entries for calculating the semi-annual payment in Example 4a):

44 $\boxed{N}$ 2.5 $\boxed{I/Y}$ −200 000 $\boxed{FV}$ 0 $\boxed{PV}$ $\boxed{CPT}$ $\boxed{PMT}$
2546.073651

Exercise 3.2

Part A

1. Determine the accumulated value of an ordinary simple annuity of $2000 per year for 5 years if money is worth a) $j_1 = 9\%$, b) $j_1 = 12\frac{1}{2}\%$.

2. Determine the accumulated value of an annuity of $500 at the end of each month for 4 years at 9% compounded monthly.

3. Lauren deposits $100 every month in a savings account that pays interest at $j_{12} = 4.5\%$. If she makes her first deposit on July 1, 2006, how much will she have in her account just after she makes her deposit on January 1, 2009?

4. A man deposits R dollars every 3 months beginning March 17, 2006 to September 17, 2009, after which he deposits $2R$ dollars beginning December 17, 2009 until June 17, 2015 at which time he will have $25 000. If he can earn $j_4 = 6\%$ on his money, what is R?

5. Jason is repaying a debt with payments of $120 a month. If he misses his payments for June, July, August and September, what payment will be required in October to put him back on schedule if interest is at 6% compounded monthly?

6. Determine the accumulated value of an annuity of $50 a month for 25 years if interest is a) 8% compounded monthly, b) $j_{12} = 11\%$.

7. Determine the accumulated value of annual deposits of $1000 each immediately after the 10th deposit if the deposits earned 5% per annum in the first 5 years and 6% per annum in the last 5 years.

8. Michael deposits $1000 at the end of each half-year for 5 years and then $2000 at the end of each half-year for 8 years. Determine the accumulated value of these deposits at the end of 13 years if interest is $j_2 = 7\%$.

9. Ashley deposits $500 into an investment fund each January 1 starting in 2005 and continuing to 2014 inclusive. If the fund has an average annual growth rate of $j_1 = 10\%$, how much will be in her account on January 1, 2019?

10. Mr. Juneau has deposited $800 at the end of each year into a RRSP investment fund for the last 10 years. His investments earned $j_1 = 10\%$ for the first 7 years and $j_1 = 9\%$ for the last 3 years. How much money does he have in his account 10 years after his last deposit if rates of return have remained level at $j_1 = 9\%$?

11. Rebecca has deposited $80 at the end of each month for 7 years. For the first 5 years the deposits earned 6% compounded monthly. After 5 years they earned 4.5% compounded monthly. Determine the value of the annuity after a) 7 years, b) 10 years.

12. What quarterly deposits should be made into a savings account paying $j_4 = 4\%$ to accumulate $10 000 at the end of 10 years?

13. It is estimated that a machine will need replacing 10 years from now at a cost of $80 000. How much must be set aside each year to provide that money if the company's savings earn interest at an 8% annual effective rate?

14. Jack has made semi-annual deposits of $500 for 5 years into an investment fund growing at $j_2 = 13\frac{1}{4}\%$. What semi-annual deposits for the next 2 years will bring the fund up to $10 000?

15. Marie deposited $150 at the end of each month into an account earning $j_{12} = 8\%$. She made these deposits for 14 years except that in the fifth year she was unable to make any deposits. Determine the value of the account two years after the last deposit.

Part B

1. Jane opened an investment account with a deposit of $1000 on January 1, 2003. She then made monthly deposits of $200 for 10 years (first deposit February 1, 2003). She then made monthly withdrawals of $300 for 5 years (first withdrawal February 1, 2013). Determine the balance in this account just after the last $300 withdrawal (i.e., January 1, 2018) if $j_{12} = 6\%$.

2. Frank has deposited $1000 at the end of each year into his Registered Retirement Savings Plan for the last 10 years. His deposits earned $j_1 = 9\%$ for the first 3 years, $j_1 = 11\%$ for the next 4 years, and $j_1 = 8\%$ for the last 3 years. What is the value of his plan after his last deposit?

3. Prove

a) $(1+i)s_{\overline{n}|i} = s_{\overline{n+1}|i} - 1$

b) $s_{\overline{m+n}|i} = s_{\overline{m}|i} + (1+i)^m s_{\overline{n}|i} = (1+i)^n s_{\overline{m}|i} + s_{\overline{n}|i}$

   Illustrate both a) and b) using a time diagram.

4. If $s_{\overline{n}|i} = 10$ and $i = 10\%$, calculate $s_{\overline{n+2}|i}$ and $s_{\overline{2n}|i}$.

5. Beginning June 30, 2006, and continuing every three months until December 31, 2010, Albert deposits $300 into a mutual fund account. Starting September 30, 2011, he makes quarterly withdrawals of $500. What is Albert's balance after the withdrawal on June 30, 2013, if growth of the mutual fund is at $j_4 = 8\%$ until March 31, 2009 and $j_4 = 6\%$ afterward?

6. It is desired to check a column of values of $s_{\overline{n}|i}$ from $n = 20$ through $n = 40$ by verifying their sum by means of an independent formula. Derive an expression for the sum of these values.

7. Deposits of $400 are made every 6 months. After 5 years, the deposits are increased to $800. After another 5 years, the deposits are decreased to $600. If the deposits earn $j_2 = 8\%$, how much has been accumulated just before the 26th deposit?

8. a) Show that $(1+i)^n = 1 + is_{\overline{n}|i}$.
   b) Verbally interpret this formula.

9. Determine an expression for an accumulation factor for n equal payments of $1 assuming simple interest at rate i per payment period.

10. Prove that $\dfrac{s_{\overline{2n}|}}{s_{\overline{n}|}} + \dfrac{s_{\overline{n}|}}{s_{\overline{2n}|}} - \dfrac{s_{\overline{3n}|}}{s_{\overline{2n}|}} = 1.$

11. a) Barbara wants to accumulate $10 000 by the end of 10 years. She starts making quarterly deposits in her investment account, which pays $j_4 = 8\%$. Determine the size of these deposits.

    b) After 4 years, the rate of return changes to $j_4 = 6\%$. Determine the size of the quarterly deposits now required if the $10 000 goal is to be met.

12. George wants to accumulate $7000 in a fund at the end of 10 years. He deposits $300 at the end of each year for the first 5 years and then $(300 + x)$ at the end of each year for the next 5 years. Determine x if $j_1 = 6\frac{1}{4}\%$.

13. You want to accumulate $100 000 at the end of 20 years. You deposit $1000 at the end of each year for the first 10 years and $(100 + x)$ at the end of each year for the second 10 years. Rate of return is $j_1 = 10\frac{1}{4}\%$.
    a) Determine x.
    b) If the last 4 payments of $1000 (at the end of years 7 through 10) were missed, what would be the value of x?

14. Beginning on June 1, 2005, and continuing until December 1, 2010, a company will need $250 000 semi-annually to retire a series of bonds. What equal semi-annual deposits in a fund paying $j_2 = 10\%$ beginning on June 1, 2000, and continuing until December 1, 2010, are necessary to retire the bonds as they fall due?

Section 3.3   ## Discounted Value of an Ordinary Simple Annuity

The discounted value A of an ordinary simple annuity is defined as the equivalent dated value of the set of payments due at the beginning of the term, i.e., **1 period before the first payment**. Below we display an ordinary simple annuity on a time diagram.

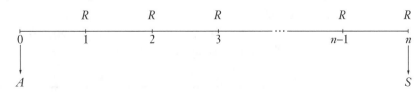

It is possible to derive the discounted value A in at least two different ways. Note first that A is the sum of a series of single discounted payments of R dollars each. That is,

$$A = R(1+i)^{-1} + R(1+i)^{-2} + \cdots + R(1+i)^{-n}$$

The value of A can be found as the sum of a geometric progression of n terms whose first term is $t_1 = R(1+i)^{-1}$ and whose common ratio is $r = (1+i)^{-1}$. We obtain:

$$A = t_1 \frac{1-r^n}{1-r} = R(1+i)^{-1} \frac{1-(1+i)^{-n}}{1-(1+i)^{-1}}$$

If we then multiply by $\frac{1+i}{1+i}$, we get:

$$A = R \frac{1-(1+i)^{-n}}{(1+i)-1} = R \frac{1-(1+i)^{-n}}{i}$$

Alternatively, we note that A and S are both dated values of the same set of payments and thus they can be made equivalent to each other using

$$A = S(1+i)^{-n}$$

Substituting for S from equation **(10)** we have:

$$A = R s_{\overline{n}|i} (1+i)^{-n} = R \frac{(1+i)^n - 1}{i} (1+i)^{-n} = R \frac{1-(1+i)^{-n}}{i}$$

If we set $R = 1$, we can denote the discounted value of this annuity as $a_{\overline{n}|i}$ (read "a angle n at i"). That is,

$$a_{\overline{n}|i} = \frac{1-(1+i)^{-n}}{i}$$

Note that this symbol $a_{\overline{n}|i}$ is the discounted, or present value of the n-payments of \$1 using the date one interest period before the first payment is due as the focal date.

If we wish to determine the discounted value of n payments of R dollars, we simply multiply R by $a_{\overline{n}|i}$. Thus, the basic formula for the discounted value A of an ordinary simple annuity is

$$\boxed{A = R a_{\overline{n}|i} = R \frac{1-(1+i)^{-n}}{i}} \qquad (11)$$

The factor $a_{\overline{n}|i} = \frac{1-(1+i)^{-n}}{i}$ is called a **discount factor for n payments**, or **the discounted value of \$1 per period**.

CALCULATION TIP:

We calculate the factor $a_{\overline{n}|i} = \frac{1-(1+i)^{-n}}{i}$ directly on a calculator and use all the digits of the display of the calculator to achieve the highest possible accuracy in our results.

EXAMPLE 1   On July 10, 2006 Mrs. Luigi buys an annuity that will provide her with payments of $1000 every three months, first payment October 10, 2006 and the final payment due on April 10, 2015. If the annuity pays interest at $j_4 = 5.2\%$, how much does Mrs. Luigi pay for the annuity?

Solution   We have $R = 1000$ and $i = 0.052/4 = 0.013$ per quarter. We note that July 10, 2006 is exactly one interest period (in this case 3 months) before the first payment is due, so we have an ordinary annuity.

To determine n, we count the number of interest periods from July 10, 2006 (designated as time 0) to April 10, 2015. There are exactly 8 years 9 months between these dates and thus $n = 8.75 \times 4 = 35$ payments. We arrange the data on a time diagram below.

	1000	1000		1000	1000	1000	1000
0	1	2	...	32	33	34	35
July 10	Oct. 10	Jan. 10		July 10	Oct. 10	Jan 10	April 10
2006	2006	2007		2014	2014	2015	2015

$\uparrow$
A

Setting up an equation of value at time 0 and using equation **(11)** we get,

$$A = 1000a_{\overline{35}|0.013} = 1000\frac{1 - (1.013)^{-35}}{0.013} \doteq \$27\,976.08$$

Note that the total value of the 35 payments of $1000 is $35 000, but Mrs. Luigi needs to invest only $27 976.08 on July 10, 2006 in order to receive the 35 quarterly payments. The difference of $7023.92 is due to compound interest.

EXAMPLE 2   Mr. Li buys some equipment and signs a contract that calls for a down payment of $1500 and for the payment of $200 a month for 10 years. The interest rate is 12% compounded monthly.
   a) What is the cash value of the contract?
   b) If Mr. Li missed the first 8 payments of $200, what must he pay at the time the ninth payment is due to bring himself up to date?
   c) If Mr. Li missed the first 8 payments of $200, what must he pay at the time the ninth payment is due to discharge his indebtedness completely?
   d) If, at the beginning of the 5th year (just after the 48th payment is made), the contract is sold to a buyer at a price that will yield $j_{12} = 15\%$, what does the buyer pay?

Solution a   Let C denote the cash value of the contract. Then C is $1500 plus the discounted value of 120 monthly payments of $200 each

1500	200	200		200	200	
0	1	2	...	119	120	$i = 1\%$

$\downarrow$
C

We calculate

$$C = 1500 + 200a_{\overline{120}|0.01} = 1500 + 200\frac{1-(1.01)^{-120}}{0.01}$$
$$\doteq 1500 + 13\,940.10 = \$15\,440.10$$

Solution b   Let X denote the required payment. Mr. Li must pay the accumulated value of the first 9 payments at the time the 9th payment is due.

We calculate

$$X = 200s_{\overline{9}|0.01} = 200\frac{(1.01)^9-1}{0.01} \doteq \$1873.71$$

Solution c   Let Y denote the required payment. Mr. Li must pay the accumulated value of the first 9 payments plus the discounted value of the last $(120-9) = 111$ payments at the time the 9th payment is due, in order to discharge his indebtedness completely.

$$Y = 200s_{\overline{9}|0.01} + 200a_{\overline{111}|0.01}$$
$$= 200\frac{(1.01)^9-1}{0.01} + 200\frac{1-(1.01)^{-111}}{0.01}$$
$$\doteq 1873.71 + 13\,372.38 = \$15\,246.09$$

Alternatively, we can calculate Y by calculating the discounted value of all 120 payments and then accumulating it to the end of the 9th period, i.e.,

$$Y = 200a_{\overline{120}|0.01}(1.01)^9 = 200\frac{1-(1.01)^{-120}}{0.01}(1.01)^9 \doteq \$15\,246.09$$

Solution d   Let Z be the price of the contract the buyer must pay. Then Z is the discounted value of the remaining $(120-48) = 72$ payments at $j_{12} = 15\%$. We calculate

$$Z = 200a_{\overline{72}|0.0125} = 200\frac{1-(1.0125)^{-72}}{0.0125} \doteq \$9458.49$$

OBSERVATION:

The solution to Example 2, part d) illustrates one of the major lessons to be learned in the mathematics of finance: to determine the price to be paid for an investment, the buyer (investor) needs to calculate the discounted value of his/her future cash flows. The interest rate used in the calculation is generally the rate of return the investor wishes to earn.

Calculating the Periodic Payment

When equation **(11)** is solved for R, we obtain

$$R = \frac{A}{a_{\overline{n}|i}} = \frac{A}{\frac{1 - (1+i)^{-n}}{i}}$$

as the periodic payment of an ordinary simple annuity whose discounted value A is given. This result is particularly useful in determining the periodic payment of an interest-bearing loan. Examples 3 and 4 illustrate this. It is also useful in determining the withdrawal that can be made every period from an initial lump sum investment. Example 5 illustrates this.

EXAMPLE 3   A bank loan of $5000 is to be repaid with quarterly payments over 4 years. Calculate the payment and the total interest paid on the loan if the bank charges interest at $j_4 = 8\%$.

Solution   The first payment is assumed to be due one period after the loan is taken out, unless otherwise stated.

We have $A = 5000$, $i = 0.08/4 = 0.02$, $n = 4 \times 4 = 16$ and calculate:

$$R = \frac{5000}{a_{\overline{16}|0.02}} = \frac{5000}{\frac{1 - (1.02)^{-16}}{0.02}} \doteq 368.25$$

Total interest paid over life of loan, $I = nR - A$
$$= 16(368.25) - 5000$$
$$= 892.00$$

The required loan payment made every 3 months is $368.25 and the total interest paid over the 4 year period is $892.00.

EXAMPLE 4   A car selling for $22 500 may be purchased by paying $2500 down and the balance in equal monthly payments for 5 years. Determine these monthly payments at a) $j_{12} = 12\%$; b) $j_{12} = 4.9\%$.

Solution a   We have $A = 20\,000$, $i = \frac{0.12}{12} = 0.01$, $n = 5 \times 12 = 60$ and calculate

$$R = \frac{20\,000}{a_{\overline{60}|0.01}} = \frac{20\,000}{\frac{1 - (1.01)^{-60}}{0.01}} \doteq \$444.89$$

Solution b   Using $A = 20\,000$, $i = \frac{0.049}{12}$, $n = 60$

$$R = \frac{20\,000}{a_{\overline{60}|i}} = \frac{20\,000}{\frac{1 - (1+i)^{-60}}{i}} \doteq \$376.51$$

Note the impact of the interest rate on the monthly payment. In a), at $j_{12} = 12\%$, total interest on the loan is $60(\$444.89) - \$20\,000 = \$6693.40$. In b), at $j_{12} = 4.9\%$, total interest on the loan is only $60(\$376.51) - \$20\,000 = \$2590.60$, more than $4100 less.

EXAMPLE 5   With the death of the insured on September 1, 2006, a life insurance policy pays out $80 000 as a death benefit. The beneficiary is to receive monthly payments, with the first payment on October 1, 2006. Determine the size of the monthly payments if interest is earned at $j_{12} = 8\%$ and the beneficiary is to receive 120 payments.

Solution   We have $A = 80\,000$, $i = \frac{0.08}{12}$, $n = 120$ and calculate

$$R = \frac{80\,000}{a_{\overline{120}|i}} = \frac{80\,000}{\frac{1-(1+i)^{-120}}{i}} \doteq 970.62$$

The size of the monthly payments is $970.62.

The next example deals with determining the discounted value of an ordinary annuity where the interest rate changes over time. In section 3.2 we discussed using the "blocking technique" to calculate the accumulated value of an annuity where either the interest rates change or the periodic payments change (or both) at some point during the term. The same technique can be used to determine the discounted value.

EXAMPLE 6   Susan has just retired and, as part of her retirement planning, she wishes to buy an annuity that pays her $2000 a month for 20 years (first payment made one month from now). How much will this annuity cost her today if the interest rate is $j_{12} = 6\%$ for the first 6 years and $j_{12} = 4.2\%$ thereafter?

Solution   We set up a time diagram

There are two "blocks" of payments. The first block consists of the 72 payments made while $i = 0.06/12 = 0.005$. The second block consists of the remaining 168 payments made while $i = 0.042/12 = 0.035$.

Both blocks need to be discounted to the focal date (time 0). Don't forget the second block must first be discounted to time 72 (one period before the first payment of the second block) and then further discounted to time 0 at $i = 0.005$, the interest rate in effect during the first 6 years.

A = discounted value of 1st block + discounted value of 2nd block

$\quad = 2000\,a_{\overline{72}|0.005} + 2000\,a_{\overline{168}|0.0035}(1.005)^{-72}$

$\quad \doteq 120\,679.028 + 253\,709.997(1.005)^{-72}$

$\quad = 120\,679.028 + 177\,166.287$

$\quad = \$297\,845.32$

Using a Financial Calculator to Calculate Discounted Values

Using the Texas Instruments BA-35 calculator, make sure the calculator is in FIN mode but is not in BGN mode (that will be needed for section 3.4).

To calculate the discounted values of an ordinary simple annuity, you will need to enter the term (N key), the periodic interest rate (I/Y key), the periodic payment entered as a negative value (PMT key) and a value of 0 for the accumulated value (FV key). The latter value is entered as a precaution to avoid incorrect answers. To obtain the discounted value, hit the CPT key followed by the PV key.

To calculate the periodic payment of an ordinary simple annuity, you will need to enter the discounted value as a negative number (PV key). Then hit the CPT key followed by the PMT key.

The following illustrates the proper calculator entries for calculating the discounted value of the annuity in Example 1:

35 $\boxed{N}$ 1.3 $\boxed{I/Y}$ –1000 $\boxed{PMT}$ 0 $\boxed{FV}$ $\boxed{CPT}$ $\boxed{PV}$
27 976.07902

The following illustrates the proper calculator entries for calculating the semi-annual payment in Example 4b):

60 $\boxed{N}$ 0.408333 $\boxed{I/Y}$ –20 000 $\boxed{PV}$ 0 $\boxed{FV}$ $\boxed{CPT}$ $\boxed{PMT}$
376.5090709

Exercise 3.3

Part A

1. Determine the discounted value of an ordinary simple annuity of $1000 per year for 5 years if money is worth a) $j_1 = 8\%$, b) $j_1 = 16\%$, c) $j_1 = 12.79\%$.

2. Determine the discounted value of an annuity of $380 at the end of each half-year for 3 years at a) $j_2 = 8\%$, b) $j_2 = 6\%$, c) $j_2 = 10.38\%$.

3. Mr. Goldberg wants to save enough money to send his two children to university. Since they are three years apart in age, he wants to have a sum of money that will provide $6000 a year for six years. Determine the single sum required one year before the first withdrawal if interest is at $j_1 = 8\%$.

4. Diana has an insurance policy whose cash value at age 65 will provide payments of $1500 a year for 15 years, first payment at age 66. If the insurance company pays $j_1 = 5\%$, on its funds, what is the cash value at age 65?

5. Alec buys a used car by paying $500 down plus $180 a month for 3 years. What was the price of the car if the interest rate on the loan is $j_{12} = 9\%$?

6. An annuity pays R dollars per month starting February 1, 2006, and ending January 1, 2009 (inclusive). If the value of this annuity on January 1, 2011, is $8000 and $j_{12} = 7.2\%$, what is its value on January 1, 2006?

7. Maria receives an inheritance of $25 000 on May 14, 2006. If she invests the money in a fund paying $j_4 = 7\%$, how much can she withdraw every 3 months if the first withdrawal is August 14, 2006 and the final withdrawal is August 14, 2021?

8. Determine the discounted value of annual payments of $1000 each over 10 years if interest is $j_1 = 6.5\%$ for the first 4 years and $j_1 = 8\%$ for the last 6 years.

9. An annuity pays $2000 at the end of each half-year for 5 years and then $1000 at the end of

each half-year for the next 8 years. Determine the discounted value of these payments if $j_2 = 10\%$.

10. An annuity pays 10 annual payments of $2000 each starting January 1, 2009. Determine the discounted value of these payments on January 1, 2006, if $j_1 = 7\%$.

11. A contract calls for payments of $250 a month for 10 years. At the beginning of the 5th year (just after the 48th payment is made) the contract is sold to a buyer at a price that will yield $j_{12} = 9\%$. What does the buyer pay?

12. A used car is purchased for $2000 down and $200 a month for 6 years. Interest is at $j_{12} = 10\%$.
   a) Determine the price of the car.
   b) If the first 4 monthly payments are missed, what payment at the time of the 5th payment will update the payments?
   c) Assuming no payments are missed, what single payment at the end of 2 years will completely pay off the debt?
   d) After 27 payments have been made, the contract is sold to a buyer who wishes to yield $j_{12} = 12\%$. Determine the sale price.

13. An insurance policy is worth $10 000 at age 65. What monthly annuity payment will this fund provide for 15 years if the insurance company pays interest at $j_{12} = 6\%$?

14. On the birth of their first child a couple puts $2000 in an investment account earning $j_1 = 6\%$. This fund is used to pay university fees and allows for three withdrawals corresponding to the 18th through 20th birthdays. What size are these withdrawals?

15. A television set worth $780 may be purchased by paying $80 down and the balance in monthly instalments for 2 years. Calculate the size of the monthly instalments if $j_{12} = 15\%$.

16. A family needs to borrow $5000 for some home renovations. The loan is to be repaid with monthly payments over 5 years. If they go to a finance company, the interest rate will be $j_{12} = 15\%$; if they use their credit card, the interest rate will be $j_{12} = 12\%$; and if they go to the bank, the rate will be $j_{12} = 9\%$. Determine the respective monthly payments and the total interest to be paid for each loan.

17. At age 65 Mrs. Bergeron takes her life savings of $120 000 and buys a 15-year annuity certain

with monthly payments. Determine the size of these payments a) at 6% compounded monthly; b) at 9% compounded monthly.

18. A person buys a boat with a cash price of $4500. She pays $500 down and the balance is financed at $j_{12} = 8.64\%$. If she is to make 24 equal monthly payments, what will be the size of each payment?

Part B

1. Prove
   a) $(1 + i)a_{\overline{n}|i} = a_{\overline{n-1}|i} + 1$
   b) $\dfrac{1}{s_{\overline{n}|i}} + i = \dfrac{1}{a_{\overline{n}|i}}$
   c) $a_{\overline{m+n}|i} = a_{\overline{m}|i} + (1 + i)^{-m} a_{\overline{n}|i} = (1 + i)^{-n} a_{\overline{m}|i} + a_{\overline{n}|i}$

2. If $a_{\overline{n}|i} = 10$ and $i = 0.08$, determine $s_{\overline{n}|i}$ and $a_{\overline{2n}|i}$.

3. Explain logically why $1 = ia_{\overline{n}|i} + (1 + i)^{-n}$ and illustrate on a time diagram.

4. If $a_{\overline{2n}|i} = 1.6a_{\overline{n}|i}$ and $i = 10\%$, determine $s_{\overline{2n}|i}$.

5. If $a_{\overline{n}|i} = 6$ when $i = \frac{1}{9}$, determine $a_{\overline{n+2}|i}$.

6. Determine an expression for a discounted factor for n equal payments of $1 assuming simple interest at rate i per payment period.

7. If money doubles itself in n years at rate i, show that $a_{\overline{n}|i}$, $a_{\overline{2n}|i}$, and $s_{\overline{n}|i}$ are in arithmetic progression.

8. Prove that $(1 - ia_{\overline{n}|i})$, 1, $(is_{\overline{n}|i} + 1)$ are in geometric progression.

9. If $X(s_{\overline{2n}|i} + a_{\overline{2n}|i}) = (s_{\overline{3n}|i} + a_{\overline{n}|i})$, what is the value of X?

10. Mrs. Cheung signed a contract that calls for payments of $150 a month for 5 years. The interest rate is $j_{12} = 6\%$.
   a) What is the cash value of the contract?
   b) If Mrs. Cheung missed making the first 6 payments, what must she pay at the time of the 7th payment to be fully up to date?
   c) If Mrs. Cheung missed the first 6 payments, what must she pay at the time of the 7th payment to fully discharge all indebtedness? (Can you find the answer to c) directly from the answer to a)?)
   d) If, at the beginning of the 3rd year (after 24 payments have been made) the contract is sold to a buyer at a price that will yield $j_{12} = 9\%$, what does the buyer pay? Is this value larger

or smaller than the discounted value of Mrs. Cheung's indebtedness at that time?

11. An annuity pays $200 at the end of each month for 2 years, then $300 at the end of each month for the next year, and then $400 at the end of each month for the next 2 years. How much does it cost to buy this annuity today if $j_{12} = 10\%$?

12. The ABC corporation borrows $100 000 on September 10, 2006. The interest rate on the loan is $j_2 = 10\%$ until March 10, 2009 when it changes to $j_2 = 7\%$ until September 10, 2013 upon which it changes to $j_2 = 5\%$ thereafter. To repay the loan, ABC pays R dollars from March 10, 2007 until September 10, 2018. What is R?

13. The Ace Manufacturing Company is considering the purchase of two machines. Machine A costs $200 000 and Machine B costs $400 000. The machines are projected to have a life of five years and to yield the following revenues:

	Cash Revenue	
End of Year	**Machine A**	**Machine B**
1	none	$90 000
2	$100 000	90 000
3	100 000	90 000
4	100 000	90 000
5	100 000	300 000

The market rate of interest is 14% per annum compounded yearly. Which machine should the company purchase?

14. A man aged 31 wishes to accumulate a fund for retirement by depositing $1000 each year for the next 35 years (ages 31 to 65 inclusive). Starting on his 66th birthday he will make 15 annual withdrawals of equal amount. Determine the amount of each withdrawal if $j_1 = 10\%$ throughout.

15. To prepare for early retirement, a self-employed consultant makes deposits of $5500 into her Registered Retirement Savings Plan each year for 20 years, starting on her 31st birthday. When she is 51 she wishes to draw out 30 equal annual payments. What is the size of each withdrawal if interest is at $j_1 = 6\%$ until the 10th deposit and at $j_1 = 5\%$ for the remaining time?

16. Mr. Horvath has been accumulating a retirement fund at an annual effective rate of 9% that will provide him with an income of $12 000 per year for 20 years, the first payment on his 65th birthday. If he now wishes to reduce the number of retirement payments to 15, what should he receive annually?

17. Today Wilma purchased a cottage and a boat worth a combined present value of $130 000. To purchase the cottage, Wilma agreed to pay $20 000 down and $700 at the end of each month for 20 years. To buy the boat, Wilma was required to pay $2000 down and R dollars at the end of each month for 4 years. Determine R if $j_{12} = 12\%$.

| *Section 3.4* | ## Other Simple Annuities |

In this section we introduce other simple annuities that can be treated as minor modifications of ordinary annuities.

Annuities Due

An **annuity due** is an annuity whose periodic payments are due at the beginning of each payment interval. The term of an annuity due starts at the time of the first payment and ends one payment period after the date of the last payment. The diagram below shows the simple case (payment intervals and interest periods coincide) of an annuity due of n payments.

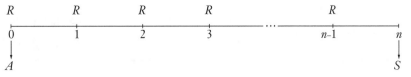

It is easy to recognize an annuity due as a "slipped" ordinary annuity, that is, each of the n payments of R has been moved one period to the left on the time diagram (compare this time diagram to the one on page 83 in section 3.3). Thus we can simply write the formulas for the accumulated value S and discounted value A of an annuity due, by adjusting equations **(10)** and **(11)** from sections 3.1 and 3.2.

Since the accumulated value of an annuity was defined as the equivalent dated value of the payments at the end of the term, it means that the accumulated value S of an annuity due is an equivalent value **due one period after the last payment**.

The accumulated value of the payments on the date of the nth payment (which is time $n - 1$) is $Rs_{\overline{n}|i}$. We then accumulate $Rs_{\overline{n}|i}$ for 1 interest period, to obtain

$$\boxed{S = Rs_{\overline{n}|i}(1+i)}$$

To determine A, we recall that the discounted value of an annuity was defined as the equivalent dated value of the payments at the beginning of the term. Thus the discounted value of an annuity due is an equivalent value **due at the time of the first payment**.

The discounted value of the payments 1 period before the 1st payment is $Ra_{\overline{n}|i}$. We then accumulate $Ra_{\overline{n}|i}$ for 1 interest period to obtain

$$\boxed{A = Ra_{\overline{n}|i}(1+i)}$$

Actuaries often use the following notation for the accumulated and discounted value of a $1 annuity due:

1. Accumulated value, $\ddot{s}_{\overline{n}|i} = s_{\overline{n}|i}(1+i)$.

2. Discounted value, $\ddot{a}_{\overline{n}|i} = a_{\overline{n}|i}(1+i)$.

EXAMPLE 1 Mary Jones deposits $100 at the beginning of each month for 3 years into an account paying $j_{12} = 4.5\%$. How much is in her account at the end of 3 years?

Solution We arrange the data on a time diagram below.

The payments are made from time 0 to time 35 (but there are $n = 3 \times 12 = 36$ payments in total). Note how we wish to determine the accumulated value at the end of 3 years, or time 36, which is one period after the final payment. Thus we have an annuity due situation.

We have $R = 100$, $i = \frac{0.045}{12} = 0.00375$, $n = 36$ and calculate

$$S = 100\ddot{s}_{\overline{36}|0.00375} = 100s_{\overline{36}|0.00375}(1.00375) = \$3861.03$$

EXAMPLE 2   The monthly rent for a townhouse is $1640 payable at the beginning of each month. If money is worth $j_{12} = 9\%$,

   a) what is the equivalent yearly rentable payable in advance,

   b) what is the cash equivalent of 5 years of rent?

Solution a   We arrange the data on a time diagram below.

We wish to determine the present value of the 12 payments of $1640 at time 0, which is the same date where the first payment is made. Thus we have an annuity due.

$$A = 1640\,\ddot{a}_{\overline{12}|0.0075} = 1640a_{\overline{12}|0.0075}(1.0075) = \$18\,893.91$$

Solution b   We calculate the discounted value A of an annuity due of 60 payments of $1640 each at $j_{12} = 9\%$

$$A = 1640\,\ddot{a}_{\overline{60}|0.0075} = 1640a_{\overline{60}|0.0075}(1.0075) = \$79\,596.87$$

In Example 1, if there was a deposit made at the end of 3 years (that is, at time 36), there would be $n = 37$ deposits in total and the accumulated value at the end of 3 years would increase by $100 to $3961.03. Another way to obtain this answer is to note that the accumulated value would now be calculated at the time of the 37th deposit, making it an ordinary annuity:

$$100s_{\overline{37}|0.00375} = \$3961.03$$

We can generalize this result (with $R = 1$) as follows:

$$\boxed{\ddot{s}_{\overline{n}|i} = s_{\overline{n+1}|i} - 1}$$

In Example 2a), we could consider the payment made at time 0 as a down payment and treat the remaining payments as an ordinary annuity. That is,

$$18\,893.91 = 1640 + \text{discounted value of other 11 payments}$$
$$= 1640 + 1640a_{\overline{11}|0.0075}$$

We can generalize this result (with $R = 1$) as follows:

$$\boxed{\ddot{a}_{\overline{n}|i} = 1 + a_{\overline{n-1}|i}}$$

EXAMPLE 3   A debt of $10\,000$ is due today. However, it is agreed that it can be paid back with 8 quarterly payments, the first due today. If $j_4 = 11\%$, determine the required quarterly payment.

Solution Arranging the data on a time diagram below:

We have $A = 10\,000$, $i = 0.0275$, $n = 8$ and calculate R one of two ways:

$$10\,000 = R\ddot{a}_{\overline{8}|0.0275} = Ra_{\overline{8}|0.0275}(1.0275)$$

$$R = \frac{10\,000}{a_{\overline{8}|0.0275}(1.0275)} = \$1371.85$$

OR

$$10\,000 = R\ddot{a}_{\overline{8}|0.0275} = R + Ra_{\overline{7}|0.0275}$$

$$R = \frac{10\,000}{1 + a_{\overline{7}|0.0275}} = \$1371.85$$

EXAMPLE 4 You wish to accumulate $20\,000 in 5 years time. To do so, you plan to make 10 semi-annual deposits, first deposit made today. If you can earn $j_2 = 6\%$, what deposit is needed?

Solution We have $S = 20\,000$, $i = 0.03$, $n = 10$, and the following time diagram:

We calculate R one of two ways:

$$20\,000 = R\ddot{s}_{\overline{10}|0.03} = Rs_{\overline{10}|0.03}(1.03)$$

$$R = \frac{20\,000}{s_{\overline{10}|0.03}(1.03)} = \$1693.80$$

OR

$$20\,000 = R\ddot{s}_{\overline{10}|0.03} = Rs_{\overline{11}|0.03} - R$$

$$R = \frac{20\,000}{s_{\overline{11}|0.03} - 1} = \$1693.80$$

Deferred Annuities

A **deferred annuity** is an annuity whose first payment is due some time later than the end of the first interest period. It is customary to analyze all deferred annuities as ordinary deferred annuities. Thus, an ordinary deferred annuity is an ordinary annuity whose term is deferred for (let's say) k periods. The time diagram below shows the simple case of an ordinary deferred annuity.

OBSERVATION:

Note that in the above diagram the period of deferment is k periods and the first payment of the ordinary annuity is $k + 1$. This is because the term of an ordinary annuity starts one period before its first payment. Thus, the period of deferment is equal to: time of first payment $- 1$.

To determine the discounted value A of an ordinary deferred annuity we calculate the discounted value of n payments one period before the first payment and discount this sum for k periods.

Discounted value one period before first payment (time k) $= Ra_{\overline{n}|i}$
Discount factor for k-periods $= (1 + i)^{-k}$

Thus

$$A = Ra_{\overline{n}|i}(1 + i)^{-k}$$

If you now return to Exercise 3.3, Part A, you will see that we have already handled questions of this nature (questions 10 and 14, for example).

EXAMPLE 5   What sum of money should be set aside on a child's birth to provide 8 semi-annual payments of \$4000 to cover the expenses for university education if the first payment is to be made on the child's 18th birthday? The fund will earn interest at $j_2 = 7\%$.

Solution   We arrange the data on a time diagram below.

We have $R = 4000$, $i = 0.035$ per half year, $n = 8$, $k = 35$, and calculate:

$$A = 4000a_{\overline{8}|0.035}(1.035)^{-35}$$
$$= 27\,495.82215(1.035)^{-35} \doteq \$8248.11$$

EXAMPLE 6   Jaclyn wins $100 000 in a provincial lottery. She takes only $20 000 in cash and invests the balance at $j_{12} = 8\%$ with the understanding that she will receive 180 equal monthly payments with the first one to be made in 4 years. Calculate the size of the payments.

Solution   The first payment is due in $4 \times 12 = 48$ months, so the deferral period is one less, or $k = 47$.

We have $A = 80\ 000$, $i = \frac{0.08}{12}$, $n = 180$, $k = 47$ and calculate R from the equation

$$80\ 000 = Ra_{\overline{180}|i}(1+i)^{-47}$$

$$R = \frac{80\ 000(1+i)^{47}}{a_{\overline{180}|i}} = \$1044.76$$

CALCULATION TIP:

In general, problems involving any simple annuities can be efficiently solved by applying equations **(10)** and **(11)** for ordinary annuities to find equivalent lump sums and then moving to a requested point in time.

EXAMPLE 7   A couple deposits $200 a month in a savings account paying interest at $j_{12} = 4\frac{1}{2}\%$. The first deposit is made on February 1, 2005 and the last deposit on July 1, 2011.
  a) How much money is in the account on
    i)   January 1, 2009 (after the payment is made)
    ii) January 1, 2010 (before the payment is made)
    iii) January 1, 2013?
  b) If they want to draw down their account with equal monthly withdrawals from February 1, 2013 to February 1, 2014, how much will they get each month?

Solution a   We arrange the data on a time diagram below.

	200	200		200		200		200		
0	1	2	...	48	...	60	...	78	...	96
Jan. 1	Feb. 1	Mar. 1		Jan. 1		Jan. 1		July 1		Jan. 1
2005	2005	2005		2009		2010		2011		2013
				S_1		S_2				S_3

i) We have $R = 200$, $i = \frac{0.045}{12}$, and calculate the accumulated value of 48 payments at the time of the 48th payment (thus we have an ordinary annuity).

$$S_1 = 200s_{\overline{48}|i} = \$10\,496.77$$

ii) We have an annuity due and we can calculate the accumulated value of 59 payments.

$$S_2 = 200\ddot{s}_{\overline{59}|i} = 200s_{\overline{59}|i}(1 + i) = \$13\,229.11$$

OR

We can calculate the accumulated value of 60 payments of an ordinary annuity and subtract the last payment.

$$S_2 = 200s_{\overline{60}|i} - 200 = \$13\,229.11$$

iii) We calculate the accumulated value of 78 payments to the time of the 78th payment ($= 200s_{\overline{78}|i}$) and then accumulate this amount for 18 more months.

$$S_3 = 200s_{\overline{78}|i}(1 + i)^{18} = \$19\,342.37$$

Solution b   Using result iii) from solution a) the accumulated value of their deposits on January 1, 2013, becomes the discounted value of their 13 future withdrawals, one month before the first withdrawal. We calculate the monthly withdrawal

$$19\,342.37 = Ra_{\overline{13}|i}$$
$$R = \frac{19\,342.37}{a_{\overline{13}|i}} = \$1527.22$$

Using a Financial Calculator for Annuities Due

For calculating periodic payments, accumulated or discounted values of an annuity due, you need to make sure your BA-35 calculator is in FIN mode and is also in BGN mode (BGN stands for "payments at the beginning of each period"). You then follow the exact same steps as given in sections 3.2 and 3.3.

The following illustrates the proper calculator entries for calculating the accumulated value of the annuity due in Example 1:

36    $\boxed{N}$ 0.375 $\boxed{I/Y}$ −100 $\boxed{PMT}$ 0 $\boxed{PV}$ $\boxed{CPT}$ $\boxed{FV}$
                                                                                                        3861.033641

The following illustrates the proper calculator entries for calculating the discounted value of the annuity due in Example 2a):

12    $\boxed{N}$ 0.75 $\boxed{I/Y}$ −1640 $\boxed{PMT}$ 0 $\boxed{FV}$ $\boxed{CPT}$ $\boxed{PV}$
                                                                                                        18\,893.390621

The following illustrates the proper calculator entries for calculating the quarterly payment in Example 3:

8   $\boxed{N}$ 2.75 $\boxed{I/Y}$ –10 000 $\boxed{PV}$ 0 $\boxed{FV}$ $\boxed{CPT}$ $\boxed{PMT}$

1371.853506

Using a Financial Calculator for Deferred Annuities

You must first get out of BGN mode. You must also have set up your equation of value so that you know the value of n (term of the annuity) and k (deferral period). The process is to first calculate the discounted value of the annuity and then discount that value k-periods. The following illustrates the proper calculator entries for calculating the discounted value of the deferred annuity in Example 5:

8   $\boxed{N}$ 3.5 $\boxed{I/Y}$ –4000 $\boxed{PMT}$ 0 $\boxed{FV}$ $\boxed{CPT}$ $\boxed{PV}$

27 495.82215

After this calculation, you add a negative sign to your answer and then push the FV key (as –$27 495.82215 represents the future value of your annuity that is supposed to start $k = 35$ periods earlier). The full sequence is:

$\boxed{FV}$ 35 $\boxed{N}$ 3.5 $\boxed{I/Y}$ 0 $\boxed{PMT}$ $\boxed{CPT}$ $\boxed{PV}$

8248.110436

Exercise 3.4

Part A

1. Determine the discounted value and the accumulated value of $500 payable semi-annually at the beginning of each half-year over 10 years if interest is 8% per annum payable semi-annually.

2. A couple wants to accumulate $10 000 by December 31, 2015. They make 10 annual deposits starting January 1, 2006. If interest is at $j_1 = 12\%$, what annual deposits are needed?

3. The premium on a life insurance policy can be paid either yearly or at the beginning of each month. If the annual premium is $120, what monthly premium would be equivalent at $j_{12} = 5\%$?

4. Deposits of $350 are made every three months from June 1, 2006 to June 1, 2009. How much has been accumulated on September 1, 2009 if the deposits earn $j_4 = 6\%$?

5. An insurance policy provides a death benefit of $100 000 or payments at the beginning of each month for 10 years. What size would these monthly payments be if $j_{12} = 5.5\%$?

6. A used car sells for $9550. Brent wishes to pay for it in 18 monthly instalments, the first due on the day of purchase. If 12% compounded monthly is charged, determine the size of the monthly payment.

7. A realtor rents office space for $5800 every three months, payable in advance. He immediately invests half of each payment in a fund paying 9% compounded quarterly. How much is in the fund at the end of 5 years?

8. A refrigerator is bought for $60 down and $60 a month for 15 months. If interest is charged at $j_{12} = 8\frac{1}{2}\%$, what is the cash price of the refrigerator?

9. Determine the discounted value of an ordinary annuity deferred 5 years paying $1000 a year for 10 years if interest is at $j_1 = 8\%$.

10. Determine the discounted value of an ordinary annuity deferred 3 years 6 months that pays

$500 semi-annually for 7 years if interest is 7% compounded semi-annually.

11. What sum of money must be set aside at a child's birth to provide for 6 semi-annual payments of $1500 to cover the expenses for a university education if the first payment is to be made on the child's 19th birthday and interest is at $j_2 = 8\%$?

12. On Mr. Pimentel's 55th birthday, the Pimentels decide to sell their house and move into an apartment. They realize $150 000 on the sale of the house and invest this money in a fund paying $j_1 = 9\%$. On Mr. Pimentel's 65th birthday they make their first of 15 annual withdrawals that will exhaust the fund. What is the dollar size of each withdrawal?

13. Mrs. Howlett changes employers at age 46. She is given $8500 as her vested benefits in the company's pension plan. She invests this money in an RRSP (Registered Retirement Savings Plan) paying $j_1 = 8\%$ and leaves it there until her ultimate retirement at age 61. She plans on 25 annual withdrawals from this fund, the first withdrawal on her 61st birthday. Determine the size of these withdrawals.

14. Determine the value on January 1, 2007, of quarterly payments of $100 each over 10 years if the first payment is on January 1, 2009, and interest is 7% compounded quarterly.

15. Determine the value on July 1, 2006, of semi-annual payments of $500 each over 6 years if the first payment is on January 1, 2010, and interest is at $5\frac{1}{4}\%$ payable semi-annually.

16. The XYZ Furniture Store sells a chesterfield for $950. It can be purchased for $50 down and no payments for 3 months. At the end of the third month you make your first payment and continue until a total of 18 payments are made. Determine the size of each payment if interest is at $j_{12} = 18\%$.

17. An 8-year-old child wins $1 000 000 from a lottery. The law requires that this money be set aside in a trust fund until the child reaches 18. The child's parents decide that the money should be paid out in 20 equal annual payments with the first payment at age 18. Calculate these payments if the trust fund pays interest at $j_1 = 10\%$.

Part B

1. A man aged 40 deposits $5000 at the beginning of each year for 25 years into an RRSP paying interest at $j_1 = 7\%$. Starting on his 65th birthday he makes 15 annual withdrawals from the fund at the beginning of each year. During this period (i.e., from his 65th birthday on) the fund pays interest at $j_1 = 6\%$. Determine the amount of each withdrawal starting at age 65.

2. Jacques signed a contract that calls for payments of $500 at the beginning of each 6 months for 10 years. If money is worth $j_2 = 13\%$, determine the value of the remaining payments
a) just after he makes the 4th payment;
b) just before he makes the 6th payment.
If after making the first 3 payments he failed to make the next 3 payments,
c) what would he have to pay when the next payment is due to bring himself back on schedule?

3. Using a geometric progression, derive the formula for the accumulated value S of an annuity due

$$S = Rs_{\overline{n}|i}(1 + i)$$

Show that it is equivalent to

$$S = R(s_{\overline{n+1}|} - 1)$$

4. Using a geometric progression derive the formula for the discounted value A of an annuity due

$$A = Ra_{\overline{n}|i}(1 + i)$$

Show that it is equivalent to

$$A = R(a_{\overline{n-1}|i} + 1)$$

5. A mutual fund promises a rate of growth of 10% a year on funds left with it. How much would an investor who makes deposits of $1000 at the beginning of each year have on deposit by the time the first deposit has grown by 159%? You may assume that the time is approximately an integral number of years and that the investor is about to make, but has not made, an annual deposit at that time.

6. Show that the discounted value A of an ordinary deferred annuity is equivalent to

$$A = R(a_{\overline{k+n}|i} - a_{\overline{k}|i})$$

7. Show that $s_{\overline{n+1}|i} - \ddot{a}_{\overline{n+1}|i} = \ddot{s}_{\overline{n}|i} - a_{\overline{n}|i}$.

8. Starting on his 45th birthday, a man deposits $1000 a year in an investment account that pays interest at $j_1 = 13\%$. He makes his last deposit on his 64th birthday. On his 65th birthday he transfers his total savings to a special retirement fund that pays $j_2 = 7\frac{1}{2}\%$. From this fund he will receive level payments of $X at the beginning of each year for 15 years (first payment on his 65th birthday). Determine X.

9. Given the following diagram

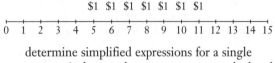

determine simplified expressions for a single sum equivalent to the seven payments calculated at times 1, 5, 8, 12, and 15, assuming rate i per period.

10. Provide symbolic answers (using $a_{\overline{n}|i}$, $s_{\overline{n}|i}$, i) in simplified form for the value of the following payments at the time indicated, assuming rate i per payment period.

11. Deposits are $100 per month for 3 years, nothing for 2 years, and then $200 per month for 3 years. Interest rates start at $j_{12} = 8\%$ and fall to $j_{12} = 6\%$ on the date of the first $200 deposit. Determine the accumulated value at the time of the final $200 deposit.

12. How much must you deposit at the end of each month for 25 years to fund an annuity of $2500 per month for 20 years? The first annuity payment is made 5 years after the last deposit, and interest changes from $j_{12} = 8\%$ to $j_{12} = 7\%$ at the time of the first annuity payment.

13. The present value of an annuity of $1000 payable for n years commencing one year from now is $6053. The annual effective rate of interest is 12.5%. Determine the present value of an annuity of $1000 commencing one year from now and payable for $(n + 2)$ years.

14. A person deposits $100 at the beginning of each year for 20 years. Simple interest at an annual rate of i is credited to each deposit from the date of deposit to the end of the 20-year period. The total amount thus accumulated is $2840. If, instead, compound interest had been credited at an annual effective rate of i, what would the accumulated value of these deposits have been at the end of 20 years?

Section 3.5   ## Determining the Term of an Annuity

In some problems the accumulated value S or the discounted value A, the periodic payment R, and the rate i are specified. This leaves the number of payments n to be determined. Formulas **(10)** and **(11)** may be solved for n by the use of logarithms. Normally, when given a value of S or A, R, and a rate i, you will not find an integer time period n for the annuity. Algebraically this means that there is usually no integer n such that $S = Rs_{\overline{n}|i}$ or $A = Ra_{\overline{n}|i}$. It is necessary to make the concluding payment different from R in order to have equivalence. One of the following procedures is followed in practice.

Procedure 1: The last regular payment is increased by a sum that will make the payments equivalent to the accumulated value S or the discounted value A. This increase is sometimes referred to as a *balloon* payment.

Procedure 2: A smaller concluding payment is made one period after the last full payment. This smaller concluding payment is sometimes referred to as a *drop* payment. Sometimes, when a certain sum of money is to be accumulated, a smaller concluding payment will not be required because the interest after the last full payment will equal or exceed the balance needed (Example 1).

CALCULATION TIP:

Unless specified otherwise, we shall use Procedure 2 throughout this book. Procedure 2 is more often used in practice.

EXAMPLE 1   A couple wants to accumulate $10 000 by making payments of $800 at the end of each half-year into an investment account that earns interest at $j_2 = 9\%$. Calculate the number of full payments required and the size of the concluding payment using both Procedures 1 and 2.

Solution   We have $S = 10\,000$, $R = 800$, $i = 4\frac{1}{2}\%$, and we want to calculate n. Substituting in equation **(10)** we obtain:

$$800s_{\overline{n}|0.045} = 10\,000$$
$$s_{\overline{n}|0.045} = 12.5$$
$$\frac{(1.045)^n - 1}{0.045} = 12.5$$
$$(1.045)^n - 1 = (12.5)(0.045)$$
$$(1.045)^n = 1.5625$$
$$n \log 1.045 = \log 1.5625$$
$$n = 10.13899776$$

Thus there will be 10 full deposits of $800, plus a final payment, needed to reach the $10 000 goal.

Procedure 1   Let X be the balloon payment that will be added to the last regular payment to make the payments equivalent to the accumulated value $S = 10\,000$. We arrange the data on a time diagram below.

Using 10 as a focal date, we obtain the equation of value for unknown X:

$$800s_{\overline{10}|0.045} + X = 10\,000$$
$$X = 10\,000 - 800s_{\overline{10}|0.045}$$
$$X \doteq 10\,000 - 9830.57$$
$$X = 169.43$$

Thus the 10th deposit will be $800 + $169.43 = $969.43.

Procedure 2   Let Y be the size of a smaller concluding payment (drop payment) made a half-year after the last full deposit. We arrange the data on a time diagram below.

Using time 11 as the focal date we obtain the equation of value for unknown Y:

$$800s_{\overline{10}|0.045}(1.045) + Y = 10\,000$$
$$10\,272.94 + Y \doteq 10\,000$$
$$Y = -272.94$$

The negative value of Y indicates that there is no concluding payment required (that is, $Y = 0$); the interest after the last full payment has increased the accumulated balance past the \$10 000 goal by \$272.94.

EXAMPLE 2   A man dies and leaves his wife an estate of \$50 000. The money is invested at $j_{12} = 12\%$. How many monthly payments of \$750 would the widow receive and what would be the size of the concluding payment?

Solution   We have $A = 50\,000$, $R = 750$, $i = 1\%$. Substituting in equation **(11)** we obtain:

$$750a_{\overline{n}|0.01} = 50\,000$$
$$a_{\overline{n}|0.01} = \frac{50\,000}{750}$$
$$\frac{1-(1.01)^{-n}}{0.01} = \frac{200}{3}$$
$$1-(1.01)^{-n} = \frac{2}{3}$$
$$(1.01)^{-n} = \frac{1}{3}$$
$$-n \log 1.01 = \log \frac{1}{3}$$
$$n \doteq 110.409624$$

Thus the widow will receive 110 full payments of \$750 and 1 smaller concluding payment, say \$Y, 1 month after the last full payment. We arrange the data on a time diagram below.

Using time 111 as the focal date, we obtain the equation of value for unknown Y:

$$750s_{\overline{110}|0.01}(1.01) + Y = 50\,000(1.01)^{111}$$
$$150\,575.63 + Y = 150\,883.76$$
$$Y = 308.13$$

Using time 0 as the focal date, we obtain the equation of value

$$750a_{\overline{110}|0.01} + Y(1.01)^{-111} = 50\,000$$
$$49\,897.89 + Y(1.01)^{-111} = 50\,000$$
$$Y(1.01)^{-111} = 102.11$$
$$Y = 102.11(1.01)^{111}$$
$$Y = 308.13$$

If the widow wanted to withdraw all remaining funds at the time of the last full $750 withdrawal, then let X be the balloon payment, made at time 110. Using time 0 as the focal date, we obtain

$$750a_{\overline{110}|0.01} + X(1.01)^{-110} = 50\,000$$
$$X(1.01)^{-110} = 102.11$$
$$X = 102.11(1.01)^{110} = 305.08$$

The final withdrawal is $750 + $305.08 = $1055.08.

Using a Financial Calculator to Determine n

We illustrate the required entries for the BA-35 calculator.

In Example 1, the steps are as follows (make sure your calculator has been set to the FIN mode):

10 000 $\boxed{FV}$ 0 $\boxed{PV}$ −800 $\boxed{PMT}$ 4.5 $\boxed{I/Y}$ $\boxed{CPT}$ $\boxed{N}$
10.13899776
(half-years)

In Example 2, the steps are as follows:

0   $\boxed{FV}$ 50 000 $\boxed{PV}$ −750 $\boxed{PMT}$ 1 $\boxed{I/Y}$ $\boxed{CPT}$ $\boxed{N}$
110.409624
(months)

Using a Computer Spreadsheet to Determine n

In some instances, a computer spreadsheet has built-in functions that allow you to calculate certain answers more quickly. Calculating the value of n for an annuity is a situation where a financial function can be used.

We will illustrate this using Microsoft's Excel and the financial function **NPER**(i, $-PMT$, PV, FV, $type$) where,

i = effective rate per compounding period (typed as a decimal)
$type$ = 0 (ordinary annuity) or 1 (annuity due)

In Example 1, you would type **NPER**(0.045, −800, 0, 10 000, 0), which would result in the answer 10.13899776 half-years.

In Example 2, you would type **NPER**(0.01, −750, 50 000, 0, 0), which would result in the answer 110.409624 months.

Exercise 3.5

Part A

1. A debt of $4000 bears interest at $j_2 = 8\%$. It is to be repaid by semi-annual payments of $400. Determine the number of full payments needed and the final smaller payment after the last full payment.

2. Melissa takes her inheritance of $25 000 and invests it at $j_{12} = 9\%$. How many monthly payments of $250 can she expect to receive and what will be the size of the concluding payment? Use both Procedure 1 and Procedure 2.

3. A couple wants to accumulate $10 000. If they deposit $250 at the end of each quarter year in an account paying $j_4 = 6\%$, how many deposits must they make and what will be the size of the final deposit? Use both Procedure 1 and Procedure 2.

4. A firm buys a machine for $30 000. They pay $5000 down and $5000 at the end of each year. If interest is at $j_1 = 10\%$, how many full payments must they make and what will be the size of the concluding smaller payment?

5. A fund of $20 000 is to be accumulated by n annual payments of $2500 plus a final smaller payment made one year after the last regular payment. If interest is at $j_1 = 8\%$, determine n and the final irregular payment.

6. A loan of $10 000 is to be repaid by monthly payments of $400, the first payment due in one year's time. If $j_{12} = 12\%$, determine the number of regular monthly payments needed and the size of the final smaller payment.

7. A fund of $8000 is to be accumulated by semi-annual payments of $2000. If $j_2 = 5\%$, determine the number of full deposits required and the final smaller payment.

8. On July 1, 2006, Shannon has $10 000 in an account paying interest at $j_4 = 6\frac{1}{2}\%$. She plans to withdraw $500 every three months with the first withdrawal on October 1, 2006. How many full withdrawals can she make and what will be the size and the date of the concluding withdrawal?

9. A parcel of land, valued at $350 000, is sold for $150 000 down. The buyer agrees to pay the balance with interest at $j_{12} = 9\%$ by paying $5000 monthly as long as necessary, the first payment due 2 years from now.
   a) Determine the number of full payments needed and the size of the concluding payment one month after the last $5000 payment.
   b) Determine the monthly payment needed to pay off the balance by 36 equal payments, if the first payment is 1 year from now and interest is at $j_{12} = 12\%$.

10. From July 1, 1998, to January 1, 2003, a couple made semi-annual deposits of $500 into an investment account paying $j_2 = 7\%$. Starting July 1, 2007, they start making semi-annual withdrawals of $800.
    a) How many withdrawals can they make and what is the size and date of the last withdrawal?
    b) If the couple decided to exhaust their savings with equal semi-annual withdrawals from July 1, 2007, to July 1, 2017, inclusive, how much will they get each half-year?

11. In October 2003, an industrialist gave your school $30 000 to be used for future scholarships of $4000 at each fall convocation starting the year the industrialist dies. If the industrialist died May 2006 and the money earns interest at $j_1 = 8\%$, for how many years will full scholarships be awarded?

12. A debt of $18 000 is to be repaid in annual instalments of $3000 with the first instalment due at the end of the second year and a final instalment of less than $3000. Interest is 9% per year compounded annually. Calculate the final payment.

Part B

1. Antonio is accumulating a $10 000 fund by depositing $100 each month, starting September 1, 2006. If the interest rate on the fund is $j_{12} = 12\%$ until May 1, 2009 and then it drops to $j_{12} = 10\frac{1}{2}\%$, determine the time and amount of the reduced final deposit.

2. A widow, as beneficiary of a $100 000 insurance policy, will receive $20 000 immediately and $1800 every three months thereafter. The

company pays interest at $j_4 = 6\%$; after 3 years, the rate is increased to $j_4 = 7\%$.
a) How many full payments of $1800 will she receive?
b) What additional sum paid with the last full payment will exhaust her benefits?
c) What payment 3 months after the last full payment will exhaust her benefits?

3. On his 25th birthday, Yves deposited $2000 in a fund paying $j_1 = 10\%$ and continued to make such deposits each year, the last on his 49th birthday. Beginning on his 50th birthday, Yves plans to make equal annual withdrawals of $20 000.
a) How many such withdrawals can be made?
b) What additional sum paid with the last withdrawal will exhaust the fund?
c) What sum paid one year after the last full withdrawal will exhaust the fund?

4. A couple bought land worth $300 000. They paid $50 000 down and signed a contract agreeing to repay the balance with interest at $j_1 = 12\%$ by annual payments of $50 000 for as long as necessary and a smaller concluding payment one year later. The contract was sold just after the 4th annual payment to an investor who wants to realize a yield of $j_1 = 13\%$. Determine the selling price.

5. A loan of $20 000 is to be repaid by annual payments of $4000 per year for the first 5 years and payments of $4500 per year thereafter for as long as necessary. Determine the total number of payments and the amount of the smaller final payment made one year after the last regular payment. Assume an annual effective rate of 7.5%.

6. Solve the equation $S = R s_{\overline{n}|i}$ for n.

7. Solve the equation $A = R a_{\overline{n}|i}$ for n.

8. A friend agrees to lend you $2000 on September 1 each year for 4 years to help with education costs. One year after the last payment you are expected to start annual repayments of $800 for as long as necessary. Interest on the loan is $j_1 = 6\frac{1}{2}\%$. Determine the number of repayments needed, and the amount of the final payment.

9. A car loan of $10 000 at $j_{12} = 12\%$ is being paid off by n payments. The first $(n-1)$ payments are $263.34 per month. The final monthly payment is $263.24. Determine n.

Section 3.6   Determining the Interest Rate

A very practical application of equations **(10)** and **(11)** is determining the interest rate. In many business transactions the true interest rate is concealed in one way or another. In order to compare different propositions (options, investments), it is necessary to determine the true interest rate of each proposition and make the decision based on true interest rates.

When R, n, and either S or A are given, the interest rate i may be determined approximately by linear interpolation. For most practical purposes, linear interpolation gives sufficient accuracy and will be used throughout this textbook.

CALCULATION TIP:

To obtain a starting value to solve the equation $s_{\overline{n}|i} = k$ by linear interpolation, we may use the formula $i = \dfrac{\left(\frac{k}{n}\right)^2 - 1}{k}$. To obtain a starting value to solve the equation $a_{\overline{n}|i} = k$ by linear interpolation, we may use the formula $i = \dfrac{1 - \left(\frac{k}{n}\right)^2}{k}$.

EXAMPLE 1   Determine the interest rate j_4 at which deposits of \$275 at the end of every 3 months will accumulate to \$5000 in 4 years.

Solution   We have $S = 5000$, $R = 275$, $n = 16$, and using equation (10) we obtain:

$$275s_{\overline{16}|i} = 5000$$
$$s_{\overline{16}|i} = 18.1818$$

We want to determine the rate $j_4 = 4i$ such that $s_{\overline{16}|i} = \frac{(1+i)^{16} - 1}{i} = 18.1818$.

A starting value to solve $s_{\overline{16}|i} = 18.1818$ is $i = \frac{\left(\frac{18.1818}{16}\right)^2 - 1}{18.1818} = 0.0160227$ or $j_4 = 4i = 6.41\%$. We suspect $6\% <$ true $j_4 < 7\%$.

By successive trials we find two factors $s_{\overline{16}|i}$, one greater than 18.1818 and one less than 18.1818. The corresponding rates $j_4 = 4i$ will provide an upper and lower bound on the unknown rate j_4, which is then approximated by a linear interpolation.

CALCULATION TIP:

The values of factors $s_{\overline{n}|i}$ and $a_{\overline{n}|i}$ will be rounded off to 4 decimal places, since additional places do not really increase the accuracy. For fixed n, factors $s_{\overline{n}|i}$ increase when i increases, whereas factors $a_{\overline{n}|i}$ decrease when i increases. Closer bounds on the nominal rate j_m generally provide better approximations of the unknown rate j_m by linear interpolation. In this textbook we will interpolate between two nominal rates that are 1% apart.

For $j_4 = 6\%$, we calculate $s_{\overline{16}|i} = 17.9324$
For $j_4 = 7\%$, we calculate $s_{\overline{16}|i} = 18.2817$
Now we have two rates, $j_4 = 6\%$ and $j_4 = 7\%$, 1% apart, that provide upper and lower bounds for interpolation.

Arranging our data in an interpolation table we have:

	$s_{\overline{16}|i}$	j_4	
	17.9324	6%	
0.3493 $\{$ 0.2494 $\{$	18.1818	j_4	$\}$ d $\}$ 1%
	18.2817	7%	

$$\frac{d}{1\%} = \frac{0.2494}{0.3493}$$
$$d = 0.7140$$
and $j_4 = 6.7140 \doteq 6.71\%$

We may check the accuracy of this answer by substituting $R = 275$, $n = 16$, and $i = \frac{0.0671}{4}$ into equation (10) and calculate the accumulated value:

$$S = 275\frac{(1+i)^{16} - 1}{i} \doteq \$4999.37$$

Linear interpolation between two nominal rates, 1% apart, gave us a very good approximation of the unknown rate j_4.

OBSERVATION:

The interest rates i and $j_m = mi$ may be computed directly using either a financial calculator or a spreadsheet.

Using a Financial Calculator to Determine i

Using the TI BA-35 calculator, we enter

5000 $\boxed{FV}$ 0 $\boxed{PV}$ –275 $\boxed{PMT}$ 16 $\boxed{N}$ $\boxed{CPT}$ $\boxed{I/Y}$

Which solves for $i = 1.679127788$

and thus $j_4 = 4i = 6.716511153 \doteq 6.72\%$

Using a Computer Spreadsheet to Determine i

We use Excel's Financial function wizard **RATE**(n, $-PMT$, PV, FV, $type$) where $type = 0$ for an ordinary annuity and $type = 1$ for an annuity due.

We type in **RATE**(16, –275, 0, 5000, 0)*4
and obtain $j_4 = 6.71651113 \doteq 6.72\%$

EXAMPLE 2   A used car sells for $6000 cash or $1000 down and $900 a month for 6 months. Determine the interest rate, j_{12}, if the purchaser buys the car on the instalment plan.

Solution   For any instalment plan, the following equation of value must hold to have the cash option equivalent to the instalment option.

cash price = down payment + discounted value of instalments

We have

$$6000 = 1000 + 900a_{\overline{6}|i}$$
$$a_{\overline{6}|i} = \frac{5000}{900}$$
$$a_{\overline{6}|i} = 5.5556$$

We want to determine the rate $j_{12} = 12i$ such that $a_{\overline{6}|i} = \frac{1-(1+i)^{-6}}{i} = 5.5556 = k$.

A starting value to solve the equation $a_{\overline{6}|i} = 5.5556$ is $i = \dfrac{1 - \left(\frac{5.5556}{6}\right)^2}{5.5556}$

$= 0.025676338$ or $j_{12} = 12i = 30.81\%$. We suspect $30\% < $ true $j_{12} < 31\%$.

By successive trials we find two factors $a_{\overline{6}|i}$, one greater than 5.5556 and one less than 5.5556, such that the corresponding rates j_{12} are 1% apart.

For $j_{12} = 26\%$, we calculate $a_{\overline{6}|i} = 5.5701$
For $j_{12} = 27\%$, we calculate $a_{\overline{6}|i} = 5.5545$

Recall that the starting point formula only provides an approximation to the value of j_m. In this example it provided a poor approximation for the value of j_{12}. The formula led us to suspect that $30\% <$ true $j_{12} < 31\%$. However, at $j_{12} = 30\%$, $a_{\overline{6}|0.025} = 5.5081$, which is too low. To raise the value of $a_{\overline{6}|0.025}$ we needed to lower the value of j_{12}, ultimately to between 26% and 27%.

Arranging our data in an interpolation table we have:

	$a_{\overline{6}|i}$	j_{12}	
	5.5701	26%	
0.0145 {	5.5556	j_{12}	} d
	5.5545	27%	

0.0156 {

$\dfrac{d}{1\%} = \dfrac{0.0145}{0.0156}$
$d = 0.93\%$
and $j_{12} = 26.93\%$

} 1%

Checking the accuracy of our answer we calculate the discounted value of the instalment plan at $j_{12} = 26.93\%$

$$1000 + 900a_{\overline{6}|i} = 6000.01$$

Note: Using the TI BA-35 calculator, we enter

0 | FV | 5000 | PV | –900 | PMT | 6 | N | CPT | I/Y

Which solves for $i = 2.244219885$
and thus $j_{12} = 12i = 26.93063862 \doteq 26.93\%$

Using Excel's Financial function wizard = **RATE**(6, –900, 5000, 0, 0)*12 gives $j_{12} = 26.93\%$.

EXAMPLE 3　Deposits of $6000 are made every 6 months into a fund starting today and continuing until 10 deposits have been made. Six months after the last deposit, there is $70 630 in the fund. What nominal rate of interest, j_2, do the deposits earn?

Solution　We have $S_n = 70\,630$, $R = 6000$, $n = 10$, and an annuity due as shown on the time diagram below.

Our equation of value is

$$70\,630 = 6000\ddot{s}_{\overline{10}|i} \text{ where } i = j_2/2$$

To use the starting point formula, we need to use the ordinary annuity symbol. We recall from section 3.4, $\ddot{s}_{\overline{n}|i} = s_{\overline{n+1}|i} - 1$.

Thus,

$$70\,630 = 6000s_{\overline{11}|i} - 6000$$
$$76\,630 = 6000s_{\overline{11}|i}$$
$$s_{\overline{11}|i} = \frac{76\,630}{6000} = 12.7717 = k \text{ (and } n \text{ is now 11)}$$

Using the starting point formula, $i = \frac{\left(\frac{12.7717}{11}\right)^2 - 1}{12.7717} = 0.02725$, which gives $j_2 \doteq 5.45\%$. We suspect $5\% < \text{true } j_2 < 6\%$.

For $j_2 = 5\%$, $s_{\overline{11}|i} = 12.4835$
For $j_2 = 6\%$, $s_{\overline{11}|i} = 12.8078$

Arranging our data in an interpolation table, we have:

		$s_{\overline{11}|i}$	j_2	
		12.4835	5%	
0.3243	0.2882	12.7717	j_{12}	d
		12.8078	6%	

$$\frac{d}{1\%} = \frac{0.2882}{0.3243}$$
$$d = 0.8887\%$$
$$\text{and } j_2 \doteq 5.89\%$$

To check,

$$6000\ddot{s}_{\overline{10}|\,0.02945} = 6000s_{\overline{10}|\,0.02945}(1.02945) = \$70\,629.85$$

Note: Using the BA-35 calculator (make sure you are in BGN mode since this is an annuity due):

70630 $\boxed{FV}$ 0 $\boxed{PV}$ –6000 $\boxed{PMT}$ 10 $\boxed{N}$ $\boxed{CPT}$ $\boxed{I/Y}$

Which gives $i = 2.945037944$ and thus $j_2 = 2i = 5.890075888 \doteq 5.89\%$.

Using Excel's Financial function wizard = **RATE**(10, – 6000, 0, 70630, 1)*2 gives $j_2 = 5.89\%$.

Exercise 3.6

Part A (Use linear interpolation; you can then use a financial calculator or spreadsheet to confirm your answers.)

1. Determine the interest rate j_2 at which semi-annual deposits of $500 will accumulate to $6000 in 5 years.

2. What rate of interest j_1 must be earned for deposits of $500 at the end of each year to accumulate to $12 000 in 10 years?

3. An insurance company will pay $80 000 to a beneficiary or monthly payments of $1000 for 10 years. What rate j_{12} is the insurance company using?

4. A television set sells for $700. Sales tax of 7% is added to that. The TV may be purchased for $100 down and monthly payments of $60 for one year. What is the interest rate j_{12}? What is the annual effective interest rate?

5. You borrow $1600 from a licensed small loan company and agree to pay $160 a month for 12 months. What nominal rate j_{12} is the company charging?

6. A store offers to sell a watch for $55 cash or $5 a month for 12 months. What nominal rate j_{12} is the store actually charging on the instalment plan, if the first payment is made immediately?

7. On February 1, 1990, Andreas made the first of a sequence of regular annual deposits of $1000 into an investment account. The last deposit was made February 1, 2006. If the account earned $j_1 = 10\frac{1}{2}\%$, the balance 1 year after the last deposit would have been $46 931.70, while it would have been $49 395.93 at $j_1 = 11\%$. In fact, the balance in the account one year after the last deposit was $48 500. What annual effective rate of interest did the account earn?

Part B

The following problems are examples of situations that could arise if there were no government legislation concerning disclosure of interest rates. In Canada, most provinces have "truth in lending" laws setting down regulations on the disclosure of the rate of interest involved in financial transactions. It is very important to check out all loan clauses fully.

1. The "Fly By Night" Used Car Lot uses the following to illustrate their 12% finance plan on a car paid for over 3 years.

   Cost of car $12 000.00
   12% finance charge   4 320.00 (12% of 12 000
   Total cost $16 320.00   × 3 years)

   Monthly payment $= \frac{\$16 320}{36} = \$453.33$

   What is the true interest rate j_{12} being charged?

2. A dealer sells an article for $6000. He will allow a customer to buy it by paying $2400 down and the balance by paying $300 a month for a year. If you pay cash for the item he will give you a 10% discount. Determine the interest rate j_{12} paid by the purchaser who uses the instalment plan described above.

3. Goods worth $1000 are purchased using the following carrying-charge plan: A down payment of $100 is required after which 9% of the unpaid balance is added on and the amount is then divided into 12 equal monthly instalments. What rate of interest j_{12} does the plan include?

4. A finance company charges 10% "interest in advance" and allows the client to repay the loan in 12 equal monthly payments. The monthly payment is calculated as one-twelfth of the total of principal and interest (10% of principal). Determine the nominal rate compounded monthly and the annual effective rate charged.

5. To buy a car costing $13 600 you can pay $1600 down and the balance in 36 monthly payments of $450 each. You can also borrow the money from a loan company and repay $13 600 by making quarterly payments of $1060 over 5 years, first payment in 3 months. Compare the annual effective rates of interest charged and determine which option is better.

6. A TV rental company uses the following illustration to prove that renting a big-screen TV at $45 a month is cheaper than buying.

   Cost of TV $1200
   Sales Tax   84
   Total $1284

   Therefore monthly payments over 3 years at 12% are $\frac{1284 + (0.12)(1284)(3)}{36} = \$48.51$. Redo this illustration properly at $j_{12} = 12\%$ and comment.

7. You are offered a loan of $10 000 with no payments for 6 months, then $600 per month for 1 year, and $500 per month for the following year. What annual effective rate of interest does this loan charge?

8. On July 1, 2005, $8500 is deposited in Fund X. On July 1, 2005, the first of 10 consecutive semi-annual payments of $1000 each is deposited in Fund Y. Both funds earn interest at a nominal rate j_2. The balances in the two funds are equal on July 1, 2010. Calculate j_2.

Section 3.7

Summary and Review Exercises

Summary — n payments of R at i per period

Annuity Type	Discounted Value	Focal Date	Accumulated Value	Focal Date
Ordinary	$Ra_{\overline{n}|i}$	One period before the first payment	$Rs_{\overline{n}|i}$	At time of nth payment
Due	$R\ddot{a}_{\overline{n}|i} =$ $Ra_{\overline{n}|i}(1+i) =$ $R(1+a_{\overline{n-1}|i})$	At time of first payment	$R\ddot{s}_{\overline{n}|i} =$ $Rs_{\overline{n}|i}(1+i) =$ $R(s_{\overline{n+1}|i} - 1)$	One period after nth payment
Deferred	$Ra_{\overline{n}|i}(1+i)^{-k}$	$k+1$ periods before the first payment		
Forborne			$Ra_{\overline{n}|i}(1+i)^{-m}$	m periods after the nth payment

where

$a_{\overline{n}|i} = \frac{1-(1+i)^{-n}}{i}$ is called a discount factor for n-payments.

$s_{\overline{n}|i} = \frac{(1+i)^{n}-1}{i}$ is called an accumulation factor for n-payments.

When calculating factors $s_{\overline{n}|i}$ and $a_{\overline{n}|i}$, do not round off the value of i. Use all digits provided by your calculator and, when necessary, store the value of i in the memory of your calculator. Note that for $i > 0$, $s_{\overline{n}|i} > n$, and $a_{\overline{n}|i} < n$.

Review Exercises 3.7

1. Determine the accumulated and the discounted value of an annuity of $500 at the end of each month at $j_{12} = 9\%$ for a) 10 years, b) 20 years.

2. At age 65 Mrs. Papadopoulos takes her life savings of $100 000 and buys a 20-year annuity certain with quarterly payments. Determine the size of these payments
   a) at 5% compounded quarterly,
   b) at 7% compounded quarterly.

3. An annuity provides $60 at the end of each month for 3 years and $80 at the end of each month for the following 2 years. If $j_{12} = 5\%$, calculate the present value of the annuity.

4. To finance the purchase of a car, Wendy agrees to pay $400 at the end of each month for 4 years.

   The interest rate is $j_{12} = 15\%$.
   a) If Wendy misses the first 4 payments, what must she pay at the time of the 5th payment to be fully up to date?
   b) Assuming Wendy has missed no payments, what single payment at the end of 2 years would completely discharge her of her indebtedness?

5. A couple needs a loan of $10 000 to buy a boat. One lender will charge $j_{12} = 9\%$ while a second lender charges $j_{12} = 7\%$. What will be the monthly savings in interest using the lower rate if the monthly payments are to run for 5 years?

6. Determine the accumulated and the discounted value of semi-annual payments of $500 at the end of every half-year over 10 years if interest is

$j_2 = 6\%$ for the first four years and $j_2 = 8\%$ for the last six years.

7. Instead of paying $900 rent at the beginning of each month for the next 10 years, a couple decides to buy a townhouse. What is the cash equivalent of the 10 years of rent at $j_{12} = 9\%$?

8. A company sets aside $15 000 at the beginning of each year to accumulate a fund for future expansion. What is the amount in the fund at the end of 5 years if the fund earns $j_1 = 8.5\%$?

9. According to Mr. Peterson's will, the $100 000 life insurance benefit is invested at $j_1 = 8\%$ and from this fund his widow will receive $15 000 each year, the first payment immediately, so long as she lives. On the payment date following the death of his wife, the balance of the fund is to be donated to a local charity. If his wife died 4 years, 3 months later, how much did the charity receive?

10. Five years from now a company will need $150 000 to replace worn-out equipment. Starting now, what monthly deposits must be made in a fund paying $j_{12} = 9\%$ for 5 years to accumulate this sum?

11. Doreen bought a car on September 1, 2006, by paying $4000 down and agreeing to make 36 monthly payments of $350, the first due on December 1, 2006. If interest is at 12% compounded monthly, determine the equivalent cash price.

12. An office space is renting for $30 000 a year payable in advance. Determine the equivalent monthly rental payable in advance if money is worth 6% compounded monthly.

13. A farmer borrowed $80 000 to buy some farm equipment. He plans to pay off the loan with interest at $j_1 = 13\frac{3}{4}\%$ in 8 equal annual payments, the first to be made 5 years from now. Determine the annual payment.

14. Charlie wants to accumulate $100 000 by making monthly deposits of $1000 into a fund that accumulates interest at $j_{12} = 12\%$. Determine the number of full deposits required and the size of the concluding deposit using both procedures 1 and 2.

15. Lise borrows $10 000 at $j_4 = 10\%$. How many $800 quarterly payments will she pay and what will be the size of the drop payment, 3 months after the last $800 payment?

16. On June 1, 2006, Ms. Kaminski purchased furniture for $2200. She paid $400 down and agreed to pay the balance by monthly payments of $100 plus a smaller final payment, the first payment due on July 1, 2006. If interest is at $j_{12} = 9\%$, when is the final payment made and what is the amount of the final payment?

17. A used car sells for $5000 cash or $1000 down and $800 a month for 6 months. Calculate the interest rate j_{12} if the purchaser buys the car on the instalment plan.

18. Determine the j_{12} at which deposits of $200 at the end of each month will accumulate to $10 000 in 3 years.

19. The XYZ Finance Company charges 10% "interest in advance" and allows the client to repay the loan in 12 equal monthly payments. Thus for a loan of $6000, they would charge $600 interest and have 12 monthly repayments of $550 each. What is the corresponding rate of interest convertible monthly?

20. A refrigerator is listed at $650. If a customer pays $200 down, the balance plus a carrying charge of $50 can be paid in 12 equal monthly payments. If the customer pays cash, he can get a discount of 15% off the list price. What is the nominal rate compounded monthly if the refrigerator is bought on time?

21. Paul wants to accumulate $5000 by depositing $300 every 3 months into an account paying 8% per annum converted quarterly. He makes the first deposit on July 1, 2006. How many full deposits should he make and what will be the size and the date of the concluding deposit?

22. How much a month for 5 years at $j_{12} = 6\%$ would you have to save in order to receive $800 a month for 3 years afterward?

23. A bank account paying $j_{12} = 5\frac{1}{2}\%$ contains $5680 on March 1, 2006. Beginning April 1, 2006, the first of a sequence of monthly withdrawals of $400 is made. What is the date of the last $400

withdrawal? By what date (first of the month) will the balance again exceed $400?

24. Jones agrees to pay Smith $800 at the end of each quarter for 5 years, but is unable to do so until the end of the 15th month when he wins $100 000 in a provincial lottery. Assuming money is worth $j_4 = 6\%$, what single payment at the end of fifteen months liquidates his debt?

25. A deposit of $1000 is made to open an account on March 1, 2006. Monthly deposits of $300 are then made for 5 years, starting April 1, 2006. Starting April 1, 2011, the first of a sequence of 20 monthly withdrawals of $1000 is made. Determine the balance in the account on December 1, 2013, assuming $j_{12} = 12\%$.

26. Fred needs a loan of $15 000 to buy a new car. The dealer offers him the loan at $j_{12} = 10\%$. Fred can get the loan at his bank at $j_{12} = 9\%$.
   a) What will be the monthly savings using the lower rate at his bank if the monthly payments are to run for 3 years?
   b) What will be the total interest on the loan at his bank?
   c) Assume that Fred takes the loan of $15 000 at his bank and decides to pay $600 at the end of each month. How many months will it take him to repay the loan, assuming a drop payment 1 month after the last $600 payment? Determine the drop payment.

27. On November 10, 2006, I.M. Broke obtained a bank loan of $4000 at 10% compounded monthly. I.M. Broke will repay the loan by making monthly payments of $250 beginning on December 10, 2006. Determine the number of full payments, the date, and the size of the smaller concluding payment required.

28. The Sound Warehouse advertises a "no interest for 1 year" option. For example, you can buy a $1200 stereo by paying $100 at the end of each month for 1 year. However, if you pay in full at the time of the purchase, you get a 10% cash discount. What rate of interest, j_{12}, is the Sound Warehouse actually charging?

29. a) Elsa wants to accumulate $20 000 by the end of 6 years by making quarterly deposits in a fund that pays interest at 10% compounded quarterly. Determine the size of these deposits.

   b) After 4 years the fund rate changes to $j_4 = 8\%$. Determine the size of the quarterly deposits now required if the $20 000 goal is to be met.
   c) What is the total interest earned on the fund over 6 years?

30. Today, Walt purchased a cottage and a yacht worth a combined present value of $600 000. To purchase the cottage, Walt agreed to pay $100 000 down and $4000 at the end of each month for 15 years. To buy the yacht, he was required to pay $20 000 down and R dollars at the end of each month for 5 years. Determine R if $j_{12} = 12\%$.

31. Erika deposited $100 monthly in a fund earning $j_{12} = 6\%$. The first deposit was made on June 1, 1996, and the last deposit on November 1, 2006.
   a) Determine the value of the fund on
      i) September 1, 2001 (after the payment is made);
      ii) December 1, 2008.
   b) From May 1, 2011, she plans to draw down the fund with monthly withdrawals of $1000. Determine the date and the size of the smaller concluding withdrawal one month after the last $1000 withdrawal.

32. Home appliances are on sale with the following payment terms: either pay cash and receive a 5% discount, or pay monthly for 15 months with no money down. To calculate the monthly payments, add a $50 finance charge per $1000 purchase price to the purchase price, then divide this amount into 15 equal payments. What annual effective rate of interest is being charged for buying on time?

33. Peter wants to invest in a mutual fund. His goal is to accumulate enough money over the next 20 years so that he can withdraw $30 000 annually for 25 years afterward. From a website **www.globefund.com** he found out that the Trimark Fund earned $j_1 = 10.84\%$ over the past 15 years (as of December 31, 2005). What annual deposits for 20 years would provide him with an annuity of $30 000 per year, if he invests in the Trimark Fund, assuming that the first withdrawal will be 1 year after the last deposit and the fund will keep earning $j_1 = 10.84\%$ over the next 45 years?

CASE STUDY 1   *Car Loans*

You are interested in buying a brand new car for a total of $22 535.60. You have the option of paying cash for the car or you can finance the purchase through the car dealership who offers a 4-year loan at 7.45% with monthly payments.

The car dealership suggests that you would be better off taking out the car loan and investing the $22 536.60 in a guaranteed investment certificate (GIC). The best interest rate on a 4-year GIC is currently 4.40%. The dealership claims that you could actually earn more on your investment than you would pay in interest on the car loan.

The dealership states that 48 months of interest on a 7.45% loan of $22 536.60 would be $3593.68, while the same principal invested at 4.40% per year would earn interest of $4235.80 — a profit of $642.12. The reason given by the dealership for this non-intuitive result is that the 7.45% is applied to a declining balance, while the 4.40% is applied to an increasing balance.

a) Verify the figures given in the third paragraph.
b) Is the dealership correct in recommending the car loan as a better option than the cash purchase? Justify your answer.

CASE STUDY 2   *Car Insurance Premiums*

Charlie changed car insurance companies and received an insurance policy covering two vehicles for 6 months for a premium of $650 plus $32.50 sales tax (total $682.50). The new policy takes effect on December 1. Charlie was given three options in which to pay this amount. The first option was to simply pay the $682.50 on December 1. The other two options consisted of paying the premium in instalments as follows:

a) Option 2 allows Charlie to pay the premium over the next 6 months. The insurance company levels a financing charge of 3% on the premium (not including the tax). The total premium ($650, plus $19.50 finance charge, plus $32.50 tax = $702) is then divided by 6 to get a monthly payment of $117. However, the company requires the first *two* months' payments up front (i.e. on December 1), with the four remaining payments made at the start of each of the next four months (Jan. 1, Feb. 1, Mar. 1, Apr. 1). The insurance company claims they are charging Charlie an annual rate of interest of only 3% (better than you could get at a bank!). However, what is the actual rate, j_1, being charged? (Use interpolation to calculate j_{12} and then calculate equivalent j_1.)

b) Charlie is buying the insurance through a broker and they provide a third option, which they claim avoids the 3% financing charge. For a $15 service fee, Charlie can pay the premium in 3 equal monthly instalments, with the first payment paid on December 1. The monthly payment would be $232.50 (i.e. $650 plus $32.50 tax plus $15 service fee all divided by 3). Is this really a better deal? To determine, calculate the actual rate, j_1, being charged. (Again, use interpolation to calculate j_{12} and then calculate equivalent j_1.)

CHAPTER 4

General and Other Annuities

Learning Objectives

In chapter 3, we discussed simple annuities where level payments were made with the same frequency that interest was compounded. For example, an annuity with interest compounded semi-annually and payments made semi-annually is a simple annuity. However, it is common for annuities to have payments that are made at different times than when interest is paid. An example would be an annuity where the payments are made quarterly, but interest is compounded annually. Such annuities are called general annuities.

Section 4.1 introduces two methods that can be used to solve problems that involve both general ordinary annuities and general annuities-due.

Section 4.2 discusses a very common type of general annuity: mortgage loans. Mortgages are large, long-term loans that are taken out to purchase a home, cottage, or property. This section will illustrate how to calculate monthly (and other frequency) mortgage payments. Since you may end up buying a home at some point in your life, you may find this section of particular interest.

Other types of simple annuities are introduced in sections 4.3 and 4.4. Section 4.3 deals with annuities where payments begin on a certain date and continue forever. These are referred to as perpetuities. Some common examples of perpetuities are given along with the methodology for determining the discounted value of perpetuities.

It is also reasonably common for an annuity to have a series of payments that are not the same each period. Section 4.4 discusses two main types of these "varying" annuities. The first type is an annuity where the payments change each period by a constant percentage. These types of annuities are common as a retirement income product where the payments are indexed to an inflation factor. The second type is an annuity where the payments change each period by a constant amount.

Section 4.1   ## General Annuities

So far, we have assumed that periodic payments have been made at the same dates as the interest is compounded. This is not always the case. In this section we will consider annuities for which payments are made more or less frequently than interest is compounded. Such a series of payments is called a **general annuity.**

One way to solve general annuity problems is to **replace the given interest rate** by an equivalent rate for which the interest compounding period is the same as the payment period. (A review of section 2.2 will reacquaint you with this process.) In effect, the general annuity problems are transformed into simple annuity problems and the methods outlined in chapter 3 can be directly used; thus no new theory is required.

The second, and historical, approach used in solving general annuity problems is to **replace the given payments** by equivalent payments made on the stated interest conversion dates.

OBSERVATION:

In this textbook we follow the "change of rate" approach, which is the preferred method of solution when calculators are used. The "change of payment" approach is illustrated in problems 2 through 5 of Part B of Exercise 4.1.

In order to solve a general annuity problem, we use the following two-step procedure:

1. Convert the general annuity into an equivalent ordinary simple annuity by replacing the given interest rate (see section 2.2).
2. Solve a simple annuity problem using the methods outlined in chapter 3.

EXAMPLE 1   Jackie makes deposits of $100 at the end of every month into an account earning 9% compounded semi-annually. Determine the value of her account at the end of 6 years.

Solution   First, determine the rate i per month equivalent to 4.5% per half-year, such that

$$(1 + i)^{12} = (1.045)^2$$
$$i = (1.045)^{1/6} - 1$$
$$i = 0.007363123$$

Second, calculate the accumulated value S of an ordinary simple annuity with $R = 100$, $n = 6 \times 12 = 72$, $i = 0.007363123$.

$$S = 100 s_{\overline{72}|i} = \$9450.90$$

CALCULATION TIP:

Do not round off the value of i but use all digits provided by your calculator. Store the value of i in the memory of your calculator.

EXAMPLE 2   A contract calls for payments of $300 at the end of every 3-month period for 5 years and an additional payment of $2000 at the end of 5 years. What is the present worth of the contract at a) 6% compounded monthly b) 8% compounded continuously?

Solution a   First, determine the rate i per quarter equivalent to $\frac{0.06}{12} = 0.005$ per month, such that

$$(1 + i)^4 = (1.005)^{12}$$
$$1 + i = (1.005)^3$$
$$i = (1.005)^3 - 1$$
$$i = 0.015075125$$

Second, determine the discounted value A of an ordinary simple annuity and of the additional payment of $2000.

$$A = 300a_{\overline{20}|i} + 2000(1 + i)^{-20} \doteq 5146.78 + 1482.74 = 6629.52$$

The present value of the contract is $6629.52.

Solution b   First, find the rate i per quarter equivalent to $j_\infty = 8\%$, such that

$$(1 + i)^4 = e^{0.08}$$
$$i = e^{0.08/4} - 1$$
$$i = 0.02020134$$

Second, calculate the discounted value A of an ordinary simple annuity and of the additional payment of $2000.

$$A = 300a_{\overline{20}|i} + 2000(1 + i)^{-20} \doteq 4895.91 + 1340.64 = 6236.55$$

The present value of the contract is $6236.55.

EXAMPLE 3   What equal monthly payments for 10 years will pay off a loan of $20 000 with interest at 10% compounded daily, if the first payment is made 6 months from now?

Solution   First, determine the rate i per month equivalent to $\frac{0.10}{365}$ per day, such that

$$(1 + i)^{12} = \left(1 + \frac{0.10}{365}\right)^{365}$$
$$i = \left(1 + \frac{0.10}{365}\right)^{365/12} - 1$$
$$i = 0.008367001$$

The monthly payment R of a simple deferred annuity with $A = 20\,000$, $n = 120$, $k = 5$, $i = 0.008367001$ is obtained from the time diagram:

From an equation of value, we solve for R.

$$Ra_{\overline{120}|i}(1+i)^{-5} = 20\,000$$

$$R = \frac{20\,000}{a_{\overline{120}|i}(1+i)^{-5}} \doteq \$276.01$$

EXAMPLE 4   A couple would like to accumulate \$20 000 in 3 years as a down payment on a house, by making deposits at the beginning of each week in an account paying interest at $j_{12} = 6\%$. Determine the size of the weekly deposit, assuming that compound interest is given for part of a conversion period.

Solution   First, determine the rate i per week equivalent to $\frac{0.06}{12} = 0.005$ per month, such that

$$(1+i)^{52} = (1.005)^{12}$$
$$1+i = (1.005)^{12/52}$$
$$i = (1.005)^{12/52} - 1$$
$$i = 0.001151634$$

Second, determine the weekly deposit R of a simple annuity due with $S = 20\,000$, $n = 3 \times 52 = 156$, and $i = 0.001151634$.

R	R	R		R	
0	1	2	$\cdots$	155	156

$$S = 20\,000$$

$$20\,000 = R\ddot{s}_{\overline{156}|i}$$

$$R = \frac{20\,000}{s_{\overline{156}|i}(1+i)} \doteq \$116.97$$

CALCULATION TIP:

When calculating the unknown interest rate in a general annuity problem, we first determine the nominal rate whose frequency of compounding matches the frequency of payments and then change it to the desired equivalent nominal rate.

EXAMPLE 5   A loan of $2000 is repaid with 8 quarterly payments of $300. What nominal rate compounded monthly is being charged?

Solution   First, we calculate the nominal rate j_4 by solving

$$300a_{\overline{8}|i} = 2000$$
$$a_{\overline{8}|i} = 6.6667$$

A starting value to solve $a_{\overline{8}|i} = 6.6667$ is

$$i = \frac{1 - (\frac{6.6667}{8})^2}{6.6667} = 0.045832063$$

or $j_4 = 4i = 18.33\%$. Using linear interpolation (as in chapter 3, section 3.6) we have

	$a_{\overline{8}|i}$	j_4
0.0660 {	6.7327	16%
	6.6667	j_4
	6.6638	17%

$$\frac{d}{1\%} = \frac{0.0660}{0.0689}$$
$$d = 0.9579\%$$
$$\text{and } j_4 \doteq 16.96\%$$

Check: $300a_{\overline{8}|0.1696/4} = \$1999.96$

Second, we calculate the nominal rate j_{12} equivalent to $j_4 = 16.96\%$.

$$(1+i)^{12} = (1 + \tfrac{0.1696}{4})^4$$
$$1+i = (1 + \tfrac{0.1696}{4})^{1/3}$$
$$i = (1 + \tfrac{0.1696}{4})^{1/3} - 1$$
$$\text{and } j_{12} = 12i = 12[(1 + \tfrac{0.1696}{4})^{1/3} - 1] \doteq 16.73\%$$

Note: Using the BA-35 calculator, we first calculate the quarterly rate of interest, $i = j_4/4$,

2000 [PV]   0 [FV]   −300 [PMT]   8 [N]   [CPT] [I/Y]
4.239464317

The equivalent nominal rate compounded monthly is,

$$j_{12} = 12[(1.04239464317)^{3/12} - 1] \doteq 16.72\%$$

Situations Where Payments Are Made More Frequently Than Interest Is Compounded

In cases in which payments are made more frequently than interest is compounded, financial institutions use different regulations for calculating interest for parts of an interest period. The two most common procedures are as follows:

1. *Simple interest* is given for part of an interest period. In these situations you cannot use the "change of rate" method. Instead, you must use the "**change**

of payment" method. In these cases the payments must be accumulated to the end of the interest period by using simple interest.

2. *Compound interest* is given for part of an interest period. (This situation is, by far, the most common in Canada.) In these situations you can use the "**change of rate**" method. This is how Examples 1 and 4 were solved.

EXAMPLE 6   Payments of $200 are made at the end of each month in an account paying $j_4 = 8\%$. How much money will be accumulated in the account at the end of 5 years if a) simple interest is paid for the fractional part of a period? b) compound interest is paid for the fractional part of a period?

Solution a   First we determine an **equivalent payment R per quarter** by accumulating monthly payments to the end of a 3-month period at a simple interest rate of 8%.

$$R = 200[1 + (0.08)(\tfrac{2}{12})] + 200[1 + (0.08)(\tfrac{1}{12})] + 200$$
$$= 600 + 200(0.08)(\tfrac{3}{12}) = \$604.00$$

We now have quarterly payments of $604.00, $n = 5 \times 4 = 20$ quarters, $i = \frac{0.08}{4} = 0.02$ per quarter.
   The accumulated value S equals

$$S = 604 s_{\overline{20}|0.02} = \$14\,675.61$$

Solution b   First, determine the rate i per month equivalent to 2% per quarter-year, such that

$$(1 + i)^{12} = (1.02)^4$$
$$1 + i = (1.02)^{1/3}$$
$$i = (1.02)^{1/3} - 1$$
$$i = 0.00662271$$

Second, determine the accumulated value S of an ordinary simple annuity with $R = 200$, $n = 60$, $i = 0.00662271$.

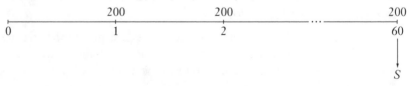

$$S = 200 s_{\overline{60}|i} \doteq \$14\,675.18$$

OBSERVATION:

Not many people are aware of the fact that simple interest brings more money for a part of a conversion period than compound interest. The difference is not large; however, it is important to know the rules that apply to the particular transaction.

Exercise 4.1

Part A

1. George deposits $200 at the beginning of each year in a bank account that earns interest at $j_4 = 6\%$. How much money will be in his bank account at the end of 5 years?

2. A car is purchased by paying $2000 down and then $300 each quarter-year for 3 years. If the interest on the loan was $j_2 = 9.2\%$, what did the car sell for?

3. An insurance policy requires premium payments of $15 at the beginning of each month for 20 years. Determine the discounted value of these payments at $j_4 = 5\%$.

4. Payments of $1000 are to be made at the end of each half-year for the next ten years. Determine their discounted value if the interest rate is 12% per annum compounded a) half-yearly; b) quarterly; c) annually; d) continuously.

5. Deposits of $100 are made at the end of each quarter to a bank account for 5 years. Determine the accumulated value of these payments if a) $j_{12} = 6\%$; b) $j_4 = 6\%$; c) $j_1 = 6\%$; d) $j_\infty = 6\%$.

6. Determine the monthly payment on a $3000 loan for 4 years at a) $j_4 = 9\%$; b) $j_\infty = 9\%$.

7. Determine the discounted value at $j_2 = 10\%$ of 20 annual payments of $200 each, the first one due five years hence.

8. Julia borrows $10 000. The loan is to be repaid with equal payments at the end of each month for the next 5 years. Determine the size of these payments if a) $j_4 = 12\%$; b) $j_1 = 12\%$.

9. Upon graduation, Scott determines that he has borrowed $8000 from the provincial loan plan over his three years of university. This loan must be repaid with monthly payments (first payment at the end of the first month) over the next 5 years. If $j_2 = 8\%$, determine the monthly payment.

10. How much must be deposited in a bank account at the end of each quarter for 4 years to accumulate $4000 if a) $j_{12} = 6\%$; b) $j_2 = 6\%$; c) $j_{365} = 6\%$?

11. Upon her husband's death, a widow finds that her husband had a $30 000 life insurance policy. One option available to her is a monthly annuity over a 10-year period. If the insurance company pays 6% per annum, what monthly income (at the end of each month) would this provide?

12. A city wants to accumulate $500 000 over the next 20 years to redeem an issue of bonds. What payment will be required at the end of each 6 months to accumulate this amount if interest is earned at 7% compounded monthly?

13. Deposits of $200 are made at the end of each month for 5 years into an account where interest is paid at $j_4 = 9\%$. Determine the accumulated value of the account at the end of 5 years if
    a) simple interest is paid for part of a period;
    b) compound interest is paid for part of a period.

14. Determine the accumulated value of $100 deposits made at the end of each month for 5 years at $j_1 = 5\%$ if a) compound interest; b) simple interest is paid for part of an interest period.

15. Which is cheaper?
    a) Buy a car for $14 000 and after three years trade it in for $4000.
    b) Rent a car for $350 a month payable at the end of each month for three years. Assume maintenance and license costs are identical and $j_1 = 7.9\%$.

16. An insurance company pays 5% per annum on money left with them. What would be the cost of an annuity certain paying $250 at the end of each month for 10 years?

17. What rate of interest j_4 must be earned for deposits of $100 at the end of each month to accumulate to $2000 in 18 months?

18. A furniture suite listing for $2100 may be purchased for $300 down and 18 monthly payments of $100. If cash is paid, a 10% discount is given. Calculate the highest interest rate j_2 at which the buyer can borrow money in order to take advantage of the cash discount.

19. Amanda's New Year's resolution is to make regular weekly deposits of $25 into her savings account earning $j_{12} = 6\%$. Determine the number of full deposits and the size of the smaller concluding deposit necessary to accumulate $3000.

20. Jack has made deposits of $250 at the end of each month for 2 years into an investment fund paying interest at $j_4 = 8\%$. What monthly deposits for the next 12 months will bring the fund up to $10 000?

21. An annuity consists of 40 payments of $300 each made at intervals of three months. Interest is at $j_1 = 12\%$. Determine the value of this annuity at each of the following times:
    a) three months before the time of the first payment;
    b) at the time of the last payment;
    c) at the time of the first payment;
    d) three months after the last payment;
    e) four years and three months before the first payment.

22. A couple made monthly deposits of $400 into an account paying interest at 5.25% compounded quarterly. The first deposit was made on August 1, 2003; the last deposit was made on December 1, 2006.
    a) How much money will be in the account on January 1, 2007?
    b) How much money will they be able to withdraw monthly, starting on February 1, 2007, and ending February 1, 2008, to pay for their expenses during their planned trip around the world?

23. Melvin borrows $1000 today at 10% compounded semi-annually. The loan is to be repaid with 10 equal monthly payments, the first due one year from today. Determine the size of the payments.

24. A university graduate must repay the government $4200 for outstanding student loans. The graduate can afford to pay $150 monthly. If the first payment is made at the end of the first year and money is worth 11% compounded quarterly, determine the number of full payments required and the size of the smaller concluding payment.

25. At age 65 a man takes his life savings of $96 000 and buys a 20-year annuity with monthly payments. Determine the size of these payments if interest is at 4% per annum compounded
    a) daily; b) continuously.

Part B

1. Using the "change of rate" method, fill in the table below to show the accumulated value of an ordinary annuity of $1, p times per year, for 10 years at $j_m = 12\%$.

	$m = 2$	$m = 4$	$m = 12$
$p = 2$			
$p = 4$			
$p = 12$	$i = (1.06)^{1/6} - 1$ $s_{\overline{120}|i}$		

2. Develop the replacement formula $R = \dfrac{W}{s_{\overline{m/p}|i}}$ to replace an ordinary general annuity with payments of W made p times a year by an equivalent ordinary simple annuity with payments of R made m times a year.

3. Using the "change of payment" method, fill in the table below to show the discounted value of an ordinary annuity of $1, p times per year, for 10 years at $j_m = 12\%$.

	$m = 2$	$m = 4$	$m = 12$
$p = 2$			$\dfrac{a_{\overline{120}|0.01}}{s_{\overline{6}|0.01}}$
$p = 4$			
$p = 12$			

4. Convert an annuity with semi-annual payments of \$500 into an equivalent annuity with
   a) annual payments if money is worth $j_1 = 8\%$;
   b) quarterly payments if money is worth $j_2 = 10\%$.

5. Convert an annuity with quarterly payments of \$1000 into an equivalent annuity with
   a) monthly payments if money is worth $j_{12} = 9\%$;
   b) annual payments if money is worth $j_4 = 7\%$.

6. Develop the following formulas for the accumulated value S and the discounted value A of an ordinary general annuity with payments W, p times per year, for k years at rate j_m.

$$S = W \frac{(1+i)^{km} - 1}{(1+i)^{m/p} - 1}$$

$$A = W \frac{1 - (1+i)^{-km}}{(1+i)^{m/p} - 1} \quad \text{where } i = \frac{j_m}{m}$$

7. Develop the following formulas for the accumulated value S and the discounted value A of a general annuity due with payments W, p times per year, for k years at rate j_m.

$$S = W \frac{s_{\overline{km}|i}}{s_{\overline{m/p}|i}} (1+i)^{m/p}$$

$$A = W \frac{a_{\overline{km}|i}}{s_{\overline{m/p}|i}} (1+i)^{m/p} \quad \text{where } i = \frac{j_m}{m}$$

8. A father has saved money in a fund that was set up to help his son to pay for his 4-year university program. The fund will pay \$300 at the beginning of each month for eight months (September through April) plus an extra \$2000 each September 1st for four years. If $j_4 = 8\%$, what is the value of the fund on the first day of university (before any withdrawals)?

9. A used car may be purchased for \$7600 cash or \$600 down and 20 monthly payments of \$400 each, the first payment to be made in 6 months. What annual effective rate of interest does the instalment plan use?

10. A \$5000 loan is repaid by 24 monthly payments of \$175 each, followed by 24 monthly payments of \$160 each. What interest rate j_1 is being charged?

11. Three years from now, a condominium owners' association will need \$100 000 to be used for major renovations. For the last 2 years they made deposits of \$4000 at the end of each quarter into a fund that earns interest at $j_{365} = 6\%$. What quarterly deposits to the fund will be needed to reach the goal of \$100 000, 3 years from now?

12. In a recent court case, the ABC Development Company sued the XYZ Trust Company. The ABC Development Company had borrowed \$8.2 million from the XYZ Trust Company at 13%. The loan was paid off over 3 years with monthly payments. The ABC Development Company thought the rate of interest was $j_1 = 13\%$. The XYZ Trust Company was using $j_{365} = 13\%$. The court sided with the Development Company and awarded them the total dollar difference (without interest). Determine the size of the award.

13. To prepare for early retirement, a self-employed businesswoman makes RRSP deposits of \$11 500 each year for 20 years, starting on her 32nd birthday. When she is 55, she plans to make the first of 30 equal annual withdrawals. What will be the size of each withdrawal if interest is at 7% compounded
   a) semi-annually; b) continuously?

14. A deposit of \$2000 is made to open an account on April 1, 2002. Quarterly deposits of \$300 are then made for 5 years, starting July 1, 2002. Starting October 1, 2008, the first of a sequence of \$1000 quarterly withdrawals is made. Assuming an interest rate of 10% compounded continuously, determine the balance in the account a) on October 1, 2005; b) on October 1, 2011.

15. Show that the accumulated value S of an ordinary annuity of n payments of R dollars each, p payments per year over t years, at rate j_∞ is

$$S = R s_{\overline{n}|j_\infty} = R \frac{e^{j_\infty t} - 1}{e^{j_\infty/p} - 1}$$

16. Show that the discounted value A of an ordinary annuity of n payments of R dollars each, p payments per year over t years, at rate j_∞ is

$$A = R a_{\overline{n}|j_\infty} = R \frac{1 - e^{-j_\infty t}}{e^{j_\infty/p} - 1}$$

Section 4.2   ## Mortgages in Canada

During a lifetime, individuals or households may borrow money for a range of purposes, including cars, education, holidays, and personal equipment. However, the biggest loan that most individuals take out is to enable them to buy their home. These housing loans are called mortgages, as the institution lending money (say, the bank) normally requires the borrower to deliver the title of the property as security for the loan. That is, should the individual be unable to repay the loan, the lender has the right to sell the property and use the proceeds to repay the loan. It is also worth noting that many housing loans are initially set for a term of 20 to 25 years, as individuals expect to repay them throughout their working lifetime.

Canadian mortgage regulations require that the interest can be compounded, at most, semi-annually, whereas mortgage payments are usually made monthly. Thus mortgage repayments in Canada are, in effect, general annuities. There are no legal ceilings on mortgage interest rates in Canada; the rates fluctuate with the price of money on the open market.*

While the monthly payment on a Canadian mortgage is usually determined using a repayment period of 20, 25, or 30 years, the interest rate stated in the mortgage is not guaranteed for that length of time. Rather, the interest rate will change after (usually) one, three, or five years depending on the mortgage chosen. At the time the interest rate is renegotiated, the mortgage is open and can be repaid in full. Refinancing of a mortgage will be discussed in chapter 5.

Note: In the United States, the interest on mortgages is compounded monthly and payments are usually made monthly.

EXAMPLE 1   In July 1990, mortgage rates in Canada averaged around $j_2 = 11\%$. In 2006, mortgage rates averaged around $j_2 = 6.60\%$. Given a $100 000 mortgage to be repaid over 25 years, determine the required monthly payment at the two different rates of interest.

Solution a   At $j_2 = 11\%$, first determine the rate i per month equivalent to $5\frac{1}{2}\%$ per half-year, such that

$$(1 + i)^{12} = (1.055)^2$$
$$1 + i = (1.055)^{1/6}$$
$$i = (1.055)^{1/6} - 1$$
$$i = 0.008963394$$

Second, determine the monthly payment R of an ordinary simple annuity with $A = 100\,000$, $n = 300$, $i = 0.008963394$.

$$R = \frac{100\,000}{a_{\overline{300}|i}} = 962.53$$

At $j_2 = 11\%$ the monthly mortgage payment required is $962.53.

*For the current mortgage rates offered by major Canadian banks, see **www.rbc.com,** **www.bmo.ca, www.td.com, www.scotiabank.com, www.cibc.com.**

Solution b At $j_2 = 6.60\%$, first determine the rate i per month equivalent to 3.30% per half-year such that

$$(1 + i)^{12} = (1.033)^2$$
$$1 + i = (1.033)^{1/6}$$
$$i = (1.033)^{1/6} - 1$$
$$i = 0.005425865$$

Second, determine the monthly payment R of an ordinary simple annuity with $A = 100\,000$, $n = 300$, and $i = 0.005425865$.

$$R = \frac{100\,000}{a_{\overline{300}|i}} = 675.90$$

At $j_2 = 6.60\%$ the monthly mortgage payment required is $675.90. Notice the significant effect the rate of interest has on a mortgage payment.

The total interest paid over the life of the mortgage can be calculated as follows:
a) At $j_2 = 11\%$, total interest $= 300(\$962.53) - \$100\,000 = \$188\,759$.
b) At $j_2 = 6.60\%$, total interest $= 300(\$675.90) - \$100\,000 = \$102\,770$.

Again, notice the significant effect the rate of interest has on the total interest paid over the life of a mortgage.

EXAMPLE 2 A couple is buying a home for $162\,500$. They make a down payment of 20% and finance the rest through a mortgage loan at 6.5% compounded semi-annually.
   a) Calculate the couple's monthly mortgage payment based on the following repayment periods: 25 years, 20 years, 15 years, and 10 years.
   b) If the couple can afford to pay $1300 monthly on their mortgage loan, how many full payments will be required and what will be the smaller concluding payment 1 month after the last full payment?

Solution a First, calculate the down payment $= \$162\,500(0.20) = \$32\,500$. The size of the mortgage loan is $\$162\,500 - \$32\,500 = \$130\,000$.

Next, determine the rate i per month equivalent to 3.25% per half-year, such that

$$(1 + i)^{12} = (1.0325)^2$$
$$1 + i = (1.0325)^{1/6}$$
$$i = (1.0325)^{1/6} - 1$$
$$i = 0.00534474$$

Then calculate the monthly payment of an ordinary simple annuity with $A = 130\,000$, $i = 0.00534474$.

For $n = 300$ (25-year period) : $R = \dfrac{130\,000}{a_{\overline{300}|i}} = \$870.77$

For $n = 240$ (20-year period) : $R = \dfrac{130\,000}{a_{\overline{240}|i}} = \$962.65$

For $n = 180$ (15-year period) : $R = \dfrac{130\,000}{a_{\overline{180}|i}} = \$1126.28$

For $n = 120$ (10-year period) : $R = \dfrac{130\,000}{a_{\overline{120}|i}} = \$1470.42$

Note that the longer the amortization period, the lower the mortgage payment. However, it is also true the longer the amortization period, the more interest that is paid over the life of the mortgage:

For $n = 300$, total interest = 300($870.77) – $130 000 = $131 231.00
For $n = 240$, total interest = 240($962.65) – $130 000 = $101 036.00
For $n = 180$, total interest = 180($1126.28) – $130 000 = $72 730.40
For $n = 120$, total interest = 120($1470.42) – $130 000 = $46 450.40

OBSERVATION:

Borrowers are advised to choose the term of the loan best suited to their particular situation.

Solution b   We have an ordinary simple annuity with $A = 130\,000$, $R = 1300$, $i = 0.00534474$ and we calculate n as follows:

$$1300a_{\overline{n}|i} = 130\,000$$
$$a_{\overline{n}|i} = 100$$
$$\frac{1 - (1.00534474)^{-n}}{0.00534474} = 100$$
$$1 - (1.00534474)^{-n} = 0.534474008$$
$$(1.00534474)^{-n} = 0.465525992$$
$$-n \log 1.00534474 = \log 0.465525992$$
$$n = 143.4361224$$

Thus there will be 143 full monthly payments and a smaller concluding (drop) payment, X dollars, 1 month after the last full payment.

A = 130 000

Using time 144 (12 years) as a focal date, we obtain the equation of value for unknown X at rate $i = 0.00534474$.

$$1300s_{\overline{143}|i}(1 + i) + X = 130\,000(1 + i)^{144}$$
$$279\,526.83 + X = 280\,094.64$$
$$X = 567.81$$

EXAMPLE 3   A home costs $166 000. A down payment of 10% is made with the remainder financed through a mortgage loan, to be repaid over 25 years. If the interest rate is $j_2 = 6\%$, what is the mortgage payment made a) once every two weeks; b) twice a month; c) weekly?

Mortgage loan $= \$166\,000 - (0.10)\$166\,000 = \$166\,000 - \$16\,600$
$= \$149\,400$.

Solution a   Determine the rate i per 2-week period equivalent to 3% per half-year, such that
$$(1 + i)^{26} = (1.03)^2$$
$$i = (1.03)^{2/26} - 1$$
$$i = 0.00227634$$

Then determine the payment R made every 2 weeks with $A = 149\,400$, $n = 25$ years $\times 26 = 650$, $i = 0.00227634$.
$$R = \frac{149\,400}{a_{\overline{650}|i}} = 440.59$$

The payment made every 2 weeks is \$440.59.

Solution b   Determine the rate i per twice a month period equivalent to 3% per half-year, such that
$$(1 + i)^{24} = (1.03)^2$$
$$i = (1.03)^{2/24} - 1$$
$$i = 0.00246627$$

Then determine the payment R made twice a month with $A = 149\,400$, $n = 25 \times 24 = 600$, $i = 0.00246627$
$$R = \frac{149\,400}{a_{\overline{600}|i}} = 477.35$$

The payment made twice a month is \$477.35.

Solution c   Determine the rate i per week equivalent to 3% per half-year, such that
$$(1 + i)^{52} = (1.03)^2$$
$$i = (1.03)^{2/52} - 1$$
$$i = 0.001137523$$

Then determine the payment R made every week with $A = 149\,400$, $n = 25 \times 52 = 1300$, $i = 0.001137523$
$$R = \frac{149\,400}{a_{\overline{1300}|i}} = 220.17$$

The payment made every week is \$220.17.

Exercise 4.2

Part A

In each question listed below, calculate the monthly mortgage payment.

No.	Mortgage Loan	Interest Rate	Repayment Period
1.	\$105 000	$j_2 = 6.25\%$	25 years
2.	\$ 93 000	$j_2 = 14.75\%$	20 years
3.	\$200 000	$j_2 = 7.50\%$	22 years
4.	\$135 000	$j_2 = 9.75\%$	12 years

5. A home selling for \$125 000 is to be purchased with a 20% down payment and the remainder financed through a mortgage with monthly payments over 25 years. Determine the monthly payment if a) $j_2 = 5\%$; b) $j_2 = 7\%$; c) $j_2 = 9\%$.

6. A \$150 000 mortgage is obtained at a rate $j_2 = 10\frac{1}{4}\%$. The mortgage can be paid over 20, 25, or 30 years. Determine the monthly payments necessary under each of these three options. Calculate the total interest paid over each of the three terms.

7. Politicians have sometimes suggested putting a ceiling on mortgage interest rates. Mr. and Mrs. Gordon want to buy a house that would require a $160 000 mortgage to be paid off in 25 years. Interest is at rate $j_2 = 9\%$. If the government guaranteed lower mortgage interest rates, then we would expect the demand for housing to increase, thus forcing house prices upward (given a constant supply). Would Mr. and Mrs. Gordon be better off if they could get a government mortgage at $j_2 = 6\%$ but the price of the house rose such that it required a $180 000 mortgage?

8. A couple is looking at buying one of two houses. The smaller house would require a $130 000 mortgage, the larger house a $160 000 mortgage. If $j_2 = 7.5\%$, what difference would there be in their monthly payments between these two houses (assume a 25-year repayment period is used in both cases)?

9. Mr. and Mrs. Battiston are considering the purchase of a house. They would require a mortgage loan of $120 000 at rate $j_2 = 6.75\%$. If they can afford to pay $900 monthly, how many full payments will be required and what will be the smaller concluding payment?

10. The Belangers can buy a certain house listed at $200 000 and pay $35 000 down. They can get a mortgage for $165 000 at $j_2 = 7\%$ payable monthly over 25 years. The seller of the house offers them the house for $210 000 and he will give them a $175 000 mortgage at $j_2 = 6\%$ with a 25-year repayment period. If these interest rates are guaranteed for 25 years, what should they do?

11. A couple requires a $120 000 mortgage loan at $j_2 = 7.6\%$ to buy a new house.
   a) Determine the couple's mortgage payment made every two weeks based on the following repayment periods: 25 years, 20 years, and 15 years.

b) If the couple can afford to pay $500 every two weeks on their mortgage loan, what repayment period (in years) should they request?

12. To purchase a house for $215 000, you make a 15% down payment and finance the rest with a mortgage at $j_2 = 6.90\%$ over 25 years. Calculate the required mortgage payment made a) weekly; b) twice a month.

Part B

In each question listed below, determine the unknown part.

No.	Mortgage Loan	Interest Rate	Repayment Period	Monthly Payment
1.	?	$j_2 = 6.75\%$	25 years	$920
2.	$100 000	$j_2 = ?$	20 years	$828
3.	$ 89 000	$j_2 = 6.45\%$	?	$750
4.	$ 80 000	$j_2 = 5.62\%$	17 years	?

5. The Friedmans have a $135 000 mortgage with monthly payments over 25 years at $j_2 = 7\%$. Because they each get paid weekly, they decide to switch to weekly payments (still at $j_2 = 7\%$ and paid over 25 years). Compare their weekly payments to their monthly payments.

6. A couple must decide between a red house and a blue house. To purchase the red house they must take a $155 000 mortgage to be repaid over 20 years at 7.8% compounded semi-annually. To purchase the blue house, they must take a mortgage to be repaid over 25 years at 7.1% compounded semi-annually. If the monthly mortgage payments are equal, determine the value of the mortgage on the blue house.

7. You want to take a $105 000 mortgage at $j_2 = 9\%$ and can afford to pay up to $300 per week. What repayment period in years should you request and what will be your weekly payment?

Section 4.3   **Perpetuities**

A **perpetuity** is an annuity whose payments begin on a fixed date and continue forever.

Illustration: Let us consider a person who invests $10 000 at rate $j_2 = 10\%$, keeps the original investment intact and collects $500 interest at the end of each half-year. As long as the interest rate does not change and the original principal of \$10 000 is kept intact, interest payments of \$500 can be collected forever. We say the interest payments of \$500 form a perpetuity.

The present value or discounted value of this infinite series of payments is \$10 000, as shown on the diagram below.

Examples of perpetuities are the series of interest payments from a sum of money invested permanently at a certain interest rate, a scholarship paid from an endowment on a perpetual basis, and the dividends on a share of preferred stock.

It is meaningless to speak about the accumulated value of a perpetuity, since there is no end to the term of a perpetuity. The discounted value, however, is well defined as the equivalent dated value of the set of payments at the beginning of the term of the perpetuity.

Discounted values of perpetuities are very useful in capitalization problems and will be discussed in chapter 7, section 7.3.

The terminology defined for annuities applies to a perpetuity as well. First we shall discuss an **ordinary simple perpetuity**, that is, a lump sum is invested and a series of level periodic payments are made, with the first payment made at the end of the first interest period and payments continuing forever. The other simple perpetuities, i.e., perpetuities due and deferred, may be handled using the concept of an equation of value.

Let A be the discounted value of an ordinary simple perpetuity; let $i > 0$ be the interest rate per period; and let R be the periodic payment of the perpetuity.

Then A must be equivalent to the set of payments R as shown on the diagram below.

From first principles,

$$A = R(1 + i)^{-1} + R(1 + i)^{-2} + R(1 + i)^{-3} + \cdots \to \infty$$

We know that the sum of an infinite geometric progression can be expressed as

$$\frac{t_1}{1 - r} \quad \text{if} \quad -1 < r < 1$$

In our infinite geometric progression $t_1 = R(1 + i)^{-1}$ and $r = (1 + i)^{-1}$. Obviously, $0 < (1 + i)^{-1} < 1$ for $i > 0$. Therefore,

$$A = \frac{R(1 + i)^{-1}}{1 - (1 + i)^{-1}} = \frac{R}{(1 + i) - 1} = \frac{R}{i}$$

Alternatively, it is evident that A will perpetually provide $R = Ai$ as interest payments on the invested capital A at the end of each interest period as long as it remains invested at rate i.

From $R = Ai$ we obtain the discounted value A of an ordinary simple perpetuity

$$\boxed{A = \frac{R}{i}}$$

(12)

OBSERVATION:

Formula **(12)** for the discounted value A of an ordinary simple perpetuity can also be obtained as the limit of the discounted value of an ordinary simple annuity

$$A = \lim_{n \to \infty} R a_{\overline{n}|i} = \lim_{n \to \infty} R \frac{1 - (1+i)^{-n}}{i} = \frac{R}{i}$$

Actuaries use the notation $a_{\overline{\infty}|i} = \lim_{n \to \infty} a_{\overline{n}|i} = \frac{1}{i}$ when referring to the discounted value of a \$1 ordinary simple perpetuity.

EXAMPLE 1   How much money is needed to establish a scholarship fund paying scholarships of \$1000 each half-year if the endowment can be invested at $j_2 = 10\%$ and if the first scholarships will be provided
   a) half-year from now;
   b) immediately;
   c) 4 years from now?

Solution a   The payments form an ordinary simple perpetuity and we have $R = 1000$ and $i = 0.05$; and using **(12)** we calculate

$$A = \frac{1000}{0.05} = \$20\,000$$

Solution b   We have a perpetuity-due, since the first payment is due at the time the lump sum deposit is made. Thus, the endowment is the sum of the above perpetuity and \$1000, i.e.

$$A = 1000 + \frac{1000}{0.05}$$
$$= 1000 + 20\,000$$
$$= \$21\,000$$

Solution c   We have a deferred perpetuity. The first scholarship is due 4 years from now, or at time 8, thus the deferral period is 7 half-years. The amount needed today is

$$A = \frac{1000}{0.05}(1.05)^{-7}$$
$$= 20\,000(1.05)^{-7}$$
$$= \$14\,213.63$$

OBSERVATION:

Since a perpetuity is an annuity with $n \to \infty$, we may develop formulas for the discounted value A of other simple perpetuities as in section 3.4:

$$A = \frac{R}{i}(1+i) = \frac{R}{i} + R \text{ for a simple perpetuity due}$$

$$A = \frac{R}{i}(1+i)^{-k} \text{ for a simple perpetuity deferred } k \text{ periods.}$$

EXAMPLE 2   A company is expected to pay $0.90 every 3 months on a share of its preferred stock. What should a share of the stock be selling for, if money is worth a) $j_4 = 6\%$; b) $j_4 = 8\%$?

Solution a   We have $R = 0.90$ and $i = 0.015$; and using **(12)** we calculate

$$A = \frac{0.90}{0.015} = \$60$$

Solution b   Using $i = 0.02$, we calculate $A = \dfrac{0.90}{0.02} = \$45$.

Note the effect of interest rates on preferred stock values.

When the payment interval and the interest period do not coincide, we have a **general perpetuity.** The simplest way to solve a general perpetuity problem is to calculate the equivalent rate of interest per payment interval and then use formula **(12)**.

EXAMPLE 3   What should a share of the stock in Example 2 be selling for if the money is worth a) $j_{12} = 6\%$; b) $j_1 = 6\%$?

Solution a   First we calculate the rate i per quarter-year equivalent to $\frac{0.06}{12} = 0.005$ per month, such that

$$(1 + i)^4 = (1 + 0.005)^{12}$$
$$1 + i = (1.005)^3$$
$$i = (1.005)^3 - 1$$
$$i = 0.015075125$$

We now have an ordinary simple perpetuity with $R = 0.90$ and $i = 0.015075125$; and using **(12)** we calculate

$$A = \frac{0.90}{i} = \$59.70$$

Solution b   First we determine the rate i per quarter-year equivalent to 0.06 per year, such that
$$(1 + i)^4 = 1.06$$
$$1 + i = (1.06)^{1/4}$$
$$i = (1.06)^{1/4} - 1$$
$$i = 0.014673846$$

We now have an ordinary simple perpetuity with $R = 0.90$ and $i = 0.014673846$; and using **(12)** we calculate

$$A = \frac{0.90}{i} = \$61.33$$

Exercise 4.3

Part A

1. Determine the discounted value of an ordinary simple perpetuity paying $50 a month if
   a) $j_{12} = 6\%$; b) $j_{12} = 7.2\%$; c) $j_{12} = 9\%$.

2. Determine the discounted value of an ordinary simple perpetuity paying $400 a year if interest is a) $j_1 = 8\%$; b) $j_1 = 12.48\%$.

3. How much money is needed to establish a scholarship fund paying $1500 annually if the fund will earn interest at $j_1 = 6\%$ and the first payment will be made a) at the end of the first year; b) immediately; c) 5 years from now?

4. On September 1, 2006, a philanthropist gives a university a fund of $50 000, which is invested at $j_2 = 10\%$. If semi-annual scholarships are awarded for 20 years from this grant, what is the size of each scholarship if the first one is awarded on a) September 1, 2006; b) September 1, 2008?

5. If the semi-annual scholarships in question 4 were to be awarded indefinitely, what would be the size of the payments for the two starting dates listed above?

6. It costs the C.N.R. $100 at the end of each month to maintain a level-crossing gate system. How much can the company contribute toward the cost of an underpass that will eliminate the level-crossing system if money is worth 9% payable monthly?

7. How much money is needed to establish a research fund paying $2000 semi-annually forever (first payment at the end of six months) if money is worth a) $j_1 = 7\%$; b) $j_2 = 7\%$; c) $j_{12} = 9\%$?

8. A family is considering putting aluminum siding on their house as it needs painting immediately. Painting the house costs $4200

and must be done every four years. What price can the family afford for the aluminum siding if they earn interest at $j_1 = 5.75\%$ on their savings?

9. The XYZ company has a stock that pays a semi-annual dividend of $4. If the stock sells for $64, what yield j_2 did the investor desire? What is the equivalent rate j_1?

10. The discounted value of a perpetuity is $20 000 and the yield on the fund is $j_2 = 8\%$. What payment will this fund provide a) at the end of each month; b) at the beginning of each year?

11. Deposits of $1000 are placed into a fund at the beginning of each year for the next 20 years. At the end of the 20th year, annual payments from the fund commence and continue forever. If $j_1 = 6\frac{1}{2}\%$, determine the value of these payments.

12. On the basis of an unspecified interest rate, i per annum, a perpetuity paying $330 at the end of each year forever may be purchased for $3000. Determine i.

13. If money is worth $j_1 = 4\%$, determine the present value of a deferred perpetuity of $1000 per year if the first payment is due at the end of 6 years.

14. What annual deposits are needed for 15 years to provide for a perpetuity of $2000 per year, with the first payment in 10 years? Assume interest is at $j_1 = 8\%$.

Part B

1. Use an infinite geometric progression to derive the formula for the discounted value of a simple perpetuity due.

2. Derive $a_{\overline{n}|i} = \frac{1-(1+i)^{-n}}{i}$ as the difference between the discounted value of an ordinary simple perpetuity of $1 per period and the discounted

value of an ordinary simple perpetuity of $1 per period deferred for n periods.

3. In 2002, a research foundation was established by a fund of $2 000 000 invested at a rate that would provide $240 000 payments at the end of each year, forever.
   a) What interest rate was being earned in the fund?
   b) After the payment in 2007, the foundation learned that the rate of interest earned on the fund was being changed to $j_1 = 10\%$. If the foundation wants to continue annual payments forever, what size will the new payments be?
   c) If the foundation continues with the $240 000 payments annually, how many full payments can be made at the new rate?

4. A university estimates that its new campus centre will require $3000 for upkeep at the end of each year for the next 5 years and $5000 at the end of each year thereafter indefinitely. If money is worth $j_1 = 8\%$, how large an endowment is necessary for the future upkeep of the campus centre?

5. You take out a loan for L at $j_{12} = 18\%$ and repay $300 at the end of each month for as long as necessary. This loan is invested at $j_1 = 10\%$ and provides for a *perpetuity due* that pays the prize in the annual "Liar's Contest." The prize is $200 for the 1st year and increases by $150 each year until it reaches $500. From then on the prize remains $500. Determine the time and amount of the final repayment on the loan.

6. A university receives a certain sum as a bequest and invests it to earn $j_1 = 8\%$. The fund can be used to pay for a lecturer at $60 000 payable at the end of each year forever, or the money can be used to pay for a new building that the university is planning to erect. The building will be paid for with 25 equal annual payments, the first of which is due 4 years from today when the building will be occupied. Calculate the amount of each building payment.

7. How much must you deposit at the end of each year for 10 years to fund a perpetuity of $2500 per year with the 1st payment in 15 years?

Interest rate is $j_1 = 6\%$ for 15 years, then $j_{12} = 9\%$.

8. A perpetuity paying $1000 at the end of each year is replaced with an annuity paying X at the end of each month for 10 years. Calculate X if $j_4 = 7\%$ in both cases.

9. If, in question 8, the annuity paid $250 at the end of each month, how long would the annuity last and what would be the size of the final smaller payment?

10. On September 1, 2006, a wealthy industrialist gives a university a fund of $100 000 which is invested at 8% compounded daily. If semi-annual scholarships are awarded for 20 years from this grant, what is the size of each scholarship if the first one is awarded on a) September 1, 2006; b) September 1, 2008?

11. If the semi-annual scholarships in question 10 were awarded indefinitely, what would be the size of the payments for the two starting dates listed above?

12. Determine the present value of a perpetuity of $362.99 payable every 4 years, the first payment 3 years hence, at the annual effective rate of 4%.

13. Determine the monthly deposit needed for 5 years to provide for a perpetuity of $400 per month. The 1st perpetuity payment is made 2 years after the last deposit, and interest changes from $j_{12} = 8\%$ to $j_{12} = 9\%$ on that date.

14. You deposit $1000 per year for 10 years at $j_1 = 8\%$. This fund then provides for a perpetuity of $3000 per year, with the first payment made n years after the final deposit. At the time of the first perpetuity payment, interest rates fall to $j_4 = 7\%$. Calculate n.

15. A perpetuity pays $4000 per year, as follows:
    a) in odd-numbered years, a payment of $4000 is made at the end of the year;
    b) in even-numbered years, a payment of $1000 is made at the end of each quarter.
    Interest is at an annual effective rate of 8%. At the beginning of an odd-numbered year, this perpetuity is exchanged for another of equal value which provides semi-annual payments, the first payment due six months hence. What is the semi-annual payment of the new perpetuity?

Section 4.4   # Annuities Where Payments Vary

Thus far, all the annuities considered have had level payments. Unfortunately, this is not always the case in real life. Thus, it is necessary to be able to handle situations where the size of the payments may vary.

First we consider situations where the annuity **payments vary in terms of a common ratio**. That is, each succeeding payment of an annuity increases or decreases by a constant percentage over the preceding payment. As a result, the payments will form a geometric progression. To calculate the present or accumulated value of the payments, we will make use of the formula for the sum of a geometric progression.

EXAMPLE 1   Mr. Fung wants to buy an annuity of $2000 a year for 10 years that is protected against inflation. The XYZ Trust Company offers to sell him an annuity where payments increase each year by exactly 5%. Determine the cost of this annuity if a) $j_1 = 6\%$; b) $j_1 = 4\%$. (Assume the payments are at the end of each year and the first payment is $2000.)

Solution a   We arrange the data on a time diagram below.

Using 0 as a focal date, we write the equation of value for the discounted value A of these payments at $j_1 = 6\%$.

$$A = 2000(1.06)^{-1} + 2000(1.05)(1.06)^{-2} + \cdots + 2000(1.05)^9(1.06)^{-10}$$

The expression on the right-hand side of the equal sign of the above equation is the sum of 10 terms of a geometric progression (see Appendix 2) with first term $t_1 = 2000(1.06)^{-1}$ and common ratio $r = (1.05)(1.06)^{-1} < 1$. Thus, applying the formula for the sum of n terms of a geometric progression $S_n = t_1 \dfrac{1 - r^n}{1 - r}$ we obtain

$$A = 2000(1.06)^{-1}\left[\frac{1 - (1.05)^{10}(1.06)^{-10}}{1 - (1.05)(1.06)^{-1}}\right] = 18\,086.75$$

The cost of the annuity is $18 086.75.

It is worth noting that a 10-year $2000 annuity purchased at $j_1 = 6\%$ with no inflation factor would cost only $2000a_{\overline{10}|6\%} = \$14\,720.17$.

Solution b   Using 0 as a focal date, we write the equation of value for the discounted value A of these payments at $j_1 = 4\%$.

$$A = 2000(1.04)^{-1} + 2000(1.05)(1.04)^{-2} + \cdots + 2000(1.05)^9(1.04)^{-10}$$

The expression on the right-hand side has $n = 10$ terms, $t_1 = 2000(1.04)^{-1}$ and common ratio $r = (1.05)(1.04)^{-1} < 1$. Thus,

$$A = 2000(1.04)^{-1}\left[\frac{(1.05)^{10}(1.04)^{-10} - 1}{(1.05)(1.04)^{-1} - 1}\right] = 20\,084.57$$

The cost of this annuity is \$20 084.57.

It is worth noting that with no inflation factor, this annuity would cost only $2000a_{\overline{10}|4\%} = \$16\,221.79$.

EXAMPLE 2   Nicholas deposits \$2500 in a savings account today. He plans to continue making deposits every 3 months, each succeeding deposit being 2% lower than the preceding deposit. If the fund earns $j_4 = 6\%$, how much has he accumulated at the end of 8 years, 3 months after his last deposit?

Solution   We arrange the data on a time diagram below.

2500	2500(0.98)	2500(0.98)^2		2500(0.98)^{30}	2500(0.98)^{31}	

```
2500    2500(0.98)   2500(0.98)²        2500(0.98)³⁰    2500(0.98)³¹
 |_____|_____|_____ ... _____|_____|_____|
 0          1            2                  30            31         32
                                                                     |
                                                                     S
```

Using time 32 as the focal date, we write the equation of value for the accumulated value S of these payments at $j_4 = 6\%$.

$$S = 2500(1.015)^{32} + 2500(0.98)(1.015)^{31} + \cdots + 2500(0.98)^{31}(1.015)$$

The right-hand side of the equation is the sum of 32 terms of a geometric progression with $t_1 = 2500(1.015)^{32}$ and $r = (0.98)(1.015)^{-1} < 1$. Thus,

$$S = 2500(1.015)^{32}\left[\frac{1 - (0.98)^{32}(1.015)^{-32}}{1 - (0.98)(1.015)^{-1}}\right] \doteq 78\,766.99$$

Nicholas has \$78 766.99 in his account at the end of 8 years.

Second, we consider situations where **payments vary in arithmetic progression**, that is, annuities where payments increase or decrease every period by a constant amount (as opposed to a constant percentage). We illustrate a popular method of solution in the following two examples.

EXAMPLE 3   Mrs. Soros has a job that pays \$25 000 a year. Each year she gets a \$1000 raise. What is the discounted value of her income for the next 15 years at $j_1 = 7\%$? (Assume payments are at the end of each year with a first payment of \$25 000.)

Solution   We arrange the data on a time diagram below.

$$
\begin{array}{ccccccc}
& 25\,000 & 26\,000 & 27\,000 & & 38\,000 & 39\,000 \\
\hline
0 & 1 & 2 & 3 & \cdots & 14 & 15
\end{array}
$$

A

Using 0 as the focal date we write the equation of value for the discounted value A of her income.

$$A = 25\,000(1.07)^{-1} + 26\,000(1.07)^{-2} + 27\,000(1.07)^{-3} + \cdots$$
$$+38\,000(1.07)^{-14} + 39\,000(1.07)^{-15}$$

If we multiply A by (1.07) we obtain

$$(1.07)A = 25\,000 + 26\,000(1.07)^{-1} + 27\,000(1.07)^{-2} + \cdots$$
$$+38\,000(1.07)^{-13} + 39\,000(1.07)^{-14}$$

Subtracting the first equation from the second gives

$$0.07A = 25\,000 + 1000[(1.07)^{-1} + (1.07)^{-2} + \cdots + (1.07)^{-14}] - 39\,000(1.07)^{-15}$$
$$0.07A = 25\,000 + 1000a_{\overline{14}|0.07} - 39\,000(1.07)^{-15}$$
$$A = \frac{1}{0.07}[25\,000 + 1000a_{\overline{14}|0.07} - 39\,000(1.07)^{-15}]$$
$$A = \$280\,143.90$$

EXAMPLE 4   Consider an annuity with a term of n periods in which payments begin at P at the end of the first period and change by Q each period thereafter. Assuming an interest rate i per period, $P > 0$, and $P + (n-1)Q > 0$ (to avoid negative payments if $Q < 0$), show that

a) the discounted value of the annuity is given by

$$\boxed{A = Pa_{\overline{n}|i} + Q\,\frac{a_{\overline{n}|i} - n(1+i)^{-n}}{i}}$$

b) the accumulated value of the annuity is given by

$$\boxed{S = Ps_{\overline{n}|i} + Q\,\frac{s_{\overline{n}|i} - n}{i}}$$

Solution a   We arrange the data on a time diagram below.

A

Using 0 as the focal date, we write the equation of value for the discounted value A of the annuity:

$$A = P(1+i)^{-1} + (P+Q)(1+i)^{-2} + (P+2Q)(1+i)^{-3} + \cdots$$
$$+ [P+(n-2)Q](1+i)^{-(n-1)} + [P+(n-1)Q](1+i)^{-n}$$

If we multiply A by $(1+i)$, we obtain:

$$(1+i)A = P + (P+Q)(1+i)^{-1} + (P+2Q)(1+i)^{-2} + (P+3Q)(1+i)^{-3} + \cdots$$
$$+ [P+(n-2)Q](1+i)^{-(n-2)} + [P+(n-1)Q](1+i)^{-(n-1)}$$

Subtracting the first equation from the second we obtain:

$$iA = P + Q[(1+i)^{-1} + (1+i)^{-2} + \cdots + (1+i)^{-(n-1)}] - P(1+i)^{-n} - (n-1)Q(1+i)^{-n}$$
$$= P[1-(1+i)^{-n}] + Q[(1+i)^{-1} + (1+i)^{-2} + \cdots + (1+i)^{-n}] - nQ(1+i)^{-n}$$
$$= P[1-(1+i)^{-n}] + Qa_{\overline{n}|i} - nQ(1+i)^{-n}$$

Thus

$$A = P\frac{1-(1+i)^{-n}}{i} + Q\frac{a_{\overline{n}|i} - n(1+i)^{-n}}{i} = Pa_{\overline{n}|i} + Q\frac{a_{\overline{n}|i} - n(1+i)^{-n}}{i}$$

Solution b   The accumulated value

$$S = A(1+i)^n = \left[Pa_{\overline{n}|i} + Q\frac{a_{\overline{n}|i} - n(1+i)^{-n}}{i} \right](1+i)^n = Ps_{\overline{n}|i} + Q\frac{s_{\overline{n}|i} - n}{i}$$

OBSERVATION:

Using the formula of Example 4 (part a) to solve Example 3, we substitute $P = 25\,000$, $Q = 1000$, $n = 15$, $i = 0.07$ to obtain

$$A = 25\,000a_{\overline{15}|0.07} + 1000\frac{a_{\overline{15}|0.07} - 15(1.07)^{-15}}{0.07} = \$280\,143.90$$

EXAMPLE 5   Mr. Smith, who just turned age 45, wishes to save money for his retirement. He decides to make monthly deposits, with his first deposit being $1500 (made today) and each succeeding deposit being $5 less. He makes deposits for 20 years. If his deposits earn $j_{12} = 6\%$, how much will he have accumulated at age 65?

Solution   We arrange the data on a time diagram below and note that we have an annuity-due.

1500	1495	1490		310	305	
0	1	2	$\cdots$	238	239	240

$$\downarrow$$
$$S$$

Using the "P & Q" formula (Example 4 b) with $P = 1500$, $Q = -5$, $n = 240$, and $i = 0.005$, we obtain the accumulated value of an ordinary annuity at the time of the 240th deposit (time 239).

$$1500 s_{\overline{240}|0.005} - 5\left[\frac{s_{\overline{240}|0.005} - 240}{0.005}\right] = \$471\,020.45$$

To obtain the accumulated value at time 240 (one month after the last deposit), we accumulate the above value for one more month:

$$S = \$471\,020.45(1.005) = \$473\,375.56$$

Mr. Smith will have $473 375.56 when he turns age 65.

Exercise 4.4

Part A

1. Determine the discounted value of a series of 20 annual payments of $500 if $j_1 = 5\%$ and we want to allow for an inflation factor of $j_1 = 2\%$. (Assume the payments are at the end of each year and the first payment is $500.)

2. A court is trying to determine the discounted value of the future income of a man paralyzed in a car accident. At the time of the accident the man was earning $45 000 a year and anticipated getting a 4% raise each year. He is 30 years away from retirement. If money is worth $j_1 = 5\%$, what is the discounted value of his future income? (Assume the payments are at the end of each year and the first payment is $45\,000(1.04) = \$46\,800$.)

3. Determine the discounted value of a series of 15 payments made at the end of each year at $j_1 = 6\%$ if the first payment is $300, the second payment is $600, the third $900, and so on.

4. Mrs. Tong makes semi-annual deposits into a fund earning interest at $j_2 = 8\%$. Her first deposit is $2000 and each succeeding deposit is 6% higher than the preceding deposit. What is the accumulated value of her fund immediately after her 15th deposit?

5. An investor deposits $1000 at the beginning of each year in a special fund paying interest at $j_1 = 10\%$. These interest payments are then deposited in a bank account paying interest at $j_1 = 6\%$. How much money has been accumulated at the end of 6 years?

6. A certain site is returning an annual rent of $5000 per year payable at the beginning of the year. It is expected that the rent will increase, on the average, 6% per year. Calculate the present value of the site at $j_1 = 10\%$.

7. Mr. Martin needs to have his house painted immediately. Painting the house will cost $1200, so he is trying to decide if he should put on aluminum siding. If we assume the house must be painted every 5th year (forever) and that the cost of painting will rise by 3% per year (forever), how much should Mr. Martin be willing to pay for aluminum siding if he can earn $j_1 = 6\%$ on his money?

8. Calculate the accumulated value of quarterly payments of $100, $110, $120, ... for 20 years if interest is at $j_{12} = 12\%$ and payments are at the end of each quarter.

9. What is the present value of quarterly payments of $100, $110, $120, $130, ... for 20 years, if $j_2 = 8\%$ and payments are at the beginning of each quarter?

10. An annuity provides for 30 annual payments. The first payment of $100 is made immediately and the remaining payments increase by 8% per annum. Interest is calculated at $j_1 = 9.4\%$. Calculate the present value of this annuity.

11. Determine the discounted value one year before the first payment of a series of 20 annual payments the first of which is $500. The payments inflate at $j_1 = 6\%$ and interest is at $j_1 = 8\%$.

12. What is the accumulated value of quarterly payments of $100, $115, $130, ... for 15 years if interest is $j_4 = 10\%$ and payments are at the beginning of each quarter?

13. A decreasing annuity will pay $800 at the end of 6 months, $750 at the end of 1 year, etc., until a final payment of $350 is made at the end of 5 years. Determine the present value of the payments if money is worth 8% compounded monthly.

14. Determine the present value of monthly payments of $20, $25, $30, $35, ... for 100 months if interest is $j_\infty = \delta = 10\%$ and payments are at the end of each month.

Part B

1. Consider a perpetuity in which payments begin at P at the end of the first period and increase by Q per period thereafter. Assuming the interest rate i per period and $P > 0$, $Q > 0$ (to avoid negative payments), show that the discounted value of this perpetuity is given by

$$\frac{P}{i} + \frac{Q}{i^2}$$

(Hint: take the limit of the formulas in Example 4a as n approaches infinity.)

2. Using the result of problem 1,
 a) show that the discounted value of a $1 increasing perpetuity, denoted by $(Ia)_{\overline{\infty}|i}$, is

$$(Ia)_{\overline{\infty}|i} = \frac{1}{i} + \frac{1}{i^2}$$

 b) calculate the present value of a perpetuity whose payments start at $100 at the end of the first month and increase by $2 per month thereafter, assuming $j_{12} = 6\%$.

3. Determine the discounted value of payments made at the beginning of each year indefinitely at $j_2 = 7\%$ if the first payment is $100; the second is $200; the third is $300; and so on.

4. Calculate the accumulated value of deposits of $1, $2, $3, ... , $98, $99, $100, $99, $98, ... , $3, $2, $1 if interest is 2% per period and deposits are at the end of periods.

5. It is desired to accumulate a fund of $18 000 at the end of 3 years by equal deposits at the beginning of each month. If the deposits earn interest at $j_{12} = 9\%$ but the interest can be

reinvested only at $j_{12} = 6\%$, determine the size of the necessary deposit.

6. Consider an annuity where payments vary as represented in the following diagram ($0 < i_1 < 1$):

$R(1 + i_1)$	$R(1 + i_1)^2$	$R(1 + i_1)^3$	$R(1 + i_1)^n$
0 1	2	3	··· n

Further, assume the interest rate is i_2 per interest period. Let i be the rate such that

$$(1 + i) = \frac{1 + i_2}{1 + i_1}$$

Show that the discounted value A of the above annuity at rate i_2 is

$$A = Ra_{\overline{n}|i}$$

7. Derive an algebraic proof of the following identities and interpret by means of time diagrams.

 a) $a_{\overline{1}|i} + a_{\overline{2}|i} + a_{\overline{3}|i} + \cdots + a_{\overline{m}|i} = \dfrac{n - a_{\overline{n}|i}}{i}$

 b) $s_{\overline{1}|i} + s_{\overline{2}|i} + s_{\overline{3}|i} + \cdots + s_{\overline{n-1}|i} = \dfrac{s_{\overline{n}|i} - n}{i}$

8. Show that the discounted value A of a decreasing annuity whose n payments at the end of each year are $nR, (n-1)R, (n-2)R, ... , 2R, R$ is $A = \dfrac{R}{i}(n - a_{\overline{n}|i})$ at rate i per year.

9. The principal on a loan of $5000 is to be repaid in equal annual instalments of $1000 each at the end of each of the next 5 years. Interest will be paid at the end of each year at $j_1 = 4\frac{1}{2}\%$ on the entire outstanding balance, including the $1000 payment then due. Determine the purchase price of the loan to yield $j_1 = 5\%$.

10. Determine the present value of an annuity where payments are $200 per month at the end of each month during the first year; $195 per month during the second year; $190 per month in the third year; etc., with monthly payments decreasing by $5 after the end of each year. Five dollars will be paid at the end of each month during the 40th year and nothing thereafter. Interest is at $j_{12} = 12\%$.

11. Mrs. Rider has just retired and is trying to decide between two retirement income options as to where she should place her life savings. Fund A will pay her quarterly payments for

25 years starting at $3000 at the end of the first quarter. Fund A will increase her payments each quarter thereafter using an inflation factor equivalent to 4% compounded quarterly. Fund B pays $4500 at the end of each quarter for 25 years with no inflation factor. Which fund should Mrs. Rider choose if she compares the funds using 6% compounded quarterly?

12. Determine the present value of a perpetuity under which an amount p is paid at the end of the second year, $p + q$ at the end of the fourth year, $p + 2q$ at the end of the sixth year, $p + 3q$ at the end of the eighth year, etc., if interest is at rate i per year.

13. Consider the perpetuity whose payments at the end of each year are $R, R + p, R + 2p, \dots,$ $R + (n-1)p, R + np, R + np, \dots$. The payments increase by a constant amount p until they reach $R + np$, after which they continue without change. Show that the discounted value A of such a perpetuity at rate i per annum is given by

$$A = \frac{R + pa_{\overline{n}|i}}{i}$$

14. A man deposits $100 at the beginning of each year into a fund paying interest to him in cash at $j_1 = 6\%$ each year on the principal in the fund. At the end of each year he deposits the interest payments into a second fund earning interest at $j_1 = 4\%$. At the end of which year will the interest fund first exceed the principal fund?

15. For the same lump-sum payment, an insurance company will provide a choice of
a) an ordinary annuity of $1000 per year for 20 years; or
b) an ordinary increasing annuity of $X per year initially, inflating at 10% per year, for 20 years.
Determine X if interest is at $j_1 = 8\%$. What is the final payment of the increasing annuity?

16. Jeanne has won a lottery that pays $1000 per month in the first year, $1100 per month in the second year, $1200 per month in the third year, etc. Payments are made at the end of each month for 10 years. Using an annual effective interest rate of 3%, calculate the present value of this prize.

17. Consider the increasing $1 annuity in the diagram below

where $(Ia)_{\overline{n}|i}$ denotes the discounted value, $(Is)_{\overline{n}|i}$ denotes the accumulated value of this annuity and i is the interest rate per period. Show that

$$(Ia)_{\overline{n}|i} = a_{\overline{n}|i} + \frac{a_{\overline{n}|i} - n(1+i)^{-n}}{i} = \frac{\ddot{a}_{\overline{n}|i} - n(1+i)^{-n}}{i}$$

$$(Is)_{\overline{n}|i} = s_{\overline{n}|i} + \frac{s_{\overline{n}|i} - n}{i} = \frac{\ddot{s}_{\overline{n}|i} - n}{i}$$

18. Consider the decreasing $1 annuity in the diagram below

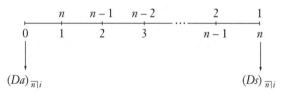

where $(Da)_{\overline{n}|i}$ denotes the discounted value, $(Ds)_{\overline{n}|i}$ denotes the accumulated value of this annuity and i is the interest rate per period. Show that

$$(Da)_{\overline{n}|i} = na_{\overline{n}|i} - \frac{a_{\overline{n}|i} - n(1+i)^{-n}}{i} = \frac{n - a_{\overline{n}|i}}{i}$$

$$(Ds)_{\overline{n}|i} = ns_{\overline{n}|i} - \frac{s_{\overline{n}|i} - n}{i} = \frac{n(1+i)^n - s_{\overline{n}|i}}{i}$$

Section 4.5   **Summary and Review Exercises**

● Change of rate approach to general annuity problems: Calculate the equivalent interest rate per payment period and then solve a simple annuity problem using the methods of chapter 3.

- For general annuities where it is stated that simple interest is paid for part of an interest period, you must use the "change of payment" approach which requires using simple interest to calculate an equivalent payment made with the same frequency as interest is compounded and then solve a simple annuity problem using the methods of chapter 3.

- Discounted value of a simple perpetuity is given by

$$A = \frac{R}{i} \qquad \text{for an ordinary perpetuity}$$

$$A = \frac{R}{i}(1+i) \quad \text{for a perpetuity due}$$

$$A = \frac{R}{i}(1+i)^{-k} \text{ for a deferred perpetuity}$$

- To calculate the discounted value A (or the accumulated value S) of an annuity with payments varying in a constant ratio, we write A as a sum of discounted values of individual payments (or S as a sum of accumulated values of individual payments) and then determine the sum of n terms of the resulting geometric progression.

- To calculate the discounted value A of an annuity with payments varying by a constant difference, we first write A as a sum of discounted values of individual payments. Then we multiply the equation for A by $(1 + i)$. Subtracting the equation for A from the equation for $A(1 + i)$ and simplifying the resulting equation for $A(1 + i) - A = Ai$, we obtain the value of A.

  Similarly we can calculate the accumulated value S.

- For an annuity with a term of n periods in which payments begin at P at the end of the first period and change by Q each period thereafter (assuming $i > 0$, $P > 0$, $P + (n - 1)Q > 0$), the discounted value A is given by

$$A = Pa_{\overline{n}|i} + Q\frac{a_{\overline{n}|i} - n(1+i)^{-n}}{i}$$

and the accumulated value S is given by

$$S = Ps_{\overline{n}|i} + Q\frac{s_{\overline{n}|i} - n}{i}$$

- For a perpetuity in which payments begin at P at the end of the first period and increase by $Q > 0$ each period thereafter, the discounted value A is given by

$$A = \frac{P}{i} + \frac{Q}{i^2}$$

Review Exercises 4.5

1. Replace an annuity with quarterly payments of $300 by an equivalent annuity with
   a) semi-annual payments if money is worth 5% compounded semi-annually;
   b) monthly payments if money is worth 7% compounded quarterly.

2. Determine the accumulated and the discounted value of payments of $100 at the end of each quarter-year for 10 years at $j_{12} = 4\%$.

3. Deposits of $100 are made at the end of each month to an account paying interest at 8% compounded semi-annually. How much money will be accumulated in the account at the end of 3 years if
   a) simple interest is paid for part of a conversion period;
   b) compounded interest is paid for part of a conversion period?

4. How many monthly deposits of $100 each and what final deposit one month later will be necessary to accumulate $3000 if interest is
   a) at $6\frac{1}{2}$ compounded semi-annually;
   b) at 9% compounded quarterly?

5. A company wishes to have $150 000 in a fund at the end of 8 years. What deposit at the end of each month must they make if the fund pays interest at 5% compounded daily?

6. Steve buys a car worth $15 000. He pays $3000 down and agrees to pay $500 at the end of each month as long as necessary. Determine the number of full payments and the final payment one month later if interest is at $j_1 = 14.2\%$.

7. If it takes $50 per month for 18 months to repay a loan of $800, what nominal rate compounded semi-annually is being charged? What annual effective rate is being charged?

8. A lot is sold for $8000 down and 6 semi-annual payments of $3000, the first due at the end of 2 years. Calculate the cash value of the lot if money is worth 6% compounded daily.

9. Determine the accumulated and discounted value of payments of $100 made at the beginning of each month for 5 years at $j_4 = 6\%$.

10. An annuity consists of 60 payments of $200 at the end of each month. Interest is at $j_1 = 11.05\%$. Determine the value of this annuity at each of the following times:
    a) at the time of the first payment;
    b) two years before the first payment;
    c) at the time of the last payment.

11. Which is cheaper?
    a) Buy a car for $13 600 and after three years trade it in for $3600.
    b) Lease a car for $318 a month payable at the beginning of each month for three years. Assume maintenance costs are identical and that money is worth $j_1 = 8\%$.

12. On November 1, 2006, a research fund of $300 000 was established to provide for equal annual grants for 10 years. What will be the size of each grant if
    a) the fund earns interest at 8% compounded daily and the first grant is awarded on November 1, 2006;

b) the fund earns interest at 10% compounded monthly and the first grant is awarded on November 1, 2009?

13. A couple requires a $95 000 mortgage loan at $j_2 = 6\frac{3}{4}\%$ to buy a new house.
    a) Calculate the couple's monthly mortgage payment based on the following repayment periods: 30 years, 20 years, and 10 years.
    b) If the couple can afford to pay up to $850 monthly on their mortgage loan, what repayment period in years should they request? What will be their monthly payment?

14. An annuity paying $200 at the end of each year for 20 years is replaced by another annuity paying $X at the end of every 6 months for 12 years. Determine X if $j_{12} = 9\%$ in both cases.

15. Starting on her 36th birthday, Ms. Gagnon deposits $2000 a year into an investment account. Her last deposit is at age 65. Starting one month later, she makes monthly withdrawals for 15 years. If $j_4 = 8\%$ throughout, determine the size of the monthly withdrawals.

16. Danielle and Sue would like to open their own business in 3 years. They estimate they will need $40 000 at that time. How much should they deposit at the end of each month into their account if they have $5000 in the account now and interest is at $j_4 = 7\%$?

17. What sum of money should be set aside to provide an income of $500 a month for a period of 3 years if money earns interest at $j_{12} = 6\%$ and the first payment is to be received a) one month from now; b) immediately; c) two years from now?

18. The proceeds of a $100 000 death benefit are left on deposit with an insurance company for seven years at an annual effective interest rate of 5%. The balance at the end of seven years is paid to the beneficiary in 120 equal monthly payments of $X, with the first payment made immediately. During the payout period, interest is credited at an annual effective interest rate of 3%. Calculate X.

19. A certain stock is expected to pay a dividend of $4 at the end of each quarter for an indefinite

period in the future. If an investor wishes to realize an annual effective yield of 10%, how much should he pay for the stock?

20. How much money is needed to establish a scholarship fund paying $1000 a year indefinitely if
    a) the fund earns interest at $j_1 = 8\%$ and the first scholarship is provided at the end of 3 years?
    b) the fund earns interest at $j_{12} = 8\%$ and the first scholarship is provided immediately?

21. On the assumption that a farm will net $15 000 annually indefinitely, what is a fair price for it if money is worth a) $j_1 = 8\%$, b) $j_{12} = 15\%$?

22. Mr. Jenkins invests $1000 at the end of each year for 10 years in an investment fund which pays $j_1 = 8\%$. The fund pays the interest out in cheque form at the end of each year and does not allow deposits of less than $1000. Mr. Jenkins deposits his annual interest payment from the fund into his bank account, which pays interest at $j_1 = 4\%$. How much money does he have at the end of 10 years?

23. Show that in question 22, if both rates of interest had been equal to $i\%$, the answer would have been $\$1000 s_{\overline{10}|i}$.

24. Calculate the discounted and the accumulated value of a decreasing annuity of 20 payments at the end of each year at $j_1 = 12\%$, if the first payment is $2000, the second $1900, and so on, the last payment being $100.

25. Calculate the discounted value of a series of payments that start at $18 000 at the end of year one and then increase by $2000 each year forever (i.e., $20 000, $22 000, etc.) if interest is at $j_1 = 10\%$.

26. Mrs. Zheng deposits R dollars today into a fund earning interest at $j_1 = 7\%$. Each succeeding deposit is 10% lower than the preceding deposit. One year after her 20th deposit, she has $150 000 in her fund. What is R?

27. Under the terms of a contract, the following payments are guaranteed:

a) $100 000 payable immediately.
b) $75 000 per year for 5 years, payable in equal monthly instalments of $6250 at the end of each month.
c) $50 000 per year, payable annually at the end of the 6th through the 10th years.

If interest is at 5% compounded annually, determine the discounted value at the beginning of the 4th year of the remaining payments due under the contract.

28. Every two years Mrs. Furtado deposits $1000 into a fund that pays interest at $j_2 = 10\%$. The first deposit is on her 53rd birthday and the last deposit is on her 65th birthday. Beginning three months after her 65th birthday and continuing every three months thereafter, she withdraws equal amounts of X dollars, which will exactly exhaust the fund on her 79th birthday. Determine X.

29. Determine the present value of an ordinary annuity paid annually for 25 years if payments are $1000 per year for the first 7 years, $5000 for the following 8 years, and $2000 in the final 10 years. Interest is $j_{12} = 6\%$ throughout this period.

30. A $5000 loan at $j_1 = 9.2\%$ is repaid by 10 quarterly payments, as shown. Calculate X.

	X	X	X	$2X$	$2X$	$2X$		$2X$
0	1	2	3	4	5	6	...	10

31. $100 is deposited in an account paying $j_{12} = 6\%$ every month for 20 years. Exactly 6 months after the last deposit the rate changes to $j_4 = 5\%$. On this date the first withdrawal is made in a series of quarterly withdrawals for 15 years. Determine the amount of each withdrawal.

32. Determine the present value of future contributions to a pension plan, for a person aged 35 earning $30 000 per year and expecting to retire at age 65. The pension plan requires contributions of 5% of salary and the employee expects to receive average annual salary increases of 3%. Use an annual effective rate of interest of 7% and assume contributions are at the end of each year.

CASE STUDY 1   *Canadian Mortgages*

Consider a purchase of a $120 000 house with a down payment of $20 000 and a $100 000 mortgage at $j_2 = 7\%$.

a) Determine the monthly payment based on the following repayment periods: 25 years, 20 years, and 15 years.

b) Using a 20-year repayment period, calculate the concluding payment, the total cost of financing, and the interest and principal parts of the first payment.

c) If you can afford to pay up to $1000 a month on the mortgage, what repayment period (in full years) should you request?

d) Compare the total payouts using monthly payments of $1000 with weekly payments of $250.

CASE STUDY 2   *Lottery Winnings*

Charlie, who is just 16 years old, won a lottery. However, the lottery does not pay out any money until a person is at least age 25. Charlie hires a financial consultant and this consultant suggests that Charlie invest the money and then begin receiving monthly payments of $2500 once he reaches age 25.

The consultant also suggests that Charlie should protect himself from inflation by having his payments increase by 2.3% each year. Thus, the 12 monthly payments in year 1 will be $2500 (age 25 to age 25, 11 months), the 12 monthly payments for year 2 will be $2500(1.023) (age 26 to age 26, 11 months), the 12 monthly payments for year 3 will be $2500(1.023)^2$ (age 27 to age 27, 11 months), and so on. (Note: This is a situation where the payments are monthly, but the percentage increase is annually.)

It turns out that Charlie has won enough money for this payment scheme to last for a total of 25 years after he turns 25. If Charlie can earn $j_1 = 8\%$ on his lottery winnings and if the consultant charges 1.5% of the winnings as a fee (payable up front when Charlie is 16), how much did Charlie win in the lottery?

CASE STUDY 3   *Scholarships*

A scholarship is set up that makes two payments a year. The first payment is $750 and the second payment, made exactly 6 months later, is $1500. This payment scheme continues forever. If money can be invested at $j_1 = 9\%$, how much money is needed to fund this scholarship six months before the first payment is to be made?

CASE STUDY 4   *Scholarships*

A university sets up two scholarship funds. The first one pays out $1200 a year, starting one year from now. The second one pays out $100 in the first year, $200 in the second year, $300 in the third year, and so on. At what interest rate would the present value of the two scholarships be the same? (BONUS: At what interest rate would the difference between the present value of the two scholarship funds be *maximized*?)

CHAPTER 5

Repayment of Debts

Learning Objectives

Many businesses and consumers will take out at least one loan in their lifetime. For many people, the largest loan they will ever see will be the mortgage on their home. As a result, it is useful to spend a bit more time taking a closer mathematical look at how loans are repaid.

This chapter will cover in some detail the three main methods used to repay a loan. Section 5.1 begins this coverage with the most common form of loan repayment: the amortization method. This is the method used to repay mortgages and most other types of consumer loans. This section will illustrate how to set up an amortization schedule which will allow you to see how much of each loan payment goes toward paying interest and how much goes toward reducing the loan. Section 5.2 shows two methods that can be used to calculate the outstanding balance of an amortized loan at any time.

For some loans, and especially for mortgages, the interest rate will change after a certain period of time. When this happens, we say the loan is refinanced and a new loan payment will need to be calculated. This is dealt with in section 5.3. Also discussed in this section are the various penalties that lenders may charge for refinancing a loan and how to take these penalties into account when determining whether or not you should refinance.

Section 5.4 deals with an alternative method for repaying a loan, called the sum-of-digits method or Rule of 78. Under this method, you start and finish at the same point as under the amortization method, but the calculations in between are different. Although most loans use the amortization method, some use this alternative method and it is important for consumers to know which method is being used for their loan and how things differ.

Section 5.5 discusses a vehicle for saving money, called sinking funds. Section 5.6 then uses this sinking fund as another method that can be used for paying off a loan called the sinking-fund method. Finally, in section 5.7, a direct comparison between the sinking-fund method and the amortization method is made which allows a business or consumer to determine which type of loan is best for them.

Section 5.1 ## Amortization of a Debt

In this chapter we shall discuss different methods of repaying interest-bearing loans, which is one of the most important applications of annuities in business transactions.

The first and most common method is the **amortization method**. When this method is used to liquidate an interest-bearing debt, a series of periodic payments, usually equal, is made. Each payment pays the interest on the unpaid balance and also repays a part of the outstanding principal. As time goes on, the outstanding principal is gradually reduced and interest on the unpaid balance decreases.

When a debt is amortized by equal payments at equal payment intervals, the debt becomes the discounted value of an annuity. The size of the payment is determined by the methods used in the annuity problems of the preceding chapters. The common commercial practice is to round the payment up to the next cent. This practice will be used in this textbook unless specified otherwise. Instead of rounding up to the next cent, the lender may round up to the next dime or dollar. In any case the rounding of the payment up to the cent, to the dime, or to the dollar will result in a smaller concluding payment. An equation of value at the time of the last payment will give the size of the smaller concluding payment.

EXAMPLE 1   A loan of \$20 000 is to be amortized with equal monthly payments over a period of 10 years at $j_{12} = 12\%$. Determine the concluding payment if the monthly payment is rounded up to a) the cent; b) the dime.

Solution   First we calculate the monthly payment R, given $A = 20\,000$, $n = 120$, and $i = 0.01$. Using equation **(11)** of section 3.3 we calculate

$$R = \frac{20\,000}{a_{\overline{120}|0.01}} = 286.9418968$$

and set up an equation of value for X at 120:

$$X + Rs_{\overline{119}|0.01}(1.01) + 20\,000(1.01)^{120}$$

Solution a   If the monthly payment is rounded up to the next cent, we have $R = \$286.95$ and calculate

$$\begin{aligned} X &= 20\,000(1.01)^{120} - 286.95s_{\overline{119}|0.01}(1.01) \\ &\doteq 66\,007.74 - 65\,722.65 \\ &= \$285.09 \end{aligned}$$

Solution b   If the monthly payment is rounded up to the next dime, we have $R = \$287$ and calculate

$$\begin{aligned} X &= 20\,000(1.01)^{120} - 287s_{\overline{119}|0.01}(1.01) \\ &\doteq 66\,007.74 - 65\,734.10 \\ &= \$273.64 \end{aligned}$$

When interest-bearing debts are amortized by means of a series of equal payments at equal intervals, it is important to know how much of each payment goes toward interest and how much goes toward the reduction of principal. For example, this may be a necessary part of determining one's taxable income or tax deductions. For example, the interest paid on some loans can be deducted for income tax purposes. Thus it is necessary to know how much interest is paid during each year of the loan. We can construct an **amortization schedule** to show how much of each loan payment goes toward interest and how much goes toward reducing the principal. It will also show the outstanding balance of the loan after each loan payment.

CALCULATION TIP:

The common commercial practice for loans that are amortized by equal payments is to round the payment up to the next cent (sometimes up to the next nickel, dime, or dollar if so specified). For each loan you should calculate the reduced final payment. For all other calculations (other than the regular amortization payment), use the normal round-off procedure. Do not round off the interest rate per conversion period. Use all the digits provided by your calculator (store the rate in a memory of the calculator) to avoid significant round-off errors. When calculating the total payout of the loan (also called the total debt in the sum-of-digits method of section 5.4), determine the total sum of all regular (rounded-up) payments and the final reduced (rounded-off) payment.

EXAMPLE 2 A debt of $22 000 with interest at $j_4 = 10\%$ is to be amortized by payments of $5000 at the end of each quarter for as long as necessary. Construct an amortization schedule showing the distribution of the payments as to interest and the repayment of principal.

Solution The following amortization schedule is obtained.

Payment Number	Monthly Payment	Interest Payment	Principal Payment	Outstanding Balance
0				$22 000.00
1	5 000.00	550.00	4 450.00	17 550.00
2	5 000.00	438.75	4 561.25	12 988.75
3	5 000.00	324.72	4 675.28	8 313.47
4	5 000.00	207.84	4 792.16	3 521.31
5	3 609.34	88.03	3 521.31	0
Totals	23 609.34	1609.34	22 000.00	

1. A payment number 0 is needed to set up the original amount of the loan.

2. The interest due at the end of the first quarter is 2.5% of $22 000, or $22 000(0.025) = $550.

3. The payment of $5000 made at the end of the first quarter (payment 1) will first pay the interest owed. This leaves $5000 − $550 = $4450 which will go toward reducing the loan balance.

4. The **outstanding principal balance*** after the first payment is $5000 − $4450 = $17 550.

5. For the next line of the table (payment 2), the interest due at the end of the second quarter is 2.5% of the current outstanding balance of $17 550, or $17 550(0.025) = $438.75. The remainder, $5000 − $438.75 = $4561.25, goes toward reducing the loan balance, which becomes $17 550 − $4561.25 = $12 988.75.

6. The next two lines are calculated using the same methodology.

7. It should be noted that the 5th and final payment is only $3609.34, which is the sum of the outstanding balance at the end of the 4th quarter plus the interest due at 2.5%.

The totals at the bottom of the schedule are for checking purposes. The total amount of principal repaid (the sum of the principal payment column) must equal the original debt. Also, the total of the periodic payments must equal the total interest plus the total principal returned. Note that the entries in the principal repaid column (except the final payment) are in the ratio $(1 + i)$. That is,

$$\frac{4561.25}{4450.00} \doteq \frac{4675.28}{4561.25} \doteq \frac{4792.16}{4675.28} \doteq 1.025.$$

EXAMPLE 3 Consider a $6000 loan that is to be repaid over 5 years with monthly payments at $j_{12} = 6\%$. Show the first three lines of the amortization schedule.

Solution First, we calculate the monthly payment R given $A = 6000$, $n = 60$, and $i = 0.005$.

$$R = \frac{6000}{a_{\overline{60}|0.005}} = \$116.00$$

To create the amortization schedule for the first three months, we follow the method outlined in Example 2 with $i = 0.005$.

Payment Number	Monthly Payment	Interest Payment	Principal Payment	Outstanding Balance
0				$6000.00
1	116.00	30.00	86.00	5914.00
2	116.00	29.57	86.43	5827.57
3	116.00	29.14	86.86	5740.71

As before, the entries in the principal repaid column are in the ratio $1 + i$. That is,

$$\frac{86.43}{86.00} \doteq \frac{86.86}{86.43} \doteq 1.005.$$

*****Outstanding principal balance** is also referred to as outstanding principal or outstanding balance.

EXAMPLE 4   Prepare a spreadsheet and show the first 3 months and the last 3 months of a complete amortization schedule for the loan of Example 3 above. Also show total payments, total interest, and total principal paid.

Solution   In any amortization schedule we reserve cells A1 through E1 for headings. The same headings will be used in all future Excel spreadsheets showing amortization schedules.

Type the loan amount, in cell E2, 6000. In cell F3 type the interest rate, $=0.06/12$. In cell F2 type the appropriate formula to calculate the periodic payment. You would type $=\text{ROUNDUP}(E2/((1-(1+F3)^{\wedge}-60)/F3),2)$. The ROUNDUP function will round the periodic payment up to the next cent.

We summarize the rest of the entries in an Excel spreadsheet and their interpretation in the table below.

	CELL	ENTER	INTERPRETATION
Headings	A1	Pmt #	'Payment number'
	B1	Payment	'Monthly payment'
	C1	Interest	'Interest payment'
	D1	Principal	'Principal payment'
	E1	Balance	'Outstanding principal balance'
Line 0	A2	0	Time starts
	E2	6000	Loan amount
Line 1	A3	=A2+1	End of month 1
	B3	$F$2	Monthly payment (up to the next cent)
	C3	=E2*$F$3	Interest 1 = (Balance 0) (0.005)
	D3	=B3–C3	Principal 1 = Payment – Interest 1
	E3	=E2–D3	Balance 1 = Balance 0 – Principal 1

To generate the complete schedule copy A3.E3 to A4.E62

To get the last payment adjust B62=E61+C62

To get totals apply Σ to B3.D62

Below are the first 3 months and the last 3 months of a complete amortization schedule together with the required totals.

	A	B	C	D	E
1	Pmt#	Payment	Interest	Principal	Balance
2	0				6,000.00
3	1	116.00	30.00	86.00	5,914.00
4	2	116.00	29.57	86.43	5,827.57
5	3	116.00	29.14	86.86	5,740.71
⋮	⋮	⋮	⋮	⋮	⋮
60	58	116.00	1.72	114.28	230.05
61	59	116.00	1.15	114.85	115.20
62	60	115.78	0.58	115.20	0.00
63		6,959.78	959.78	6,000.00	

If you want to see the amortization schedule for a loan amount of $15 000 at $j_{12} = 8\%$ (but still a 5-year loan), all you have to do is type 15000 in E2 and =0.08/12 into F3. Your periodic payment becomes $304.15 and all other values in the amortization table will automatically change.

EXAMPLE 5 A couple purchases a home and signs a mortgage contract for $80 000 to be paid in equal monthly payments over 25 years with interest at $j_2 = 6.60\%$. Determine the monthly payment and make out a partial amortization schedule showing the distribution of the first six payments as to interest and repayment of principal.

Solution Since the interest is compounded semi-annually and the payments are paid monthly we have a general annuity problem. First we calculate rate i per month equivalent to 3.3% per half-year and store it in a memory of the calculator.

$$(1+i)^{12} = (1.033)^2$$

$$(1+i) = (1.033)^{\frac{1}{6}}$$

$$i = (1.033)^{\frac{1}{6}} - 1$$
$$i = 0.005425865$$

The monthly payment $R = \dfrac{80\,000}{a_{\overline{300}|i}} \doteq \$540.72$.

To make out the amortization schedule for the first 6 months, we follow the same method as in the previous two examples with $i = 0.005425865$.

Payment Number	Monthly Payment	Interest Payment	Principal Payment	Outstanding Balance
0				$80 000.00
1	540.72	434.07	106.65	79 893.35
2	540.72	433.49	107.23	79 786.12
3	540.72	432.91	107.81	79 678.31
4	540.72	432.32	108.40	79 569.91
5	540.72	431.74	108.98	79 460.93
6	540.72	431.14	109.58	79 351.35
Totals	3244.32	2595.67	648.65	

During the first 6 months only $648.65 of the original $80 000 debt is repaid. It should be noted that about 80% of the first six payments goes for interest and only 20% for the reduction of the outstanding balance.

Again, the entries in the principal repaid column are in the ratio of $(1 + i)$. That is:

$$\frac{107.23}{106.65} \doteq \frac{107.81}{107.23} \doteq \cdots \doteq \frac{109.58}{108.98} \doteq 1 + i$$

EXAMPLE 6   Prepare an Excel spreadsheet and show the first 6 months and the last 6 months of a complete amortization schedule for the mortgage loan of Example 5 above. Also show total payments, total interest, and total principal paid.

Solution   Type the loan amount in cell E2, 80 000. In cell F3 type the given semi-annual interest rate, =0.066/2. In cell F4 calculate the equivalent monthly interest rate by typing =(1+F3)^(1/6)−1. In cell F2 calculate the monthly payment by typing in =ROUNDUP(E2/((1−(1+F4)^−300)/F4),2). We summarize the entries for line 0 and line 1 of an Excel spreadsheet.

CELL	ENTER
A2	0
E2	80 000
A3	=A2+1
B3	$F$2
C3	=E2*$F$4
D3	=B3−C3
E3	=E2−D3

To generate the complete schedule copy A3.E3 to 4.E302

To get the last payment adjust B302=E301+C302

To get the totals apply Σ to B3.D302

Below are the first 6 months and the last 6 months of a complete amortization schedule together with the required totals.

	A	B	C	D	E	F
1	Pmt#	Payment	Interest	Principal	Balance	
2	0				80,000.00	540.72
3	1	540.72	434.07	106.65	79,893.35	0.033
4	2	540.72	433.49	107.23	79,786.12	0.005426
5	3	540.72	432.91	107.81	79,678.31	
6	4	540.72	432.32	108.40	79,569.91	
7	5	540.72	431.74	108.98	79,460.93	
8	6	540.72	431.14	109.58	79,351.35	

	A	B	C	D	E	F
298	:	:	:	:	:	
299	297	540.72	11.57	529.15	1,602.99	
300	298	540.72	8.70	532.02	1,070.96	
301	299	540.72	5.81	534.91	536.06	
302	300	538.97	2.91	536.06	-	
303		162,211.34	82,214.24	80,000.00		

EXAMPLE 7   **General amortization schedule**

Consider a loan of A dollars to be repaid with level payments of R dollars at the end of each period for n periods, at rate i per period. Show that in the kth line of the amortization schedule ($1 \le k \le n$)

a) Interest payment $I_k = iRa_{\overline{n-k+1}|i} = R[1-(1+i)^{-(n-k+1)}]$

b) Principal payment $P_k = R(1+i)^{-(n-k+1)}$

c) Outstanding balance $B_k = Ra_{\overline{n-k}|i}$

Verify that

d) Sum of principal repaid column = original loan amount = $A = Ra_{\overline{n}|i}$

e) Sum of interest payments column = total interest paid = $nR - A$

f) Principal payments are in the ratio of $(1 + i)$:

$$\frac{P_{k+1}}{P_k} = (1+i)$$

Solution a   The outstanding balance after the $(k-1)$st payment is the discounted value of the remaining $n - (k-1) = n - k + 1$ payments, that is

$$B_{k-1} = Ra_{\overline{n-k+1}|i}$$

Interest paid in the kth payment is

$$I_k = iB_{k-1} = iRa_{\overline{n-k+1}|i} = iR\frac{1-(1+i)^{-(n-k+1)}}{i} = R[1-(1+i)^{-(n-k+1)}]$$

Solution b   Principal repaid in the kth payment is

$$P_k = R - I_k = R - R[1-(1+i)^{-(n-k+1)}] = R(1+i)^{-(n-k+1)}$$

Solution c   The outstanding balance after the kth payment is the discounted value of the remaining $(n-k)$ payments, that is

$$B_k = Ra_{\overline{n-k}|i}$$

Solution d   The sum of the principal payments is

$$\sum_{k=1}^{n} P_k = \sum_{k=1}^{n} R(1+i)^{-(n-k+1)} = R[(1+i)^{-n} + \cdots + (1+i)^{-1}] = Ra_{\overline{n}|i} = A$$

Solution e   The sum of the interest payment is

$$\sum_{k=1}^{n} I_k = \sum_{k=1}^{n} R[1-(1+i)^{-(n-k+1)}] = nR - Ra_{\overline{n}|i} = nR - A$$

Solution f
$$\frac{P_{k+1}}{P_k} = \frac{R(1+i)^{-[n-(k+1)+1]}}{R(1+i)^{-(n-k+1)}} = (1+i)^{(-n+k)+(n-k+1)} = (1+i)$$

EXAMPLE 8   A loan of \$10 000 at $j_2 = 6.5\%$ is to be repaid over 10 years.
   a) How much interest is paid in the 14th payment?
   b) How much principal is repaid as part of the 5th payment?
   c) What is the outstanding balance of the loan after 13 payments?

Solution a   First we need to calculate the semi-annual payment as

$$R = \frac{10\,000}{a_{\overline{20}|0.0325}} = \$687.79$$

The interest portion of the 14th payment is

$$\begin{aligned} I_{14} &= 687.79[1 - (1.0325)^{-(20-14+1)}] \\ &= 687.79[1 - (1.0325)^{-7}] \\ &\doteq \$137.96 \end{aligned}$$

Solution b   The principal portion of the 5th payment is

$$\begin{aligned} P_5 &= 687.79(1.0325)^{-(20-5+1)} \\ &= 687.79(1.0325)^{-16} \\ &\doteq \$412.30 \end{aligned}$$

Solution c   The outstanding balance immediately after the 13th payment is

$$B_{13} = 687.79 a_{\overline{20-13}|0.0325} = \$4245.04$$

Note: From this value you can calculate the outstanding balance after the 14th payment as follows. From **a)**, we can calculate $P_{14} = \$687.79 - \$137.96 = \$549.83$. Thus

$$B_{14} = B_{13} - P_{14} = \$4245.04 - \$549.83 = \$3695.21$$

EXAMPLE 9   A loan of A dollars is to be repaid with 20 payments. The principal repaid in the 9th and 10th payments are \$278.00 and \$282.17 respectively. What is A?

Solution   We calculate the periodic interest rate by taking the ratio of the principal repaid values

$$\frac{P_{10}}{P_9} = \frac{282.17}{278.00} = 1.015$$

Thus, $i = 0.015$ (Note: we do not know at what frequency this interest rate is compounded, but we do not need this information.)
   We calculate the periodic payment,

$$\begin{aligned} P_9 &= R(1 + i)^{-(20-9+1)} \\ 278.00 &= R(1.015)^{-12} \\ R &= 278.00(1.015)^{12} \doteq \$332.38 \end{aligned}$$

From this we calculate the loan amount,

$$A = 332.38 a_{\overline{20}|0.015} \doteq \$5706.51$$

Exercise 5.1

Part A

1. A loan of $5000 is to be amortized with equal quarterly payments over a period of 5 years at $j_4 = 12\%$. Determine the concluding payment if the quarterly payment is rounded up to a) the cent; b) the dime.

2. A loan of $20 000 is to be amortized with equal monthly payments over a 3-year period at $j_{12} = 8\%$. Determine the concluding payment if the monthly payment is rounded up to a) the cent; b) the dime.

3. A $5000 loan is to be amortized with 8 equal semi-annual payments. If interest is at $j_2 = 9\%$, determine the semi-annual payment and construct an amortization schedule.

4. A loan of $900 is to be amortized with 6 equal monthly payments at $j_{12} = 12\%$. Determine the monthly payment and construct an amortization schedule.

5. A loan of $1000 is to be repaid over 2 years with equal quarterly payments. Interest is at $j_{12} = 6\%$. Determine the quarterly payment required and construct an amortization schedule to show the interest and principal portion of each payment.

6. A debt of $50 000 with interest at $j_4 = 8\%$ is to be amortized by payments of $10 000 at the end of each quarter for as long as necessary. Create an amortization schedule.

7. A $10 000 loan is to be repaid with semi-annual payments of $2500 for as long as necessary. If interest is at $j_{12} = 12\%$, create a complete amortization schedule.

8. A debt of $2000 will be repaid by monthly payments of $500 for as long as necessary, the first payment to be made at the end of 6 months. If interest is at $j_{12} = 9\%$, calculate the size of the debt at the end of 5 months and create the complete schedule starting at that time.

9. A couple buys some furniture for $1500. They pay off the debt at $j_{12} = 15\%$ by paying $200 a month for as long as necessary. The first payment is at the end of 3 months. Do a complete amortization schedule for this loan.

10. A $16 000 car is purchased by paying $1000 down and then equal monthly payments for 3 years at $j_{12} = 8.4\%$. Determine the size of the monthly payments and complete the first three lines of the amortization schedule.

11. A mobile home worth $46 000 is purchased with a down payment of $6000 and monthly payments for 15 years. If interest is $j_2 = 10\%$, determine the monthly payment and complete the first 6 lines of the amortization schedule.

12. A couple purchases a home worth $256 000 by paying $86 000 down and then taking out a mortgage at $j_2 = 7\%$. The mortgage will be amortized over 25 years with equal monthly payments. Determine the monthly payment and create a partial amortization schedule showing the distribution of the first 6 payments as to interest and principal. How much of the principal is repaid during the first 6 months?

13. In September 1981, mortgage interest rates in Canada peaked at $j_2 = 21\frac{1}{2}\%$. Redo question 12 using $j_2 = 21\frac{1}{2}\%$.

Part B

1. On a loan with $j_{12} = 12\%$ and monthly payments, the amount of principal in the 6th payment is $40.
   a) Determine the amount of principal in the 15th payment.
   b) If there are 36 equal payments in all, determine the amount of the loan.

2. A loan is being repaid over 10 years with equal annual payments. Interest is at $j_1 = 7\%$. If the amount of principal repaid in the third payment is $100, determine the amount of principal repaid in the 7th payment.

3. The ABC Bank develops a special scheme to help their customers pay their loans off quickly. Instead of making payments of X dollars once a month, mortgage borrowers are asked to pay $\frac{X}{4}$ dollars once a week (52 times a year).

   The Gibsons are buying a house and need a $180 000 mortgage. If $j_2 = 8\%$, determine
   a) the monthly payment required to amortize the debt over 25 years;
   b) the weekly payment $\frac{X}{4}$ suggested in the scheme;
   c) the number of weeks it will take to pay off the debt using the suggested scheme.
   Compare these results and comment.

4. A loan is being repaid by monthly instalments of $100 at $j_{12} = 18\%$. If the loan balance after the fourth month is $1200, determine the original loan value.

5. A loan is being repaid with 20 annual instalments at $j_1 = 15\%$. In which instalment are the principal and interest portions most nearly equal to each other?

6. A loan is being repaid with 10 annual instalments. The principal portion of the seventh payment is $110.25 and the interest portion is $39.75. What annual effective rate of interest is being charged?

7. A loan at $j_1 = 9\%$ is being repaid by monthly payments of $750 each. The total principal repaid in the twelve monthly instalments of the 8th year is $400. What is the total interest paid in the 12 instalments of the 10th year?

8. Below is part of a mortgage amortization schedule.

Payment	Interest	Principal	Balance
	243.07	31.68	
	242.81	31.94	

Determine
a) the monthly payment;
b) the effective rate of interest per month;
c) the nominal rate of interest j_2, rounded to nearest $\frac{1}{8}\%$ (Note: Use this rounded nominal rate from here on);
d) the outstanding balance just after the first payment shown above;
e) the remaining period of the mortgage if interest rates don't change.

9. On mortgages repaid by equal annual payments covering both principal and interest, a mortgage company pays as a commission to its agents 10% of the portion of each scheduled instalment, which represents interest. What is the total commission paid per $1000 of original mortgage loan if it is repaid with n annual payments at rate i per year?

10. Fred buys a personal computer from a company whose head office is in the United States. The computer includes software designed to calculate mortgage amortization schedules. Fred has a $75 000 mortgage with 20-year amortization at $j_2 = 6\frac{1}{2}\%$. According to his bank statement, his monthly payment is $555.38. When Fred uses his software, he enters his original principal balance of $75 000, the amortization period of 20 years, and the nominal annual rate of interest of $6\frac{1}{2}\%$. The computer produces output that says the monthly payment should be $559.18. Which answer is correct? Can you explain the error?

11. As part of the purchase of a home on January 1, 2006, you have just negotiated a mortgage in the amount of $150 000. The amortization period for calculation of the level monthly payments (principal and interest) has been set at 25 years and the interest rate is 9% per annum compounded semi-annually.
a) What level monthly payment is required, assuming the first one to be made at February 1, 2006?
b) It has been suggested that if you multiply the monthly payment [calculated in a)] by 12, divide by 52 then pay the resulting amount each week, with the first payment at January 8, 2006, then the amortization period will be shortened. If the lender agrees to this, at what time in the future will the mortgage be fully paid?
c) What will be the size of the smaller, final weekly payment, made 1 week after the last regular payment [as calculated for part b)]?

12. Part of an amortization schedule shows

Payment	Interest	Principal	Balance
	440.31	160.07	
	438.71	161.67	

Complete the next two lines of this schedule.

13. You lend a friend $15 000 to be amortized by semi-annual payments for 8 years, with interest at $j_2 = 9\%$. You deposit each payment in an account paying $j_{12} = 7\%$. What annual effective rate of interest have you earned over the entire 8-year period?

14. A loan of $10 000 is being repaid by 10 semi-annual principal payments of $1000. Interest on the outstanding balance at j_2 is paid in addition to the principal repayments. The total of all payments is $12 200. Determine j_2.

15. A loan of A dollars is to be repaid by 16 equal semi-annual instalments, including principal and interest, at rate i per half-year. The principal

in the first instalment (six months hence) is $30.83. The principal in the last is $100. Determine the annual effective rate of interest.

16. A loan is to be repaid by 16 quarterly payments of $50, $100, $150, ... , $800, the first payment due three months after the loan is made. Interest is at 8% compounded quarterly. Calculate the total amount of interest contained in the payments.

17. A loan of $20 000 with interest at $j_{12} = 6\%$ is amortized by equal monthly payments over 15 years. In which payment will the interest portion be less than the principal portion, for the first time?

18. You are choosing between two mortgages for $160 000 with a 20-year amortization period. Both charge $j_2 = 7\%$ and permit the mortgage to be paid off in less than 20 years. Mortgage A allows you to make weekly payments, with each payment being $\frac{1}{4}$ of the normal monthly payment. Mortgage B allows you to make double the usual monthly payment every 6 months. Assuming that you will take advantage of the mortgage provisions, calculate the total interest charges over the life of each mortgage to determine which mortgage costs less.

19. In the United States, in an effort to advertise low rates of interest, but still achieve high rates of return, lenders sometimes charge *points*. Each point is a 1% discount from the face value of the loan. Suppose a home is being sold for $220 000 and that the buyer pays $60 000 down and gets a $160 000 15-year mortgage at $j_{12} = 8\%$. The lender charges 5 points, that is 5% of $160 000 = $8000, so the loan is $152 000, but $160 000 is repaid. What is the true interest rate, j_{12}, on the loan?

Section 5.2   ## Outstanding Balance

It is quite important to know the amount of principal remaining to be paid at a certain time. The borrower may want to pay off the outstanding balance of the debt in a lump sum, the borrower or lender may want to refinance the loan, or the lender may wish to sell the contract.

One could determine the outstanding balance by making out an amortization schedule. This becomes rather tedious without a spreadsheet when a large number of payments are involved. In this section we shall calculate the outstanding balance directly from an appropriate equation of value.

Let B_k denote the outstanding balance immediately after the kth payment has been made.

Two methods for finding B_k are available.

The Retrospective Method: This method uses the past history of the debt — the payments that have been made already. The outstanding balance B_k is calculated as

B_k = Accumulated value of original debt – Accumulated value of payments made to date

$$B_k = A(1 + i)^k - Rs_{\overline{k}|i} \qquad (13)$$

Equation **(13)** always gives the correct value of the outstanding balance B_k and can be used in all cases, but is particularly useful when the number of payments is not known or the last payment is an irregular one.

The Prospective Method: This method uses the future prospects of the debt — the payments yet to be made. The outstanding balance B_k is calculated as

B_k = Discounted value of the remaining $(n - k)$ payments

If all the payments, including the last one, are equal, we obtain

$$\boxed{B_k = Ra_{\overline{n-k}|i}}\qquad\qquad\textbf{(14)}$$

While equations **(13)** and **(14)** are algebraically equivalent (see problem B8 in Exercise 5.2), equation **(14)** cannot be used when the concluding payment is an irregular one. However, it is useful if you don't know the original value of the loan or if there have been several interest rate changes in the past. When the concluding payment is an irregular one, equation **(14)** is still applicable if suitably modified, but it is usually simpler to use the retrospective method than to discount the $(n - k)$ payments yet to be made.

EXAMPLE 1   A loan of $2000 with interest at $j_{12} = 12\%$ is to be amortized by equal payments at the end of each month over a period of 18 months. Determine the outstanding balance at the end of 8 months.

Solution   First we calculate the monthly payment R, given $A = 2000$, $n = 18$, $i = 0.01$,

$$R = \frac{2000}{a_{\overline{18}|0.01}} \doteq \$121.97$$

The retrospective method We have $A = 2000$, $R = 121.97$, $k = 8$, $i = 0.01$, and calculate B_8 using equation **(13)**

$$B_8 = 2000(1.01)^8 - 121.97 s_{\overline{8}|0.01}$$
$$\doteq 2165.71 - 1010.60 = \$1155.11$$

The prospective method We have $R = 121.97$, $n - k = 10$, $i = 0.01$ and calculate B_8 using equation **(14)**

$$B_8 = 121.97 a_{\overline{10}|0.01} \doteq \$1155.21$$

The difference of 10 cents is due to rounding the monthly payment R up to the next cent. The concluding payment is, in fact, slightly smaller than the regular payment $R = 121.97$, so the value of B_8 under the prospective method is not accurate.

EXAMPLE 2 On July 15, 2006, a couple borrowed $10\,000$ at $j_{12} = 7.2\%$ to start a business. They plan to repay the debt in equal monthly payments over 8 years with the first payment on August 15, 2006. a) How much principal did they repay during 2006? b) How much interest can they claim as a tax deduction during 2006?

Solution We arrange our data on a time diagram below.

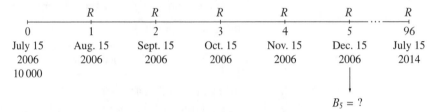

First we calculate the monthly payment R, given $A = 10\,000$, $n = 96$, $i = 0.006$

$$R = \frac{10\,000}{a_{\overline{96}|0.006}} \doteq 137.34$$

Then we calculate the outstanding balance B_5 on December 15, 2006, after the 5th payment has been made. We have $A = 10\,000$, $R = 137.34$, $k = 5$, $i = 0.006$, and using equation **(13)** we calculate

$$B_5 = 10\,000(1.006)^5 - 137.34 s_{\overline{5}|0.006}$$
$$= 10\,303.62 - 694.99$$
$$= \$9608.63$$

The total reduction in principal in 2006 is the difference between the outstanding balance on December 15, 2006, after the 5th payment has been made, and the original debt of $10\,000$. Thus, they repaid $10\,000 - \$9608.63 = \$391.37$ of principal during 2006.

To get the total interest paid in 2006, we subtract the amount they repaid on principal from the total of the 5 payments, i.e., total interest $= 5 \times \$137.34 - \$391.37 = \$295.33$. They can deduct $295.33 as an expense on their 2006 income tax return.

This method of amortization is quite often used to pay off loans incurred in purchasing a property. In such cases, the outstanding balance is called the **seller's equity**. The amount of principal that has been paid already plus the down payment is called the **buyer's equity**, or **owner's equity**. At any point in time we have the following relation:

> **Buyer's equity + Seller's equity = Original selling price**

The buyer's equity starts with the down payment and is gradually increased with each periodic payment by the part of the payment which is applied to reduce the outstanding balance. It should be noted that the buyer's equity, as defined above, does not make any allowance for increases or decreases in the value of the property.

EXAMPLE 3 The Mancinis buy a cottage worth $178\,000$ by paying $38\,000$ down and the balance, with interest at $j_2 = 6.75\%$, in monthly instalments of 2000 for as long as necessary. Determine the Mancinis' equity at the end of 5 years.

Solution The monthly payments form a general annuity. First, we calculate a monthly rate of interest i equivalent to $3\frac{3}{8}\%$ each half-year.

$$(1+i)^{12} = (1.03375)^2$$
$$(1+i) = (1.03375)^{\frac{1}{6}}$$
$$i = (1.03375)^{\frac{1}{6}} - 1$$
$$i = 0.005547491$$

Using the retrospective method, we calculate the seller's equity as the outstanding balance at the end of 60 months.

$$B_{60} = 140\,000(1+i)^{60} - 2000s_{\overline{60}|i}$$
$$= 195\,111.68 - 141\,921.73 = \$53\,189.95$$

The Mancinis' equity is then

$$\text{Buyer's equity} \doteq 178\,000 - 53\,189.95 = \$124\,810.05$$

Exercise 5.2

Part A

1. To pay off the purchase of a car, Chantal got a $15\,000$, 3-year bank loan at $j_{12} = 12\%$. She makes monthly payments. How much does she still owe on the loan at the end of two years (24 payments)? Use both the retrospective and prospective methods.

2. A debt of $10\,000$ will be amortized by payments at the end of each quarter of a year for 10 years. Interest is at $j_4 = 10\%$. Determine the outstanding balance at the end of 6 years.

3. On July 1, 2006, Brian borrowed $30\,000$ to be repaid with monthly payments (first payment August 1, 2006) over 3 years at $j_{12} = 8\%$. How much principal did he repay in 2006? How much interest?

4. A couple buys a house worth $156\,000$ by paying $46\,000$ down and taking out a mortgage for $110\,000$. The mortgage is at $j_2 = 7\%$ and will be repaid over 25 years with monthly payments. How much of the principal does the couple pay off in the first year?

5. On May 1, 2006, the Morins borrow 4000 to be repaid with monthly payments over 3 years at $j_{12} = 9\%$. The 12 payments made during 2007 will reduce the principal by how much? What was the total interest paid in 2007?

6. To pay off the purchase of home furnishings, a couple takes out a bank loan of 2000 to be repaid with monthly payments over 2 years at $j_{12} = 9\%$. What is the outstanding debt just after the 10th payment? What is the principal portion of the 11th payment?

7. A couple buys a piece of land worth $200\,000$ by paying $50\,000$ down and then taking a loan out for $150\,000$. The loan will be repaid with quarterly payments over 15 years at $j_4 = 8\%$. Determine the couple's equity at the end of 8 years.

8. A family buys a house worth $326\,000$. They pay $110\,000$ down and then take out a 5-year mortgage for the balance at $j_2 = 6\frac{1}{2}\%$ to be amortized over 20 years. Payments will be made monthly. Determine the outstanding balance at the end of 5 years and the owners' equity at that time.

9. Land worth $80\,000$ is purchased by a down payment of $12\,000$ and the balance in equal monthly instalments for 15 years. If interest is

at $j_{12} = 9\%$, determine the buyer's and seller's equity in the land at the end of 9 years.

10. A loan of $10 000 is being repaid by instalments of $200 at the end of each month for as long as necessary. If interest is at $j_4 = 8\%$, determine the outstanding balance at the end of 1 year.

11. A debt is being amortized at an annual effective rate of interest of 10% by payments of $5000 made at the end of each year for 11 years. Determine the outstanding balance just after the 7th payment.

12. A loan is to be amortized by semi-annual payments of $802, which includes principal and interest at 8% compounded semi-annually. What is the original amount of the loan if the outstanding balance is reduced to $17 630 at the end of 3 years?

13. A loan is being repaid with semi-annual instalments of $1000 for 10 years at 10% compounded semi-annually. Determine the amount of principal in the 6th instalment.

14. Jones purchased a cottage, paying $10 000 down and agreeing to pay $500 at the end of every month for the next ten years. The rate of interest is $j_2 = 12\%$. Jones discharges the remaining indebtedness without penalty by making a single payment at the end of 5 years. Determine the extra amount that Jones pays in addition to the regular payment then due.

Part B

1. With mortgage rates at $j_2 = 11\%$, the XYZ Trust Company makes a special offer to its customers. It will lend mortgage money and determine the monthly payment as if $j_2 = 9\%$. The mortgage will be carried at $j_2 = 11\%$ and any deficiency that results will be added to the outstanding balance. If the Moras are taking out a $100 000 mortgage to be repaid over 25 years under this scheme, what will their outstanding balance be at the end of 5 years?

2. The Hwangs can buy a home for $190 000. To do so would require taking out a $125 000 mortgage from a bank at $j_2 = 7.25\%$. The loan will be repaid over 25 years with the rate of interest fixed for 5 years.

   The seller of the home is willing to give the Hwangs a mortgage at $j_2 = 6.25\%$. The monthly payment will be determined using a 25-year repayment schedule. The seller will guarantee the rate of interest for 5 years at which time the Hwangs will have to pay off the seller and get a mortgage from a bank. If the Hwangs accept this offer, the seller wants $195 000 for the house, forcing the Hwangs to borrow $130 000. If the Hwangs can earn $j_{12} = 4\%$ on their money, what should they do?

3. The Smiths buy a home and take out a $160 000 mortgage on which the interest rate is allowed to float freely. At the time the mortgage is issued, interest rates are $j_2 = 6\%$ and the Smiths choose a 25-year amortization schedule. Six months into the mortgage, interest rates rise to $j_2 = 8\%$. Three years into the mortgage (after 36 payments) interest rates drop to $j_2 = 7\%$ and four years into the mortgage, interest rates drop to $j_2 = 5\frac{1}{2}\%$. Determine the outstanding balance of the mortgage after 5 years. (The monthly payment is set at issue and does not change.)

4. A young couple buys a house and assumes a $90 000 mortgage to be amortized over 25 years. The interest rate is guaranteed at $j_2 = 8\%$. The mortgage allows the couple to make extra payments against the outstanding principal each month. By saving carefully the couple manages to pay off an extra $100 each month. Because of these extra payments, how long will it take to pay off the mortgage and what will be the size of the final smaller monthly payment?

5. A loan is made on January 1, 1990, and is to be repaid by 25 level annual instalments. These instalments are in the amount of $3000 each and are payable on December 31 of the years 1990 through 2014. However, just after the December 31, 1994, instalment has been paid, it is agreed that, instead of continuing the annual instalments on the basis just described, henceforth instalments will be payable quarterly with the first such quarterly instalment being payable on March 31, 1995, and the last one on December 31, 2014. Interest is at an annual effective rate of 10%. By changing from the old repayment schedule to the new one, the borrower will reduce the total amount of payments made over the 25-year period. Determine the amount of this reduction.

6. The ABC Trust Company issues loans where the monthly payments are determined by the rate of interest that prevails on the day the loan

is made. After that, the rate of interest varies according to market forces but the monthly payments do not change in dollar size. Instead, the length of time to full repayment is either lengthened (if interest rates rise) or shortened (if interest rates fall).

Medhaf takes out a 10-year, $20 000 loan at $j_2 = 8\%$. After exactly 2 years (24 payments) interest rates change. Determine the duration of the remaining loan and the final smaller payment if the new interest rate is a) $j_2 = 9\%$; b) $j_2 = 7\%$.

7. Big Corporation built a new plant in 2003 at a cost of $1 700 000. It paid $200 000 cash and assumed a mortgage for $1 500 000 to be repaid over 10 years by equal semi-annual payments due each June 30 and December 31, the first payment being due on December 31, 2003. The mortgage interest rate is 5.5% per annum compounded semi-annually and the original date of the loan was July 1, 2003.
   a) What will be the total of the payments made in 2005 on this mortgage?
   b) Mortgage interest paid in any year (for this mortgage) is an income tax deduction for that year. What will be the interest deduction on Big Corporation's 2005 tax form?
   c) Suppose the plant is sold on January 1, 2007. The buyer pays $700 000 cash and assumes the outstanding mortgage. What is Big Corporation's capital gain (amount realized less original price) on the investment in the building?

8. Given a loan L to be repaid at rate i per period with equal payments R at the end of each period for n periods, give the Retrospective and Prospective expressions for the outstanding balance of the loan at time k (after the kth payment is made) and prove that the two expressions are equal.

9. A 5-year loan is being repaid with level monthly instalments at the end of each month, beginning with January 2005 and continuing through December 2009. A 12% interest rate compounded monthly was used to determine the amount of each monthly instalment. On which date will the outstanding balance of this loan first fall below one-half of the original amount of the loan?

10. A debt is amortized at $j_4 = 10\%$ by payments of $300 per quarter. If the outstanding principal is

$2853.17 just after the kth payment, what was it just after the $(k-1)$st payment?

11. A loan of $3000 is to be repaid by annual payments of $400 per annum for the first 5 years and payments of $450 per year thereafter for as long as necessary. Determine the total number of payments and the amount of the smaller final payment made one year after the last regular payment. Assume an annual effective rate of 7%.

12. Five years ago, Justin deposited $1000 into a fund out of which he draws $100 at the end of each year. The fund guarantees interest at 5% on the principal on deposit during the year. If the fund actually earns interest at a rate in excess of 5%, the excess interest earned during the year is paid to Justin at the end of the year in addition to the regular $100 payment. The fund has been earning 8% each year for the past 5 years. What is the total payment Justin now receives?

13. An advertisement by Royal Trust said,
   Our new Double-Up mortgage can be paid off faster and that dramatically reduces the interest you pay. You can double your payment any or every month, with no penalty. Then your payment reverts automatically to its normal amount the next month. What this means to you is simple. You will pay your mortgage off sooner. And that's good news because you can save thousands of dollars in interest as a result.
   Consider a $120 000 mortgage at 8% compounded semi-annually, amortized over 25 years with no anniversary pre payments.
   a) Determine the required monthly payment for the above mortgage.
   b) What is the total amount of interest paid over the full amortization period (assuming $j_2 = 8\%$)?
   c) Suppose that payments were "Doubled-Up," according to the advertisement, every 6th and 12th month.
      i) How many years and months would be required to pay off the mortgage?
      ii) What would be the total amount of interest paid over the full amortization period?
      iii) How much of the loan would still be outstanding at the end of 3 years, just after the Doubled-Up payment then due?
      iv) How much principal is repaid in the payment due in 37 months?

| Section 5.3 | **Refinancing a Loan — The Amortization Method** |

It is common to want to renegotiate a long-term loan after it has been partially paid off. In this section, we are interested in two situations:

1. At the end of the guaranteed interest rate period, a loan is often refinanced; that is, the loan is renewed at whatever interest rates are effective in the market at that time. We will calculate the revised loan payment based on the new interest rate (which may have gone up or down).

2. Sometimes loans are refinanced *before* the maturity date of the loan or before the end of the guaranteed interest rate period. This is generally initiated by the borrower if interest rates have fallen. However, there is often a penalty involved in refinancing a loan early in these situations. We need to take this penalty into account when determining whether or not the borrower should refinance.

EXAMPLE 1   Mr. Bouchard buys $5000 worth of home furnishings from the ABC Furniture Mart. He pays $500 down and agrees to pay the balance with monthly payments over 5 years at $j_{12} = 12\%$. The contract he signs stipulates that if he pays off the contract early there is a penalty equal to three months' payments. After two years (24 payments) Mr. Bouchard realizes that he could borrow the money from the bank at $j_{12} = 8.4\%$. He realizes that to do so means he will have to pay the three-month penalty on the ABC Furniture Mart contract. Should he refinance?

Solution   First, calculate the monthly payments required under the original contract.

$$R_1 = \frac{4500}{a_{\overline{60}|0.01}} \doteq \$100.10$$

Now, calculate the outstanding balance B_{24} on the original contract at the end of two years.

$$B_{24} = 4500(1.01)^{24} - 100.10 s_{\overline{24}|0.01} \doteq \$3013.76$$

If Mr. Bouchard repays the loan he will also pay a penalty equal to $3 \times R = \$300.30$. Therefore, the amount he must borrow from the bank is

$$\$3160.52 + \$300.30 = \$3314.06$$

To calculate the new monthly payment, we take the outstanding balance after 24 payments (including the penalty) and treat it like a brand new loan. That is, we use $A = B_{24} = 3314.06$, $n = 36$, and $i = 0.084/12 = 0.007$.

Thus, the new monthly payments on the bank loan are

$$R_2 = \frac{3314.06}{a_{\overline{36}|0.007}} \doteq \$104.46$$

Therefore, he should not refinance since $104.46 is larger than $100.10.

The largest single loan the average Canadian is likely to make will be the mortgage on one's home. At one time, interest rates on mortgages were guaranteed for the life of the repayment schedule, which could be as long as 25 or 30 years. Now, the longest period of guaranteed interest rates available is usually 5 years, although homeowners may choose mortgages where the interest rate is adjusted every three years, every year, or even daily to current interest rates.

A homeowner who wishes to repay the mortgage in full before the defined renegotiation date may sometimes have to pay a penalty (although in cases where you refinance your mortgage early with the same institution, there usually is no penalty). In some cases, this penalty is defined as three months of interest on the amount prepaid. In other cases the penalty varies according to market conditions and can be determined by the lender at the time of prepayment (the formula that the lender must use may be defined in the mortgage contract, however). This situation is illustrated in Example 3.

With the high interest rates of the late 1980s and early 1990s and the drop in rates throughout the 1990s and early 2000s, many new and different mortgages are being offered to the prospective borrower. It is important that students are capable of analyzing these contracts fully. Several examples are illustrated in the exercises contained in this chapter.

EXAMPLE 2   A couple purchased a home and signed a mortgage contract for $180 000 to be paid with monthly payments calculated over a 25-year period at $j_2 = 10\%$. The interest rate is guaranteed for 5 years. After 5 years, they renegotiate the interest rate and refinance the loan at $j_2 = 6\frac{1}{2}\%$. There is no penalty if a mortgage is refinanced at the end of an interest rate guarantee period. Calculate
    a) the monthly payment for the initial 5-year period;
    b) the new monthly payments after 5 years;
    c) the accumulated value of the savings for the second 5-year period (at the end of that period) at $j_{12} = 4\frac{1}{2}\%$; and
    d) the outstanding balance at the end of 10 years.

Solution a   First we calculate a monthly rate of interest i equivalent to $j_2 = 10\%$:

$$(1+i)^{12} = (1.05)^2$$
$$(1+i) = (1.05)^{\frac{1}{6}}$$
$$i = (1.05)^{\frac{1}{6}} - 1$$
$$i \doteq 0.008164846$$

Now $A = 180\,000$, $n = 300$, $i = 0.008164846$ and we calculate the monthly payment R_1 for the initial 5-year period.

$$R_1 = \frac{180\,000}{a_{\overline{300}|i}} \doteq \$1610.08$$

Solution b   First we calculate the outstanding balance of the loan after 5 years.

$$180\,000(1+i)^{60} - 1610.08 s_{\overline{60}|i}$$
$$= 293\,201.03 - 124\,015.89 = \$169\,185.12$$

This outstanding balance is refinanced at $j_2 = 6\frac{1}{2}\%$ over a 20-year period. First, calculate the rate i per month equivalent to $j_2 = 6\frac{1}{2}\%$.

$$(1+i)^{12} = (1.0325)^2$$
$$(1+i) = (1.0325)^{\frac{1}{6}}$$
$$i = (1.0325)^{\frac{1}{6}} - 1$$
$$i \doteq 0.00534474$$

Now $A = 169\,185.12$, $n = 240$, $i = 0.00534474$ and we calculate the new monthly payment R_2.

$$R_2 = \frac{169\,185.12}{a_{\overline{240}|i}} = \$1252.82$$

Solution c   The monthly savings after the loan is renegotiated after 5 years at $j_2 = 6\frac{1}{2}\%$ is

$$1610.08 - 1252.82 = \$357.26$$

If these savings are deposited in an account paying $j_{12} = 4\frac{1}{2}\%$, the accumulated value of the savings at the end of the 5-year period is:

$$357.26 s_{\overline{60}|0.00375} \doteq \$23\,988.42$$

Solution d   The outstanding balance of the loan at the end of 10 years at $i = 0.00534474$ is

$$169\,185.12(1+i)^{60} - 1252.82 s_{\overline{60}|i}$$
$$= 232\,950.03 - 88\,344.94 = \$144\,605.09$$

The outstanding balance at the end of 10 years is $\$144\,605.09$. That means that only $\$180\,000 - \$144\,605.09 = \$35\,394.91$ of the loan was repaid during the first 10 years (they still owe 80.3% of the original $\$180\,000$ loan). This is despite the fact that payments in the first 10 years totalled $(60 \times \$1610.08 + 60 \times \$1252.82)$ or $\$171\,774$.

EXAMPLE 3   The Knapps buy a house and borrow $\$145\,000$ from the ABC Insurance Company. The loan is to be repaid with monthly payments over 30 years at $j_2 = 9\%$. The interest rate is guaranteed for 5 years. After exactly two years of making payments, the Knapps see that interest rates have dropped to $j_2 = 7\%$ in the market place. They ask to be allowed to repay the loan in full so they can refinance. The Insurance Company agrees to renegotiate but sets a penalty exactly equal to the money the company will lose over the next 3 years. Calculate the value of the penalty.

Solution   First, calculate the monthly payments R required on the original loan at $j_2 = 9\%$. Determine i such that

$$(1+i)^{12} = (1.045)^2$$
$$(1+i) = (1.045)^{\frac{1}{6}}$$
$$i = (1.045)^{\frac{1}{6}} - 1$$
$$i \doteq 0.007363123$$

Now $A = 145\,000$, $n = 360$, $i = 0.007363123$, and

$$R = \frac{145\,000}{a_{\overline{360}|i}} = \$1149.61$$

Next we calculate the outstanding balance after 2 years:

$$= 145\,000(1+i)^{24} - 1149.61 s_{\overline{24}|i}$$
$$= 172\,915.20 - 30\,058.08 = \$142\,857.12$$

Also, we determine the outstanding balance after 5 years if the loan is not renegotiated.

$$145\,000(1+i)^{60} - 1149.61 s_{\overline{60}|i}$$
$$= 225\,180.57 - 86\,335.54 = \$138\,845.03$$

If the insurance company renegotiates, it will receive $142\,857.12 plus the penalty of X dollars now. If they do not renegotiate, they will receive $1149.61 a month for 3 years plus $138\,845.03 at the end of 3 years. These two options should be equivalent at the current interest rate $j_2 = 7\%$.

```
                    +X
Option 1:   142 857.12
           ├──────────┼──────────┼────···────┼──────────┤
           0          1          2           35         36
Option 2:          1149.61    1149.61      1149.61    1149.61
                                                     +138 845.03
```

Determine the monthly rate i equivalent to $j_2 = 7\%$.

$$(1+i)^{12} = (1.035)^2$$
$$(1+i) = (1.035)^{\frac{1}{6}}$$
$$i = (1.035)^{\frac{1}{6}} - 1$$
$$i \doteq 0.00575004$$

Using 0 as the focal date we solve an equation of value for X.

$$X + 142\,857.12 = 1149.61 a_{\overline{36}|i} + 138\,845.03(1+i)^{-36}$$
$$X + 142\,857.12 = 37\,286.97 + 112\,950.52$$
$$X = 7380.37$$

Thus the penalty at the end of 2 years is $7380.37.

Should the Knapps refinance? Using $A = 142\,857.12 + 7380.37 = 150\,237.49$, $i = 0.00575004$, and $n = 336$ we calculate the revised monthly payment:

$$R_2 = \frac{150\,237.49}{a_{\overline{336}|0.00575004}} \doteq \$1011.16$$

If the only goal of the Knapps is lower monthly payments, then they should refinance. However, it is not clear whether they should actually refinance. Let's calculate the outstanding balance of the loan after 5 years and assume that the loan is refinanced at that time at $j_2 = 6\%$ (equivalent monthly rate $= 0.004938622$).

i) If they do not refinance,

$$B_{60} = 145\,000(1.007363123)^{60} - 1149.61 s_{\overline{60}|i} \doteq \$138\,845.03$$

and the new monthly payment will be,

$$R = \frac{138\,845.03}{a_{\overline{300}|0.004938622}} \doteq \$888.34$$

Total payments over mortgage $= 60(\$1149.61) + 300(\$888.34) = \$335\,478.60$.

ii) If they refinance and pay the penalty,

$$B_{60} = 150\,237.49(1.00575004)^{36} - 1011.16 s_{\overline{36}|i} \doteq \$144\,365.07$$

and the new monthly payment will be,

$$R = \frac{144\,365.07}{a_{\overline{300}|0.004938622}} \doteq \$923.66$$

Total payments over mortgage $= 24(\$1149.61) + 36(\$1011.16) + \$300(923.66)$
$= \$341\,090.40$.

The Knapps would end up paying $5611.80 more in interest over the 30 years of the life of the mortgage if they refinanced after the first 2 years and paid the penalty. This will not always be the case. Sometimes it will be better to refinance and pay the penalty. It depends on the size of the penalty and how low is the refinanced interest rate.

Before deciding whether or not to refinance early and pay a penalty, you need to carry out calculations similar to those given above.

Note: Another common penalty is 3 times the monthly interest due on the outstanding balance at the time of refinancing. In this example, the penalty would have been

$$3 \times \$142\,857.12 \times 0.007363123 = \$3155.62.$$

EXAMPLE 4 The Wongs borrow $10 000 from a bank to buy some home furnishings. Interest is $j_{12} = 9\%$ and the term of the loan is 3 years. After making 15 monthly payments, the Wongs miss the next two monthly payments. The bank forces them to renegotiate the loan at a new, higher interest rate $j_{12} = 10\frac{1}{2}\%$. Determine
a) the original monthly payments R_1;
b) the outstanding balance of the loan at the time the 17th monthly payment would normally have been made.
c) the new monthly payments R_2 if the original length of the loan term is not extended.

Solution a Using $A = 10\,000$, $n = 36$, $i = \frac{0.09}{12} = 0.0075$ we calculate the original monthly payment

$$R_1 = \frac{10\,000}{a_{\overline{36}|i}} \doteq \$318.00$$

Solution b The first 15 monthly payments of $318 were made. Therefore at the end of 15 months the outstanding balance was

$$10\,000(1+i)^{15} - 318 s_{\overline{15}|i}$$
$$= 11\,186.03 - 5028.75 = \$6157.28$$

Then no payments were made for 2 months. Therefore the outstanding balance grows with interest and at the end of 17 months is

$$\$6157.28(1 + i)^2 = \$6249.99$$

Solution c We have $A = 6249.99$, $n = 19$, $i = \frac{0.105}{12} = 0.00875$ and we calculate the new monthly payment

$$R_2 = \frac{6249.99}{a_{\overline{19}|i}} = \$358.49$$

Exercise 5.3

Part A

1. A borrower is repaying a $5000 loan at $j_{12} = 9\%$ with monthly payments over 3 years. Just after the 12th payment (at the end of 1 year) he has the loan refinanced at $j_{12} = 6\%$. If the number of payments remains unchanged, what will be the new monthly payment and what will be the monthly savings in interest?

2. A 5-year, $6000 loan is being amortized with monthly payments at $j_{12} = 10\%$. Just after making the 30th payment, the borrower has the loan refinanced at $j_{12} = 8\%$ with the number of payments to remain unchanged. What will be the monthly savings in interest?

3. A borrower has a $5000 loan with the "Easy-Credit" Finance Company. The loan is to be repaid over 4 years at $j_{12} = 18\%$. The contract stipulates an early repayment penalty equal to 3 months' payments. Just after the 20th payment, the borrower determines that his local bank would lend him money at $j_{12} = 12\%$. Should he refinance?

4. The Jones family buys a fridge and stove totalling $1400 from their local appliance store. They agree to pay off the total amount with monthly payments over 3 years at $j_{12} = 13\%$. If they wish to pay off the contract early they will experience a penalty equal to 3 months' interest on the outstanding balance. After 12 payments they see that interest rates at their local bank are $j_{12} = 9\%$. Should they refinance?

5. Consider a couple who bought a house in Canada in 1976. Assume they needed a $60 000 mortgage, which was to be repaid with monthly payments over 25 years. In 1976, interest rates were $j_2 = 10\frac{1}{2}\%$. What was their monthly payment? In 1981 (on the 5th anniversary of their mortgage) their mortgage was renegotiated to reflect current market rates. The repayment schedule was to cover the remaining 20 years and interest rates were now $j_2 = 22\%$. What was the new monthly payment? What effect might this have on homeowners?

6. The Steins buy a house and take out an $85 000 mortgage. The mortgage is amortized over 25 years at $j_2 = 9\%$. After $3\frac{1}{2}$ years, the Steins sell their house and the buyer wants to set up a new mortgage better tailored to his needs. The Steins find out that in addition to repaying the principal balance on their mortgage, they must pay a penalty equal to three months' interest on the outstanding balance. What total amount must they repay?

7. A couple borrows $15 000 to be repaid with monthly payments over 48 months at $j_4 = 10\%$. They make the first 14 payments and miss the next three. What new monthly payments over 31 months would repay the loan on schedule?

8. A loan of $20 000 is to be repaid in 13 equal annual payments, each payable at year-end. Interest is at $j_1 = 8\%$. Because the borrower is having financial difficulties, the lender agrees that the borrower may skip the 5th and 6th payments. Immediately after the 6th payment would have been paid, the loan is renegotiated to yield $j_1 = 10\%$ for the remaining 7 years. Determine the new level annual payment for each of the remaining 7 years.

9. A loan of $50 000 was being repaid by monthly level instalments over 20 years at $j_{12} = 9\%$ interest. Now, when 10 years of the repayment period are still to run, it is proposed to increase

the interest rate to $j_{12} = 10\frac{1}{2}\%$. What should the new level payment be so as to pay off the loan on its original due date?

10. The Mosers buy a camper trailer and take out a $15 000 loan. The loan is amortized over 10 years with monthly payments at $j_2 = 9\%$.
   a) Determine the monthly payment needed to amortize this loan.
   b) Determine the amount of interest paid by the first 36 payments.
   c) After 3 years (36 payments) they could refinance their loan at $j_2 = 7\%$ provided they pay a penalty equal to three months' interest on the outstanding balance. Should they refinance? (Show the difference in their monthly payments.)

Part B

1. A couple buys a home and signs a mortgage contract for $120 000 to be paid with monthly payments over a 25-year period at $j_2 = 10\frac{1}{2}\%$. After 5 years, they renegotiate the interest rate and refinance the loan at $j_2 = 7\%$; determine
   a) the monthly payment for the initial 5-year period;
   b) the new monthly payment after 5 years;
   c) the accumulated value of the savings for the second 5-year period at $j_{12} = 3\%$ valued at the end of the second 5-year period;
   d) the outstanding balance at the end of 10 years.

2. Mrs. McDonald is repaying a debt with monthly payments of $100 over 5 years. Interest is at $j_{12} = 12\%$. At the end of the second year she makes an extra payment of $350. She then shortens her payment period by 1 year and renegotiates the loan without penalty and without an interest change. What are her new monthly payments over the remaining two years? How much interest does she save by doing this?

3. Mr. Fisher is repaying a loan at $j_{12} = 12\%$ with monthly payments of $1500 over 3 years. Due to temporary unemployment, Mr. Fisher missed making the 13th through the 18th payments inclusive. Determine the value of the revised monthly payments needed starting in the 19th month if the loan is still to be repaid at $j_{12} = 12\%$ by the end of the original 3 years.

4. Mrs. Metcalf purchased property several years ago, (but she cannot remember exactly when). She has a statement in her possession, from the mortgage company, which shows that the outstanding loan amount on January 1, 2006, is $28 416.60 and that the current interest rate is 11% compounded semi-annually. It further shows that monthly payments are $442.65.

   Assuming continuation of the interest rate until maturity and that monthly payments are due on the 1st of every month:
   a) What is the final maturity date of the mortgage?
   b) What will be the amount of the final payment?
   c) Show the amortization schedule entries for January 1 and February 1, 2006.
   d) Calculate the new monthly payment required (effective after December 31, 2005) if the interest rate is changed to 8% compounded semi-annually and the other terms of the mortgage remain the same.
   e) Calculate the new monthly payment if Mrs. Metcalf decides that she would like to have the mortgage completely repaid by December 31, 2015 (i.e., last payment at December 1, 2015). Assume the 11% compounded semi-annually interest rate, and that new payments will start on February 1, 2006.

5. A loan effective January 1, 2005, is being amortized by equal monthly instalments over 5 years using interest at a nominal annual rate of 12% compounded monthly. The first such instalment was due February 1, 2005, and the last such instalment was to be due January 1, 2010. Immediately after the 24th instalment was made on January 1, 2007, a new level monthly instalment is determined (using the same rate of interest) in order to shorten the total amortization period to $3\frac{1}{2}$ years, so the final instalment will fall due on July 1, 2008. Determine the ratio of the new monthly instalment to the original monthly instalment.

6. A $150 000 mortgage is to be amortized by monthly payments for 25 years. Interest is $j_2 = 9\frac{1}{2}\%$ for 5 years and could change at that time. No penalty is charged for full or partial payment of the mortgage after 5 years.

a) Calculate the regular monthly payment and the reduced final mortgage payment assuming the $9\frac{1}{2}\%$ rate continues for the entire 25 years.

b) What is the outstanding balance after
   i) 2 years; ii) 5 years?

c) During the 5-year period, there is a penalty of 6 months' interest on any principal repaid early. After 2 years, interest rates fall to $j_2 = 8\%$ for 3-year mortgages. Calculate the new monthly payment if the loan is refinanced and set up to have the same outstanding balance at the end of the initial 5-year period. Would it pay to refinance? (Exclude consideration of any possible refinancing costs other than the penalty provided in the question.)

7. A \$200 000 mortgage is taken out at $j_2 = 6\frac{1}{2}\%$, to be amortized over 25 years by monthly payments. Assume that the $6\frac{1}{2}\%$ rate continues for the entire life of the mortgage.

a) Calculate the regular monthly payment and the reduced final payment.

b) Calculate the accumulated value of all the interest payments on the mortgage, at the time of the final payment.

c) Calculate the outstanding principal after 5 years.

d) If an extra \$5000 is paid off in 5 years (no penalty) and the monthly payments continue as before, how much less will have to be paid over the life of the mortgage?

8. Two years ago the Tongs took out a \$175 000 mortgage that was to be amortized over a 25-year period with monthly payments. The initial interest rate was set at $j_2 = 11\frac{1}{4}\%$ and guaranteed for 5 years. After exactly two years

of payments, the Tongs see that mortgage interest rates for a 3-year term are $j_2 = 7\frac{1}{2}\%$. They ask the bank to let them pay off the old mortgage in full and take out a new mortgage with a 23-year amortization schedule with $j_2 = 7\frac{1}{2}\%$ guaranteed for 3 years. The bank replies that the Tongs must pay a penalty equal to the total dollar difference in the interest payments over the next three years. The mortgage allows the Tongs to make a 10% lump-sum principal repayment at any time (i.e., 10% of the remaining outstanding balance). The Tongs argue that they should be allowed to make this 10% lump-sum payment first and then determine the interest penalty. How many dollars will they save with respect to the interest penalty if they are allowed to make the 10% lump-sum repayment?

9. Mr. Adams has just moved to Waterloo. He has been told by his employer that he will be transferred out of Waterloo again in exactly three years. Mr. Adams is going to buy a house and requires a \$150 000 mortgage. He has his choice of two mortgages with monthly payments and 25-year amortization period.

Mortgage A is at $j_2 = 10\%$. This mortgage stipulates, however, that if you pay off the mortgage any time before the fifth anniversary, you will have to pay a penalty equal to three months' interest on the outstanding balance at the time of repayment.

Mortgage B is at $j_2 = 10\frac{1}{2}\%$ but can be paid off at any time without penalty. Given that Mr. Adams will have to repay the mortgage in three years and that he can save money at $j_1 = 6\%$, which mortgage should he choose?

Section 5.4   ## Refinancing a Loan — The Sum-of-Digits Method

A few Canadian lending institutions, when determining the outstanding principal on a consumer loan, do not use the amortization method outlined in the previous two sections, but rather they use an approximation to the amortization method called the **Sum-of-Digits Method** or the **Rule of 78**.

We know that under the amortization method, each payment made on a loan is used partly to pay off interest owing and partly to pay off principal owing. We also know that the interest portion of each payment is largest at the early instalments and gets progressively smaller over time. Thus, if a consumer borrowed $1000 at $j_{12} = 12\%$ and repaid the balance over 12 months, we would get the following amortization schedule:

Payment Number	Monthly Payment	Interest Payment	Principal Payment	Outstanding Balance
				$1000.00
1	88.85	10.00	78.85	921.15
2	88.85	9.21	79.64	841.51
3	88.85	8.42	80.43	761.08
4	88.85	7.61	81.24	679.84
5	88.85	6.80	82.05	597.79
6	88.85	5.98	82.87	514.92
7	88.85	5.15	83.70	431.22
8	88.85	4.31	84.54	346.68
9	88.85	3.47	85.38	261.30
10	88.85	2.61	86.24	175.06
11	88.85	1.75	87.10	87.96
12	88.84	0.88	87.96	0
Totals	1066.20	66.20	1000.00	

Under the sum-of-digits approximation, we calculate the interest portion of each payment by taking a defined proportion of the total interest paid — that is, $66.20. The proportion used is calculated as follows.

The loan is paid off over 12 months. If we sum the digits from 1 to 12 we get 78. We now say that the amount of interest assigned to the first payment is $\frac{12}{78} \times 66.20 = \$10.18$. The amount of interest assigned to the second payment is $\frac{11}{78} \times 66.20 = \$9.34$. This process continues until the amount of interest assigned to the last payment is $\frac{1}{78} \times \$66.20 = \$0.85$. In general, the interest portion of the kth payment, I_k, is given by:

$$I_k = \frac{n - k + 1}{s_n} I$$

where n = number of payments

s_n = sum of digits from 1 to $n = \frac{n(n + 1)}{2}$

I = total interest to be paid over life of loan

OBSERVATION:

Notice that the total of the interest column is still $66.20 since $(\frac{12}{78} + \frac{11}{78} + \cdots + \frac{1}{78}) = \frac{78}{78}$. Since many consumer loans are paid off over 12 months, the alternative name, the Rule of 78, is sometimes used.

If we apply the sum-of-digits method to the loan described above, we will get the repayment schedule shown as follows.

Payment Number	Monthly Payment	Interest Payment	Principal Payment	Outstanding Balance
				$1000.00
1	88.85	10.18	78.67	921.33
2	88.85	9.34	79.51	841.82
3	88.85	8.49	80.36	761.46
4	88.85	7.64	81.21	680.25
5	88.85	6.79	82.06	598.19
6	88.85	5.94	82.91	515.28
7	88.85	5.09	83.76	431.52
8	88.85	4.24	84.61	346.91
9	88.85	3.39	85.46	261.45
10	88.85	2.55	86.30	175.15
11	88.85	1.70	87.15	88.00
12	88.85	0.85	88.00	0
Totals	1066.20	66.20	1000.00	

OBSERVATION:

One important point to notice here is that while the error is small, the use of the sum-of-digits approximation leads to an outstanding balance that is always larger than that obtained by using the amortization method. Thus, if you want to refinance your loan to repay the balance early, there is a penalty attached because of the use of the sum-of-digits approximation.

In the above illustration we can see that if the consumer paid his loan off in full after one month the lending institution would have realized an interest return of $10.18 on $1000 over one month, or $i = 1.018\%$. This corresponds to $j_{12} = 12.216\%$ as opposed to $j_{12} = 12\%$.

EXAMPLE 1   Consider a $6000 loan that is to be repaid over 5 years at $j_{12} = 6\%$. Show the first three lines of the repayment schedule using: a) the amortization method; b) the sum-of-digits method.

Solution   First we calculate the monthly payment R required

$$R = \frac{6000}{a_{\overline{60}|0.005}} \doteq \$116.00$$

Solution a   From Example 3 in section 5.1 we have the repayment schedule using the amortization method as shown below.

Payment Number	Monthly Payment	Interest Payment	Principal Payment	Outstanding Balance
				$6000.00
1	116.00	30.00	86.00	5914.00
2	116.00	29.57	86.43	5827.57
3	116.00	29.14	86.86	5740.71

Solution b Using the sum-of-digits approach we first calculate the total dollar value of all interest payments. We calculate the smaller concluding payment X at the end of 5 years using the method of section 5.1,

$$X = 6000(1.005)^{60} - 116.00s_{\overline{59}|0.005}(1.005)$$
$$= 8093.10 - 7977.32 = \$115.78$$

and then calculate the total interest in the loan as the difference between the total dollar value of all payments and the value of the loan; i.e.,

$$I = (59 \times \$116.00 + \$115.78) - \$6000 = \$959.78$$

The sum of the digits from 1 to 60 is 1830. Thus,

$$I_1 = \text{Interest in first payment} = \frac{60}{1830} \times 959.78 = \$31.47$$

$$I_2 = \text{Interest in second payment} = \frac{59}{1830} \times 959.78 = \$30.94$$

$$I_3 = \text{Interest in third payment} = \frac{58}{1830} \times 959.78 = \$30.42$$

This leads to the following entries in our repayment schedule:

Payment Number	Monthly Payment	Interest Payment	Principal Payment	Outstanding Balance
				$6000.00
1	116.00	31.47	84.53	5915.47
2	116.00	30.94	85.06	5830.41
3	116.00	30.42	85.58	5744.83

Example 1 illustrates the penalty involved in refinancing a loan, where the lending institution uses the sum-of-digits approximation, as the values in the outstanding balance column are all larger than when using the amortization method. The penalty can be quite significant on long-term loans at high interest rates. In fact, it is possible under the sum-of-digits approximation for the interest portion of early payments to exceed the dollar size of these payments, which leads to an outstanding balance that is actually larger than the original loan (see problem 7 in Exercise 5.4, Part A).

In the above illustration, if the consumer repaid the loan after one month the lending institution would earn $31.47 of interest on their $6000 over one month, or $i = 0.5245\%$. This corresponds to $j_{12} = 6.294\%$ as opposed to $j_{12} = 6\%$.

We pointed out in section 3.6 that most provinces in Canada have "Truth-in-Lending" Acts to protect the consumer. Unfortunately, these acts apply only if the loan is not renegotiated before the normal maturity date. Paying off a loan early constitutes "breaking the contract" and the Truth-in-Lending laws do not apply once the contract is broken.

As of January 1, 1983, the Rule of 78 method became illegal for consumer loans issued by federally chartered Canadian banks. However, loans financed through agencies like furniture companies or car dealers will sometimes use the Rule of 78. It is important that the borrower is aware of whether their loan is financed using the amortization or the Rule of 78 method, especially if they plan to repay the loan in full, or refinance the loan, before maturity.

Calculating the Outstanding Balance

If you have a consumer loan from an institution using the Rule of 78, to determine the outstanding balance, the loans officer will not go through an entire repayment schedule but rather will use the method outlined below.

The outstanding balance, B_k, of a loan of A over n-periods with $(n - 1)$ periodic payments of R and a smaller concluding payment of X at i per period using the sum-of-digits method is determined as follows:

Total debt $= (n - 1)R + X = A + I$

Less: Interest rebate $= \left(\dfrac{s_{n-k}}{s_n}\right)I$

Less: Payments to date $= kR$

where

$$s_{n-k} = 1 + 2 + \cdots + (n - k)$$

EXAMPLE 2   To pay off the purchase of a mobile home, a couple takes out a loan of \$45 000 to be repaid with monthly payments over 10 years at $j_{12} = 9\%$. Using the sum-of-digits method determine the outstanding debt at the end of 2 years.

Solution   The regular monthly payment R and the final payment X are

$$R = \frac{45\,000}{a_{\overline{120}|0.0075}} = \$570.05$$

$$X = 45\,000(1.0075)^{120} - 570.05 s_{\overline{119}|0.0075}(1.0075)$$
$$\doteq 110\,311.07 - 109\,742.76 = \$568.31$$

$$\text{Total interest} = (119 \times \$570.05 + \$568.31) - \$45\,000 = \$23\,404.26$$

The total interest to be repaid over the remaining 96 months is called the **interest rebate** and is calculated as

$$\frac{\text{sum of digits 1 to 96}}{\text{sum of digits 1 to 120}} \times \$23.404.26 = \frac{4656}{7260} \times \$23\,404.26 = \$15\,009.67$$

The couple would be given the following figures:

Original total debt $= 119R + X$	$= 68\,404.26$
Less interest rebate	$= 15\,009.67$
Less payments to date $= 24 \times 570.05$	$= \underline{13\,681.20}$
Outstanding balance at the end of 2 years	$= \$39\,713.39$

It is interesting to note that the outstanding balance at the end of 2 years under the amortization method is

$$45\,000(1.0075)^{24} - 570.05 s_{\overline{24}|0.0075} = 53\,838.61 - 14\,928.74$$
$$= \$38\,909.87$$

The "penalty" of using the sum-of-digits method to the borrower is the difference in the outstanding balances under the two methods: $39 713.39 – $38 909.87 = $803.52.

EXAMPLE 3   Prepare an Excel spreadsheet and show the first three months and last three months of a complete repayment schedule for the $6000 loan of Example 1 using the sum-of-digits method. Also show total payments, total interest, and total principal paid.

Solution   We use the same headings in cells A1 through E1 as in the amortization schedule of Example 1. Type the loan amount in cell E2, 6000. In cell F3 type the given semi-annual interest rate, = 0.06/12. In cell F2 calculate the monthly payment by typing, =E2/((1–(1+F3)^–60)/F3). We do not need to round up the periodic payment, as we will use the nonrounded payment when calculating the total interest. In cell F4, calculate the total interest by typing, =60*F2–E2. In cell F5 calculate the sum of the digits from 1 to 60 by typing, =60*61/2. We summarize the entries for line 0 and line 1 of an Excel spreadsheet.

CELL	ENTER
A2	0
E2	6000
A3	=A2+1
B3	=$F$2
C3	=((60–A3+1)/$F$5)*$F$4
D3	=B3–C3
E3	=E2–D3

To generate the complete schedule copy A3.E3 to A4.E62

To get the last payment adjust B62=E61+C62

To get the totals apply Σ to B3.D62

Below are the first 3 months and the last 3 months of a complete repayment schedule with required totals, using the sum-of-digits method.

	A	B	C	D	E
1	Pmt#	Payment	Interest	Principal	Balance
2	0				6,000.00
3	1	116.00	31.47	84.53	5,915.47
4	2	116.00	30.94	85.06	5,830.41
5	3	116.00	30.42	85.58	5,744.83
⋮	⋮	⋮	⋮	⋮	⋮
60	58	116.00	1.57	114.43	230.31
61	59	116.00	1.05	114.95	115.26
62	60	115.78	0.52	115.26	–
63		6,959.78	959.78	6,000.00	

Exercise 5.4

Part A

1. A loan of $900 is to be repaid with 6 equal monthly payments at $j_{12} = 12\%$. Determine the monthly payment and construct the repayment schedule using the sum-of-digits method. (Compare this answer to Exercise 5.1, Part A, question 4.)

2. A loan of $1000 is to be repaid over one year with equal monthly payments at $j_{12} = 9\%$. Determine the monthly payment and construct the repayment schedule using the sum-of-digits method.

3. To pay off the purchase of a car, Derek obtained a $15 000 3-year loan at $j_{12} = 9\%$. He makes equal monthly payments. Determine the outstanding balance on the loan just after the 24th payment using the sum-of-digits method.

4. Christine borrows $20 000 to be repaid by monthly payments over 3 years at $j_{12} = 10\frac{1}{2}\%$. Determine the outstanding balance at the end of 16 months using the sum-of-digits method.

5. Raymond is repaying a $5000 loan at $j_{12} = 9\%$ with monthly payments over 3 years. Just after the 12th payment he has the balance refinanced at $j_{12} = 6\%$. The balance is determined by the sum-of-digits method. If the number of payments remains unchanged, what will be the new monthly payments and what will be the monthly savings in interest? (Compare this to Exercise 5.3, Part A, question 1.)

6. A 5-year $6000 loan is to be repaid with monthly payments at $j_{12} = 10\%$. Just after making the 30th payment, the borrower has the balance refinanced at $j_{12} = 8\%$ with the term of the loan to remain unchanged. If the balance is determined by the sum-of-digits method, what will be the monthly savings in interest? (Compare this to Exercise 5.3, Part A, question 2.)

7. Consider a $10 000 loan being repaid with monthly payments over 15 years at $j_{12} = 15\%$. Determine the outstanding balance at the end of 2 years and at the end of 5 years using both the sum-of-digits method and the amortization method.

8. Michelle has a $5000 loan that is being repaid by monthly payments over 4 years at $j_{12} = 9\%$. The lender uses the sum-of-digits method to determine outstanding balances. After 1 year of payments the lender's interest rate on new loans has dropped to $j_{12} = 6\%$. Will Michelle save money by refinancing the loan? (The term of the loan will not be changed.)

Part B

1. Matthew can borrow $15 000 at $j_4 = 15\%$ and repay the loan with monthly payments over 10 years. If he wants to pay the loan off early, the outstanding balance will be determined using the sum-of-digits method.

   He can also borrow $15 000 with monthly payments over 10 years at $j_4 = 16\%$ and pay the loan off at any time without penalty. The outstanding balance will be determined using the amortization method.

   Matthew has an endowment insurance policy coming due in 4 years that could be used to pay off the outstanding balance at that time in full. Which loan should he take if he earns $j_{12} = 6\%$ on his savings?

2. A loan of $18 000 is to be repaid with monthly payments over 10 years at $j_2 = 8\frac{1}{2}\%$. Using the sum-of-digits method,
   a) construct the first two and the last two lines of the repayment schedule;
   b) determine the interest and the principal portion of the 10th payment;
   c) calculate the outstanding balance at the end of 2 years and compare it with the outstanding balance at the same time calculated by the amortization method;
   d) advise whether the loan should be refinanced at the end of 2 years at current rate $j_2 = 8\%$ with the term of the loan unchanged.

3. A $20 000 home renovation loan is to be amortized over 10 years by monthly payments, with each regular payment rounded up to the next dollar, and the last payment reduced accordingly. Interest on the loan is at $j_4 = 10\%$. After 4 years the loan is fully paid off with an extra payment. Determine the amount of this final payment if the sum-of-digits method is used to calculate the outstanding principal.

Section 5.5   Sinking Funds

When a specified amount of money is needed at a specified future date, it is a good practice to accumulate systematically a fund by means of equal periodic deposits. Such a fund is called a **sinking fund**. Sinking funds are used to pay off debts (see section 5.6), to redeem bond issues, to replace worn-out equipment, or to buy new equipment.

Because the amount needed in the sinking fund, the time the amount is needed, and the interest rate that the fund earns are known, we have an annuity problem in which the size of the payment, the sinking-fund deposit, is to be determined. A schedule showing how a sinking fund accumulates to the desired amount is called a **sinking-fund schedule**.

EXAMPLE 1   An eight-storey condominium apartment building consists of 146 two-bedroom apartment units of equal size. The Board of Directors of the Homeowners' Association estimated that the building will need new carpeting in the halls at a cost of $25 800 in 5 years.

Assuming that the association can invest their money at $j_{12} = 8\%$, what should be the monthly sinking-fund assessment per unit?

Solution   The sinking-fund deposits form an ordinary simple annuity with $S = 25\ 800$, $i = \frac{2}{3}\%$, $n = 60$.

We calculate the total monthly sinking-fund deposit

$$R = \frac{25\ 800}{s_{\overline{60}|2/3\%}} = \$351.13 \textbf{ (rounded off)}$$

Per-unit assessment should be

$$\frac{351.13}{146} = \$2.41$$

EXAMPLE 2   Show the first three lines and the last two lines of the sinking-fund schedule, explaining the growth of the fund in Example 1.

Solution   At the end of the first month, a deposit of $351.13 is made and the fund contains $351.13. This amount earns interest at $\frac{2}{3}\%$ for 1 month, i.e., $351.13 \times \frac{2}{300} = \$2.34$. Thus the total increase at the end of the second month is the second payment plus interest on the amount in the fund, i.e., $351.13 + \$2.34 = \$353.47$, and the fund will contain $704.60. This procedure may be repeated to complete the entire schedule.

In order to complete the last two lines of the sinking-fund schedule without running the complete schedule, we may calculate the amount in the fund at the end of the 58th month as the accumulated value of 58 payments, i.e.,

$$351.13 s_{\overline{58}|2/3\%} = \$24\,764.04$$

and complete the schedule from that point. The calculations are tabulated below.

End of the Month	Interest on Fund at $\frac{2}{3}\%$	Deposit	Increase in Fund	Amount in Fund
1	—	351.13	351.13	351.13
2	2.34	351.13	353.47	704.60
3	4.70	351.13	355.83	1060.43
⋮	⋮	⋮	⋮	⋮
58				24 764.04
59	165.09	351.13	516.22	25 280.26
60	168.54	351.20*	519.67	25 800.00

*The last deposit is adjusted to have the final amount in the fund equal $25 800.

In General — Sinking-Fund Schedules

Consider an amount S dollars to be accumulated with level deposits of R dollars into a sinking fund at the end of each period for n periods, at rate i per period. The kth line of the sinking-fund schedule ($1 \leq k < n$) is:

a) Interest on fund $= iRs_{\overline{k-1}|i} = R[(1+i)^{k-1} - 1]$

b) Increase in fund $= R + R[(1+i)^{k-1} - 1] = R(1+i)^{k-1}$

c) Amount in fund $= Rs_{\overline{k}|i}$

In Example 2, the 3rd line of the sinking fund schedule can be calculated as:

   Interest on fund $= \$351.13[(1.0066666)^2 - 1] = \$4.70$

   Increase in fund $= \$351.13(1.0066666)^2 = \$355.83$

   Amount in fund $= \$351.13 s_{\overline{3}|.006666} = \$1060.43$

EXAMPLE 3   Prepare an Excel spreadsheet and show the first 3 months and the last 3 months of the sinking-fund schedule of Example 2 above.

Solution   We reserve cells A1 through E1 for headings. In cell F3, enter the final amount, 25 800. In cell F2, enter the interest rate earned by the sinking fund by typing =0.08/12. In cell F4, calculate the sinking fund deposit by typing =ROUND(F3/(((1+F2)^60−1))/F2,2). The entries are summarized in the table below.

	CELL	ENTER	INTERPRETATION
Headings	A1	Deposit #	'Deposit number' or 'End of the month #'
	B1	Interest	'Interest on fund'
	C1	Deposit	'Monthly deposit'
	D1	Increase	'Increase in fund'
	E1	Amount	'Amount in fund'
Line 0	A2	0	Time starts
	E2	0	Amount in fund at the beginning of month 1
Line 1	A3	=A2+1	End of month 1
	B3	=E2*$F$2	Interest on fund at the end of month 1
	C3	$F$4	Monthly deposit
	D3	=B3+C3	Increase in fund at the end of month 1
	E3	=E2+D3	Amount in fund at the end of month 1

To generate the complete schedule copy A3.E3 to A4.E62
To get the last deposit adjust C62=E62−E61−B62

Below are the first 3 months and the last 3 months of the sinking-fund schedule.

	A	B	C	D	E
1	Deposit#	Interest	Deposit	Increase	Amount
2	0				0
3	1	0	351.13	351.13	351.13
4	2	2.34	351.13	353.47	704.60
5	3	4.70	351.13	355.83	1,060.43
⋮	⋮	⋮	⋮	⋮	⋮
60	58	161.67	351.13	512.80	24,764.04
61	59	165.09	351.13	516.22	25,280.26
62	60	168.54	351.20	519.74	25,800.00

Exercise 5.5

Part A

1. A couple is saving a down payment for a home. They want to have $15 000 at the end of 4 years in an account paying interest at $j_1 = 6\%$. How much must be deposited in the fund at the end of each year? Make out a schedule showing the growth of the fund.

2. A company wants to save $100 000 over the next 5 years so they can expand their plant facility. How much must be deposited at the end of each year if their money earns interest at $j_1 = 8\%$? Make out a schedule for this problem.

3. What quarterly deposit is required in a bank account to accumulate $2000 at the end of 2 years if interest is at $j_4 = 4\%$? Prepare a schedule for this problem.

4. A sinking fund earning interest at $j_4 = 6\%$ now contains $1000. What quarterly deposits for the next 5 years will cause the fund to grow to $10 000? How much interest is earned by the sinking fund during the 12th deposit? What is the increase in the sinking fund after the 12th deposit? How much is in the sinking fund at the end of 3 years?

5. A cottagers' association decides to set up a sinking fund to save money to have their cottage road widened and paved. They want to have $250 000 at the end of 5 years and they can earn interest at $j_1 = 9\%$. What annual deposit is

required per cottager if there are 30 cottages on the road? Show the complete schedule.

6. Determine the quarterly deposits necessary to accumulate $10 000 over 10 years in a sinking fund earning interest at $j_4 = 6\%$. Determine the amount in the fund at the end of 9 years and complete the rest of the schedule.

7. A city needs to have $200 000 at the end of 15 years to retire a bond issue. What annual deposits will be necessary if their money earns interest at $j_1 = 7\%$? Make out the first three and last three lines of the schedule.

8. What monthly deposit is required to accumulate $3000 at the end of 2 years in a bank account paying interest at $j_4 = 5\%$?

9. A couple wants to save $200 000 to buy some land. They can save $3500 each quarter-year in a bank account paying $j_4 = 9\%$. How many years (to the nearest quarter) will it take them and what is the size of the final deposit?

10. In its manufacturing process, a company uses a machine that costs $75 000 and is scrapped at the end of 15 years with a value of $5000. The company sets up a sinking fund to finance the replacement of the machine, assuming no change in price, with level payments at the end of each year. Money can be invested at an annual

effective interest rate of 4%. Determine the value of the sinking fund at the end of the 10th year.

Part B

1. A homeowners' association decided to set up a sinking fund to accumulate $50 000 by the end of 3 years to improve recreational facilities. What monthly deposits are required if the fund earns 5% compounded daily? Show the first three and the last two lines of the sinking-fund schedule.

2. Consider an amount that is to be accumulated with equal deposits R at the end of each interest period for 5 periods at rate i per period. Hence, the amount to be accumulated is $Rs_{\overline{5}|i}$. Do a complete schedule for this sinking fund. Verify that the sum-of-the-interest column plus the sum-of-the-deposit column equals the sum of the increase-in-the-fund column, and both sums equal the final amount in the fund.

3. A sinking fund is being accumulated at $j_{12} = 6\%$ by deposits of $200 per month. If the fund contains $5394.69 just after the kth deposit, what did it contain just after the $(k - 1)$st deposit?

The Sinking-Fund Method of Retiring a Debt

An alternative method of paying off a loan is to pay the interest on the loan at the end of each interest period and to pay back the principal in one lump sum at the end of the term of the loan. To ensure that the borrower has enough money at the end of the term to repay the original principal in one lump sum, a sinking fund is often set up to accumulate the required amount. At the end of the term of the loan, the borrower returns the whole principal by transferring the accumulated value of the sinking fund to the lender.

This type of loan is often referred to as a **sinking-fund loan**. Sinking-fund loans are not commonly used for consumer loans, but are reasonably common for long-term corporate or government loans. The sinking-fund method of retiring a debt is also used by corporations and governments that raise money by issuing bonds and is discussed in chapter 6.

Under a sinking-fund loan, the borrower is making two series of payments. One is the interest payment to the lender and the other is the deposit into the sinking fund. Usually, the deposits into the sinking fund are made at the same times as the interest payments on the debt are made to the lender. This leads to one of the two main values that we are interested in calculating in this section:

**Periodic cost of the debt = Interest payment to lender
+ Sinking-fund deposit**

The periodic cost of the debt (also referred to as the periodic expense of the debt) represents the total cash outlay the borrower must make each period.

Borrowers are also interested in how much of the loan remains to be repaid at any time. Technically, the outstanding balance of the loan is always equal to the original principal because the borrower is not making any payments toward reducing the principal (as is done for an amortized loan). However, the borrower is accumulating money in a sinking fund. In theory, the accumulated value of the sinking fund can be used to partially pay off the principal at any time. This leads to the following definition:

**Book value of the debt = Original principal
– Accumulated value of the sinking fund**

The book value of the debt can be thought of as the outstanding balance of the loan. It should also be noted that there are two interest rates associated with sinking-fund loans and you need to fully understand which rate is for what use. One interest rate is associated with paying interest on the loan and can be thought of as the lending rate that is paid by the borrower. The other interest rate is the rate that the sinking fund earns and can be thought of as a savings rate that is earned by the borrower.

A sinking-fund schedule can be set up using the same method and headings as shown in section 5.5. The only difference is that you would usually add an extra column to show the book value of the debt.

EXAMPLE 1　A city issues \$1 000 000 of bonds paying interest at $j_2 = 9\frac{1}{8}\%$, and by law it is required to create a sinking fund to redeem the bonds at the end of 8 years. If the fund is invested at $j_2 = 8\%$, calculate a) the semi-annual expense of the debt; b) the book value of the city's indebtedness at the beginning of the 7th year.

Solution a　Semi-annual interest payment on the debt: \$1 000 000 × 0.045625 = \$45 625

Semi-annual deposit into the sinking fund:　　$R = \dfrac{\$1\,000\,000}{s_{\overline{16}|0.04}} \doteq \$45\,820$

Semi-annual expense of the debt　　　　　　　　　　　　$= \$91\,445$

Solution b　The amount in the sinking fund at the end of the 6th year is the accumulated value of the deposits; i.e.,

$$\$45\,820s_{\overline{12}|0.04} \doteq \$688\,482.41$$

The book value of the city's indebtedness at the beginning of the 7th year is then

$$\$1\,000\,000 - \$688\,482.41 = \$311\,517.59$$

EXAMPLE 2 A loan of $15 000 is taken out. Interest payments are due every three months. A sinking fund is set up to pay back the $15 000 in one lump sum at the end of 6 years. The sinking fund earns $j_4 = 4\%$ and deposits are made quarterly. The quarterly expense of the debt is $867.35. Calculate a) the interest rate on the loan, j_4; b) the book value of the debt after 2 years.

Solution a The quarterly sinking fund deposit is

$$\frac{15\,000}{s_{\overline{24}|0.01}} \doteq \$556.10$$

Let the quarterly loan interest rate be i. The quarterly expense of the debt is

$$867.35 = 15\,000i + 556.10$$

which when solved for i gives

$$i = (867.35 - 556.10)/15\,000 = 0.02075$$

Hence, for j_4:

$$j_4 = 4i = 8.30\%$$

The interest rate on the sinking-fund loan is 8.30% compounded quarterly.

Solution b The book value of the debt after 2 years (8 payments) is

$$\$15\,000 - \$556.10s_{\overline{8}|0.01} = \$15\,000 - \$4607.66 = \$10\,392.34$$

Exercise 5.6

Part A

1. A borrower of $5000 agrees to pay interest semi-annually at $j_2 = 10\%$ on the loan and to build up a sinking fund, which will repay the loan at the end of 5 years. If the sinking fund accumulates at $j_2 = 4\%$, determine his total semi-annual expense. How much is in the sinking fund at the end of 4 years?

2. A city borrows $250 000, paying interest annually on this sum at $j_1 = 9\frac{1}{2}\%$. What annual deposits must be made into a sinking fund earning interest at $j_1 = 3\frac{1}{2}\%$ in order to pay off the entire principal at the end of 15 years? What is the total annual expense of the debt?

3. A company issues $500 000 worth of bonds, paying interest at $j_2 = 8\%$. A sinking fund with semi-annual deposits accumulating at $j_2 = 4\%$ is established to redeem the bonds at the end of 20 years. Determine
   a) the semi-annual expense of the debt;
   b) the book value of the company's indebtedness at the end of the 15th year.

4. A city borrows $2 000 000 to build a sewage treatment plant. The debt requires interest at $j_2 = 10\%$. At the same time, a sinking fund is established, which earns interest at $j_2 = 4\frac{1}{2}\%$ to repay the debt in 25 years. Determine
   a) the semi-annual expense of the debt;
   b) the book value of the city's indebtedness at the beginning of the 16th year.

5. On a debt of $4000, interest is paid monthly at $j_{12} = 12\%$ and monthly deposits are made into a sinking fund to retire the debt at the end of 5 years. If the sinking fund earns interest at $j_4 = 3.6\%$, what is the monthly expense of the debt?

6. On a debt of $10 000, interest is paid semi-annually at $j_2 = 10\%$ and semi-annual deposits are made into a sinking fund to retire the debt at the end of 5 years. If the sinking fund earns interest at $j_{12} = 6\%$, what is the semi-annual expense of the debt?

7. Interest at $j_2 = 12\%$ on a loan of $3000 must be paid semi-annually as it falls due. A sinking

fund accumulating at $j_4 = 8\%$ is established to enable the debtor to repay the loan at the end of 4 years.
a) Determine the semi-annual sinking-fund deposit and construct the last two lines of the sinking fund schedule, based on semi-annual deposits.
b) Determine the semi-annual expense of the loan.
c) What is the outstanding principal (book value of the loan) at the end of 2 years?

8. A 10-year loan of $10 000 at $j_1 = 11\%$ is to be repaid by the sinking-fund method, with interest and sinking fund payments made at the end of each year. The rate of interest earned in the sinking fund is $j_1 = 5\%$. Immediately after the 5th year's payment, the lender requests that the outstanding principal be repaid in one lump sum. Calculate the amount of extra cash the borrower has to raise in order to extinguish the debt.

Part B

1. A company issues $2 000 000 worth of bonds paying interest at $j_{12} = 10\frac{1}{2}\%$. A sinking fund accumulating at $j_4 = 6\%$ is established to redeem the bonds at the end of 15 years. Determine
a) the monthly expense of the debt;
b) the book value of the company's indebtedness at the beginning of the 6th year.

2. A man is repaying a $10 000 loan by the sinking-fund method. His total monthly expense is $300. Out of this $300, interest is paid to the lender at $j_{12} = 12\%$ and a deposit is made to a sinking fund earning $j_{12} = 9\%$. Determine the duration of the loan and the final smaller payment.

3. A $100 000 loan is to be repaid in 15 years, with a sinking fund accumulated to repay principal *plus interest*. The loan charges $j_2 = 12\%$, while the sinking fund earns $j_2 = 5\%$. What semi-annual sinking fund deposit is required?

4. A loan of $20 000 bears interest on the amount outstanding at $j_1 = 10\%$. A deposit is to be made in a sinking fund earning interest at $j_1 = 4\%$, which will accumulate enough to pay one-half of the principal at the end of 10 years. In addition, the debtor will make level payments to the creditor, which will pay interest at $j_1 = 10\%$ on the outstanding balance first and the remainder will repay the principal. What is the total annual payment, including that made to the creditor and that deposited in the sinking fund, if the loan is to be completely retired at the end of 10 years?

5. John borrows $10 000 for 10 years and uses a sinking fund to repay the principal. The sinking-fund deposits earn an annual effective interest rate of 5%. The total required payment for both the interest and the sinking-fund deposit made at the end of each year is $1445.05. Calculate the annual effective interest rate charged on the loan.

6. A company borrows $10 000 for five years. Interest of $600 is paid semi-annually. To repay the principal of the loan at the end of 5 years, equal semi-annual deposits are made into a sinking fund that credits interest at a nominal rate of 8% compounded quarterly. The first payment is due in 6 months. Calculate the annual effective rate of interest that the company is paying to service and retire the debt.

7. On August 1, 1998, Mrs. Chan borrows $20 000 for 10 years. Interest at 11% compounded semi-annually must be paid as it falls due. The principal is replaced by means of level deposits on February 1 and August 1 in years 1999 to 2008 (inclusive) into a sinking fund earning $j_1 = 7\%$ in 1999 through December 31, 2003, and $j_1 = 6\%$ January 1, 2004, through 2008.
a) Calculate the semi-annual expense of the loan.
b) How much is in the sinking fund just after the August 1, 2007, deposit?
c) Show the sinking-fund schedule entries at February 1, 2008, and August 1, 2008.

8. Mr. White borrows $15 000 for 10 years. He makes total payments, annually, of $2000. The lender receives $j_1 = 10\%$ on his investment each year for the first 5 years and $j_1 = 8\%$ for the second 5 years. The balance of each payment is invested in a sinking fund earning $j_1 = 7\%$.
a) Determine the amount by which the sinking fund is short of repaying the loan at the end of 10 years.
b) By how much would the sinking-fund deposit (in each of the first 5 years only) need to be increased so that the sinking fund at the end of 10 years will be just sufficient to repay the loan?

| *Section 5.7* | # Comparison of Amortization and Sinking-Fund Methods |

We have discussed the two most common methods of paying off long-term loans: the amortization method and the sinking-fund method. When there are several sources available from which to borrow money, it is important to know how to compare the available loans and choose the cheapest one. The borrower should choose that source for which the periodic expense of the debt is the lowest. When the amortization method is used, the periodic expense of the debt is equal to the periodic amortization payment. When the sinking-fund method is used, the periodic expense of the debt is the sum of the interest payment and the sinking-fund deposit.

To study the relationship between the amortization and sinking-fund methods, we define the following:

A = principal of the loan

n = number of interest periods during the term of the loan

i_1 = loan rate per interest period using amortization

i_2 = loan rate per interest period using the sinking fund

i_3 = sinking-fund rate per interest period

R_A = periodic expense using amortization = $\dfrac{A}{a_{\overline{n}|i_1}} = A\left(\dfrac{1}{s_{\overline{n}|i_1}} + i_1\right)$
    (See Exercises 3.3 Part B question 1b.)

R_S = periodic expense using sinking fund = $\dfrac{A}{s_{\overline{n}|i_3}} + Ai_2 = A\left(\dfrac{1}{s_{\overline{n}|i_3}} + i_2\right)$

We shall examine the relationship between R_A and R_S for different levels of rates i_1, i_2, i_3.

Case I: $i_1 = i_2$ (Interest rate on amortized loan = interest rate on sinking-fund loan)

a) Let $i_1 = i_2 = i_3 \equiv i$, then $R_A = R_S$

b) Let $i_3 > i_1 = i_2$, then $i_3 > i_1$ implies

$$s_{\overline{n}|i_3} > s_{\overline{n}|i_1}$$

$$\frac{1}{s_{\overline{n}|i_1}} > \frac{1}{s_{\overline{n}|i_3}}$$

$$\frac{1}{s_{\overline{n}|i_1}} + i_1 > \frac{1}{s_{\overline{n}|i_3}} + i_2$$

$$R_A > R_S$$

c) Let $i_3 < i_1 = i_2$, then $i_3 < i_1$ implies

$$s_{\overline{n}|i_3} < s_{\overline{n}|i_1}$$

$$\frac{1}{s_{\overline{n}|i_1}} < \frac{1}{s_{\overline{n}|i_3}}$$

$$\frac{1}{s_{\overline{n}|i_1}} + i_1 < \frac{1}{s_{\overline{n}|i_3}} + i_2$$

$$R_A < R_S$$

Case c) is the most common situation, where savings rate < lending rate. This means the amortized loan will always be cheaper. So, why would anyone take out a loan and pay it back using the sinking-fund method? There are two potential reasons:

1. Under a sinking-fund loan, the sinking-fund deposit usually remains under the control of the borrower. That means the borrower can miss making a sinking-fund deposit (as long as they make it up later). Also, the borrower can take some risk in investing the deposits and perhaps earn a higher rate of return on the sinking fund.

2. The borrower can usually negotiate a lower rate of interest on a sinking-fund loan. This situation is covered in *Case II* below.

Case II: $i_1 > i_2$ (interest rate on amortized loan > interest rate on sinking-fund loan)

Let $i_3 < i_2 < i_1$. In this case, which is the most common, we can't tell which method is cheaper. We must calculate the actual periodic costs to determine the cheaper source of money, i.e., the source with the smallest periodic expense.

EXAMPLE 1   A company wishes to borrow $500 000 for 5 years. One source will lend the money at $j_2 = 10\%$ if it is amortized by semi-annual payments. A second source will lend the money at $j_2 = 8\%$ if only the interest is paid semi-annually and the principal is returned in a lump sum at the end of 5 years. If the second source is used, a sinking fund will be established by semi-annual deposits that accumulate at $j_{12} = 4.2\%$. How much can the company save semi-annually by using the better plan?

Solution   When the first source is used, the semi-annual expense of the debt is

$$R_A = \frac{\$500\,000}{a_{\overline{10}|0.05}} \doteq \$64\,752.29.$$

When the second source is used, the interest on the debt paid semi-annually is 4% of $500 000 = $20 000.00.

To calculate the semi-annual deposit into the sinking fund, we must first calculate the semi-annual rate i equivalent to $j_{12} = 4.2\%$

$$(1 + i)^2 = (1.0035)^{12}$$
$$i = (1.0035)^6 - 1$$
$$i = 0.021184609$$

Now we calculate the semi-annual deposit R into the sinking fund

$$R = \frac{\$500\,000}{s_{\overline{10}|i}} = \$45\,416.52$$

The semi-annual expense of the debt using the second source is

$$R_S = \$20\,000 + \$45\,416.52 = \$65\,416.52$$

Thus, the first source, using amortization, is cheaper and the company can save

$$\$65\,416.52 - \$64\,752.29 \text{ or } \$664.23 \text{ semi-annually.}$$

EXAMPLE 2   A firm wants to borrow $500 000. One source will lend the money at $j_4 = 10\%$ if interest is paid quarterly and the principal is returned in a lump sum at the end of 10 years. The firm can set up a sinking fund at $j_4 = 7\%$. At what rate j_4 would it be less expensive to amortize the debt over 10 years?

Solution   We calculate the quarterly expense of the debt.

Interest payment: $500 000 \times 0.025 = \$12\,500.00$

Sinking-fund deposit: $\dfrac{\$500\,000}{s_{\overline{40}|0.0175}} \doteq \$\,8\,736.05$

Quarterly expense: $= \$21\,236.05$

The amortization method will be as expensive if the quarterly amortization payment is equal to $21\,236.05$. Thus, we want to determine the interest rate i per quarter (and then j_4) given $A = 500\,000$, $R = 21\,236.05$, $n = 40$.
We have

$$500\,000 = 21\,236.05 a_{\overline{40}|i}$$
$$a_{\overline{40}|i} = 23.544868$$

We want to determine the rate $j_4 = 4i$ such that $a_{\overline{40}|i} = 23.5449$. A starting value to solve $a_{\overline{40}|i} = 23.5449$ is

$$i = \frac{1 - (\frac{23.5449}{40})^2}{23.5449}$$

or $j_4 = 4i = 11.10\%$. Using linear interpolation, we calculate

	$a_{\overline{40}|i}$	j_4	
	24.0781	11%	
	23.5449	j_4	
	23.1148	12%	

$$\frac{d}{1\%} = \frac{0.5332}{0.9663}$$
$$d \doteq 0.55\%$$
$$\text{and } j_4 = 11.55\%$$

with brackets: 0.9633, 0.5332, d, 1%

If the firm can borrow the money and amortize the debt at less than $j_4 = 11.55\%$, then it will be less expensive than a straight loan at $j_4 = 10\%$ with a sinking fund at $j_4 = 7\%$.

Exercise 5.7

Part A

1. A company borrows $50\,000$ to be repaid in equal annual instalments at the end of each year for 10 years. Determine the total annual cost under the following conditions:
   a) the debt is amortized at $j_1 = 9\%$;
   b) interest at 9% is paid on the debt and a sinking fund is set up at $j_1 = 9\%$;
   c) interest at 9% is paid on the debt and a sinking fund is set up at $j_1 = 6\%$.

2. A company can borrow $180\,000$ for 15 years. They can amortize the debt at $j_1 = 10\%$, or they can pay interest on the loan at $j_1 = 9\%$ and set up a sinking fund at $j_1 = 7\%$ to repay the loan. Which plan is cheaper and by how much per annum?

3. A firm wants to borrow $60 000 to be repaid over 5 years. One source will lend them the money at $j_2 = 10\%$ if it is amortized by semi-annual payments. A second source will lend them money at $j_2 = 9\frac{1}{2}\%$ if only the interest is paid semi-annually and the principal is returned in a lump sum at the end of 5 years. The firm can earn $j_2 = 4\%$ on their savings. Which source should be used for the loan and how much will be saved each half-year?

4. A company can borrow $100 000 for 10 years by paying the interest as it falls due at $j_2 = 9\%$ and setting up a sinking fund at $j_2 = 7\%$ to repay the debt. At what rate, j_2, would an amortization plan have the same semi-annual cost?

5. A city can borrow $500 000 for 20 years by issuing bonds on which interest will be paid semi-annually at $j_2 = 9\frac{1}{8}\%$. The principal will be paid off by a sinking fund consisting of semi-annual deposits invested at $j_2 = 8\%$. Determine the nominal rate, j_2, at which the loan could be amortized at the same semi-annual cost.

6. A firm can borrow $200 000 at $j_1 = 9\%$ and amortize the debt for 10 years. From a second source, the money can be borrowed at $j_1 = 8\frac{1}{2}\%$ if the interest is paid annually and the principal is repaid in a lump sum at the end of 10 years. What yearly rate, j_1, must the sinking fund earn for the annual expense to be the same under the two options?

7. A company wants to borrow $500 000. One source of funds will agree to lend the money at $j_4 = 8\%$ if interest is paid quarterly and the principal is paid in a lump sum at the end of 15 years. The firm can set up a sinking fund at $j_4 = 6\%$ and will make quarterly deposits.
   a) What is the total quarterly cost of the loan?
   b) At what rate, j_4, would it be less expensive to amortize the debt over 15 years?

8. You are able to repay an $80 000 loan by either
   a) amortization at $j_{12} = 7\%$ with 12 months payments; or b) at $j_{12} = 6\frac{1}{2}\%$ using a sinking fund earning $j_{12} = 4\%$, and paid off in 1 year. Which method is cheaper?

Part B

1. A company needs to borrow $200 000 for 6 years. One source will lend them the money at $j_2 = 10\%$ if it is amortized by monthly payments. A second source will lend the money at $j_4 = 9\%$ if only the interest is paid monthly and the principal is returned in a lump sum at the end of 6 years. The company can earn interest at $j_{365} = 6\%$ on the sinking fund. Which source should be used for the loan and how much will be saved monthly?

2. Tanya can borrow $10 000 by paying the interest on a loan as it falls due at $j_2 = 12\%$ and by setting up a sinking fund with semi-annual deposits that accumulate at $j_{12} = 9\%$ over 10 years to repay the debt. At what rate, j_4, would an amortization scheme have the same semi-annual cost?

3. A loan of $100 000 at 8% per annum is to be repaid over 10 years; $20 000 by the amortization method and $80 000 by the sinking-fund method, where the sinking fund can be accumulated with annual deposits at $j_4 = 5\%$. What extra annual payment does the above arrangement require as compared to repayment of the whole loan by the amortization method?

4. A company wants to borrow a large amount of money for 15 years. One source would lend the money at $j_2 = 9\%$, provided it is amortized over 15 years by monthly payments. The company could also raise the money by issuing bonds paying interest semi-annually at $j_2 = 8\frac{1}{2}\%$ and redeemable at par in 15 years. In this case, the company would set up a sinking fund to accumulate the money needed for the redemption of the bonds at the end of 15 years. What rate, j_{12}, on the sinking fund would make the monthly expense the same under the two options?

5. A $10 000 loan is being repaid by the sinking-fund method. Total annual outlay (each year) is $1400 for as long as necessary, plus a smaller final payment made 1 year after the last regular payment. If the lender receives $j_1 = 8\%$ and the sinking fund accumulates at $j_1 = 6\%$, determine the time and amount of the irregular final payment.

6. A $5000 loan can be repaid quarterly for 5 years using amortization and an interest rate of $j_{12} = 10\%$ or by a sinking fund to repay both principal and accumulated interest. If paid by a sinking fund, the interest on the loan will be $j_{12} = 9\%$. What annual effective rate must the sinking fund earn to make the quarterly cost the same for both methods?

| Section 5.8 | **Summary and Review Exercises** |

- Outstanding balance B_k (immediately after the kth payment has been made) by the retrospective method (looking back)

$$B_k = A(1+i)^k - Rs_{\overline{k}|i}$$

by the prospective method (looking ahead) assuming all payments equal

$$B_k = Ra_{\overline{n-k}|i}$$

- Total interest = Total payments – Amount of Loan

- For a loan of A dollars to be amortized with level payments of R dollars at the end of each period for n periods, at rate i per period, in the kth line of the amortization schedule ($1 \le k \le n$):
Interest payment $I_k = R[1 - (1 + i)^{-(n-k+1)}]$
Principal payment $P_k = R(1 + i)^{-(n-k+1)}$
Outstanding balance $B_k = Ra_{\overline{n-k}|i}$
Successive principal payments are in the ratio $1 + i$, that is $\dfrac{P_{k+1}}{P_k} = (1+i)$.

- In the sum-of-digits approximation to the amortization method, the interest portion of the kth payment is given by

$$I_k = \frac{n - k + 1}{s_n} I$$

where n = number of payments
s_n = sum of digits from 1 to $n = \dfrac{n(n+1)}{2}$
I = total interest

- For a sinking fund designed to accumulate a specified amount of S dollars by equal deposits of R dollars at the end of each period for n periods, at rate i per period, in the kth line of the sinking-fund schedule ($1 \le k \le n$):
Interest on fund $= iRs_{\overline{k-1}|i} = R[(1 + i)^{k-1} - 1]$
Increase in fund $= R + R[(1 + i)^{k-1} - 1] = R(1 + i)^{k-1}$
Amount in fund $= Rs_{\overline{k}|i}$

- When a loan A is paid off by the sinking-fund method, the borrower pays interest at i on the loan at the end of each period and accumulates the principal of the loan in a sinking fund earning r. The principal of the loan is repaid at the end of the term of the loan as a lump sum from the sinking fund.

Periodic expense of the loan = Interest payment + Sinking-fund deposit
$$= Ai + \frac{A}{s_{\overline{n}|r}}.$$

Book value of the loan after k periods = Principal of the loan – Amount in the sinking fund $= A - \left(\dfrac{A}{s_{\overline{n}|r}}\right)s_{\overline{k}|r}.$

Review Exercises 5.8

1. The Roberts borrow $15 000 to be repaid with monthly payments over 10 years at $j_{12} = 9\%$.
   a) Determine the monthly payment required.
   b) Determine the outstanding balance of the loan after three years (36 payments) and split the 37th payment into principal and interest under
   i) the amortization method;
   ii) the sum-of-digits method.

2. A loan of $20 000 is to be amortized by 20 quarterly payments over 5 years at $j_{12} = 7\frac{1}{2}\%$. Split the 9th payment into principal and interest.

3. A loan of $10 000 is repaid by 5 equal annual payments at $j_2 = 14\%$. What is the total amount of interest paid?

4. A company wants to borrow a large sum of money to be repaid over 10 years. The company can issue bonds paying interest at $j_2 = 8\frac{1}{2}\%$ redeemable at par in 10 years. A sinking fund earning $j_{12} = 7\frac{1}{2}\%$ can be used to accumulate the amount needed in 10 years to redeem the bonds. At what rate, j_{12}, would the semi-annual cost be the same if the debt were amortized over 10 years?

5. Interest at $j_2 = 10\%$ on a debt of $3000 must be paid as it falls due. A sinking fund accumulating at $j_4 = 4\%$ is established to enable the debtor to repay the loan at the end of four years. Calculate the semi-annual sinking-fund deposit and construct the last two lines of the sinking-fund schedule.

6. For a $60 000 mortgage at $j_2 = 10\%$ amortized over 25 years, determine
   a) the level monthly payment required;
   b) the outstanding balance just after the 48th payment;
   c) the principal portion of the 49th payment; and
   d) the total interest paid in the first 48 payments.

7. A $100 000 loan is being amortized over 12 years with monthly payments at $j_2 = 8\%$. After 5 years you want to renegotiate the loan. You discover that the outstanding balance will be calculated using the sum-of-digits method. You can refinance by borrowing the money needed to pay off the outstanding balance at $j_2 = 7\%$ and repay this new loan by accumulating the total principal and interest that will be due in 7 years in a sinking fund earning $j_{12} = 6\%$. Should you refinance?

8. As part of the purchase of a home on January 1, 2002, you negotiated a mortgage in the amount of $110 000. The amortization period for calculation of the level payments (principal and interest) was 25 years and the initial interest rate was 6% compounded semi-annually.
   a) What was the initial monthly payment?
   b) During 2002–2006 inclusive (and January 1, 2007) all monthly mortgage payments were made as they became due. What was the balance of the loan owing just after the payment made January 1, 2007?
   c) At January 1, 2007 (just after the payment then due) the loan was renegotiated at 8% compounded semi-annually (with the end date of the amortization period unchanged). What was the new monthly payment?
   d) All payments, as above, have been faithfully made. How much of the September 1, 2007, payment will be principal and how much represents interest?

9. A couple has a $150 000, 5-year mortgage at $j_2 = 9\%$ with a 20-year amortization period. After exactly 3 years (36 payments) they could renegotiate a new mortgage at $j_2 = 7\%$. If the bank charges an interest penalty of three times the monthly interest due on the outstanding balance at the time of renegotiation, what will their new monthly payment be?

10. Janet wants to borrow $10 000 to be repaid over 10 years. From one source, money can be borrowed at $j_1 = 10\%$ and amortized by annual payments. From a second source, money can be borrowed at $j_1 = 9\%$ if only the interest is paid annually and the principal repaid at the end of 10 years. If the second source is used, a sinking fund will be established by annual deposits that accumulate at $j_4 = 7\%$. How much can Janet save annually by using the better plan?

11. Given the following information, find the original value of the loan.

Payment #	Interest	Principal
1		10.00
2	389.00	
3		
4		13.31

12. A loan is paid off over 19 years with equal monthly payments. The total interest paid over the life of the loan is $5681.17. Using the

sum-of-digits method, determine the amount of interest paid in the 163rd payment.

13. The XYZ Mortgage Company lends you $100 000 at 9% compounded semi-annually. The loan is to be repaid by monthly payments at the end of each month for 20 years and the rate is guaranteed for 5 years.
    a) Determine the monthly payment.
    b) Determine the total amount of interest paid over the first 5 years.
    c) Split the first monthly payments into principal and interest portions
       i) based on the amortization method and
       ii) based on the sum-of-digits approximation method.
    d) If after 5 years of payments interest rates have increased to 11% compounded semi-annually, determine the new monthly payment at time of mortgage renegotiation exactly 5 years after the original loan agreement based on the amortization method.

14. A loan of $2000 is being repaid by equal monthly payments for an unspecified length of time. Interest on the loan is $j_{12} = 15\%$.
    a) If the amount of principal in the 4th payment is $40, what amount of the 18th payment will be principal?
    b) Determine the regular monthly payment.

15. On a loan at $j_{12} = 12\%$ with monthly payments, the amount of principal in the 8th payment is $62.
    a) Find the amount of principal in the 14th payment.
    b) If there are 48 equal payments in all, calculate the amount of the loan.

16. Given the following part of an amortization schedule, determine X.

Payment #	Interest	Principal	Balance
1	50 000	180 975	819 025
2			
3			X

17. A couple purchases a home worth $150 000 by paying $30 000 down and taking out a 5-year mortgage for $120 000 at $j_2 = 7.25\%$. The mortgage will be amortized over 25 years with equal monthly payments. How much of the principal is repaid during the first year?

18. You take out an $80 000 mortgage at $j_2 = 9\%$ with a 25-year amortization period.
    a) Determine the monthly payment required, rounded up to the next dime.
    b) Determine the reduced final payment.
    c) Determine the total interest paid during the 4th year.
    d) At the end of 4 years, you pay down an additional $2500 (no penalty).
       i) How much sooner will the mortgage be paid off?
       ii) What would be the difference in total payments over the life of the mortgage?

19. You take out a car loan of $10 000 at $j_{12} = 12\%$. It is to be paid off by monthly payments for 50 months. Payments are rounded up to the next dollar and the final payment is reduced accordingly. After 15 months you decide to pay off the loan. How much is outstanding after your 15th payment if the sum-of-digits method is used?

20. A company decides to borrow $100 000 at $j_1 = 12\%$ in order to finance a new equipment purchase. One of the conditions of the loan is that the company must make annual payments into a sinking fund (the sinking fund will be used to pay off the loan at the end of 20 years). The sinking-fund investment will earn $j_1 = 6\%$.
    a) What is the amount of each sinking-fund payment if they are all to be equal?
    b) What is the total annual cost of the loan?
    c) What overall annual effective compound interest rate is the company paying to borrow the $100 000 when account is taken of the sinking-fund requirement?

21. A $50 000 loan at $j_1 = 7\%$ is to be amortized over 15 years by annual payments.
    a) Determine the regular payment and the reduced final payment.
    b) The borrower accumulates the money for each annual payment by making 12 monthly deposits into a sinking fund earning $j_{12} = 6\%$. Determine the size of each deposit for the first 14 years.

c) If the sum-of-digits method is used to calculate the outstanding principal, what is the outstanding balance after 6 years?

22. A loan of $15 000 is to be paid off over 12 years by equal monthly payments at $j_{12} = 18\%$.

a) Compare the outstanding balance at the end of 2 years using the amortization and the sum-of-digits methods.

b) Should the borrower refinance the loan without penalty at the end of 2 years at $j_{12} = 16\%$ if the lender uses the sum-of-digits method?

CASE STUDY 1   *Comparison of amortization, sum-of-digits, and sinking-fund methods*

A $10 000 loan at $j_{12} = 12\%$ is to be paid off by monthly payments for 5 years. Using
  a) the amortization method,
  b) the sum-of-digits method,
  c) the sinking-fund method, with $j_{365} = 6\frac{1}{2}\%$ on the sinking fund, calculate and compare
    i) the monthly expense of the loan;
    ii) the outstanding balance of the loan at the end of 2 years; and
    iii) the interest and principal payment at the end of the 1st month and at the end of 2 years.

CASE STUDY 2   *Increasing extra annual payments*

A $100 000 mortgage is taken out at $j_2 = 8\%$, to be amortized over 25 years by monthly payments. Payments are rounded up to the *next dime* and the final payment is reduced accordingly.
  a) Calculate the regular monthly payment and the reduced final payment.
  b) Suppose extra payments are made at the end of every year to get the mortgage paid off sooner. Determine the time and amount of the last payment on the mortgage if these extra payments are:
  $300 at the end of year 1, $350 at the end of year 2, $400 at the end of year 3, $450 at the end of year 4, ... (increasing by $50 each year).

CASE STUDY 3   *Mortgage amortization*

A $90 000 mortgage at $j_2 = 9\%$ is amortized over 25 years by monthly payments.
  a) Determine the regular monthly payment and the smaller final payment.
  b) Determine the total interest (total cost of financing).
  c) Show the first three lines of the amortization schedule.
  d) Determine the outstanding balance after 2 years.
  e) Determine the total principal and the total interest paid in the first 2 years.
  f) Suppose you paid an extra $1000 after 2 years. How much interest would this save over the life of the mortgage?
  g) How much less interest would be paid if the mortgage could be amortized over 20 years rather than 25 years?
  h) In the 25-year mortgage, after 2 years, interest rates drop to $j_2 = 8.5\%$. There is a penalty of 3 months' interest on the outstanding balance for early repayment. Does it pay to refinance?

CASE STUDY 4   *Accelerated mortgage payments*

"Invest" that extra money back into your mortgage. (from Royal Trust)
Does it pay to accelerate mortgage payments in a low interest rate environment?

Interest rates have dropped so low, relative to what they were a few years ago, that you have to wonder if there's any merit to stepping up the mortgage payments on your home. After all, there's a temptation to invest — or spend — the difference between today's payments and the ones you made a few years ago. With the stock market so hot, you may be tempted to try to make a buck or two from stocks or mutual funds.

Forget it. Your humble, terribly dull mortgage is a far better investment.

The reason: our tax system will force you to pay tax on any earnings from your investment. If you pay down your mortgage, there's no tax on the interest you save.

"Whether the interest rate of your mortgage is 6 percent or 12 percent, the best investment is to pay off your mortgage," says Tom Alton, president of Bank of Montreal Mortgage Corp.

Jack Quinn, president of CIBC Mortgage Corp., agrees. "On an after-tax basis, it's pretty hard to find something that's as good as a mortgage." Someone in a 50 percent tax bracket would have to earn at least 16 percent just to net 8 percent after tax on an investment.

Most lenders offer a number of strategies to save you money.

- Provided you can afford it, consider a shorter amortization period when your mortgage comes up for renewal. For instance, if you had an 11 percent mortgage and renewed at 8 percent, continue to pay at the old rate, instead of the reduced new one. It will shorten the amortization because the difference will be applied to the principal.

  Assuming you had a 25-year $100 000 mortgage at 11 percent, your monthly payment would be $962.50. If the rate drops to 8 percent, the payment would be $763.20, for a difference of $199.30 a month.

  What difference is another couple of hundred bucks going to make? Plenty. If you continue to make the old monthly payments, you can reduce the amortization to 14.6 years, according to Mr. Alton.

- Another strategy is to take advantage of any opportunity to make larger monthly payments. For instance, under Bank of Montreal's "10 plus 10" plan, you can increase your monthly payments by up to 10 percent. Royal Trust goes a bit further and allows borrowers to "double up" their monthly mortgage payments — that is, pay up to an additional 100 percent of the payment any or every month of the year (see accompanying chart).

- Most institutions let you make an annual lump-sum payment of up to 10 percent of the original principal. TD Canada Trust has a higher maximum: 15 percent.

- Finally, consider an accelerated weekly mortgage. Take your monthly payment, divide it by four, and pay that amount on a weekly basis. That means that you will be painlessly paying the equivalent of 13 months in the space of a year. "If you do that you'll make larger payments, but knock about seven years of payments off a 25-year mortgage," Mr. Alton says.

HOW TO SAVE ON MORTGAGES
$100 000 mortgage, 8% interest rate
By shortening the term:

Amortization	Payment	Interest paid over life of mortgage	Interest saved versus 25-year amortization
25 years	$763	$129 098.54	—
20 years	$828	$98 927.31	$30 171.23
15 years	$948	$70 692.37	$58 406.17
10 years	$1206	$44 794.25	$84 304.29

By doubling-up payments	Interest paid over life of mortgage	Interest saved versus no double-up payments	Time paid off sooner
No double-up payments	$129 098.54	—	
1 double-up payment a year (month 4)	$98 863.53	$30 285.06	4 years and 11 months
2 double-up payments a year (months 4, 10)	$81 925.83	$47 172.71	7 years and 11 months
4 double-up payments a year (months 3, 6, 9, 12)	$61 486.75	$67 611.69	11 years and 9 months

Data: Royal Trust

Required:
a) Verify the figures in the first 2 lines of the first table (i.e., by shortening the term).
b) Verify the figures in the second and fourth line of the second table (i.e., by doubling up payments).

CHAPTER 6

Bonds

Learning Objectives

One of the primary ways for governments and publicly listed corporations to raise capital is to issue bonds. Bonds are a method used to borrow money from a large number of investors to help raise funds to finance long-term debt. From the investor's point of view, bonds provide steady periodic interest payments along with returning the amount borrowed at some point in the future.

This chapter begins with an introduction to the terminology used when dealing with bonds in section 6.1. Section 6.2 introduces one of the main goals of this chapter which is to determine the price to be paid for a bond. This section presents two formulas that can be used to determine the price along with showing how the price, or value, of a bond changes as the desired rate of return (called the yield rate) goes up or down.

Bonds can be purchased for more or for less than what the investor will receive when the bond matures. That is, bonds can be purchased at a premium or a discount. Section 6.3 analyzes this in more detail while providing some context as to the tax consequences of premiums and discounts.

Some corporations offer bonds which allow them to pay the maturity value of the bond before the stated maturity date. These are referred to as callable bonds and they are discussed in section 6.4. The main goal from the investor's point of view is to determine the correct price to pay for these types of bonds to ensure the investor earns his/her desired rate of return.

There is an active bond market in Canada and bonds can be bought and sold at any time during the year. As a result, it is important to know how to determine the price or value of a bond at any time. Section 6.5 shows how to do this.

Also of importance to the bond investor is the ability to determine the rate of return, or yield rate, when considering buying a bond for a certain price. Section 6.6 illustrates two methods that can be used to determine the yield rate when the price of a bond is given, along with showing how to use your calculator or a computer spreadsheet to obtain the rate. This section also discusses the yield curve and shows how an investor can earn a higher rate of return by "riding the yield curve."

The chapter concludes with section 6.7 where other types of bonds that are available in the investment market are introduced.

| Section 6.1 | ## Introduction and Terminology

When a corporation, municipality, or government needs a large sum of money for a long period of time, they issue **bonds**, sometimes called debentures, which are sold to a number of investors.

A bond is a written contract between the issuer (borrower) and the investor (lender) that specifies:

- The **face value**, or the **denomination**, of the bond, which is stated on the front of the bond. This is usually a multiple of 100 such as $100, $500, $1000, $5000, or $10 000.
- The **redemption date**, or **maturity date**; that is, the date on which the loan will be repaid.
- The **bond rate**, or **coupon rate**; that is, the rate at which the bond pays interest on its face value at equal time intervals until the maturity date. In most cases this rate is compounded semi-annually.

The amount of money that will be paid on the redemption date is called the **redemption value**. In most cases it is the same as the face value, and in such cases we say the bond is **redeemed at par**. Bonds can be redeemed at values other than par. On rare occasions, bonds are redeemable at a premium (redemption value > face value). In these situations the redemption value is often stated in units of 100. For example, a $500 bond redeemable at 105 would have a redemption value that is 105% of the face value, or 1.05($500) = $525. A $2000 bond redeemable at 101.5 would have a redemption value that is 101.5% of the face value, or 1.015($2000) = $2030.

Some bonds are **callable**; they contain a clause that allows the issuer to pay off the loan at a date earlier than the redemption date. Most callable bonds are called at a premium and the redemption value of a bond called before maturity is a previously specified percentage of the face value.

A distinction should be made between savings bonds and marketable bonds. Savings bonds (such as the popular Canada Savings Bonds — discussed in section 6.7) can be cashed in at any time before the redemption date and you will receive the full face value plus accrued interest. Marketable bonds (such as corporate bonds or Government of Canada bonds) do not allow the bond owner to cash the bond in before maturity. If you no longer wish to own the bond, you must sell the bond on the open "bond market," where the price you receive will be influenced by current interest rates. It is marketable bonds that we will be dealing with in this chapter.

Bonds (as a contract) may be transferred from one investor to another. Bonds may be bought or sold on the bond market at any time. The buyer of the bond, as an investor, wants to realize a certain return on his investment, specified by the **investment** or **yield rate**. This desired rate of return will vary with the financial climate and will affect the price at which bonds are traded.

As an illustration, consider a $1000 bond redeemable at par in 5 years, paying interest at bond rate or coupon rate $j_2 = 8\%$. If the buyer paid $1000 for the bond, then he receives $40 every half-year in interest and we say his yield rate is

$j_2 = 8\%$, that is, the same as the bond rate (coupon rate). If the buyer paid less than the face value, his yield rate will be higher than the bond rate $j_2 = 8\%$ because he receives \$40 every half-year in interest and on the redemption date he receives the face value of \$1000, i.e., more than he invested. Similarly, if the buyer paid more than the face value, his yield rate will be lower than the bond rate. In the latter case, his interest payments at $j_2 = 8\%$ will be partially offset by the loss incurred when the bond is redeemed.

In this chapter we shall use the following notation:

F = the face value or par value of the bond.
C = the redemption value of the bond.
r = the bond rate per interest period (coupon rate).
i = the yield rate per interest period (assume $i > 0$).
n = the number of interest periods until the redemption date.
P = the purchase price of the bond to yield rate i.
Fr = the bond interest payment or coupon.

The two fundamental problems relating to bonds, which will be discussed in this chapter, are

1. to determine the purchase price P of a bond to yield a given investment (yield) rate i to maturity;

2. to determine the investment rate i that a bond will yield when bought for a given price P.

OBSERVATION:

In this chapter, the yield rate means the yield rate to maturity unless specified otherwise.

Section 6.2

Purchase Price to Yield a Given Investment Rate to Maturity

We want to determine the purchase price of a bond on a bond interest date n interest periods before maturity so that it earns interest at a specified yield rate i. We shall assume that the bond rate and the yield rate have the same conversion period.

A bond is a financial asset. When purchasing any financial asset, you pay a lump sum of money at the time of purchase and in return you receive future payments, or cash flows, from the asset. As we have seen before, to determine the price paid to buy an asset, you discount each future cash flow to the date of sale at some rate of interest. That is, the price of any financial asset is equal to the discounted value of future payments.

For a bond, the buyer will receive two types of payments or cash flows:

1. a bond interest payment, or coupon Fr, at the end of each interest period;

2. the redemption value C on the redemption date.

The buyer of a bond who wishes to realize a yield rate i on the investment should pay a price equal to the discounted value of the above payments at rate i. Thus,

P = discounted value of coupons + discounted value of redemption value

$$P = Fra_{\overline{n}|i} + C(1 + i)^{-n} \tag{15}$$

It is common practice to express the price of a bond as a price per $100 face value, even when the face value is not $100.

EXAMPLE 1   A $1000 bond that pays interest at $j_2 = 8\%$ is redeemable at par at the end of 5 years. Determine the purchase price to yield an investor
a) 10% compounded semi-annually;
b) 6% compounded semi-annually.

Solution   We have $F = C = 1000$, $r = 0.08/2 = 0.04$, $Fr = 40$, $n = 5$ years $\times 2 = 10$.

a) The purchase price P to yield $j_2 = 10\%$ is the discounted value of the above payments at $i = 0.05$.

$$P = 40a_{\overline{10}|0.05} + 1000(1.05)^{-10} \doteq \$308.87 + \$613.91 = \$922.78$$

The purchase price of $922.78 will yield a buyer a return of $j_2 = 10\%$ on the investment. Since the buyer is buying the bond for less than the redemption value, that is $P < C$, we say the bond is purchased at a **discount**.

b) The purchase price P to yield $j_2 = 6\%$ is

$$P = 40a_{\overline{10}|0.03} + 1000(1.03)^{-10} \doteq \$341.21 + \$744.09 = \$1085.30$$

The purchase price of $1085.30 will yield a buyer a return of $j_2 = 6\%$ on the investment. Since the buyer is buying the bond for more than the redemption value, that is $P > C$, we say the bond is purchased at a **premium**.

Using a Financial Calculator to Determine the Price

Using the Texas Instruments BA-35 calculator,

$PMT = $ coupon, Fr
$FV = $ redemption value, C
$N = $ time to redemption (in bond interest periods)
$I/Y = $ yield rate per bond interest period (typed as a number, not a decimal)
$PV = $ price of bond

In Example 1a), the steps are as follows (make sure your calculator has been set to the FIN mode):

40 $\boxed{PMT}$ 1000 $\boxed{FV}$ 10 $\boxed{N}$ 5 $\boxed{I/Y}$ $\boxed{CPT}$ $\boxed{PV}$
-922.78265

Notice how the final price is negative. Taking the absolute value gives the final price of the bond, $922.78.

To obtain the price in Example 1b), all the steps and values are the same except that the yield rate is 3%, which means you key in the value 3 for I/Y.

Example 2   A $5000 bond maturing at 105 on September 1, 2028, has semi-annual coupons at 7%. Determine the purchase price on March 1, 2007, to guarantee a yield of $j_2 = 6.8\%$.

Solution   We have $F = 5000$, $r = 0.07/2 = 0.035$, $Fr = 5000 \times 0.035 = 175$, $C = 1.05(5000)$ $= 5250$ and $i = 0.068/2 = 0.034$. To determine n, we know from March 1, 2007 to March 1, 2028 is 21 years, or 42 interest periods. Since the redemption date is one period later, September 1, 2028, $n = 43$.

The purchaser receives 43 coupons plus the maturity value. The purchase price P on March 1, 2007, to guarantee a yield of $j_2 = 6.8\%$ is

$$P = 175.00a_{\overline{43}|0.034} + 5250(1.034)^{-43}$$
$$\doteq \$3924.76 + \$1246.74 = \$5171.50$$

or $\frac{\$5171.50}{50} = \$103.43$ per $100 unit.

In this example, the buyer is content with a yield rate smaller than the coupon rate on the bond and yet, since the price is less than the redemption value, the bond has been purchased at a discount. This apparent contradiction can be explained by remembering that while the bond is redeemed for $5250, which affects the price of the bond, the coupons are determined by taking $3\frac{1}{2}\%$

of \$5000, not $3\frac{1}{2}\%$ of \$5250. In fact, if we determine the bond interest rate per unit of redemption, we get $\frac{175}{5250} = 3.3\%$. It is because 3.3% is less than the desired yield rate of 3.4% each half-year that results in the purchase of the bond at a discount.

We will study the concepts of premium and discount in more detail in section 6.3.

The above two examples illustrate that in the bond investment market the price of a bond depends on the bond rate, the yield rate acceptable to investors, the time to maturity, and the redemption value.

> **OBSERVATION:**
>
> Note that unless it is specified otherwise, we assume that bonds are redeemed at par.

An Alternative Purchase-Price Formula

We shall develop an alternative formula for the purchase price of a bond sold on a bond interest date, which is somewhat simpler than formula **(15)**. Using the identity $a_{\overline{n}|i} = \frac{1 - (1+i)^{-n}}{i}$ from chapter 3, we can get the factor $(1 + i)^{-n}$ as $(1+i)^{-n} = 1 - ia_{\overline{n}|i}$ and eliminate it in formula **(15)**. Thus,

$$P = Fra_{\overline{n}|i} + C(1+i)^{-n} = Fra_{\overline{n}|i} + C(1 - ia_{\overline{n}|i})$$

or

$$\boxed{P = C + (Fr - Ci)a_{\overline{n}|i}} \tag{16}$$

Formula **(16)** is often more efficient than formula **(15)** since it requires only one calculation, $a_{\overline{n}|i}$, whereas formula **(15)** requires two: $a_{\overline{n}|i}$ and $(1 + i)^{-n}$. It also tells us immediately whether the bond is purchased at a premium or a discount and the size of the premium or discount.

EXAMPLE 3   A corporation decides to issue 15-year bonds in the amount of \$10 000 000. Under the contract, interest payments will be made at the rate $j_2 = 10\%$. The bonds are priced to yield $j_2 = 8\%$ to maturity. What is the issue price of the bond? What is the price of a \$1000 bond to yield $j_2 = 8\%$?

Solution   We have $F = C = 10\ 000\ 000$, $r = 0.10/2 = 0.05$, $Fr = 500\ 000$, $n = 30$, $i = 0.08/2 = 0.04$, $Ci = 400\ 000$.

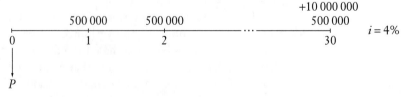

The alternative purchase-price formula will give us

$$P = 10\ 000\ 000 + (500\ 000 - 400\ 000)a_{\overline{30}|0.04} \doteq \$11\ 729\ 203$$

The issue price of the bonds to the public is $11 729 302. The bonds will provide the investor with a yield $j_2 = 8\%$ if held to maturity. An issue of $10 000 000 is just like issuing 10 000 bonds of $1000 each. Thus, the price of a $1000 bond is

$$\frac{\$11\,729\,203}{10\,000} = \$1172.92$$

In all examples so far we have considered the case where the bond interest payments, Fr, form an ordinary simple annuity, that is, where the bond interest period coincides with the period the yield rate is compounded. In cases when these periods are different, the bond interest payments form a general annuity and the interest yield rate is recalculated to coincide with the bond coupon period. The following example will illustrate the procedure.

EXAMPLE 4   Determine the issue price of the bonds in Example 3 to yield a) 8% per annum compounded monthly; b) 8% per annum compounded annually.

Solution a   Calculate rate i per half-year such that

$$(1+i)^2 = (1 + \tfrac{0.08}{12})^{12}$$
$$1+i = (1 + \tfrac{0.08}{12})^6$$
$$i = (1 + \tfrac{0.08}{12})^6 - 1$$
$$i = 0.040672622$$

Now
$$P = 10\,000\,000 + (500\,000 - 406\,726.22)a_{\overline{30}|i} \doteq \$11\,599\,802$$

The issue price of the bonds to the public is $11 599 802. The purchase price of a $1000 bond is then $1159.98.

Solution b   Calculate rate i per half-year such that

$$(1+i)^2 = 1.08$$
$$(1+i) = (1.08)^{1/2}$$
$$i = (1.08)^{1/2} - 1$$
$$i = 0.039230485$$

Now
$$P = 10\,000\,000 + (500\,000 - 392\,304.85)a_{\overline{30}|i} \doteq \$11\,879\,792$$

The issue price of the bonds to the public is $11 879 792. The purchase price of a $1000 bond is then $1187.98.

EXAMPLE 5   A 10-year $2000 bond pays semi-annual coupons at $j_2 = 6\%$ and is purchased to yield $j_2 = 6\%$. What is the purchase price if the bond is redeemable at a) par; b) 101.5?

Solution   We have $F = 2000$, $r = 0.03$, $Fr = 60$, $n = 20$. This is a situation where the bond rate is the same as the yield rate, $i = 0.03$.

Solution a   We have $C = 2000$ and $Ci = 60$. From formula **(16)**, we obtain

$$P = 2000 + (60 - 60)a_{\overline{20}|0.03} = 2000$$

Note that when the yield rate is equal to the bond rate and the bond is redeemable at par, the price is equal to the redemption value, $P = C$.

Solution b   We have $C = 2000(1.015) = 2030$ and $Ci = 60.90$. From formula **(16)**, we obtain

$$P = 2030 + (60 - 60.90)a_{\overline{20}|0.03} \doteq 2016.61$$

When the yield rate is equal to the bond rate, but $F \neq C$, then the price is not equal to the redemption value, that is $P \neq C$. In this case, since $P < C$, the bond is said to be purchased at a discount.

EXAMPLE 6   To see the impact the yield rate has on the purchase price of a bond, take the bond given in Example 5a) and calculate the price for nominal yield rates compounded semi-annually starting at 2% and increasing by 1% to 12%. Graph the results.

Solution   The prices are given in the table below.

Yield Rate, j_2	Price
2%	$2721.82
3%	$2515.06
4%	$2327.03
5%	$2155.89
6%	$2000.00
7%	$1857.88
8%	$1728.19
9%	$1609.76
10%	$1501.51
11%	$1402.48
12%	$1311.80

OBSERVATION:

Bond prices move in the opposite direction to yield rates. That is, when yield rates rise, bond values (prices) go down. This means that in a rising interest rate environment, bond values fall.

Exercise 6.2

Part A

Problems 1 to 8 use the information in the table below. Using either formula (**15**) or formula (**16**), determine the purchase price of the bond.

No.	Face Value	Redemption	Bond Interest Rate	Years to Redemption	Yield Rate
1.	$ 500	at par	$j_2 =$ 9%	20	$j_2 =$ 8%
2.	$ 1 000	at par	$j_2 =$ 9%	15	$j_2 =$ 10%
3.	$ 2 000	at par	$j_2 = 6\frac{1}{2}$%	15	$j_4 =$ 7%
4.	$ 5 000	at par	$j_2 =$ 12%	20	$j_2 =$ 10%
5.	$ 1 000	at 110	$j_2 =$ 9%	18	$j_2 =$ 12%
6.	$ 2 000	at 105	$j_2 =$ 7%	20	$j_2 =$ 5%
7.	$10 000	at 102.5	$j_2 = 10\frac{1}{2}$%	15	$j_{12} =$ 7%
8.	$ 5 000	at 103	$j_2 =$ 6%	17	$j_4 =$ 4%

9. The XYZ Corporation needs to raise some funds to pay for new equipment. They issue $1 000 000 worth of 20-year bonds with semi-annual coupons at $j_2 = 6$%. These bonds are redeemable at 105. At the time of issue, interest rates in the market place are $j_{12} = 5\frac{1}{2}$%. How much money did they raise?

10. Mr. Simpson buys a $1000 bond paying bond interest at $j_2 = 6\frac{1}{2}$% and redeemable at par in 20 years. Mr. Simpson's desired yield rate is $j_4 = 7$%. How much did he pay for the bond? After exactly five years he sells the bond. Interest rates have dropped and the bond is sold to yield a buyer $j_1 = 5$%. Determine the sale price.

11. A corporation issues $600 000 worth of 12-year bonds with semi-annual coupons at $j_2 = 10$%. The bonds are priced to yield $j_2 = 9$%. Determine the issue price per $100 unit.

12. A $1000 bond paying coupons at $j_2 = 6$% is redeemable at par in 20 years. Determine the price to yield an investor a) $j_2 = 7$%; b) $j_2 = 6$%; c) $j_2 = 5$%.

Part B

1. Show that if a bond is redeemable at par and $i = r$, then $P = C$.

2. Prove the following formula for a *par value* bond

$$P = F(1+i)^{-n} + \frac{r}{i}[F - F(1+i)^{-n}]$$

This purchase-price formula is known as Makeham's formula and requires the use of only $(1 + i)^{-n}$ factors.

3. An $X bond quoted as redeemable at 105 in 10 years is purchased to yield $j_2 = 10$%. If this same bond was redeemable at par, the actual purchase price would be $113.07 less. Determine the value of X.

4. The XYZ Corporation issues a special 20-year bond issue that has no coupons. Rather, interest will accumulate on the bond at rate $j_2 = 11$% for the life of the bond. At the time of maturity, the total value of the loan will be paid off, including all accumulated interest. Determine the price of a $1000 bond of this issue to yield $j_2 = 10$%. This type of bond is sometimes referred to as an **accumulation bond**.

5. A $1000 bond bearing coupons at $j_2 = 6\frac{1}{2}$% and redeemable at par is bought to yield $j_2 = 6$%. If the present value of the redemption value at this yield is $412, what is the purchase price? (Do not calculate n.)

6. Two $1000 bonds redeemable at par at the end of n years are bought to yield $j_2 = 10\%$. One bond costs $1153.72 and has semi-annual coupons at $j_2 = 12\%$. The other bond has semi-annual coupons at $j_2 = 8\%$. Determine the price of the second bond.

7. A $1000 bond with semi-annual coupons at $j_2 = 6\%$ and redeemable at the end of n years at $1050 sells at $980 to yield $j_2 = 7\frac{1}{2}\%$. Determine the price of a $1000 bond with semi-annual coupons at $j_2 = 5\%$ redeemable at the end of $2n$ years at $1040 to yield $j_2 = 7\frac{1}{2}\%$. (Do not calculate n.)

8. A bond with a par value of $100\,000 has coupons at the rate $j_2 = 6\frac{1}{2}\%$. It will be redeemed at par when it matures a certain number of years hence. It is purchased for a price of $96\,446.90. At this price, the purchaser who holds the bond to maturity will realize a yield rate $j_2 = 7\%$. Determine the number of years to maturity.

9. A $1000 bond with annual coupons at $8\frac{1}{2}\%$ and maturing in 20 years at par is purchased to yield an annual effective rate of interest of 9% if held to maturity. The book value of the bond at any time is the discounted value of all remaining payments, using the 9% rate. Ten years later, just after a coupon payment, the bond is sold to yield the new purchaser a 10% annual effective rate of interest if held to maturity. Calculate the excess of the book value over the second sale price.

10. A corporation has an issue of bonds with annual coupons at $j_1 = 5\%$ maturing in five years at par that are quoted at a price that yields $j_1 = 6\%$.
a) What is the price of a $1000 bond?
It is proposed to replace this issue of bonds with an issue of bonds with annual coupons at $j_1 = 5\frac{1}{2}\%$.
b) How long must the new issue run so that the bond holders will still yield $j_1 = 6\%$? Express your answer to the nearest year.

11. A $1000 bond bearing semi-annual coupons at $j_2 = 10\%$ is redeemable at par. What is the minimum number of whole years that the bond should run so that a person paying $1100 for it would earn at least $j_2 = 8\%$?

12. If the coupon rate on a bond is $1\frac{1}{2}$ times the yield rate when it sells for a premium of $10 per $100, determine the price per $100 for a bond with the same number of coupons to run and the same yield with coupons equal to $\frac{3}{4}$ of the yield rate.

Section 6.3 # Premium and Discount

A bond is just a loan agreement between the bond issuer (the borrower) and the investor (the lender). The bond issuer sets a bond interest rate (the coupon rate) and the redemption value and date, and the investor determines the amount of the loan (the purchase price of the bond).

Bond Purchased at a Premium

We have seen that if $P > C$ (the purchase price of a bond exceeds its redemption value), the bond is said to have been purchased **at a premium**. In fact, from the alternative purchase price formula, the size of the premium must be

$$\boxed{\text{Premium} = P - C = (Fr - Ci)a_{\overline{n}|i}}$$

That is, a premium occurs when $Fr > Ci$. In other words, each coupon Fr exceeds the interest desired by the investor Ci, which allows the price P to exceed the redemption value C. For par value bonds (i.e., $C = F$) the bond is purchased at a premium when $r > i$.

When the bond is purchased at a premium, then only C of the original principal is returned on the redemption date. There will be a loss, equal to the premium, at the redemption date.

This loss can be applied against an investor's income at the time of redemption which would result in less tax being owed at that time. However, it would be more efficient, from a tax point of view, if an investor could take the tax savings which occurs at redemption and allocate it over each bond interest period. Bond interest payments are considered taxable income to the investor, so this would lead to paying less tax each period (paying tax on approximately Ci instead of Fr), instead of getting the tax break at redemption.

The government allows bond investors to do this if they so choose. In these cases the premium (or loss at redemption), $P - C$, is amortized over the term of the bond. That is, small "pieces" of the premium are allocated to each bond coupon.

Each coupon payment, in addition to paying interest on the investment (at a yield rate), provides a partial return of the principal P. These payments of principal will continually reduce the value of the bond from the price on the purchase date to the redemption value on the redemption date. These adjusted values of the bond are called the **book values** of the bond and are used by many investors in reporting the asset values of bonds for financial statements. The process of gradually decreasing the value of the bond from the purchase price to the redemption value is called **amortization of a premium** or **writing down a bond**. A **bond amortization schedule** is a table that shows the division of each interest payment into the interest paid on the book value (at a yield rate) and the decrease in the book value of the bond (or the book value adjustment) along with the book value after each bond interest payment is paid.

EXAMPLE 1 A $1000 bond, redeemable at par on December 1, 2007, pays interest at $j_2 = 6\frac{1}{2}\%$. The bond is bought on June 1, 2005, to yield $j_2 = 5\frac{1}{2}\%$. Determine the purchase price and construct the bond schedule.

Solution The purchase price P on June 1, 2005 can be determined using the alternative purchase-price formula **(16)**.

$$P = 1000 + (32.50 - 27.50)a_{\overline{5}|0.0275} \doteq \$1000 + \$23.06 = \$1023.06$$

The premium is $23.06 and this is the amount of the loss that occurs on December 1, 2007. This amount could be applied against the investor's income for 2007 and would result in less tax being owed. (We will ignore the fact that the tax savings would be very small in this case due to this being a relatively small bond.) Instead, we will amortize this premium and allocate small "pieces" of it to each of the 5 coupons.

To construct the amortization schedule for this bond, we shall calculate how much of each coupon is used as return on the investment at the desired yield rate and how much is used to adjust the book value or the principal (i.e., amortize the premium).

At the end of the first half-year, on December 1, 2005, the investor's yield should be $1023.06 × 0.0275 = $28.13. Since he actually receives $32.50, the difference of $4.37 can be regarded as part of the original principal being returned and is used to adjust (reduce) the principal, or amortize the premium. The adjusted value, or book value, after the coupon payment is $1023.06 − $4.37 = $1018.69. This book value can be computed independently by the alternative purchase-price formula using $F = C = 1000$, $r = 3\frac{1}{4}\%$, $i = 2\frac{3}{4}\%$, and $n = 4$. The above procedure is continued until the bond matures.

The following is a complete bond schedule with $F = C = 1000$, $r = 0.0325$, $i = 0.0275$, and $n = 5$.

Schedule for a Bond Purchased at a Premium

Date (1)	Time t (2)	Coupon $F \cdot r$ (3)	Interest on Book Value $I_t = B_{t-1} \cdot i$ $(4) = (6)_{t-1} \cdot i$	Book Value Adjustment $(5) = (3) - (4)$	Book Value B_t $(6) = B_{t-1} - (5)$
June 1, 2005	0	—	—	—	1023.06
Dec. 1, 2005	1	32.50	28.13	4.37	1018.69
June 1, 2006	2	32.50	28.01	4.49	1014.20
Dec. 1, 2006	3	32.50	27.89	4.61	1009.59
June 1, 2007	4	32.50	27.76	4.74	1004.85
Dec. 1, 2007	5	32.50	27.63	4.87	999.98*
Totals		162.50	139.42*	23.08*	

* The 2¢ error is from the accumulation of round-off.

OBSERVATIONS:

1. All the book values can be reproduced using either of the purchase price formulas with $n =$ term remaining.

2. The sum of the book value adjustments is equal to the original amount of the premium.

3. The book value is gradually adjusted from the original purchase price down to the redemption value.

4. Successive book value adjustments are in the ratio $(1 + i)$,
   i.e., $\frac{4.49}{4.37} \doteq \frac{4.61}{4.49} \doteq \frac{4.74}{4.61} \doteq \frac{4.87}{4.74} \doteq 1.0275$.

5. The investor would end up claiming the values "Interest on Book Value" as interest income over the term of the bond. That is, he/she would pay income tax on $139.42 in total as opposed to paying tax on the actual amount received, $162.50. However, he/she would not be allowed to claim the premium of $23.06 against his/her income at the time of redemption.

Bond Purchased at a Discount

Similarly, if $P < C$ (the purchase price is less than the redemption value) the bond is said to have been purchased **at a discount**. From the alternative purchase-price formula, the size of the discount is

$$\text{Discount} = C - P = (Ci - Fr)a_{\overline{n}|i}$$

That is, a discount occurs when $Fr < Ci$. In other words, each coupon, Fr, is less than the interest desired by the investor Ci. For a par value bond (i.e., $C = F$) the bond is purchased at a discount when $i > r$.

When the bond is purchased at a discount, the investor's return is more than just the bond interest payment. There will be a gain, equal to the discount, at the redemption date. This gain must be reported as income in the year it occurs, which would result in increased income taxes being owed. But, similar to when a bond is purchased at a premium, it would be more efficient, from a tax point of view, if an investor could take the gain which occurs at redemption and allocate part of it over each bond interest period. This would lead to paying more tax each period (paying tax on approximately Ci instead of Fr), but not having a higher tax bill at redemption.

Again, the government allows bond investors to do this if they so choose. In these cases the discount (or gain at redemption), $P - C$, is accumulated over the term of the bond. That is, small "pieces" of the discount are allocated to each bond coupon.

The process of gradually increasing the value of the bond from the purchase price up to the redemption value is called **accumulation of a discount** or **writing up a bond**. A **bond accumulation schedule** is a table that shows the division of the investor's interest (at a yield rate) into the bond interest payment and the increase in the book value of the bond (or the book value adjustment) along with the book value after each bond interest payment is paid.

EXAMPLE 2 A $1000 bond, redeemable at par on December 1, 2008, pays interest at $j_2 = 9\%$. The bond is bought on June 1, 2006, to yield $j_2 = 10\%$. Determine the price and construct a bond schedule.

Solution The purchase price P on June 1, 2006, can be determined by the alternative purchase-price formula (**16**):

$$P = 1000 + (45 - 50)a_{\overline{5}|0.05} \doteq 1000 - 21.65 = \$978.35$$

The discount is $21.65 and this is the amount of the gain that occurs on December 1, 2008. This amount would be added to the investor's income for 2008, which would result in more tax being owed. Instead, we will accumulate this discount and allocate small "pieces" of it to each of the 5 coupons, much like we did in Example 1.

To construct the accumulation schedule for this bond, we shall calculate the investor's interest at the end of each half-year and gradually increase the book value of the bond by the difference between investor's interest and the bond interest payment.

At the end of the first half-year, on December 1, 2006, the investor's interest should be $978.35 × 0.05 = $48.92. Since the bond interest payment is only $45, we increase the book value of the bond by $48.92 – $45.00 = $3.92. We say $3.92 is used for accumulation of a discount or –$3.92 is the principal adjustment (book value adjustment). You should be able to see that a bond accumulation schedule works exactly the same as a bond amortization schedule, except that the book value adjustment column consists of negative values.

The adjusted value, or book value, after the bond interest payment on December 1, 2006, is $978.35 – (–$3.92) = $978.35 + $3.92 = $982.27. This book value can be computed independently by the alternative purchase-price formula using $F = C = 1000$, $r = 4\frac{1}{2}\%$, $i = 5\%$, and $n = 4$. The above procedure is continued until the bond matures.

The following is a complete bond schedule with $F = C = 1000$, $r = 0.045$, $i = 0.05$, and $n = 5$.

Schedule for a Bond Purchased at a Discount

Date (1)	Time t (2)	Coupon $F \cdot r$ (3)	Interest on Book Value $I_t = B_{t-1} \cdot i$ (4) = (6)$_{t-1} \cdot i$	Book Value Adjustment (5) = (3) − (4)	Book Value B_t (6) = B_{t-1} − (5)
June 1, 2006	0	—	—	—	978.35
Dec. 1, 2006	1	45.00	48.92	−3.92	982.27
June 1, 2007	2	45.00	49.11	−4.11	986.38
Dec. 1, 2007	3	45.00	49.32	−4.32	990.70
June 1, 2008	4	45.00	49.54	−4.54	995.24
Dec. 1, 2008	5	45.00	49.76	−4.76	1000.00
Totals		225.00	246.65	−21.65	

The five observations that followed Example 1 hold here as well, keeping in mind that the investor would end up paying tax on $246.65 over the term of the bond, as opposed to paying tax on the actual total amount of coupons received, $225.00. However, the investor would not have to claim the discount of $21.65 as interest income at the time of redemption.

The payments made during the term of a bond can be regarded as loan payments made by the borrower (bond issuer) to the lender (the bondholder) to repay a loan amount equal to the purchase price of the bond. The bond purchase price is calculated as the discounted value of those payments (coupons plus redemption value) at a certain yield rate (the interest rate on the loan). Thus the bond transaction can be regarded as the amortization of a loan and an amortization schedule for the bond can be constructed like the general loan amortization schedule in section 5.1.

Also, the first four observations with respect to bond schedules shown in Examples 1 and 2 follow from the general loan amortization schedule and may be summarized as follows:

OBSERVATIONS:

1. The outstanding principal (the book value of the bond) can be computed as the discounted value of the remaining payments (the purchase price of the bond) at any payment date (coupon date).

2. The sum of the principal repaid (the book value adjustments) is equal to the amount of the loan (the redemption value plus the amount of the premium or the discount).

3. The outstanding principal of the loan is gradually adjusted from the original amount to zero balance after the last payment (last coupon plus redemption value) is paid.

4. Successive principal repayments (book value adjustments) are in the ratio $1 + i$. (Last principal repaid must be reduced by redemption value to satisfy the condition that the last ratio is equal to $1 + i$.)

EXAMPLE 3   Construct the amortization schedule for the loan of a) Example 1; b) Example 2.

Solution a

Date	Payment	Interest Due (at $i = 0.0275$)	Principal Repaid	Outstanding Principal
June 1, 2005	—	—	—	1023.06
Dec. 1, 2005	32.50	28.13	4.37	1018.69
June 1, 2006	32.50	28.01	4.49	1014.20
Dec. 1, 2006	32.50	27.89	4.61	1009.59
June 1, 2007	32.50	27.76	4.74	1004.85
Dec. 1, 2007	1032.50	27.63	1004.87	−0.02*
Totals	1162.50	139.42	1023.08*	

*Each calculation is rounded to the nearest 1¢ and then carried forward at its rounded-off value. This results in an accumulated 2¢ error in the final balance.

Solution b

Date	Payment	Interest Due (at $i = 0.05$)	Principal Repaid	Outstanding Principal
June 1, 2006	—	—	—	978.35
Dec. 1, 2006	45.00	48.92	−3.92	982.27
June 1, 2007	45.00	49.11	−4.11	986.38
Dec. 1, 2007	45.00	49.32	−4.32	990.70
June 1, 2008	45.00	49.54	−4.54	995.24
Dec. 1, 2008	1045.00	49.76	995.24	0
Totals	1225.00	246.65	978.35	

EXAMPLE 4   A $2000 bond is redeemable at 102 in 6 years. The absolute value of the sum of the write-downs (book value adjustment column) is $53.42. What is the price of the bond?

Solution   We have $F = 2000$, $C = 1.02(2000) = 2040$. We are also given the absolute value of the sum of the write-downs is 53.42.

When a bond is being "written down," the book value starts at P and gets adjusted down to C. This means $P > C$, or in other words the bond is purchased at a premium. Thus,

$$P = C + \text{premium}$$
$$= \$2040 + \$53.42$$
$$= \$2093.42$$

EXAMPLE 5   A 3-year bond pays semi-annual coupons and is bought to yield $j_2 = 15\%$. The interest portion of the first coupon is $57.40. The absolute value of the write-up in the book value in the last period (6th coupon) is $46.51. What is the coupon, Fr, paid each period?

Solution   We are given $n = 6$ and $i = 0.075$. Also, since the bond is being "written up," bond values start at P and get adjusted up to C. This means $P < C$, the bond is purchased at a discount.

Using the notation of section 5.1, this means $P_6 = -46.51$ is the book value adjustment at the time of the 6th coupon. To calculate the book value adjustment in the 1st coupon, P_1, we recognize that the values in the book value adjustment column are in the ratio of $(1 + i)$. Thus,

$$P_1 = P_6(1.075)^{-5} = -46.51(1.075)^{-5} \doteq -\$32.40$$

The coupon is equal to the interest paid plus the book value adjustment. Thus,

$$\text{Coupon} = Fr = \$57.40 + (-\$32.40) = \$25.00$$

EXAMPLE 6   Prepare an Excel spreadsheet for the bond from Example 1.

Solution   You should first type in some of the given values. In cell G2, type in the face value, 1000. In cell G3, type in the bond rate, =0.065/2. In cell G4, type in the redemption value, 1000. In cell G5, type in the yield rate, =0.055/2. In cell G6, we will get the computer to calculate the purchase price by typing in the alternative purchase formula as =G4+(G2*G3−G4*G5)*(1−(1+G5)^−5)/G5.

The rest of the entries in an Excel spreadsheet are summarized below.

	CELL	ENTER	INTERPRETATION
Headings	A1	Time	'Time value for a coupon date'
	B1	Coupon	'Bond interest payment'
	C1	Interest on BV	'Interest on book value'
	D1	Adjustment	'Book value adjustment'
	E1	Book value	'Book value of the bond'
Line 0	A2	0	Time starts
	E2	=G6	Purchase price at time 0
Line 1	A3	=A2+1	Time for coupon 1
	B3	=$G$2*$G$3	Semi-annual bond interest payment
	C3	=E2*$G$5	Interest on book value at time 1
	D3	=B3−C3	Book value adjustment at time 1
	E3	=E2−D3	Book value at time 1

To generate the complete schedule copy A3.E3 to A4.E7

To get totals apply Σ to B3.D7

Below is the bond schedule by an Excel spreadsheet.

	A	B	C	D	E
1	Time	Coupon	Interest on BV	Adjustment	Book Value
2	0				1,023.06
3	1	32.50	28.13	4.37	1,018.69
4	2	32.50	28.01	4.49	1,014.21
5	3	32.50	27.89	4.61	1,009.60
6	4	32.50	27.76	4.74	1,004.86
7	5	32.50	27.63	4.87	1,000.00
8		162.50	139.44	23.06	

Note: All output is rounded to the nearest 1¢ but carried internally to several decimals. Thus the correct final balance is produced, but some columns appear not to add up.

Exercise 6.3

Part A

For problems 1 to 6 in the table that follows, determine logically, before calculation, if the bond is purchased at a premium or a discount. Then determine the purchase price of the bond and make out a complete bond schedule showing the amortization of the premium or the accumulation of the discount.

No.	Face Value	Redemption	Bond Interest Rate	Years to Redemption	Yield Rate
1.	$ 1 000	at par	$j_2 = 10\%$	3	$j_2 = 9\%$
2.	$ 5 000	at par	$j_2 = 6\%$	3	$j_2 = 7\%$
3.	$ 2 000	at par	$j_2 = 6\frac{1}{2}\%$	2.5	$j_2 = 5\frac{1}{2}\%$
4.	$ 1 000	at 105	$j_2 = 10\%$	2.5	$j_2 = 12\%$
5.	$ 2 000	at 103	$j_2 = 7\%$	3	$j_2 = 6\%$
6.	$10 000	at 110	$j_2 = 7\%$	2.5	$j_2 = 8\%$

7. A $1000 par value bond paying interest at $j_2 = 6\%$ has book value $1100 on March 1, 2006, at a yield rate of $j_2 = 4\frac{1}{2}\%$. Determine the amount of amortization of the premium on September 1, 2006, and the new book value on that date.

8. When $C \neq F$, we define a **modified coupon rate** $g = \dfrac{Fr}{C}$, so $Fr = Cg$. Then

$$P = C + (Cg - Ci)a_{\overline{n}|i} = C + C(g - i)a_{\overline{n}|i}.$$

When a bond is purchased at a premium, $P - C = C(g - i)a_{\overline{n}|i} > 0$ if $g > i$.

When a bond is purchased at a discount, $C - P = C(i - g)a_{\overline{n}|i} > 0$ if $i > g$.

Using the above, calculate the price of a $100 2-year bond with bond interest at $j_2 = 9\%$, redeemable at 105 to yield $j_4 = 10\%$. Produce a bond schedule.

Part B

1. A 20-year bond with annual coupons is bought at a premium to yield $j_1 = 8\%$. If the amount of write-down of the premium in the 3rd payment is $6, determine the amount of write-down of the premium in the 16th payment.

2. A $1000 bond, redeemable at par, with annual coupons at 10% is purchased for $1060. If the write-down in the book value is $7 at the end of the first year, what is the write-down at the end of the 4th year?

3. A bond with $80 annual coupons is purchased at a discount to yield $j_1 = 7\frac{1}{2}\%$. The write-up for the first year is $22. What was the purchase price?

4. A $1000 bond redeemable at $1050 on December 1, 2008, pays interest at $j_2 = 6\frac{1}{2}\%$. The bond is bought on June 1, 2006. Determine the price and construct a bond schedule if the desired yield is a) $j_{12} = 6\%$; b) $j_1 = 5\frac{1}{2}\%$.

5. A $1000 20-year par value bond with semi-annual coupons is bought at a discount to yield $j_2 = 10\%$. If the amount of the write-up of the discount in the last entry in the schedule is $5, determine the purchase price of the bond.

6. A bond with $40 semi-annual coupons is purchased at a premium to yield $j_2 = 7\%$. If the first write-down is $4.33, determine the purchase price of the bond.

7. A $1000 bond pays coupons at $j_2 = 7\%$ on January 1 and July 1 and will be redeemed at par on July 1, 2009. If the bond was bought on January 1, 2001, to yield 6% per annum compounded semi-annually, determine the interest due on the book value on January 1, 2005.

8. A $1000 bond providing annual coupons at $j_1 = 9\%$ is redeemable at par on November 1, 2009. The write-up in the first year was $5.63. The write-up in the eleventh year was $19.08. Determine the book value of the bond on November 1, 2005.

9. A $2000 bond with annual coupons matures at par in 5 years. The first interest coupon is $400, with subsequent coupons reduced by 25% of the previous year's coupon, each year.
   a) Calculate the price to yield $j_1 = 10\%$.
   b) Draw up the bond schedule.

10. A 10-year bond matures for $2000 and has annual coupons. The first coupon is $100, and each increases by 10%. The bond is priced to yield $j_1 = 9\%$. Determine the price and draw up the bond schedule.

11. A $1000 bond with semi-annual coupons at $j_2 = 5\%$ is redeemable for $1100. If the amount for the 16th write-up is $2.50, calculate the purchase price to yield $j_2 = 6\%$.

12. You are told that a $1000 bond with semi-annual coupons at $j_2 = 8\%$ redeemable at par will be sold at $700 to an investor requiring 12% per annum compounded semi-annually.
   a) Determine the price of this bond to the same investor if the above coupon rate were changed to $j_2 = 11\%$.
   b) Is the 11% bond purchased at a premium or a discount? Explain.
   c) For the 11% bond show the write-up (or write-down) entries at the first two coupon dates.

13. A $10 000 15-year bond is priced to yield $j_4 = 12\%$. It has quarterly coupons of $200 each the 1st year, $215 each the 2nd year, $230 each the 3rd year,..., $410 each the 15th year.
   a) Show that the price is $9267.05.
   b) Determine the book value after 14 years.
   c) Draw up a partial bond schedule showing the first and last year's entries only.

Section 6.4   Callable Bonds

Some bonds contain a clause that allows the issuer to redeem the bond prior to the maturity date. These bonds are referred to as **callable bonds**. A bond issuer would "call" a bond early if interest rates fall. This way, they could pay off the old issue and replace it with a new series of bonds with a lower coupon rate.

Callable bonds present a problem with respect to the calculation of the price since the term of the bond is not certain. Since the corporation issuing the bond controls when the bond is redeemed (or called), the investor must determine a price that will guarantee the desired yield regardless of the call date.

EXAMPLE 1   The XYZ Corporation issues a 20-year $1000 bond with coupons at $j_2 = 6\%$. The bond can be called, at par, at the end of 15 years. Determine the purchase price that will guarantee an investor a return of a) $j_2 = 7\%$; b) $j_2 = 5\%$.

Solution a   The bond matures at the end of 20 years but may be called at the end of 15 years. Given a desired yield rate of $j_2 = 7\%$, we calculate the price of the bond for these two different dates using formula **(16)**.

i) If it is called after 15 years,
$$P = 1000 + (30 - 35)a_{\overline{30}|0.035} \doteq \$1000 - \$91.96 = \$908.04$$

ii) If it matures after 20 years,
$$P = 1000 + (30 - 35)a_{\overline{40}|0.035} \doteq \$1000 - \$106.78 = \$893.22$$

The purchase price to guarantee a return of $j_2 = 7\%$ is the lower of these two answers, or \$893.22. If the investor pays \$893.22 and the bond runs the full 20 years to maturity, the investor's yield will be exactly $j_2 = 7\%$. If the investor pays \$893.22 and the bond is called after 15 years, the investor's return will exceed $j_2 = 7\%$.

If the investor pays \$908.04 for the bond, however, it will yield $j_2 = 7\%$ only if the bond is called after 15 years. If the bond runs to its full maturity, the rate of return will be less than $j_2 = 7\%$.

Solution b Again we calculate the price of the bonds at the two different dates using a yield of $j_2 = 5\%$ and formula **(16)**.

i) If it is called after 15 years,
$$P = 1000 + (30 - 25)a_{\overline{30}|0.025} \doteq \$1000 - \$104.65 = \$1104.65.$$

ii) If it matures after 20 years,
$$P = 1000 + (30 - 25)a_{\overline{40}|0.025} \doteq \$1000 + \$125.51 = \$1125.51.$$

The purchase price to guarantee a return of $j_2 = 5\%$ is \$1104.65. If the bond is called after 15 years, the investor's yield will be exactly $j_2 = 5\%$. If the bond is called any time after 15 years, or if the bond is held to maturity, the investor's yield will exceed $j_2 = 5\%$.

In the above example, we have shown, in effect, that the investor must assume that the issuer of the bond will exercise his call option to the disadvantage of the investor and must calculate the price accordingly. The example above also illustrates a useful principle *for bonds that are callable at par*. That is,

> If the yield rate is less than the coupon rate (if the bond sells at a premium), then you use the earliest possible call date in your calculation.
>
> If the yield rate is greater than the coupon rate (if the bond sells at a discount), then you use the latest possible redemption date in your calculation.

These examples can be explained logically. For a bond purchased at a premium, the earliest call date is the worst for the investor since she gets only \$1000 for her bond whenever it is called. On the other hand, for a bond purchased at a discount, the earliest call date is the best for the investor, since at that early call date she will get a full \$1000 for a bond that she values at something less than \$1000. Thus, the most unfavourable situation is the latest possible redemption.

Unfortunately, these guidelines cannot be applied often since, when a bond is called early, it is usually done so at a premium. In that case, we are forced to calculate all possible purchase prices and pay the lowest price calculated.

EXAMPLE 2   The ABC Corporation issues a 20-year $1000 par value bond with bond interest at $j_2 = 6\%$. The bond is callable at the end of 10 years at $1100 or at the end of 15 years at $1050. Determine the price to guarantee an investor a yield rate of $j_2 = 5\%$.

Solution   Calculate the purchase price using formula **(16)**
  i) If the bond is called after 10 years,

$$P = 1100 + (30 - 27.50)a_{\overline{20}|0.025} \doteq \$1100 + \$38.97 = \$1138.97$$

  ii) If the bond is called after 15 years,

$$P = 1050 + (30 - 26.25)a_{\overline{30}|0.025} \doteq \$1050 + \$78.49 = \$1128.49$$

  iii) If the bond is redeemed at par after 20 years,

$$P = 1000 + (30 - 25)a_{\overline{40}|0.025} \doteq \$1000 + \$125.51 = \$1125.51$$

In this case, despite the fact that the desired yield rate is less than the bond coupon rate, the correct answer is found by using the latest possible redemption date. That is because of the premium value in the early call dates.

There also exist debt securities called **extendible** or **retractable bonds**. These bonds are somewhat like a callable bond in that they allow the option of redeeming the bond at a time other than the stated redemption date. The difference between callable bonds and extendible/retractable bonds is that the bond owner, not the issuer, has the option.

An extendible bond allows the owner to extend the redemption date of the bond for a specified additional period. A retractable bond allows the owner to sell back the long-term bond to the issuer at a date earlier than the normal redemption date at par.

Canada Savings Bonds are an example of retractable bonds.

Because the option to extend or retract lies with the bond owner, no new mathematical analysis needs to be introduced.

Exercise 6.4

Part A

1. A $2000 bond paying interest at $j_2 = 10\%$ is redeemable at par in 20 years. It is callable at par in 15 years. Determine the price to guarantee a yield rate of
a) $j_2 = 8\%$; b) $j_2 = 12\%$.

2. A $5000 bond paying interest at $j_2 = 6\%$ is redeemable at par in 20 years. It is callable at 105 in 15 years. Determine the price to guarantee a yield rate of
a) $j_2 = 5\%$; b) $j_2 = 7\%$.

3. A $1000 bond with coupons at $j_2 = 9\%$ is redeemable at par in 20 years. It is callable after 10 years at 110 and after 15 years at 105. Determine the price to guarantee a yield rate of a) $j_2 = 8\%$; b) $j_2 = 10\%$.

4. A bond, paying interest at $j_2 = 5.5\%$, is redeemable at par in 10 years. It is callable at par in 5 years. What date should you use to calculate the purchase price of the bond if you desire a yield of
a) $j_2 = 5.5\%$; b) $j_2 = 6.5\%$; c) $j_2 = 5\%$?

5. A $2000 bond is redeemable at par in 12 years and is callable at par after 8 years. The price of the bond to yield $j_2 = 8\%$ is
• $2076.23 assuming the bond is held to maturity
• $2058.26 assuming the bond is called after 8 years
How will the actual yield rate compare with the desired yield rate (do not calculate the actual yield rate) if an investor pays
a) $2058.26 and the bond is called early?
b) $2058.26 and the bond is held to maturity?
c) $2076.23 and the bond is called early?
d) $2076.23 and the bond is held to maturity?

Part B

1. A $2000 bond with semi-annual coupons at $j_2 = 6\frac{1}{2}\%$ is redeemable at par in 20 years. It is callable at a 5% premium in 15 years. Determine the price to guarantee a yield rate of a) $j_4 = 8\%$; b) $j_1 = 5\frac{1}{2}\%$.

2. A $1000 bond with coupons at $j_2 = 6\%$ is redeemable at par in 20 years. It also has the following call options:

Call Date	Redemption
15 years	105
16 years	104
17 years	103
18 years	102
19 years	101

Determine the price to guarantee a yield rate of a) $j_1 = 5\%$; b) $j_{12} = 7\%$.

3. A $5000 callable bond pays $j_2 = 9\frac{1}{2}\%$ and matures at par in 20 years. It may be called at the end of years 10 to 15 (inclusive) for $5200. Determine the price to yield at least $j_2 = 8\frac{1}{2}\%$.

4. A special callable bond with semi-annual coupons at $j_2 = 10\%$ and a face value of $1000 is sold by the issuer for a purchase price P. The redemption amount is a little unusual in that it is described as $(1200 - 20t)$ during the first 10 years and $[1000 + 20(t - 10)]$ after 10 years, where t is the number of years after issue.
a) What is the purchase price P to yield 9% per annum compounded semi-annually assuming the bond is called at the end of 6 years?
b) Is the bond
   i) redeemed at a premium or at a discount? Specify the amount.
   ii) purchased at a premium or at a discount? Specify the amount.
c) Using the purchase price in a), at what other time point could the bond be called to produce the same yield rate? (Answer to the closest integral number of years n from issue.)

| Section 6.5 | **Price of a Bond Between Bond Interest Dates** |

The bond purchase-price formulas **(15)** and **(16)** were derived for bonds purchased on bond interest dates. In that case, the seller keeps the bond interest payment due on that date, and the buyer receives all the future bond interest payments. In actuality, bonds are purchased at any time and, consequently, we need a method of valuation of bonds between bond interest dates.

In most cases, bonds are purchased on the bond market (bond exchange) where they are sold to the highest bidder. Trading of bonds is done through agents acting on behalf of the buyer and seller. The seller indicates the minimum price he or she is willing to accept (ask) and the buyer the maximum price he or she is willing to pay (bid). The agents, who work for a commission, try to get the best possible price for their client. Many newspapers publish tables of bond information, as illustrated on page 237. The columns describe the bonds as to issuer, bond interest rate and date of redemption or maturity. The yields listed are calculated assuming the bond is purchased for the price bid and held to maturity.

When a bond is sold between bond interest dates, the buyer receives all future bond interest payments. However, part of the next bond interest payment really "belongs" to the seller, for the seller owned the bond for part of the bond interest period. We need to calculate the fractional part of the interest period for which the seller owned the bond, and take this into account when determining the price of the bond on the actual purchase date.

We will use the following notation in determining the value of a bond purchased between bond interest dates to yield the buyer interest at rate i.

P_0 = the purchase price of a bond on the preceding bond interest date to yield i

k = the fractional part of the interest period that has elapsed since the preceding bond interest date. $(0 < k < 1)$

$$= \frac{no.\ of\ days\ between\ preceding\ bond\ coupon\ date\ and\ date\ of\ sale}{no.\ of\ days\ between\ preceding\ bond\ coupon\ date\ and\ next\ bond\ coupon\ date}$$

P = the **flat price** or total value of the bond on the actual purchase date.

There are two ways to calculate the flat price.

1. $P = P_0(1 + ki)$

This formula assumes simple interest for the fractional period of time k. However, in Canada (and the United States) this formula is seldom used in practice any more.

2. $P = P_0(1 + i)^k$

This formula assumes compound interest for the fractional period of time, k, and is the formula used in practice.

EXAMPLE 1   A $1000 bond, redeemable at par on October 1, 2008, pays bond interest at $j_2 = 10\%$. Determine the purchase price on June 16, 2006, to yield $j_2 = 9\%$ assuming a) compound interest; b) simple interest, for the fractional duration.

Solution   Bond coupons are paid on April 1 and October 1. The preceding bond interest date is April 1, 2006. The exact time elapsed from April 1, 2006, to June 16, 2006, is 76 days. The exact time from April 1, 2006, to the next bond interest date on October 1, 2006, is 183 days. Thus, $k = \frac{76}{183}$.

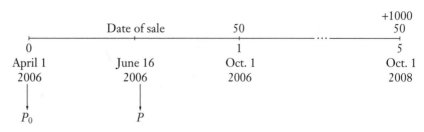

Using formula **(16)**,

$$P_0 = 1000 + (50 - 45)a_{\overline{5}|0.045} \doteq \$1021.95$$

a) Using the compound interest formula

$$P = P_0(1 + i)^k = 1021.95(1.045)^{\frac{76}{183}} \doteq \$1040.80$$

b) Using the simple interest formula

$$P = P_0(1 + ki) = 1021.95[1 + (0.045)(\tfrac{76}{183})] \doteq \$1041.05$$

The simple interest calculation will always give a larger answer than the compound interest calculation. (For a proof of this, see Exercise 2.4, question 1 in Part B).

OBSERVATION:

Unless otherwise specified, we will assume the compound interest formula for the flat price of the bond in this text.

If we were to graph the flat price of a bond, we would see a "sawtoothed" effect, as presented on the following page. As we approach each bond interest date, the flat price or actual selling price of the bond increases to give the seller the accrued value of the next bond interest payment or the **accrued bond interest**, which is equal to

$$\boxed{I = k \cdot Fr}$$

In our example,

$$I = \tfrac{76}{183}(50) = \$20.77$$

At each bond interest payment date, the accrued bond interest is zero and the price of the bond returns to the lower line marked Q. Q is called the **market price** or **quoted price** of the bond and is the price that is quoted in the daily paper. Q does not rise and fall as P does.

From the graph, we can see that $P = Q + I$ or

$$\boxed{Q = P - I}$$

In our example,

$$Q = \$1040.80 - \$20.77 = \$1020.03$$

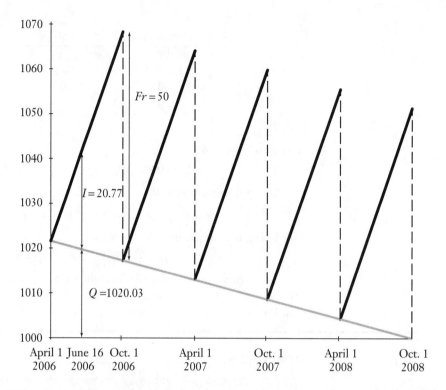

Note that under the compound interest for fractional durations assumption the value of Q moves along a straight line from one coupon date to the next. The value of Q does not, however, move in a straight line from April 1, 2006, to October 1, 2008, as it may appear; Q is, in fact, a piece-wise linear function.

Since bonds are issued in different denominations, it is customary to give the **market quotation** q on the basis of a $100 bond.

EXAMPLE 2 A $1000 bond, paying interest at $j_2 = 9\frac{1}{2}\%$ is redeemable at par on August 15, 2027. This bond was sold on September 1, 2006, at a market quotation of 103.13. What did the buyer pay?

Solution We have $q = 103.13$. The market price is $Q = 10 \times \$103.13 = \$1031.30$.

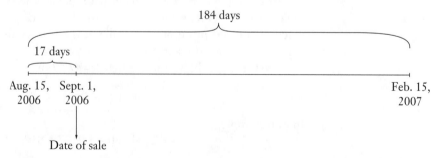

The accrued bond interest from August 15, 2006, to September 1, 2006, is

$$I = \tfrac{17}{184} \times \$47.50 = \$4.39$$

and the total purchase (flat) price is
$$P = Q + I = \$1031.30 + \$4.39 = \$1035.69$$

EXAMPLE 3   A \$500 bond, paying interest at $j_2 = 8\%$, is redeemable at par on February 1, 2015. What should the market quotation be on November 15, 2006, to yield the buyer 9% compounded semi-annually?

Solution

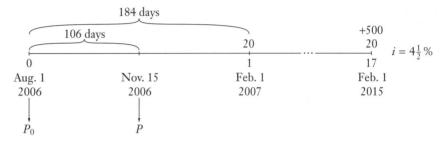

The purchase price on August 1, 2006, to yield $j_2 = 9\%$, would be
$$P_0 = 500 + (20 - 22.50)a_{\overline{17}|0.045} \doteq \$500 - \$29.27 = \$470.73$$

The purchase price on November 15, 2006, to yield $j_2 = 9\%$ would be
$$P = P_0(1+i)^k = 470.73(1.045)^{\frac{106}{184}} = \$482.82$$

The accrued bond interest from August 1, 2006, to November 15, 2006, is
$$I = \tfrac{106}{184} \times \$20 = \$11.52$$

The market price on November 15, 2006, would be
$$Q = P - I = \$482.82 - \$11.52 = \$471.30$$

Reducing Q to a \$100 bond we get the so-called **market quotation**
$$q = \tfrac{471.30}{5} = 94.26$$

Canadian Bonds

Bond quotations supplied by CBID-ATS, Perimeter Markets Inc. Closing prices and yields as of 4 p.m. end-of-week. Prices are ask prices. Most active based on volume traded. Yields are semi-annual compound to maturity.

Gov. of Canada and Agencies

CMHC	5.250	2006-Dec-01	100.31	3.62
CMHC	5.300	2007-Dec-03	101.48	4.02
CMHC	5.500	2012-Jun-01	107.16	4.08
CMHC	4.900	2013-Dec-01	104.74	4.13
CMHC	4.300	2015-Apr-01	100.65	4.21
CMHC	4.250	2016-Feb-01	100.29	4.21
Canada	3.250	2006-Dec-01	99.83	4.04
Canada	7.000	2006-Dec-01	100.57	4.00
Canada	3.000	2007-Jun-01	99.25	4.10
Canada	7.250	2007-Jun-01	102.14	4.10
Canada	4.500	2007-Sep-01	100.38	4.09
Canada	13.000	2007-Oct-01	109.00	4.01
Canada	2.750	2007-Dec-01	98.48	4.06
Canada	10.000	2008-Jun-01	109.82	3.96

Provincials and Agencies

Alberta	4.250	2012-Jun-01	100.60	4.13
AlbertaTreas	4.100	2011-Jun-01	99.94	4.11
AltaCapFinAu	5.850	2012-Jun-01	108.56	4.15
AltaCapFinAu	5.000	2013-Dec-02	105.07	4.18
AltaCapFinAu	4.350	2016-Jun-15	100.45	4.29
AltaCapFinAu	5.100	2023-Dec-01	106.20	4.57
BC	5.250	2006-Dec-01	100.23	3.96

Continued

Canadian Bonds (continued)

BC	6.000	2008-Jun-09	103.08	4.12
BC	4.300	2008-Dec-18	100.52	4.05
BC	5.700	2009-Jun-01	103.92	4.15
BC	6.250	2009-Dec-01	106.30	4.12
BC	6.375	2010-Aug-23	108.12	4.11

Municipalities

BC MFA	4.250	2011-Apr-06	100.75	4.07
BC MFA	5.900	2011-Jun-01	107.36	4.16
Chambly	4.350	2009-Jul-06	100.08	4.32
Durham Reg	5.400	2010-Nov-01	104.49	4.20
GrandeVallee	3.450	2009-Apr-20	97.84	4.34
Laval	5.400	2009-Jan-07	102.30	4.34
McGill U RI	6.150	2042-Sep-22	120.50	4.93
Metro Toronto	6.100	2007-Aug-15	101.76	4.09
Montreal	4.900	2011-Sep-26	102.31	4.38
Montreal	5.350	2012-Apr-25	104.62	4.41
Montreal	5.950	2012-May-17	107.62	4.41
Montreal	5.250	2012-Nov-08	104.32	4.44
Mtl UrbComTr	4.950	2007-Nov-15	100.56	4.44
PrSeigneurSB	5.000	2007-Jun-28	100.46	4.38
Quebec City	6.000	2012-Apr-25	107.81	4.41
Repentigny	6.350	2011-Aug-01	108.56	4.38

Sherbrooke	5.050	2008-Jul-24	101.21	4.35
Winnipeg	10.000	2009-Dec-14	117.16	4.26
Winnipeg	4.900	2010-Jan-17	102.37	4.13
York Region	4.400	2010-Jun-01	100.97	4.11

Corporates

407 Intl	6.900	2007-Dec-17	103.13	4.27
407 Intl	6.050	2009-Jul-27	104.74	4.26
55 Sch Trust	5.900	2033-Jun-02	114.50	4.92
Aliant Telec	5.350	2007-Jan-15	100.29	4.33
AmianteCEGEP	4.350	2008-Mar-06	99.97	4.37
BC Gas Util	6.500	2007-Oct-16	102.28	4.30
BC Gas Util	6.200	2008-Jun-02	103.02	4.33
BCE Inc.	6.750	2007-Oct-30	102.44	4.46
BMO	5.750	2008-Feb-04	101.94	4.27
BMO	4.450	2008-Oct-13	100.37	4.26
BMO	4.660	2009-Mar-31	100.87	4.29
BMO	4.300	2009-Sep-04	100.23	4.22
BMO	7.000	2010-Jan-28	108.40	4.28
BMO	4.690	2011-Jan-31	101.56	4.29
BMO	4.000	2010-Jan-21	99.01	4.32
BMO	4.870	2015-Aug-22	101.50	4.66

(Taken from Monday, Sept. 18/06, *The Globe and Mail*, business section.)

This information can also be found at:
www.globeandmail.ca/servelet/page/document/v5/templates/hub or
www.rbcinvestments.com/ds

Exercise 6.5

Part A

Determine the purchase price and the quoted price of the bonds in problems 1 to 6 in the table below.

No.	Face Value	Redemption	Bond Interest Rate	Yield Rate	Redemption Date	Date of Purchase
1.	$ 1 000	at par	$j_2 = 8\%$	$j_2 = 10\%$	Jan. 1, 2026	May 8, 2006
2.	$ 500	at par	$j_2 = 12\%$	$j_2 = 11\%$	Jan. 1, 2021	Oct. 3, 2006
3.	$ 2 000	at par	$j_2 = 9\%$	$j_2 = 10\%$	Nov. 1, 2016	July 20, 2006
4.	$10 000	at par	$j_2 = 6\frac{1}{2}\%$	$j_2 = 7\%$	Feb. 1, 2024	Oct. 27, 2006
5.	$ 1 000	at 105	$j_2 = 10\%$	$j_2 = 8\%$	July 1, 2017	July 30, 2006
6.	$ 2 000	at 110	$j_2 = 5\frac{1}{2}\%$	$j_2 = 6\frac{1}{2}\%$	Oct. 1, 2022	Apr. 17, 2007

Determine the purchase price of the following $1500 bonds if bought at the given market quotation.

No.	Redemption Value	Bond Interest Rate	Market Quotation	Redemption Date	Date of Purchase
7.	par	$j_2 = 6\%$	98.50	Sept. 1, 2023	June 8, 2005
8.	par	$j_2 = 11\%$	104.25	Feb. 1, 2019	Oct. 2, 2005
9.	$1575	$j_2 = 9\%$	101.75	Oct. 1, 2019	Nov. 29, 2006
10.	$1600	$j_2 = 13\%$	112.50	Apr. 1, 2019	Jan. 12, 2004

What would be the market quotation on the following $2000 bonds?

No.	Redemption Value	Bond Interest Rate	Yield Rate	Redemption Date	Date of Purchase
11.	par	$j_2 = 11\%$	$j_2 = 8\%$	Nov. 1, 2022	Feb. 8, 2004
12.	par	$j_2 = 12\%$	$j_2 = 10\%$	Mar. 1, 2024	Aug. 19, 2005
13.	$2100	$j_2 = 5\frac{1}{2}\%$	$j_2 = 6\%$	June 1, 2018	Oct. 30, 2003
14.	$2050	$j_2 = 9\%$	$j_2 = 7\%$	Oct. 1, 2014	Nov. 2, 2006

15. A $1000 bond, redeemable at par on October 1, 2008, is paying bond interest at rate $j_2 = 9\%$. Determine the purchase price on August 7, 2006, to yield $j_2 = 10\%$. Do a diagram similar to that found in section 6.5 for this bond.

Part B

1. Let: P_t be the value of a bond on a coupon date at time t to yield i.

P_{t+1} be the value of a bond on the following coupon date to yield i.

Show that $P_{t+1} = P_t(1 + i) - Fr$.

2. A $1000 bond, redeemable at $1100 on November 7, 2015, has coupons at $j_2 = 7\%$. Determine the purchase price on April 18, 2006, if the desired yield is a) $j_{12} = 8\%$; b) $j_1 = 6\%$.

3. An investment company is being audited and must locate the complete records of a specific bond transaction. The bond was a $500 bond with bond interest at rate $j_2 = 12\%$ redeemable at par on January 1, 2021. It was purchased for $550.89 sometime between July 1, 2006, and January 1, 2007. Determine the exact date if the bond was purchased to yield $j_2 = 11\%$.

4. Repeat Part A, problem 6, but assume simple interest for the fractional period.

5. A National Auto Company Limited $1000 bond is due at par on December 1, 2017. Interest is payable at $j_2 = 7\%$ on June 1 and December 1. The bond may be called at 104 on December 1, 2011. Determine the flat (purchase) price and the market price for this bond on August 8, 2006 if the yield is to be $j_2 = 6\%$,
a) assuming the bond is called at December 1, 2011;

b) assuming the bond matures at par on December 1, 2017.

6. A $5000 bond with semi-annual coupons at $j_2 = 9\%$ is redeemable at par on November 1, 2026.
a) Determine the price on November 1, 2006, to yield $j_4 = 10\%$.
b) Determine the book value of the bond on May 1, 2009 (just after the coupon is cashed).
c) What should the market quotation of this bond be on August 17, 2009, if the buyer wants a yield of $j_1 = 7\%$?

7. For one of the bonds from the newspaper listing shown earlier, confirm the bid price given the other information about that bond.

8. a) A $1000 bond paying interest at $j_2 = 7\%$ is redeemable at par on September 1, 2026. Determine the price on its issue date of September 1, 2006, to yield $j_2 = 9\%$.
b) Determine the book value of the bond on September 1, 2008, (just after the coupon is cashed).
c) Determine the sale price of this bond on September 1, 2008, if the buyer wants a yield of
 i) 6% compounded semi-annually;
 ii) 12% compounded semi-annually.
d) What should the market quotation of this bond be on October 8, 2008, to yield a buyer $j_2 = 8\%$?

9. The ABC Corporation $5000 bond that pays interest at $j_2 = 7\%$ matures at par on October 1, 2017.
a) What did the buyer pay for the bond if it was sold on July 28, 2005, at a market quotation of 89.38?
b) What should the market quotation of this bond be on July 28, 2005, to yield a buyer $j_{12} = 6\%$?
c) What should the market quotation of this bond be on December 13, 2007, to yield a buyer $j_1 = 8\%$?

Note: For b) and c) assume simple interest.

Section 6.6 Determining the Yield Rate

One of the fundamental problems relating to bonds is to determine the investment rate i a bond will give to the buyer when bought for a given price P. In practice, the market price is often given without stating the yield rate. The investor is interested in determining the true rate of return on his or her investment, i.e., the yield rate. Based on the yield rate, the investor can decide whether the purchase of a particular bond is an attractive investment or not, and also determine which of several bonds available is the best investment.

There are different methods available for calculating the yield rate. In this section we will calculate the yield rate in two ways. We will also show how to calculate the yield rate using a financial calculator and a spreadsheet.

Note that in the examples that follow, we calculate the yield rate assuming that the bond will be held to maturity unless specifically stated otherwise.

The Method of Averages

This method is simple and usually leads to fairly accurate results. It calculates an approximate value of the yield rate i as the ratio of the average interest payment over the average amount invested.

EXAMPLE 1 A \$500 bond, paying interest at $j_2 = 9\frac{1}{2}\%$, redeemable at par on August 15, 2018, is quoted at 109.50 on August 15, 2006. Determine the approximate value of the yield rate j_2 to maturity.

Solution The purchase price is $P = 5 \times \$109.50 = \$547.50$, since the bond is sold on a bond interest date. If the buyer holds the bond until maturity, she will receive 24 bond interest payments of \$23.75 each plus the redemption price \$500, in total $24 \times \$23.75 + \$500 = \$1070$. She pays \$547.50 and receives \$1070. The net gain $\$1070 - \$547.50 = \$522.50$ is realized over 24 interest periods, so that the average interest per period is

$$\tfrac{\$522.50}{24} = \$21.77$$

The average amount invested is the average of the purchase price (the original value) and the redemption value (the final value), i.e., $\frac{1}{2}(\$547.50 + \$500) = \$523.75$. The approximate value of the yield rate is

$$i = \tfrac{21.77}{523.75} = 0.0416 = 4.16\% \text{ or } j_2 = 8.32\%.$$

If n is the number of interest periods from the date of sale until the redemption date we can conclude that

$$\text{The average interest payment} = \frac{n \times Fr + C - P}{n}$$

$$\text{The average amount invested} = \frac{P + C}{2}$$

$$\boxed{\text{The approximate value of } i = \frac{\text{the average interest payment}}{\text{the average amount invested}}}$$

In most cases the answer is correct to the nearest 10th of a percent. If a more accurate answer is desired, the method of averages should be followed by the interpolation technique described below.

The Method of Interpolation

This method of determining the yield rate consists of calculating two adjacent nominal rates such that the market price of the bond lies between the prices determined. The standard method of interpolation between the two adjacent rates is then used to determine i or j_2. Usually the method of averages is used to get a starting value to be used in the method of interpolation.

EXAMPLE 2   Compute the yield rate j_2 in Example 1 by the method of interpolation.

Solution   By the method of averages we determined that $j_2 = 8.32\%$. Now we compute the market prices (which are equal to purchase prices) to yield $j_2 = 8\%$ and $j_2 = 9\%$.

$$Q(\text{to yield } j_2 = 8\%) = 500 + (23.75 - 20)a_{\overline{24}|0.04} \doteq \$557.18$$
$$Q(\text{to yield } j_2 = 9\%) = 500 + (23.75 - 22.50)a_{\overline{24}|0.045} \doteq \$518.12$$

Arranging the data in the interpolation table, we have

	Q	j_2
	557.18	8%
	547.50	j_2
	518.12	9%

$$\frac{d}{1\%} = \frac{9.68}{39.06}$$
$$d = 0.2478238\%$$
$$\text{and } j_2 = 8.2478238\%$$
$$\doteq 8.25\%$$

Check: $Q(\text{to yield } j_2 = 8.25\%) = 500 + (23.75 - 20.63)a_{\overline{24}|0.04125} \doteq \$546.97$.

EXAMPLE 3   A $1000 bond paying interest at $j_2 = 11\%$ matures at par on November 15, 2017. On November 15, 2002, it was purchased at 104. On November 15, 2006, it was sold at 97.50. What was the yield rate, j_2?

Solution   We have $F = 1000$, $r = 0.11/2 = 0.055$, $Fr = 55$. The bond was purchased on November 15, 2002 for $P = 10 \times 104 = 1040$ and is sold on November 15, 2006 for $C = 10 \times 97.50 = 975.00$. The number of interest periods between the date of purchase and the date of sale is $n = 4 \times 2 = 8$. Using the method of averages, we find

The average interest payment $= \frac{8 \times 55 + 975 - 1040}{8} = \$46.875$

The average amount invested $= \frac{975 + 1040}{2} = \$1007.50$

The approximate value of $i = \frac{46.875}{1007.50} = 0.0465$ or 4.65%

The approximate value of $j_2 = 9.30\%$.

If we want a more accurate answer, we select two rates, $j_2 = 9\%$ and $j_2 = 10\%$, and use them in the following formula:

$$1040 = 55a_{\overline{8}|i} + 975(1+i)^{-8}$$

At $j_2 = 9\%$, the right-hand side equals: $362.77 + 685.61 = \$1048.38$
At $j_2 = 10\%$, the right-hand side equals: $355.48 + 659.22 = \$1015.40$
Arranging the data in an interpolation table, we have

	Q	j_2
8.38 {	1048.38	9% } d
32.98 {	1040.00	j_2 } 1%
	1015.40	10%

$$\frac{d}{1\%} = \frac{8.38}{32.98}$$
$$d = 0.254093389\%$$
and $j_2 = 9.25409\%$
$$\doteq 9.25\%$$

Using a Financial Calculator to Determine the Yield Rate

We will use the notation that was introduced when using the Texas Instruments BA-35 calculator to determine the price of a bond in section 6.2.
For Example 2, the steps are as follows:

23.75 $\boxed{PMT}$ 500 $\boxed{FV}$ −547.50 $\boxed{PV}$ 24 $\boxed{N}$ $\boxed{CPT}$ $\boxed{I/Y}$
4.11929

This rate is the yield per half-year. To obtain the nominal yield rate, double this value. Thus, $j_2 = 2(4.11929) = 8.23858 \doteq 8.24\%$. You can see the yield rate obtained using linear interpolation, 8.25%, turned out to be very accurate.
For Example 3, the steps are as follows:

55 $\boxed{PMT}$ 975 $\boxed{FV}$ −1040 $\boxed{PV}$ 8 $\boxed{N}$ $\boxed{CPT}$ $\boxed{I/Y}$
4.62512

Thus, $j_2 = 2(4.62512) = 9.250243 \doteq 9.25\%$.

Using a Spreadsheet to Determine the Yield Rate

Excel has a function called YIELD which will calculate the nominal yield rate of a bond:

YIELD(settlement date, maturity date, rate, price, redemption, frequency, basis)

where
settlement date = date of purchase
maturity date = date of sale or redemption
rate = nominal bond rate, typed as a decimal
price = price bond was purchased at, in units of $100
redemption = price the bond was sold at, in units of $100

frequency = type '1' if bond has annual coupons, '2' if semi-annual coupons

basis = type '1' if any fractional period uses actual number of days

For the settlement and maturity dates, they should be typed using the DATE function. This function works even for situations where the bond is purchased in between coupon dates (see Examples 4 and 5).

In Example 2, to calculate the yield rate, j_2, you would type:

=YIELD(date(2006,8,15),date(2018,8,15),0.095,109.5,100,2,1)

This will produce the answer 0.0823858, or $j_2 \doteq 8.24\%$.

In Example 3,

=YIELD(date(2002,11,15),date(2006,11,15),0.11,104,97.50,2,1)

This will produce the answer 0.0925024, or $j_2 \doteq 9.25\%$.

The two methods described in this section apply equally well to bonds purchased between interest dates. The computations are more tedious, as is illustrated in the following example.

EXAMPLE 4   A $5000 bond paying interest at $j_2 = 11\%$ matures at par on June 1, 2016. On February 3, 2006, this bond is quoted at 95.38. What is the yield rate j_2?

Solution   First we use the method of averages to get an estimate of the yield rate assuming that the bond was quoted on the **nearest** coupon date, in this case December 1, 2005, or 21 interest periods before maturity. The market price on February 3, 2006, is $Q = 50 \times 95.38 = \$4769.00$.

The average interest payment $= \frac{21 \times 275 + 5000 - 4769}{21} = \$286.00$.

The average amount invested $= \frac{5000 + 4769}{2} = \$4884.50$.

The approximate value of $i = \frac{286.00}{4884.50} = 0.058552564$.

The approximate value of $j_2 = 11.71\%$.

If we want a more accurate answer, we select 2 rates, $j_2 = 11\%$ and $j_2 = 12\%$, and compute the corresponding market prices on February 3, 2006, using the method outlined in section 6.5.

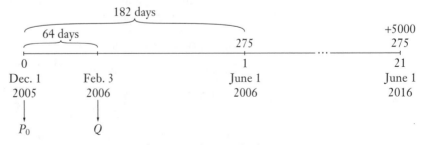

At $j_2 = 11\%$: $P_0 = Q = \$5000$ without calculation.

At $j_2 = 12\%$: $P_0 = 5000 + (275 - 300)a_{\overline{21}|0.06} = 5000 - 294.10 = \$4705.90$

$$P = 4705.90(1.06)^{\frac{64}{182}} = \$4803.32$$

$$Q = P - I = 4803.32 - \tfrac{64}{182}(275) = \$4706.62$$

Arranging the data in an interpolation table, we have

Q on Feb. 3, 2000		j_2
	5000.00	11%
231.00 4769.00		j_2
293.38		
	4706.62	12%

$$\frac{d}{1\%} = \frac{231.00}{293.38}$$

$$d = 0.7924256\%$$

and $j_2 = 11.7924256\%$

$$\doteq 11.79\%$$

Note: Using Excel's yield function,

=YIELD(date(2006,2,3),date(2016,6,1),0.11,95.38,100,2,1)

will produce the answer 0.1177894, or $j_2 = 11.78\%$.

Note: Suppose the bond was quoted at 95.38 on April 12, 2006. The nearest coupon date would be June 1, 2006 or 20 interest periods before maturity. You should confirm that the yield rate using the method of averages becomes $i = 0.058665$, or $j_2 = 11.73\%$. Using the method of interpolation, use the same method as shown above but with $n = 20$. Also, when calculating the flat price, P, and the quoted price, Q, the numerator of k is the number of days between December 1 and April 12 (132 days) and the denominator is the number of days between December 1 and June 1 (182 days). Thus $k = \frac{132}{182}$. You should confirm this leads to $j_2 = 11.82\%$.

EXAMPLE 5   A \$1000 bond paying interest at $j_2 = 12\%$ matures on June 1, 2021. On October 10, 2004, it was purchased for \$1042.50 plus accrued bond interest (i.e., $q = 104.25$). On February 8, 2007, it was sold for \$968.70 plus accrued bond interest (i.e., $q = 96.87$). Estimate the yield rate j_2 by the method of averages.

Solution

Using the method of averages, we assume that both transactions took place at the nearest respective coupon date. That is, we assume a purchase price of \$1042.50 on December 1, 2004, and a sale price of \$968.70 on December 1, 2006. In this period, there would be four coupons of \$60 each.

The average interest payment $= \frac{4 \times 60 + 968.70 - 1042.50}{4} = \$41.55$.

The average amount invested $= \frac{968.70 + 1042.50}{2} = \$1005.60$.

The approximate value of $i = \frac{41.55}{1005.60} = 0.0413$ or 4.13%.

The approximate value of $j_2 = 8.26\%$.

The calculation of the answer using the method of interpolation is left for Part B, problem 9 in Exercise 6.6.

Note: Using Excel's yield function,

=YIELD(date(2004,10,10),date(2007,2,8),0.12,104.25,96.87,2,1)

will produce the answer 0.0868954, or $j_2 \doteq 8.69\%$.

The Yield Curve

One interesting aspect of the bond market is the yield curve. This is a graph showing the current yield-to-maturity of bonds of different maturities. The yield-to-maturity assumes the investor holds the bonds until redemption and is the yield used in previous sections. Of course, many investors may choose to sell their bond before maturity and in this case their rate of return will depend on both the purchase and the selling prices and not the yield-to-maturity at purchase.

The yield curve shows how interest rates vary for different maturities. That is, it is a visual representation of interest rates for different terms. Before looking at an example, it is important to note that each yield curve should consider bonds of similar risk.

At the time of writing, the longer-term bonds have a higher yield so that the yield curve is upward sloping (as you can see in the graph below). This is a normal or positive yield curve and represents the usual market position. However, sometimes the shorter maturities have higher yields so that the yield curve is known as downward sloping or concave. In these situations, the yield curve is said to be inverted. There was an inverted yield curve in Canada in 1990–91.

Yield Curve of Sept. 18, 2006

Source: CBID – Perimeter Markets Inc. *The Globe and Mail.*

A normal yield curve highlights the fact that if you purchase a bond, hold on to the investment for a period of time and then sell it, it is likely that your selling yield will be lower that your purchase yield, assuming that other market forces have not changed. This provides investors with the opportunity to obtain a yield in excess of the yield-to-maturity and is known as "riding the yield curve." The next example illustrates this approach.

EXAMPLE 6   Mrs. Noori purchases a $1000 bond, paying bond interest at $j_2 = 8\%$ and redeemable at par in 10 years. The price she pays will yield $j_2 = 7\%$ if held to maturity. After holding the bond for 3 years, she sells the bond to yield the new purchaser $j_2 = 6\%$. Calculate Mrs. Noori's yield rate, j_2, over the 3-year investment period.

Solution   Using the bond pricing formula (**15**), $Fr = 40$, $C = 1000$, $n = 20$, and $i = 0.035$.

$$\text{Purchase price} = 40a_{\overline{20}|0.035} + 1000(1.035)^{-20} \doteq \$1071.06$$

After 3 years, the selling price can be calculated using $Fr = 40$, $C = 1000$, $n = 14$, and $i = 0.03$.

$$\text{Selling price} = 40a_{\overline{14}|0.03} + 1000(1.03)^{-14} \doteq \$1112.96$$

Now consider her 3-year investment. She paid $1071.06 for the bond, received a $40 coupon payment every 6 months for 3 years and then $1112.96 when she sold the bond. Therefore, her equation of value at rate i per half-year is:

$$1071.06 = 40a_{\overline{6}|i} + 1112.96(1 + i)^{-6}$$

We first calculate the approximate yield and then use linear interpolation to obtain a more accurate answer.

Using $Fr = 40$, $n = 6$, $C = 1112.96$, and $P = 1071.06$ and the method of averages, we calculate the approximate value of i:

$$i = \frac{(6 \times 40 + 1112.96 - 1071.06)/6}{(1112.96 + 1071.06)/2} \doteq 0.043 \text{ or } j_2 = 8.6\%$$

$$Q(\text{to yield } j_2 = 8\%) = 40a_{\overline{6}|0.04} + 1112.96(1.04)^{-6} \doteq \$1089.27$$

$$Q(\text{to yield } j_2 = 9\%) = 40a_{\overline{6}|0.045} + 1112.96(1.045)^{-6} \doteq \$1060.95$$

Arranging the data in the interpolation table, we have

		Q	j_2	
		1089.27	8%	
28.32	18.21	1071.06	j_2	1%
		1060.95	9%	

$$\frac{d}{1\%} = \frac{18.21}{28.32}$$
$$d \doteq 0.64\%$$
$$\text{and } j_2 = 8.64\%$$

Hence, in this example, the investor obtains a yield in excess of 8% because she was able to sell at a lower yield. This could have been due to the shape of the yield curve or a change in market conditions.

Current and historical Government of Canada yield rates can be found at:
www.bankofcanada.ca/en/rates

Exercise 6.6

In the questions that follow, assume that the bond will be held to maturity unless specifically stated otherwise.

Part A

In problems 1 to 4, determine the yield rate, j_2, by the method of averages.

No.	Face Value	Redemption Value	Bond Interest	Years to Redemption	Purchase Price
1.	$2000	at par	$j_2 = 11\%$	12	$1940
2.	$5000	at par	$j_2 = 7\%$	10	$5340
3.	$1000	at 105	$j_2 = 12\%$	15	$1120
4.	$ 500	at 110	$j_2 = 6\%$	11	$ 450

5-8. Determine the yield rate, j_2, in problems 1 to 4 by the method of interpolation. Confirm your answers using a financial calculator or using the YIELD function in Excel.

9. A $1000 bond paying bond interest at $j_2 = 6\%$ matures at par on August 1, 2013. If this bond was quoted at 92 on August 1, 2006, what was the yield rate j_2
a) using the method of averages;
b) using the method of interpolation;
c) using a calculator or spreadsheet?

10. A $1000 bond redeemable at par at the end of 20 years and paying bond interest at $j_2 = 11\%$ is callable in 15 years at $1050. Determine the yield rate j_2 if the bond is quoted now at 110 assuming
a) it is called;
b) it is not called.

11. A $1000 bond redeemable at par in 20 years pays bond interest at $j_2 = 10\%$. It is callable at the end of 10 years at 105. If it is quoted at 96, determine the yield rate j_2 assuming
a) it is called;
b) it is not called.

12. A $1000 bond paying interest at $j_2 = 10\%$ matures at par on June 1, 2022. On August 17, 2006, this bond is quoted at 98.50. What is the yield rate?

13. A $1000 bond paying interest at $j_2 = 7\%$ matures at par on October 1, 2017. On April 28, 2006, this bond is quoted at 102. What is the yield rate?

14. The XYZ Corporation has a $1000 bond that pays bond interest at $j_2 = 8\%$. The bond is redeemable at par on June 1, 2016. On June 1, 2000, an investor buys this bond on the open market at 97. On June 1, 2008, he sells this bond on the open market at 101. Determine the investor's yield rate j_2.

15. Ms. Holman buys a $1000 bond that pays bond interest at $j_2 = 7\%$ and is redeemable at par in 15 years. The price she pays will give her a yield of $j_2 = 8\%$ if held to maturity. After 5 years, Ms. Holman sells this bond to Mr. Dawson, who desires a yield of $j_2 = 6\%$ on his investment.
a) What price did Ms. Holman pay?
b) What price did Mr. Dawson pay?
c) What yield j_2 did Ms. Holman realize? (Use interpolation)

16. A $1000 bond paying interest at $j_2 = 11\%$ matures at par on July 15, 2022. On January 29, 2003, it was purchased for $972.50 plus accrued bond interest (i.e., 97.25). On May 7, 2006, it was sold for $1003.80 plus accrued bond interest (i.e., 100.38). Estimate the yield rate j_2 by the method of averages.

17. Bond interest, paid in the form of coupons, is taxable in full in the hands of the individual who owns the bond. However, the difference between your purchase price and your sale price (or redemption value) is either a capital gain (if sold at a profit) or a capital loss (if sold at a loss). Only one-half of any realized capital gain enters one's taxable income, while capital losses can be used to offset capital gains in the same year before determining one's taxable income.

On January 1, 2006, Fred buys a $1000 corporate bond paying interest at $j_2 = 8\%$ (payable June 30 and December 31) and redeemable at par in exactly 10 years. His purchase price is $980. On December 31, 2008, Fred sells the bond on a day where its market quote is 104.

By purchasing this bond, how much additional taxable income does Fred incur in:
a) 2006; b) 2007?

Part B

1. The XYZ Corporation issues a $1000 bond with semi-annual coupons at $j_2 = 7\%$ redeemable at par in 20 years or callable at par in 15 years. Mr. LaBelle buys the bond to guarantee a yield rate $j_{12} = 9\%$.
a) Determine the purchase price.
b) After 15 years, the XYZ Corporation calls the bond in and pays Mr. LaBelle his $1000. Calculate his overall yield stated as a rate j_{12}.

2. In our "method of averages" formula we said

$$\text{Average amount invested} = \frac{P+C}{2}$$

A slightly more accurate formula uses

$$\text{Average amount invested} = C + \frac{n+1}{2n}(P-C)$$

Using this latter modification, repeat problems 1 to 4 in Part A above and see if your approximations improve.

3. The XYZ Corporation has a bond due December 4, 2019, paying bond interest at $j_2 = 10\frac{3}{8}\%$. The price bid on December 14, 2006, is 104. What yield j_{12} does the investor desire?

4. Mr. Hunter buys a $1000 bond with semi-annual coupons at $j_2 = 6\%$. The bond is redeemable at par in 20 years. The price he pays will guarantee him a yield of $j_4 = 8\%$ if held to maturity. After 5 years, Mr. Hunter sells this bond to Miss Schnarr, who desires a yield of $j_1 = 5\frac{1}{2}\%$ on her investment.
   a) What price did Mr. Hunter pay?
   b) What price did Miss Schnarr pay?
   c) What yield, j_4, did Mr. Hunter realize?

5. The ABC Corporation issues a $1000 bond, with coupons payable at $j_2 = 7\%$ on January 1 and July 1, redeemable at par on July 1, 2016.
   a) How much would an investor pay for this bond on September 1, 2006, to yield $j_2 = 8\%$?
   b) Given the purchase price from part a), if each coupon is deposited in a bank account paying interest at $j_4 = 6\%$ and the bond is held to maturity, what is the effective annual yield rate j_1 on this investment?

6. A bond paying semi-annual coupons at $j_2 = 8\%$ matures at par in n years and is quoted at 110 to yield rate j_2. A bond paying semi-annual coupons at $j_2 = 8\frac{1}{2}\%$ matures at par in n years and is quoted at 112 on the same yield basis.
   a) Determine the unknown yield rate, j_2.
   b) Determine n to the nearest half-year.

7. An issue of bonds, redeemable at par in n years, is to bear coupons at $j_2 = 9\%$. An investor offers to buy the entire issue at a premium of 15%. At the same time, she advises the issuer that if the coupon rate were raised from $j_2 = 9\%$ to $j_2 = 10\%$, she would offer to buy the entire issue at a premium of 25%. At what yield rate j_2 are these two offers equivalent?

8. In August 1991, interest rates in the bond markets were such that an investor could expect a yield of $j_2 = 10\%$. On August 1, 1991, an investor bought a bond with semi-annual coupons at $j_2 = 9\%$ which was to mature in 20 years at par. By August 1, 1992, interest rates had fallen to $j_2 = 8\%$. This same investor sold his bond on August 1, 1992, on the bond market. Determine the yield j_2 on this investment.

9. For the bond question solved in Example 5 in section 6.6, use the method of interpolation to calculate the yield rate, j_2.

10. The ABC Corporation issues a very unusual type of bond on July 1, 2006. It is issued in units where the face amount is $1000 and the redemption amount is $1500 at July 1, 2016. Semi-annual coupons are payable January 1 and July 1 and are as follows:

	2007	2008	2009	2010	2011
Jan. 1	$60	64	68	72	76
July 1	60	64	68	72	76

	2012	2013	2014	2015	2016
Jan. 1	$80	84	88	92	96
July 1	80	84	88	92	96

   a) What should the initial offering price per unit be if the yield to maturity is to be 10% per annum compounded semi-annually?
   b) Is this a premium or a discount? Specify the amount.
   c) If a purchaser on July 1, 2006, buys a bond at a price as calculated in a), then sells one unit of the bond at July 1, 2008, for $1300, what interest rate j_2 would be realized?

Section 6.7   **Other Types of Bonds**

Canada Savings Bonds

Every autumn since the end of World War II, the Canadian government has borrowed the savings of individual Canadians through the issuance of Canada Savings Bonds. These bonds are available in values ranging from $100 to $10 000 and are the favourite investment of the average citizen. In fact, they account for one-quarter of the total value of all bonds — both corporate and government. Two interest options are available. Regular interest bonds pay simple interest each November by cheque or direct deposit to the customer's account. Compound interest bonds pay compound interest on maturity or redemption. Canada Savings Bonds are redeemable on any banking day at any bank for their full face value, plus any interest accrued up to that time. The bonds are guaranteed by the federal government and are registered. They are nontransferable and there is a limit on the value that can be held by any person, partnership, or corporation. Canada Savings Bonds are heavily advertised every year. Any Canadian resident can buy them without any formality at any branch of any chartered bank or trust company, as well as through a stockbroker or investment dealer. They can also be purchased through payroll deductions. Since Canada Savings Bonds are redeemable at par on any banking day, purchase-price formula (**15**) or (**16**) does not apply to their valuation. For more information, see: *www.csb.gc.ca*.

Indexed Bonds

The relationship between inflation and interest rates was explained in section 2.8, Example 4. The yields obtained from fixed interest investments (such as bonds) are normally in excess of the inflation rate so that a "real" yield is obtained. Yet, despite a positive "real" yield overall, investments in bonds produce a constant income during the term of the loan that diminishes in "real" value (i.e., after inflation is taken into account) and a redeemed principal that has lost a considerable amount of its "real" value. These disadvantages may be particularly relevant for retired people who invest their life savings for future income. An alternative type of bond that overcomes these difficulties is an inflation-indexed bond where the interest and the redemption value increase with a specific index (e.g., consumer price index or CPI) and therefore maintain their "real" values.

Both Canada and the United States (and many other nations) issue inflation-indexed bonds. Every six months, the face value of the bond is adjusted by an amount equal to the CPI adjustment. Bond interest, or coupons, are still payable semi-annually, but are effective on the adjusted face value of the bond. For example, assume a $1000 inflation-indexed bond with coupons at $j_2 = 3\%$. After six months, the CPI has risen 1%. At that time, the face value of the bond would rise to $1010 and the first coupon would be $15.15 (i.e., 1.5% of $1010).

By year end, the CPI is up 3% from the time the bond was issued. The face value of the bond would now be $1030 and the second coupon would be $15.45. Similar adjustments would occur over the lifetime of the bond. Note that at the time of redemption, the maturity value would be the full inflation-adjusted face value, not $1000.

In Canada, the amount of outstanding inflation-indexed bonds (sometimes called Real Return Bonds) is small, but growing. These bonds are of particular interest to insurance companies and pension funds that have promises that may have to be paid in real value benefits (e.g., inflation-indexed retirement income). At the end of March 2004, there were $20.6 billion in Real Return Bonds outstanding in Canada (see *www.fin.gc.ca/* and then go to Glossary — The Government of Canada, Ministry of Finance).

As at October 2, 2006, Government of Canada Real Return Bonds due December 1, 2031, were paying bond interest at 4.00% and yielding 1.67% (see ***www.bankofcanada.ca/en/rates***).

It should be noted that the interest rate payable on indexed bonds is considerably lower than that payable on conventional bonds as the "real" values of each interest payment and the principal are maintained throughout the term of the loan. These bonds may be valued using similar principles to those developed in earlier sections.

Serial Bonds

When municipal governments borrow by means of an issue of bonds, they occasionally issue a series of bonds with staggered redemption dates instead of with a common redemption date. Such bonds are called **serial bonds**. Serial bonds can be thought of simply as several bonds covered under one bond contract. If the redemption date of each individual bond is known, then the valuation of any one bond can be performed by methods already described. The value of the entire issue of the bonds is just the sum of the values of the individual bonds.

EXAMPLE 1   A city has authorized the issuance of $30 000 000 of serial bonds on September 1, 2006. Interest is to be paid annually on September 1 at a nominal rate of 9%. The indenture provides the following redemption provisions:

  i) $5 000 000 of the issue is to be redeemed on September 1, 2011;
 ii) $10 000 000 of the issue is to be redeemed on September 1, 2016;
iii) $15 000 000 of the issue is to be redeemed on September 1, 2021.

    a) Determine the purchase price of the issue on September 1, 2006, which would yield $j_1 = 8\%$.

    b) What would be the value of the bonds on September 1, 2013?

Solution a   We consider the serial issue to be composed of 3 issues, represented by the following diagrams:

```
                                  +5 000 000
               450 000              450 000
      |-----------|----------...------|
      0           1                   5
    Sept. 1    Sept. 1             Sept. 1
     2006       2007                2011


                                           +10 000 000
               900 000         900 000        900 000
      |-----------|----...--------|----...------|
      0           1               5            10
    Sept. 1    Sept. 1         Sept. 1      Sept. 1
     2006       2007            2011         2016


                                                        +15 000 000
              1 350 000      1 350 000     1 350 000      1 350 000
      |-----------|----...------|----...------|----...------|
      0           1             5            10            15
    Sept. 1    Sept. 1       Sept. 1      Sept. 1       Sept. 1
     2006       2007          2011         2016          2021
```

The purchase price of the entire serial issue P on September 1, 2006, is the sum of the purchase prices of the 3 individual issues $P^{(1)}$, $P^{(2)}$, $P^{(3)}$.

$$
\begin{aligned}
P^{(1)} &= 5\,000\,000 + (450\,000 - 400\,000)a_{\overline{5}|0.08} &&= \$\ 5\,199\,635.50 \\
P^{(2)} &= 10\,000\,000 + (900\,000 - 800\,000)a_{\overline{10}|0.08} &&= \$10\,671\,008.14 \\
P^{(3)} &= 15\,000\,000 + (1\,350\,000 - 1\,200\,000)a_{\overline{15}|0.08} &&= \$16\,283\,921.80 \\
\hline
P &= P^{(1)} + P^{(2)} + P^{(3)} &&= \$32\,154\,565.44
\end{aligned}
$$

Solution b   The value of the entire serial issue P on September 1, 2013, is the sum of the values of the 2nd and 3rd individual cases $P^{(2)}$ and $P^{(3)}$. (The first individual issue was already redeemed at that time.)

$$
\begin{aligned}
P^{(2)} &= 10\,000\,000 + (900\,000 - 800\,000)a_{\overline{3}|0.08} &&= \$10\,257\,709.70 \\
P^{(3)} &= 15\,000\,000 + (1\,350\,000 - 1\,200\,000)a_{\overline{8}|0.08} &&= \$15\,861\,995.84 \\
\hline
P &= P^{(2)} + P^{(3)} &&= \$26\,119\,705.54
\end{aligned}
$$

Strip Bonds

Investors have several reasons for choosing one investment over another. They look for high yields and safety. They also look for cash flows whose timing matches their needs. For some investors, the coupons on a bond match their cash flow needs (e.g., a corporation responsible for paying monthly retirement benefits to a worker). For other investors, the redemption value of a bond matches their cash flow needs (e.g., an insurance company that needs to satisfy the maturity value of an endowment insurance contract).

For these reasons, some investors separate the coupons from the redemption value of the bond. In some instances, an investor buys the bond contract, "strips" the coupons from the bond and sells the remainder of the asset — namely, the redemption value. This redemption-value-only bond is called a "strip" bond and would sell for a price $C(1 + i)^{-n}$. The original buyer may also then sell each coupon as a separate asset. Each coupon has value $Fr(1 + i)^{-n}$ where n is the number of interest conversion periods from now to the time the coupon is payable.

In rare cases, corporations issue zero-coupon bonds where the bond interest rate is 0%. Obviously, the value of this bond is the discounted value of the redemption value, i.e., $C(1 + i)^{-n}$.

EXAMPLE 2   There exists a $1000 corporate bond with bond interest at $j_2 = 9\%$ redeemable at par in 20 years. Investor A buys the bond to yield $j_2 = 8\frac{1}{2}\%$. Investor A strips the coupons from the bond and sells the remaining "strip" bond to Investor B, who wishes a yield rate of $j_{12} = 9\%$.

Determine a) the price Investor B paid for the strip bond; b) the yield rate j_2 realized by Investor A; c) the profit Investor A makes if, in addition to selling the strip bond, the first 10 coupons are sold to Investor C who wishes to yield $j_2 = 8\%$ and the last 30 coupons are sold to Investor D who wishes to yield $j_2 = 7\%$.

Solution a   Investor B will pay the discounted value of $1000 payable in 20 years at $j_{12} = 9\%$, or $i = 0.0075$, per month over 240 months.

$$P = 1000(1.0075)^{-240} \doteq \$166.41$$

Solution b   First determine the price Investor A paid for the bond. With $F = C = 1000$, $r = 0.045$, $i = 0.0425$, and $n = 40$,

$$P = 1000 + (45.00 - 42.50)a_{\overline{40}|0.0425} \doteq \$1047.69$$

In return for the investment of $1047.69, Investor A gets 40 coupons worth $45 each over 20 years plus $166.41 payable immediately from Investor B. That is,

$$1047.69 = 166.41 + 45a_{\overline{40}|i}$$
$$a_{\overline{40}|i} = 19.5840$$

A starting value to solve $a_{\overline{40}|i} = 19.5840$ (see section 3.6) is

$$i = \frac{1 - \left(\frac{19.5840}{40}\right)^2}{19.5840} = 0.038822092 \text{ or } j_2 = 2i = 7.76\%.$$

At $j_2 = 7\%$, $a_{\overline{40}|0.035} = 21.3551$.
At $j_2 = 8\%$, $a_{\overline{40}|0.04} = 19.7928$.

We obviously need to proceed to $j_2 = 9\%$.

At $j_2 = 9\%$, $a_{\overline{40}|0.045} = 18.4016$.

Now we have two rates, $j_2 = 8\%$ and $j_2 = 9\%$, 1% apart, that provide upper and lower bounds for interpolation.

Arranging our data in an interpolation table, we have

		$a_{\overline{40}|i}$	j_2		
		19.7928	8%		
1.3912	0.2088	19.5840	j_2	d	1%
		18.4016	9%		

$$\frac{d}{1\%} = \frac{0.2088}{1.3919}$$
$$d \doteq 0.15001078\%$$
$$\text{and } j_2 = 8.15\%$$

Solution c   The price Investor C pays for the first 10 coupons is

$$P = 45a_{\overline{10}|0.04} \doteq \$364.99$$

The price Investor D pays for the last 30 coupons is

$$P = 45a_{\overline{30}|0.035}(1.035)^{-10} \doteq \$586.73$$

Total received by Investor A = $(166.41 + 364.99 + 586.73) = \$1118.13$
Total paid by Investor A $= \$1047.69$
Net Profit earned by Investor A $= \$\quad 70.44$

Exercise 6.7

Part A

1. A $10 000 serial bond is to be redeemed in instalments of $2000 at the end of each of the 21st through 25th year from the date of issue. The bonds pay interest at $j_2 = 11\%$. What is the price to yield 9% per annum compounded semi-annually?

2. A $100 000 issue of serial bonds issued July 1, 2006, and paying interest at rate $j_2 = 9\%$ is to be redeemed in instalments of $25 000 each on the first day of July in 2011, 2013, 2015, and 2017. Determine the price to yield 7% per annum compounded semi-annually.

3. A corporation issues a $1000 20-year bond with bond interest at $j_2 = 10\%$. It is purchased by an investor A who wishes a yield of $j_2 = 9\frac{1}{2}\%$. This investor A keeps the coupons but sells the strip bond to another investor whose desired yield is $j_{12} = 10\frac{1}{2}\%$. Determine the overall rate j_2 to investor A.

4. A corporation issues a $1000 15-year zero coupon bond redeemable at par. Determine the price paid by an investor whose desired yield is $j_{365} = 8\%$.

5. Investor A buys a $2500 10-year bond paying interest at $j_2 = 6\%$, redeemable at 105, to yield $j_2 = 7\%$. She sells the coupons to Investor B who wishes to yield $j_2 = 6.25\%$ and she sells the strip bond to Investor C who wishes to yield $j_4 = 6.5\%$. What profit does Investor A make?

Part B

1. In Part B, problem 2 of Exercise 6.2 we introduced Makeham's formula for a bond redeemable at par.

$$P = F(1+i)^{-n} + \frac{r}{i}[F - F(1+i)^{-n}]$$

For serial bonds with k individual issues, we have

$$P^{(k)} = F_k(1+i)^{-n_k} + \frac{r}{i}[F_k - F_k(1+i)^{-n_k}]$$

and $\sum_k P^{(k)} = \sum_k F_k(1+i)^{-n_k} + \frac{r}{i}\left[\sum_k F_k - \sum_k F_k(1+i)^{-n_k}\right]$

where $\sum_k P^{(k)}$ ... purchase price of the entire serial issue.

$\sum_k F_k(1+i)^{-n_k}$ ... total present value of all redemptions.

$\sum_k F_k$ ... total face value of k individual issues.

Try this formula on questions 1 and 2 of Part A.

2. To finance an expansion of services, the city of Aurora will issue on March 15, 2006, $30 000 000 of serial bonds. Bond interest at 13% per annum is payable half yearly on March 15 and September 15, and the contract provides for redemption as follows:
$10 000 000 of the issue to be redeemed March 15, 2011;
$10 000 000 of the issue to be redeemed March 15, 2016;
$10 000 000 of the issue to be redeemed March 15, 2021.
Calculate the purchase price of the issue to the public to yield $j_1 = 12\%$ on those bonds redeemable in 5 years and $j_1 = 14\%$ on the remaining bonds.

3. A $210 000 issue of serial bonds with annual coupons of 10% on the balance outstanding is to be redeemed in 20 annual instalments beginning at the end of 1 year. The amount redeemed at the end of 1 year is to be $1000; at the end of 2 years, $2000; at the end of 3 years, $3000; and so on, so that the last redemption amount is $20 000 at the end of 20 years. Determine the price to be paid for this issue to yield $j_1 = 8\%$. [Note that Makeham's formula may prove to be useful.]

4. A $10 000 serial bond is to be redeemed in $1000 instalments of principal per year over the next 10 years. Coupons at the rate of 9% on the outstanding balance over the next 10 years are also to be paid annually. Calculate the purchase price to yield an investor a yield a) $j_1 = 10\%$; b) $j_2 = 8\%$.

5. A corporation issues a $1000 15-year bond with bond interest at $j_2 = 9\frac{1}{2}\%$ and redeemable at 105. It is purchased by Investor A who wishes a yield of $j_2 = 10\%$. Investor A sells the coupons to Investor B whose desired yield is $j_2 = 10\frac{1}{2}\%$ and Investor A keeps the strip bond. Determine the overall yield rate, j_2, to Investor A.

| Section 6.8 | **Summary and Review Exercises** |

- Purchase price P of a bond with face value F, redemption value C, and bond rate r, on a bond interest date n interest periods prior to maturity, to yield rate i until maturity is given by

$$P = Fra_{\overline{n}|i} + C(1+i)^{-n} \qquad \text{basic formula}$$

or

$$P = C + (Fr - Ci)a_{\overline{n}|i} \qquad \text{premium/discount formula}$$

- For par value bonds with $C = F$

$$\text{premium } P - C = (Fr - Ci)a_{\overline{n}|i} = F(r - i)a_{\overline{n}|i}$$
$$\text{discount } C - P = (Ci - Fr)a_{\overline{n}|i} = F(r - i)a_{\overline{n}|i}$$

- For other bonds with $C \neq F$ and modified coupon rate $g = \dfrac{Fr}{C}$

$$\text{premium } P - C = (Fr - Ci)a_{\overline{n}|i} = C(g - i)a_{\overline{n}|i}$$
$$\text{discount } C - P = (Ci - Fr)a_{\overline{n}|i} = C(i - g)a_{\overline{n}|i}$$

- Properties of a bond schedule:
  1. All book values can be reproduced by a purchase price formula.
  2. Book value adjustments add up to the amount of discount (or the amount of premium).
  3. Book values are gradually adjusted from P to C. In the case of a discount, we accumulate the discount or write the bond up from P to C; in the case of a premium, we amortize the premium or write the bond down from P to C.
  4. Successive book value adjustments are in the ratio $(1 + i)$.

- In the bond schedule:
  Book value adjustment at time k = Coupon – Interest on book value at time $(k - 1)$.
  For bonds purchased at a discount, book value adjustments are negative and the bond is written up.
  For bonds purchased at a premium, book value adjustments are positive and the bond is written down.

- If the bond is purchased between bond interest dates, where k is the fractional part of the interest period that has elapsed since the preceding bond interest date $(0 < k < 1)$ the flat price P is given by

$$P = P_0 (1 + i)^k$$

  where P_0 is the price on the preceding bond interest date.

- Market price Q is the flat price P less accrued bond interest $I = k(Fr)$

$$Q = P - I = P_0 (1 + i)^k - kFr$$

- To estimate the yield rate by the Method of Averages we calculate

$$i \doteq \frac{\text{average income per period}}{\text{average value invested}} = \frac{[n(Fr) + C - P]/n}{(P + C)/2}$$

To obtain a more accurate value of i, we follow the Method of Interpolation, or use a spreadsheet.

Review Exercises 6.8

1. The Acme Corporation issues $10 000 000 of 20-year bonds on March 15, 2006, with semi-annual coupons at 7%. The contract requires Acme to set up a sinking fund earning interest at $j_2 = 5\%$ to redeem the bonds at maturity; the first sinking-fund deposit is to be made September 15, 2006. Determine
   a) the purchase price of the bond issue to yield $j_2 = 6\%$;
   b) the necessary sinking-fund payment.

2. Refer to Problem 1. Rather than issuing 20-year bonds, assume that Acme Corporation decided to issue serial bonds on March 15, 2006, with the following redemption schedule:
   $5 000 000 on March 15, 2012;
   $3 000 000 on March 15, 2017;
   $2 000 000 on March 15, 2022.
   Compute the purchase price of this serial bond issue to the public on March 15, 2006, to yield $j_2 = 6\%$.

3. The XYZ Corporation issues a $1000 bond with coupons at $j_2 = 8\%$ and redeemable at par on August 1, 2021.
   a) How much should be paid for this bond on February 1, 2006, to yield $j_2 = 6\%$?
   b) If the purchase price was $1050, and the bond is held to maturity, determine the overall yield, j_2.

4. A $1000 bond with semi-annual coupons at $j_2 = 10\%$ payable January 1 and July 1 each year matures on July 1, 2011, for $1050.
   a) Determine the price on January 1, 2006, to yield $j_2 = 10\frac{1}{2}\%$.
   b) Is the bond purchased at a premium or a discount?
   c) Calculate the entries in the bond schedule on July 1, 2006, and January 1, 2007.

5. The ABC Corporation $2000 bond, paying bond interest at $j_2 = 8\%$, matures at par on September 1, 2019.
   a) What did a buyer pay for this bond on July 20, 2006, if the market quotation for the bond was 104.75?
   b) Estimate, using linear interpolation, the yield rate for the buyer in part a).

   c) What should the market quotation for this bond be on July 20, 2006, if the desired yield is $j_2 = 7\%$?

6. The ABC Corporation issues a 20-year par value bond on February 1, 2006, with coupons at $j_2 = 8\%$ payable February 1 and August 1. Mr. Kelly buys a $1000 bond from this issue on February 1, 2006 to yield $j_2 = 9\%$. On August 1, 2010, Mr. Kelly sells this bond to Ms. Quinn, who wants a yield $j_2 = 7\%$.
   a) Determine the original purchase price.
   b) Determine the sale price on August 1, 2010.
   c) What yield, j_2, did Mr. Kelly realize?
   d) Determine the sale price if the transaction took place on September 1, 2010.

7. Ms. Machado invested $10 000 in the Ace Manufacturing Company four years ago. She was to be paid interest on the loan at $j_2 = 11\%$. The principal amount of $10 000 was to be returned after 10 years. Now, having just received the 8th interest payment in full, Ms. Machado has been informed that Ace has just been declared bankrupt. Ms. Machado has been offered, as a settlement, 25% of the present value of all monies due to her, determined at $j_1 = 13\%$. How much can she expect to receive?

8. A $1000 bond has semi-annual coupons at $j_2 = 7\%$. The bond matures after 20 years at par but can be called after 15 years at $1050.
   a) Determine the price to guarantee a yield of $j_2 = 8\%$.
   b) What maturity date was assumed in answering part a)?
   c) Determine the yield, j_2, realized if the bond is redeemed other than anticipated in part a). (Your answer must be larger than $j_2 = 8\%$.)

9. A bond with face value $10 000 pays $j_2 = 9\%$. An investor buys it for $10 500 and sells it 4 years later for $10 200. Calculate the yield rate, j_2, earned by the investor over this period using a) the method of averages; b) interpolation.

10. A $1000 bond with coupons at $j_2 = 10\%$ is redeemable at par in n years. It is purchased at

a premium of $300. Another $1000 bond with coupons at $j_2 = 8\%$ is also redeemable at par in n years. It is purchased at a premium of $100 on the same yield basis.
a) Calculate the unknown yield rate, j_2.
b) Determine n.

11. A $1000 callable bond pays $j_2 = 10\%$ and matures at par in 20 years. It may be called at $1100 at the end of years 5–9 inclusive. Determine the price to yield at least $j_2 = 9\%$.

12. A $10 000 bond has semi-annual coupons, and matures at par in 15 years. It is bought at a discount to yield $j_2 = 11\%$. The adjustment in book value at the end of 5 years is $25. Determine the purchase price.

13. Calculate the price on Dec. 8, 2006, of a $5000 bond maturing at par on July 2, 2016, paying $j_2 = 6\%$. It is priced to yield $j_2 = 7\%$.

14. A 20-year bond with a par value of $1000, paying $j_2 = 7\%$, and a maturity value of $1100 is bought on December 20, 2003, to yield $j_2 = 6\%$ to the investor.
a) What is the price of the bond?
b) How much of the coupon received on June 20, 2007, can be considered as interest income by the purchaser?
c) If the bond were sold on July 20, 2007, to yield $j_2 = 5\%$ to the purchaser, how much would the seller receive?
d) Assume the bond is bought for the price calculated in a) and sold for the price calculated in c) on July 20, 2007. What rate, j_2, has the original investor earned? Use the method of averages.

15. A $2000 bond matures at par in 10 years and pays $j_2 = 10\%$. Determine the purchase price to yield to maturity a) $j_2 = 11\%$; b) $j_{12} = 9\%$.

16. A $1000 bond matures for $1050 in 2 years and pays $j_2 = 9\%$. Determine the price P to yield $j_2 = 10\%$ to maturity and construct the bond schedule.

17. A $2000 bond with semi-annual coupons at $j_2 = 7\%$ is redeemable for $2100. If the amount for the 10th write-down is $6.50, calculate the purchase price to yield $j_2 = 5.8\%$.

18. For a $2000 bond redeemable at par on February 1, 2021, with bond interest at $j_2 = 8\%$, determine the purchase price on May 8, 2006 to yield $j_2 = 7\%$ until maturity.

19. For a $5000 bond redeemable at 101.75 on May 15, 2013, paying bond interest at $j_2 = 8.5\%$, determine the purchase price on March 7, 2006 at a market quotation of 91.25.

20. For a $2000 bond redeemable at par on April 18, 2015, paying bond interest at $j_2 = 7\%$, calculate the market quotation on June 6, 2006, that would give a yield rate to maturity $j_2 = 8.2\%$.

21. A $2000 bond maturing at par in 16 years, with bond interest at $j_2 = 9\%$, is purchased to yield $j_2 = 10\%$ to maturity. After 4 years the bond is sold to yield $j_2 = 8\%$ to maturity. Determine the yield rate over the 4-year period using interpolation.

CASE STUDY 1   *Callable bond*

A $5000 callable bond matures on September 1, 2015, at par. It is callable on September 1, 2010, 2012, or 2014 at $5250. Interest on the bond is $j_2 = 8\%$.
a) Calculate the price on September 1, 2006, to yield an investor $j_2 = 6\%$.
b) Draw up the bond schedule for the year September 1, 2006, to September 1, 2007.
c) If the bond was called on September 1, 2012, what yield, j_2, would the investor have earned? Use the method of averages, followed by interpolation.
d) On November 1, 2008, the bond is sold to yield $j_2 = 7\%$ until maturity.
   i) Determine the purchase price.
   ii) What is the market quotation?

CHAPTER 7

Business Decisions, Capital Budgeting, and Depreciation

Learning Objectives

In this chapter we discuss some common methods and financial tools that are used by companies and individuals to help them make business decisions. These methods basically consist of estimating future income streams or future cash flows and then calculating their present value.

Section 7.1 introduces the concept of net present value. Here we calculate the present value of future cash flows and then subtract the initial investment amount. If the resulting net present value is positive, that indicates that the investment will be profitable and should proceed.

Section 7.2 introduces a related concept called the internal rate of return. This is the interest rate at which the net present value is zero. This rate is considered to be the actual rate of return that an investment will earn assuming that the estimated future cash flows turn out to be realized.

Both the net present value and the internal rate of return are values that are calculated by companies and individuals when assessing their investment opportunities. In section 7.2 we attempt to give the reader some thoughts about which of the two is the better tool.

Throughout this text, we have focused on financial assets, in which an investment is made and future income is received. Sections 7.3 and 7.4 switch the focus to physical assets. These are assets that are used to run a business and they cost money to purchase and maintain. Section 7.3 calculates the present value of the future costs of a physical asset. The resulting value is called the capitalized cost and it can be used as an analytic tool by a company when they are faced with a decision about which of several assets to purchase to perform the same job.

Section 7.4 concludes the chapter by discussing how physical assets depreciate over time and how this depreciation is expensed by the company. The two most common methods that are used in Canada to depreciate assets over their useful lifetime are introduced.

Section 7.1 — Net Present Value

Most business enterprises and investors are required to decide, on a fairly regular basis, whether a particular business venture or investment is worthwhile and should proceed. In many cases, a comparison between alternative projects is also required. That is, a financial assessment of each proposal is necessary before it commences so that the appropriate decision may be made.

One method of assessing a project that involves future cash flows is to use compound interest and calculate the present value of these cash flows at a particular interest rate. The interest rate used is known as the **cost of capital** and can be considered to be the cost of borrowing money by the business or the rate of return that an investor may obtain if the money is invested with security. The cost of capital can also be thought of as the minimum rate of return required by the investor if they are to undertake the investment or business venture. This process is known as calculating the **net present value** for the project and may be represented by the following equation:

$$\text{Net Present Value (or NPV)} = F_0 + F_1(1 + i)^{-1} + F_2(1 + i)^{-2} +$$
$$F_3(1 + i)^{-3} + \cdots + F_n(1 + i)^{-n}$$

where F_t = estimated cash inflows – estimated cash outflows (for period t) and i is the cost of capital per period. F_t is commonly referred to as the estimated net cash flow for the project at the end of period t. When $F_t > 0$, the cash inflows for period t exceed the cash outflows and the opposite is true when $F_t < 0$.

The net present value can be used to make a business decision. If $\text{NPV} \geq 0$, we can conclude that the rate of return from the cash inflows is greater than or equal to the cost of the cash outflows and the project has economic merit and should proceed. If $\text{NPV} < 0$, we conclude that the return for the cash inflows is lower than the cost of the cash outflows and the project should not proceed (as the cost cannot be recovered by the income).

In many examples the first cash flow (namely F_0) is negative, while all future cash flows during the term of the project are positive. However, in other cases, additional funds may be required such that some later F_ts are negative.

EXAMPLE 1   Determine the net present value of a $100 000 investment that is estimated to have the following estimated yearly cash flows (all assumed to occur at the end of each year) if the cost of capital is a) $j_1 = 7\%$; b) $j_1 = 14\%$.

Year End	1	2	3	4
Cash Inflow	$80 000	$70 000	$65 000	$70 000
Cash Outflow	$40 000	$40 000	$35 000	$35 000

Solution a   We have $F_0 = -100\,000$, $F_1 = 40\,000$, $F_2 = 30\,000$, $F_3 = 30\,000$, $F_4 = 35\,000$, and $i = 0.07$,

$$\text{NPV at } 7\% = -100\,000 + 40\,000(1.07)^{-1} + 30\,000(1.07)^{-2}$$
$$+ 30\,000(1.07)^{-3} + 35\,000(1.07)^{-4}$$
$$\doteq +\$14\,777$$

This result indicates that if the cost of capital is 7%, then the project should proceed, because its profit in present value terms is $14 777.

Solution b   With the same values for F_t but with $i = 0.14$,

$$\text{NPV at 14\%} = -100\,000 + 40\,000(1.14)^{-1} + 30\,000(1.14)^{-2}$$
$$+ 30\,000(1.14)^{-3} + 35\,000(1.14)^{-4}$$
$$\doteq -\$856$$

This negative net present value indicates that if the cost of capital is 14%, then this project will not return as high a rate as the cost of capital and therefore should not proceed.

OBSERVATION:

The following points should be noted.

1. Due to the uncertainty of the future, the cash-flow figures used are normally estimates and therefore the net present value can be rounded to the nearest dollar, or in some cases the nearest hundred or thousand dollars.

2. As the future cash flows are only estimates and may vary with changing circumstances, it is common for at least three different sets of cash flows to be used representing the expected situation as well as an optimistic and pessimistic view, which in turn provides three net present values.

As shown in previous chapters, problems involving cash flows over several periods can be presented in a spreadsheet. The following spreadsheet shows how Example 1 could be calculated at both interest rates.

	A	B	C	D	E	F
			Factor at 7% p.a.	PV at 7% p.a.	Factor at 14% p.a.	PV at 14% p.a.
1	Year End	Cash Flow				
2	0	−100,000	1.00000	−100,000	1.00000	−100,000
3	1	+40,000	0.93458	+37,383	0.87719	+35,088
4	2	+30,000	0.87344	+26,203	0.76947	+23,084
5	3	+30,000	0.81630	+24,489	0.67497	+20,249
6	4	+35,000	0.76290	+26,702	0.59208	+20,723
7			NPV	+$14,477		−$856

In a spreadsheet, it is also possible to place a variable (say the interest rate) in a particular cell and to set up the table in terms of this cell. This means that when the variable is changed, all the relevant cells change automatically. This process enables the user to see the results at different interest rates quickly.

Most spreadsheets also have an inbuilt function to calculate the net present value. For instance, in Excel it is *NPV* (rate, value 1, value 2, ...). However, this assumes that each value is spaced equally and that the first payment (i.e., value 1) is in one period's time. Using Example 1, we could type the interest rate in cell G1 (0.07) and then the function in the spreadsheet would be:

$$= NPV(\text{G1, B3 : B6}) - 100\,000$$

Note that the $100 000 that is paid immediately is subtracted from the function to obtain the correct answer. To see what the net present value becomes when the cost of capital is 14%, you need only change the value of cell G1 to 0.14.

One of the major advantages in calculating net present values is that they enable comparisons to be made between two alternative projects that require the same investment. However, as shown in the following example, the preferred choice may depend on the cost of capital.

EXAMPLE 2   The following data provide the estimated end-of-year net cash flows that will be received from alternative projects A and B for an investment of $200 000. Which project should be adopted if the cost of capital is a) $j_1 = 6\%$; b) $j_1 = 8\%$?

Year	1	2	3	4
Project A	$80 000	$70 000	$60 000	$ 35 000
Project B	$30 000	$40 000	$40 000	$150 000

Solution a

NPV of project A at 6% $= -200\,000 + 80\,000(1.06)^{-1}$
$+70\,000(1.06)^{-2} + 60\,000(1.06)^{-3}$
$+35\,000(1.06)^{-4}$
$\doteq +\$15\,871$

NPV of project B at 6% $= -200\,000 + 30\,000(1.06)^{-1}$
$+40\,000(1.06)^{-2} + 40\,000(1.06)^{-3}$
$+150\,000(1.06)^{-4}$
$\doteq +\$16\,301$

Both net present values are positive so that both projects would be profitable and could proceed. However, with the higher NPV at 6%, project B is to be slightly preferred.

Solution b

NPV of project A at 8% $= -200\,000 + 80\,000(1.08)^{-1}$
$+70\,000(1.08)^{-2} + 60\,000(1.08)^{-3}$
$+35\,000(1.08)^{-4}$
$\doteq +\$7444$

NPV of project B at 8% $= -200\,000 + 30\,000(1.08)^{-1}$
$+40\,000(1.08)^{-2} + 40\,000(1.08)^{-3}$
$+150\,000(1.08)^{-4}$
$\doteq +\$4079$

On this occasion project A returns the higher profit, although again both projects would be acceptable.

OBSERVATION:

This example highlights the fact that the actual interest rate used is important when using *NPV*s to make investment decisions.

EXAMPLE 3   An insurance company has $1 million to invest. Two investment options are available: the first is an investment in a 4-year 12% government bond paying half-yearly interest, redeemable at par and priced at $95; the second is the purchase of a 4-year lease on a coal mine priced at $1 million, which is likely to return the following year-end cash flows:

Year	1	2	3	4
Cash Flow	$400 000	$600 000	$500 000	−$200 000

The net cash outflow in the fourth year is shown as a negative payment and is the cost of land restoration. Which option should the company follow?

Solution   In this problem we will calculate the yield obtained on the government bond investment (which we assume to be secure) and then use this figure as the cost of capital to calculate the net present value of the mining investment. Using formula (**15**) the equation of value for the bond is

$$95 = 6a_{\overline{8}|i} + 100(1 + i)^{-8}$$

Using the Texas Instruments BA-35 calculator, with the following steps

6 $\boxed{PMT}$ 100 $\boxed{FV}$ −95 $\boxed{PV}$ 8 $\boxed{N}$ $\boxed{CPT}$ $\boxed{I/Y}$

results in $i = 6.831892\%$, or $j_2 = 13.663784\%$.
Then determine i per year equivalent to $j_2 = 13.663784\%$

$$1 + i = \left(1 + \tfrac{0.13663784}{2}\right)^2$$
$$i \doteq 14.13\%$$

We now use $i = 14.13\%$ as the cost of capital for the alternative coal mine lease. (Note that at this cost of capital, the net present value of the government bond is equal to 0.)

$$\begin{aligned}
\text{NPV at } 14.13\% &= -1\,000\,000 + 400\,000(1.1413)^{-1} \\
&\quad + 600\,000(1.1413)^{-2} + 500\,000(1.1413)^{-3} \\
&\quad - 200\,000(1.1413)^{-4} \\
&= +\$29\,563
\end{aligned}$$

As the NPV is positive, it indicates that the mining investment will be more profitable than the bond investment; the insurance company should choose the mining investment over the government bond based on these estimated cash flows.

It should be added that this example makes no allowance for the different risks involved in these two investment options. That will be analyzed in chapter 8.

EXAMPLE 4 A mining company is considering whether to develop a mining property. It is estimated that an immediate expenditure of $7 000 000 will be needed to bring the property into production. Thereafter, the net cash inflow will be $1 700 000 at the end of each year for the next 10 years. An additional expenditure of $3 200 000 at the end of 11 years will have to be made to restore the property to an attractive condition. On projects of this type the company would expect to earn at least $j_1 = 20\%$. Advise whether the company should proceed.

Solution The net present value of the project at $j_1 = 20\%$ is

$$\text{NPV at } 20\% = -7\,000\,000 + 1\,700\,000a_{\overline{10}|0.20} - 3\,200\,000(1.20)^{-11}$$
$$\doteq -7\,000\,000 + 7\,127\,202.55 - 430\,681.55$$
$$= -\$303\,479$$

The negative net present value of the project means that the project will not yield a 20% return per annum and therefore should be rejected. If the above calculations are repeated using a desired rate of 15%, the net present value of the project will be

$$-7\,000\,000 + 1\,700\,000a_{\overline{10}|0.15} - 3\,200\,000(1.15)^{-11} \doteq \$844\,088$$

The positive net present value of the project means that the project is earning more than 15% per annum.

Exercise 7.1

Part A

Calculate the net present value for a $100 000 investment in problems 1 to 4 and determine whether the investment should proceed.

		End-of-Year Net Cash Flow			
No.	Cost of Capital per Annum	Year 1	Year 2	Year 3	Year 4
1.	10%	$40 000	$30 000	$40 000	$30 000
2.	7%	$50 000	$60 000	$20 000	—
3.	12%	$15 000	$20 000	$40 000	$60 000
4.	9%	$80 000	$60 000	$20 000	–$20 000

5. A company is considering a $200 000 investment. It is expected that project A will return $50 000 at the end of each year for the next 5 years. On the other hand, it is expected that project B will return nothing for the next 2 years but $100 000 at the end of years 3, 4, and 5. Which project should be chosen if the cost of capital is $j_1 = 4\%$? Do you obtain the same answer if the cost of capital is $j_1 = 7\%$?

6. Which of the following projects should a company choose if each proposal costs $50 000 and the cost of capital is $j_1 = 10\%$?

	End-of-Year Net Cash Flow				
	Year 1	Year 2	Year 3	Year 4	Year 5
Project A	$20 000	$10 000	$5 000	$10 000	$20 000
Project B	$5 000	$20 000	$20 000	$20 000	$5 000

7. The Northeast Mining Company is considering the exploitation of a mining property. If the company goes ahead, the estimated cash flows are as follows:

	Cash Inflow	Cash Outflow
Now	0	$3 000 000
End of year 1	$1 000 000	$2 000 000
End of year 2	$1 500 000	$500 000
End of year 3	$1 400 000	$400 000
End of year 4	$1 300 000	$300 000
End of year 5	$1 200 000	$200 000
End of year 6	$1 100 000	$100 000
End of year 7	$1 100 000	$100 000
End of year 8	$1 100 000	$100 000

The project would be financed out of working capital, on which Northeast expects to earn at least 16% per annum. Advise whether Northeast should proceed.

8. A pension fund is able to earn $j_2 = 10\%$ on its investments in government bonds. Should it proceed with an investment that costs $100 000 and returns $17 000 at the end of each half-year for the next 4 years?

9. A company is able to borrow money at $j_2 = 8\%$. A new machine costing $60 000 is now available and is estimated to produce the following savings over the next 6 years.

End of Year	1	2	3	4	5	6
Saving	$20 000	$16 000	$14 000	$12 000	$8000	$4000

Should the company borrow money to buy this machine?

Part B

1. A company is able to borrow money at $j_1 = 9\frac{1}{2}\%$. It is considering the purchase of a machine costing $110 000, which will save the company $5000 at the end of every quarter for 7 years and may be sold for $14 000 at the end of the term. Should it borrow the money to buy the machine?

2. An insurance company can invest in government bonds to obtain a yield of $j_2 = 12\%$. There are two other investments available. The first is a perpetuity paying $3300 at the end of each quarter, which may be purchased for $100 000. The second is a $100 000 investment, which will return $20 000 at the end of every year for the next 10 years. Which investment provides the company with the highest profit?

3. An investment of $100 000 produces the following year-end net cash flows.

Year	1	2	3	4	5
Cash Flow	$30 000	$30 000	$20 000	$30 000	$20 000

Calculate the net present value for this project if the cost of capital is $j_1 = 2\%$, 4%, 6%, 8%, 10%, or 12%. Graph your six answers showing the NPV against the cost of capital.

Section 7.2   Internal Rate of Return

The calculation of the net present value for a proposed investment is one method used to assess whether it ought to proceed. For example, in Example 4 of section 7.1, we determined that the project should not proceed if the cost of capital is $j_1 = 20\%$ (since NPV < 0) but should proceed if the cost of capital is $j_1 = 15\%$. It might be interesting to determine the rate of interest for which the net present value turns from positive to negative. In other words, at what rate of interest is NPV = 0.

The interest rate that produces a zero net present value is called the **internal rate of return** and its calculation is another financial tool that can be used to determine whether or not to proceed with a project. In terms of the estimated cash flows, it may be expressed as the rate of interest that solves the following equation:

$$F_0 + F_1(1 + i)^{-1} + F_2(1 + i)^{-2} + F_3(1 + i)^{-3} + \cdots + F_n(1 + i)^{-n} = 0$$

where i is the internal rate of return (or IRR) or, in terms of compound interest, the yield required to solve this equation of value.

In many instances F_0 is the only cash outflow (or negative net cash flow) so that the equation may be rewritten as

$$F_1(1 + i)^{-1} + F_2(1 + i)^{-2} + F_3(1 + i)^{-3} + \cdots + F_n(1 + i)^{-n} = -F_0$$

or $\quad F_1(1 + i)^{-1} + F_2(1 + i)^{-2} + F_3(1 + i)^{-3} + \cdots + F_n(1 + i)^{-n} = A$

where A is the initial investment.

EXAMPLE 1 Determine the internal rate of return for an investment costing $10 000 that is expected to produce net cash flows of $5000 at the end of year 1, $3000 at the end of year 2, and $5000 at the end of year 3.

Solution We have $F_0 = -10\,000$, $F_1 = 5000$, $F_2 = 3000$, $F_3 = 5000$, and

$$-10\,000 + 5000(1 + i)^{-1} + 3000(1 + i)^{-2} + 5000(1 + i)^{-3} = 0$$

or $\quad 5000(1 + i)^{-1} + 3000(1 + i)^{-2} + 5000(1 + i)^{-3} = 10\,000$

With trial and error, we determine that:

value of left hand side at 14% = 10 069
value of left hand side at 14.5% = 9986

As the cash flows are estimated we do not use linear interpolation to obtain a more accurate answer. Instead we choose the interest rate, to the nearest 0.5%, that is closest to $10 000. Since the value of the left hand side at 14.5% is only $14 off $10 000 (versus $69 off at 14%), we conclude that the internal rate of return is about 14.5%.

Using a Spreadsheet to Calculate the IRR

Excel has a function called IRR which will calculate the internal rate of return of a series of current and future net cash flows.

In Example 1, suppose cells B1 to E1 contain the cash flow values: −10 000, 5000, 3000, and 5000 respectively. To calculate the IRR of these cash flows, you would type =IRR(B1:E1), which would return a value of 14.41507% which could be rounded to two decimal points, 14.42%.

OBSERVATION:

When calculating IRRs by hand, rounding your answer to the nearest 0.5% is sufficient. When using a spreadsheet to calculate IRRs, you should round your answer to two decimal points.

Internal rates of return may also be calculated directly with a preprogrammed financial calculator. However, before using this approach, students should fully understand this section.

From our definition of the internal rate of return we know that the net present value for the investment in Example 1 at about 14.5% will be zero. The following table and graph show the NPVs for this investment for various costs of capital.

Cost of Capital	NPV for Example 1
4%	+$2026
8%	+$1171
12%	+$ 415
14%	+$ 69
14.5%	−$ 14
15%	−$ 96
16%	−$ 257
20%	−$ 856

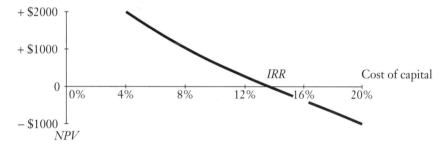

It will be noticed that if the cost of capital is less than the internal rate of return, then there is a positive NPV and hence the investment should proceed. On the other hand, when the cost of capital is greater than the internal rate of return, the NPV is negative and the investment should not proceed. This example leads us to the following relationships, which apply in most cases.

> Let i_c be the cost of capital and i_r be the internal rate of return.
>
> Where $i_c < i_r$, then $NPV > 0$ and the project will return a profit.
> $i_c = i_r$, then $NPV = 0$.
> $i_c > i_r$, then $NPV < 0$ and the project will not return the minimum required rate of return, i_c.

Although the above discussion has highlighted the similarities between NPV and IRR, the following is a list of disadvantages in using internal rates of return in assessing financial projects.

1. Multiple solutions are possible as shown by Example 3. This problem applies when the cumulative summation of F_ts changes sign more than once during the term of the investment.

2. No reference is made to the existing interest rates in the market place. Hence it is "internal" as it only refers to the cash flows of that particular investment.

3. Should the investment need to accumulate funds for a final payment (such as land restoration) then it is implied by the IRR calculation that this positive fund will earn the internal rate of return. This is extremely unlikely.

4. The use of internal rates of return to compare alternative projects may lead to conclusions different from those found by the use of NPVs. This is shown in Example 2.

EXAMPLE 2   In Example 2 from section 7.1, calculate the internal rate of return for both project A and project B. Which investment should you choose based on the IRR? Compare your decision to the one made in Example 2 from section 7.1 when the cost of capital is 6%.

Solution

Cost of Capital	NPV for A	NPV for B
6%	+$15 871	+$16 301
8%	+$ 7 444	+$ 4 079
8.5%	+$ 5 424	+$ 1 180
9%	+$ 3 438	−$ 1 659
9.5%	+$ 1 484	−$ 4 440
10%	−$ 437	−$ 7 164

The IRR for project A is about 10% (9.89% to be exact) and the IRR for project B is about 8.5% (8.71% to be exact). If the decision is to be based on the IRR, we would choose project A. However, as can be seen from the above table, if the cost of capital is 6%, we would choose project B since it has the higher NPV.

Which is the correct decision? The answer depends on the cost of capital. If the desired cost of capital is 6%, then project B would be chosen. If the cost of capital is anywhere from 8% to 9.5%, then project A would be preferable.

Remember, we ultimately want to choose a profitable investment, and the project with the higher NPV is the one that is the most profitable, regardless of the IRRs.

EXAMPLE 3   An investment company has been offered an investment that costs $7200 now and $27 000 in 2 years' time for an estimated return of $24 200 in 1 year's time and $10 000 in 3 years' time. Calculate the net present values for this investment at 5% intervals from 0% to 30% inclusive. Show that there exist three internal rates of return.

Solution   We have $F_0 = -7200$, $F_1 = 24\,200$, $F_2 = -27\,000$, and $F_3 = 10\,000$.

$$NPV = -7200 + 24\,200(1 + i)^{-1} - 27\,000(1 + i)^{-2} + 10\,000(1 + i)^{-3}$$

The following table sets out the NPVs for the required rates.

Cost of Capital	Net Present Value
0%	0
5%	– $4
10%	– $1
15%	+ $3
20%	+ $4
25%	0
30%	– $9

As the internal rate of return is the interest rate that provides a zero net present value, we can immediately see that 0% and 25% are both internal rates of return. In addition, there is a third solution between 10% and 15% (actually 11.1%). The reason for these multiple solutions is that the cumulative F_ts change sign more than once. That is, $F_0 < 0$, $F_0 + F_1 > 0$, $F_0 + F_1 + F_2 < 0$, and $F_0 + F_1 + F_2 + F_3 = 0$. In all our previous examples there had only been one change of sign and this is the condition for a single IRR.

Although this particular investment is a little unusual, it highlights the possibility of multiple IRR solutions and the difficulty that may exist in the interpretation of the internal rate of return.

Despite the possible existence of multiple IRRs and the fact that IRRs can lead to different decisions than NPVs do when comparing different investment options, internal rates of return are still frequently calculated and used by companies to assist in making business decisions. The reason is that IRRs are generally easier to understand and easier to communicate than net present values. Stating that "The project will return 13.2%" is much simpler than stating that "At a 12% cost of capital, the net present value of the project is $5000".

Exercise 7.2

Part A

1-4. Having calculated net present values for problems 1–4 in Part A of Exercise 7.1, calculate the internal rate of return in each case using the same data.

5. An investment of $10 000 provides an estimated net cash flow of $3000 for the next 2 years and $3500 for the following 2 years. Calculate this investment's internal rate of return.

6. Determine the internal rate of return for a project that costs $100 000 and is estimated to return the following year-end net cash flows:

Year	1	2	3	4	5
Cash Flow	$10 000	$20 000	$30 000	$40 000	$50 000

Part B

1. An insurance company must choose between two investments, each of which costs $10 000 and produces the following net cash flows at the end of each year.

Year	1	2	3	4	5
Project A	$5000	$4000	$3000	$2000	$1000
Project B	$1000	$3000	$4000	$5000	$6000

Calculate the internal rate of return for each project and their respective net present values at $j_1 = 15\%$ and $j_1 = 25\%$. Which project should be chosen?

2. An investment of $100 000 generates income of $75 000 at the end of the first and second years but requires an outlay of $25 000 at the end of the third year.

a) Calculate this project's internal rate of return.

b) As the final cash flow is a negative one, a sinking fund is set up at the end of the second year so that this payment will be met. If the sinking fund earns $j_1 = 5\%$ (and not the IRR), what is the project's rate of return under this condition?

Section 7.3 Capitalized Costs

In sections 7.3 and 7.4 we turn our attention away from financial assets and concentrate on physical assets. Physical assets are assets that are needed to run a business. Examples include: manufacturing equipment and machines, furniture, photocopiers, vans, trucks, tractors, and buildings. What all these assets have in common is that they do not last forever and eventually they will need to be replaced.

Many business decisions involve comparing the costs of owning or operating physical assets that depreciate over the long term and eventually need replacing. One method of comparison is that of capitalization. The **capitalized cost** of a particular asset is the present value of the total costs involved with the asset for an infinite term.

EXAMPLE 1 A manufacturer buys a machine for $25 000. It is expected to last 10 years at which time it can be sold for $2000. It is expected to cost $800 a year for maintenance. If money is worth $j_1 = 8\%$, what is the capitalized cost of the machine?

Solution We will arrange the current and future costs of the machine on a time diagram. The asset costs $25 000 today. At the end of every 10 years, the asset will be re-purchased for $25 000 and the old asset will be sold for $2000. We assume maintenance costs of $800 are paid at the end of each year.

Thus,

$K =$ original cost $+$ present value of replacement cost $+$ present value of
     of asset   of asset every 10 years   maintenance cost

In other words, the capitalized cost of the machine is defined as the original cost of the asset, plus the present value of an infinite number of replacements and the present value of the maintenance costs in perpetuity. This may be expressed as the sum of the initial cost and the value of the two perpetuities.

$$K = 25\,000 + \frac{25\,000 - 2000}{i^*} + \frac{800}{i}$$

where i^* is the nominal rate compounded once every 10 years that is equivalent to $j_1 = 8\%$. Thus,

$$K = 25\,000 + \frac{25\,000 - 2000}{(1.08)^{10} - 1} + \frac{800}{0.08}$$

$$= 25\,000 + 19\,845.98 + 10\,000$$

$$\doteq \$54\,845.98$$

To calculate the capitalized cost of any asset, we will use the following notation:

K = the capitalized cost of the asset,
C = the original cost of the asset,
S = the scrap value of the asset at the end of n years,
M = the maintenance costs per annum (assumed at the end of each year),
i = the annual interest rate,
i^* = the equivalent interest rate convertible every n years,
n = the useful life of the asset.

The relationship between i and i^* may be written as

$$1 + i^* = (1 + i)^n$$
$$i^* = (1 + i)^n - 1$$

Hence, the above equation for K may be expressed as

$$\boxed{K = C + \frac{C - S}{(1 + i)^n - 1} + \frac{M}{i}} \tag{17}$$

In theory, a company can invest the capitalized cost of an asset today in a fund earning i per year. This fund will provide enough money to allow the company to buy the asset today, to replace the asset every n years (after selling off the old asset), and to pay maintenance costs at the end of every year forever.

The concept of capitalized cost is useful in capital budgeting, when the objective is the selection of the lowest cost alternative to provide a specific level of benefits to the owner. In making comparisons between two physical assets that are employed for the same purpose but that vary with respect to original costs, scrap values, expected useful lifetimes and maintenance costs, we may compare the capitalized costs of the assets.

Some investors prefer to consider a related definition, namely the **annual cost** of each asset. As the capitalized cost is the present value of the total costs in perpetuity, the annual cost may be found as the annual interest on the capitalized cost.

$$\boxed{\textbf{Annual Cost} = Ki = Ci + \frac{C - S}{s_{\overline{n}|i}} + M}$$

OBSERVATION:

The annual cost may also be regarded as the sum of the annual opportunity (or interest) cost, the annual sinking fund deposit required for the asset's replacement, and the annual maintenance cost.

It should be noted that the above formulas make no direct allowance for inflation. However, the concepts are applicable in an inflationary period with adjustments to the interest rate.

EXAMPLE 2   A farmer can purchase a steel barn with an estimated lifetime of 20 years. It will cost $200 000 and will require $1000 a year to maintain. Alternatively, he can purchase a wooden barn with an estimated lifetime of 14 years. It will cost $160 000 and require $2000 a year to maintain. If the farmer requires a return of $j_1 = 15\%$ on his investment, what should he do?

Solution   Capitalized cost K_1 of the steel barn is

$$K_1 = 200\,000 + \frac{200\,000}{(1.15)^{20} - 1} + \frac{1000}{0.15}$$

$$\doteq 200\,000 + 13\,015.29 + 6666.67$$

$$= \$219\,681.96$$

Capitalized cost K_2 of the wooden barn is

$$K_2 = 160\,000 + \frac{160\,000}{(1.15)^{14} - 1} + \frac{2000}{0.15}$$

$$\doteq 160\,000 + 26\,334.39 + 13\,333.33$$

$$= \$199\,667.72$$

The farmer should purchase the wooden barn.

Note: The annual cost of the steel barn = $\$219\,681.96 \times 0.15 = \$32\,952.29$ and the annual cost of the wooden barn = $\$199\,667.72 \times 0.15 = \$29\,950.16$.

In comparing assets and deciding which one should be chosen, we do not need to estimate the future income that will be generated from each asset. This is because it is assumed that each asset will provide the same level of income or the same level of output. When that is not true, we need to take output into account in our analysis.

Different assets may produce items at a different rate per unit of time. In that case, it is necessary to divide the capitalized cost by the number of items produced per unit of time. If U_1 and U_2 are the numbers of items produced per unit of time by asset 1 and asset 2 with capitalized cost K_1 and K_2 respectively, then the two assets are economically equivalent if

$$\frac{K_1}{U_1} = \frac{K_2}{U_2}$$

EXAMPLE 3   A machine costing $4000 has an estimated useful lifetime of 10 years and an estimated salvage value of $500. It produces 1600 items per year and has an annual maintenance cost of $800. How much can be spent on increasing its productivity to 2000 units per year if its lifetime, salvage value, and maintenance costs remain the same? The owners want a rate of return of $j_1 = 8\%$ on their investment.

Solution   Let X dollars be the maximum amount to be spent on increasing the productivity of the machine. It is assumed that X dollars will also be spent every time the machine is replaced.

The capitalized cost K_1 of the original machine is

$$K_1 = 4000 + \frac{3500}{(1.08)^{10} - 1} + \frac{800}{0.08}$$
$$\doteq 4000 + 3020.04 + 10\,000$$
$$= \$17\,020.04$$

The capitalized cost K_2 after remodelling is

$$K_2 = (4000 + X) + \frac{3500 + X}{(1.08)^{10} - 1} + \frac{800}{0.08}$$
$$= 17\,020.04 + X + \frac{X}{(1.08)^{10} - 1}$$
$$= 17\,020.04 + 1.862868609X$$

After remodelling, the machine will be economically equivalent to the original one if

$$\frac{K_1}{1600} = \frac{K_2}{2000}$$
$$K_2 = \frac{2000}{1600} K_1$$
$$17\,020.04 + 1.862868609X = \frac{2000}{1600}(17\,020.04)$$
$$1.862868609X = 4255.01$$
$$X \doteq 2284.12$$

Hence, if the improvements cost less than $2284, they should go ahead.

Exercise 7.3

1. A certain machine costs $8000; it has an expected lifetime of 10 years and scrap value of $1000. The annual maintenance cost is $1500. Determine the capitalized cost of the machine if $j_1 = 12\%$.

2. A company can build a steel warehouse with an estimated lifetime of 25 years at a cost of $200\,000 plus annual maintenance of $1500 a year. Alternatively, they can build a cement block warehouse with an estimated lifetime of 20 years at a cost of $180\,000 plus annual maintenance of $1200 a year. If money is worth $j_1 = 7\%$, what should they do?

3. A company uses batteries costing $45 with a useful lifetime of 2 years. Another model, which cost $60, has a useful lifetime of 3 years. If money is worth $j_1 = 11\%$, which should be purchased?

4. Widget-producing machines can be purchased from Manufacturer A or Manufacturer Z. Machine A costs $18 000, will last 15 years and will have a salvage value of $2400 at that time. The cost of maintenance is $1500 a year. Machine Z costs $30 000, will last 20 years and will have a salvage value of $2000 at that time. The annual maintenance cost is $1000. Machine A produces 8000 widgets per year while Machine Z produces 9000 widgets per year. If money is worth $j_1 = 7\%$, which machine should be purchased?

5. Ontario Hydro uses poles costing $200 each. These poles last 15 years and have no salvage value. How much per pole would Ontario Hydro be justified in spending on a preservative to lengthen the life of the pole to 20 years? Assume that the annual maintenance costs are equal and that money is worth $j_1 = 8\%$.

6. A town is putting a new roof on its arena. One type of roof costs $600 000 and has an expected lifetime of 20 years with no salvage value. Another type costs $700 000 but will last 30 years with no salvage value. Maintenance costs are equal. If money is worth $j_1 = 7\%$, how much can be saved each year by purchasing the more economical roof?

7. A new car can be purchased for $29 000. If it is kept for 4 years, its trade-in value will be $5200. What should the trade-in value be at the end of 3 years so that trading would be economically equivalent to keeping it 4 years, if money is worth $j_1 = 6\%$?

8. Machine 1 sells for $100 000, has an annual maintenance expense of $2000 and an estimated lifetime of 25 years with a salvage value of $5000. Machine 2 has an annual maintenance expense of $4000 and an estimated lifetime of 20 years with no salvage value. Machine 2 produces output twice as fast as Machine 1. If money is worth $j_1 = 8\%$, determine the price of Machine 2 so that it would be economically equivalent to Machine 1.

9. A machine costing $40 000 has a scrap value of $5000 after 10 years. It produces 2000 units of output per year. The annual maintenance cost is $1500. How much can be spent on increasing its productivity to 3000 units per year if its period of service, scrap value, and maintenance cost remain unchanged? Assume money is worth $j_1 = 7\%$.

10. An oil furnace should be serviced annually to maintain efficient combustion.
    a) Calculate the capitalized cost of this servicing one year before the next servicing, assuming interest is $j_1 = 6\%$ and the cost of servicing is $100.
    b) If the first servicing is due right now, costing $100, and the cost of servicing increases by 2% per year, what is the capitalized cost at $j_1 = 6\%$?

11. A building that costs $100 000 will have a salvage value of S at the end of 5 years. The annual maintenance cost is $5000, and the total annual cost is $6380.50. The sinking fund rate and the yield rate are equal to $j_1 = 5\%$. Calculate S.

Part B

1. Egbert can purchase a car with an estimated lifetime of 7 years. It will cost $20 000 and will require $1000 a year to maintain. Alternatively, he can purchase a car with an estimated lifetime of 10 years. It will cost $25 000 and will require $750 a year to maintain. Using $j_1 = 8\%$, how much can be saved by purchasing the more economical car?

2. A company is thinking of buying a machine that will replace five skilled workers. These workers are paid $3600 each at the end of each month. The machine costs $2400 a month to maintain, will last 20 years, and will have no scrap value at that time. If money is worth $j_1 = 8\%$, what is the largest amount (in thousands of dollars) that can be spent for the machine while remaining profitable?

3. Show that the capitalized cost K of an asset with zero salvage value is

$$K = \frac{1}{i}\left[\frac{C}{a_{\overline{n}|i}} + M\right].$$

4. An asset, which costs C dollars when new, has a service life of n years. At the rate of interest i per year, show that the maximum amount to

be spent to extend the life of this asset by an additional m years, given $S = 0$, is

$$\frac{Ca_{\overline{m}|i}}{s_{\overline{n}|i}} \text{ dollars.}$$

5. A machine that costs $8000 when new has a salvage value of $1000 after 5 years of service. How much could be spent on increasing its output by 40% and extending its service life by 20%? Assume that the salvage value remains the same and that money is worth $j_1 = 10\%$.

6. Machine A lasts for 10 years with a salvage value of 25% of its original cost. Machine B sells for 80% of the cost of Machine A and lasts for 10 years with no salvage value. At what annual effective interest rate would a buyer be indifferent comparing the two machines? (Assume equal maintenance costs.)

7. A person buying a house under construction has the option of paying an extra $1500 to have a more efficient gas furnace installed. Gas bills for the standard furnace are expected to be $100 per month for the first year and increase by 5% each year. For the more efficient furnace, gas bills are expected to be $60 per month the first year and also have 5% annual increases. If money could be invested at $j_2 = 8\%$, how long (to the nearest month) would it take for the more efficient furnace to pay for itself?

8. An industrial plant could recover waste heat from its production process with a heat exchanger and use this heat to reduce its fuel costs. Installing the heat exchanger would cost

$25 000. The system is estimated to last 15 years and have a scrap value of $100 at that time. Assume interest rates are $j_2 = 8\%$ and that inflation causes fuel and electricity costs to rise by 6% each year (i.e., an increase of 6% at the end of each year, with costs being constant during each year). Electricity costs to run the heat exchanger are $30 per month the first year. Fuel savings are $400 per month the first year.
   a) Determine the equivalent constant monthly fuel savings over the 15-year period.
   b) Based on monthly costs, would the heat exchanger be cost effective?

9. Plastic trays last 8 years and cost $20. Metal trays last 24 years and cost X dollars. Trays are needed for 48 years, and inflation will increase the cost of the trays 5% per year. At $j_1 = 6\%$, determine X so that the buyer is indifferent to purchasing plastic or metal trays, assuming no salvage value.

10. A town pays $100 000 per year (at the end of the year, for simplicity) to operate its landfill site. In the future, this is expected to increase by 10% per year. It would cost X dollars, paid now, to set up a composting program, but this would save $10 000 at the end of the 1st year, with savings increasing by 10% per year (e.g., after 1 year it would cost $90 000 rather than $100 000 for landfill; after 2 years it would cost $99 000 rather than $110 000 for landfill; and so on). Based on capitalized cost, what is the maximum value of X which would make composting cost effective? Assume interest is $j_1 = 11\%$ (and ignore environmental factors!).

Section 7.4   **Depreciation**

Assets, purchased at a particular point in time, provide services over a finite future accounting period. Since the economic life of most assets (land being a notable exception) is limited, it is necessary to allocate the cost of the asset to the accounting periods in which it generates revenues. This periodic charge to income to measure the consumption of the asset is called **depreciation** and, from an accounting standpoint, is an expense to the owner of the asset. Although depreciation does not require an actual cash outlay, failure to take account of the depreciation of assets that are used to run a business will, at least temporarily, understate expenses and overstate profits which will result in higher income taxes.

An account, which usually bears the name **accumulated depreciation**, or allowance for depreciation expense, is used to record the total depreciation expense from period to period. The difference between the original cost of an asset and its accumulated depreciation is its **book value**. The book value is not necessarily the same as its market value or resale value. Rather, the book value represents the remaining amount of the original cost of the asset which has yet to be charged as an expense.

At the end of its useful lifetime, the book value of an asset will equal its estimated **scrap** or **salvage value**. Both the economic lifetime of the asset and its salvage value are estimates made by persons familiar with the particular asset. The **depreciation base** of an asset is its original cost less its estimated scrap value and represents the total amount that should be recorded as depreciation over the useful lifetime of the asset.

There are many accounting methods for handling depreciation as an operating expense. We shall consider the two methods used in Canada: the straight-line method and the constant-percentage method (also called the declining-balance method); we will also consider the physical service method and depletion.

In this section we will use the following notation:

C = the original cost of the asset

S = the estimated scrap, salvage, or residual value of the asset at the end of its useful lifetime (this could be negative)

n = the estimated useful lifetime of the asset in years

R_k = the yearly depreciation expense or yearly depreciation for the kth year

B_k = the book value of the asset at the end of k years, $k \leq n$. Note that $B_0 = C$, and $B_n = S$

D_k = the accumulated depreciation expense or accumulated depreciation at the end of k years, $k \leq n$. Note that $D_k = R_1 + R_2 + \cdots + R_k$, $D_0 = 0$, and $D_n = C - S$

OBSERVATION

In Canada, the yearly depreciation expense, R_k, that a business is allowed to deduct from its income for tax purposes is referred to as the Capital Cost Allowance (CCA).

For every method of depreciation we shall set up a **depreciation schedule** showing the status of the depreciation expense at various stages during the lifetime of the asset, namely the yearly depreciation expense, the book value at the end of each year, and the accumulated depreciation to date. For all methods, the accumulated depreciation, D_k, plus the book value of the asset, B_k, must equal the original cost of the asset C. That is, $D_k + B_k = C$.

The Straight-Line Method

The simplest and by far most popular method for depreciating an asset is the straight-line method. As a matter of fact, this is the method used to report depreciation expenses under generally accepted accounting principles, GAAP, although in Canada other depreciation methods are required to be used to calculate the CCA for income tax purposes.

This method assumes that the asset contributes its services equally to each year's operation so that the total depreciation base is evenly allocated over the lifetime of the asset and the yearly depreciation expense, R_k, is a constant, R, given by

$$\boxed{R = R_k = \frac{C - S}{n}} \qquad \text{(18)}$$

The accumulated depreciation, D_k, at the end of k years is then given by

$$D_k = k\left(\frac{C - S}{n}\right) = k \cdot R$$

If we think of k as changing continuously, and not merely taking integral values, then the graph of D_k as a function of k is a straight line (see page **259**). This accounts for the name given to this method.

The book value, B_k, of the asset at the end of k years is

$$B_k = C - k\left(\frac{C - S}{n}\right) = C - k \cdot R$$

EXAMPLE 1 Equipment costing $5000 is estimated to have a useful lifetime of 5 years and scrap value of $500. Prepare a depreciation schedule using the straight-line method.

Solution The depreciation base of the asset is $5000 – $500 = $4500 and the yearly depreciation is

$$R_k = \frac{4500}{5} = \$900$$

The accumulated depreciation increases by $900 each year and the book value of the asset decreases by $900 each year. For example, the book value after 4 years is $B_4 = \$5000 – 4(\$900) = \$1400$. The complete depreciation schedule is given below.

End of Year	Yearly Depreciation	Accumulated Depreciation	Book Value
0	0	0	5000
1	900	900	4100
2	900	1800	3200
3	900	2700	2300
4	900	3600	1400
5	900	4500	500

While the straight-line method is the most popular, the next depreciation method, which charges a greater proportion of the depreciation base to the early years, is used for income tax purposes because it may match more suitably the perceived service consumption of the asset.

The Constant-Percentage Method

The constant-percentage method or declining-balance method is used for income tax purposes in Canada for almost all depreciation (capital-cost allowance) calculations. The regulations in Canada state that all items in a certain class may be pooled together and depreciated at a fixed percentage of the total capital cost (book value) in that particular pool during that year. The percentage to be used is defined by the Canada Tax Act and varies from class to class.

In general, under the constant-percentage method, each year's depreciation is a fixed percentage of the preceding book value. When this method is used, it is customary to assign a value to the **rate of depreciation,** d, rather than to estimate the useful lifetime, n, and scrap value, S. As mentioned, values of d are stated in the Canada Tax Act and vary by class of asset. Here are some examples:

Class	Rate, d	Description
1	4%	Buildings acquired after 1987
3	5%	Buildings acquired before 1988
7	15%	Boats and other vessels
9	25%	Aircraft
10	30%	Automobiles, vans, wagons, trucks, buses, tractors
13	straight line	Leasehold property
38	30%	Construction equipment acquired after 1987
39	25%	Manufacturing equipment acquired after 1987

The yearly depreciation for the kth year, R_k, is different for each year and is given by

$$R_k = B_{k-1}d$$

At the end of the 1st year:
the depreciation is $\qquad$ Cd
the book value is $\qquad$ $C - Cd = C(1 - d)$

At the end of the 2nd year:
the depreciation is $\qquad$ $C(1 - d)d$
the book value is $\qquad$ $C(1 - d) - C(1 - d)d$
$\qquad\qquad\qquad$ $= C(1 - d)(1 - d) = C(1 - d)^2$

At the end of the 3rd year:
the depreciation is $\qquad$ $C(1 - d)^2 d$
the book value is $\qquad$ $C(1 - d)^2 - C(1 - d)^2 d$
$\qquad\qquad\qquad$ $= C(1 - d)^2(1 - d) = C(1 - d)^3$

Continuing in this manner for k years, the book value, B_k, at the end of k years is given by

$$\boxed{B_k = C(1 - d)^k} \tag{19}$$

The accumulated depreciation, D_k, at the end of k years may then be calculated by $D_k = C - B_k$ or

$$D_k = C - C(1 - d)^k$$

EXAMPLE 2 A car costing \$26 500 depreciates 30% of its value each year. Make out a depreciation schedule for the first 3 years; calculate the book value at the end of 5 years and the depreciation expense for the 6th year.

Solution   A depreciation schedule is set up below.

End of Year	Yearly Depreciation	Accumulated Depreciation	Book Value
0	0	0	26 500.00
1	7950.00	7 950.00	18 550.00
2	5565.00	13 515.00	12 985.00
3	3895.50	17 410.50	9 089.50

We calculate the book value, B_5, by equation **(19)**

$$B_5 = 26\,500(1 - 0.3)^5$$
$$= 26\,500(0.7)^5$$
$$= 26\,500(0.16807)$$
$$\doteq \$4453.86$$

The depreciation expense for the 6th year is

$$R_6 = dB_5$$
$$= 0.3(4453.86)$$
$$\doteq \$1336.16$$

If we estimate the useful lifetime, n, and the scrap value, S, of the asset, it is necessary first to compute the rate of depreciation d. This is shown in Example 3. The constant-percentage method can be used only if S is positive.

EXAMPLE 3   Determine the rate of depreciation and construct the depreciation schedule for the equipment in Example 1 if the constant-percentage method is used.

Solution   We have $C = 5000$, $S = 500$, $n = 5$. Noting that $S = B_5$, i.e., the scrap value is the book value at the end of 5 years, we substitute into equation **(19)** to obtain

$$B_5 = C(1 - d)^5$$
$$500 = 5000(1 - d)^5$$
$$(1 - d)^5 = 0.1$$
$$(1 - d) = (0.1)^{1/5}$$
$$(1 - d) = 0.630957344$$
$$d = 0.369042656$$

The schedule can now be set up using the rate of depreciation $d = 0.369042656$.

End of Year	Yearly Depreciation	Accumulated Depreciation	Book Value
0	0	0	5000.00
1	1845.21	1845.21	3154.79
2	1164.25	3009.46	1990.54
3	734.59	3744.05	1255.95
4	463.50	4207.55	792.45
5	292.45	4500.00	500.00

The Physical-Service Method and Depletion

If assets are purchased to supply a service, the cost of using any asset should be spread in relation to the amount of service received in each period. The asset's useful lifetime is expressed in terms of service units and the depreciation expense is then expressed in dollars per service unit. The depreciation charge per period will then fluctuate with the amount of activity of the asset. The service units can be expressed in many ways. Examples include hours, units of production, and mileage.

EXAMPLE 4   A machine costing $5000 is estimated to have a useful lifetime of 5 years and a scrap value of $500. It is expected to run for 20 000 hours. Determine the depreciation rate per hour of useful service and prepare a depreciation schedule assuming the actual hours worked are as follows:

Year	Production Hours
1	5000
2	4400
3	4000
4	3400
5	3200

Solution   The depreciation base of the asset is $5000 − $500 = $4500. The depreciation rate is $\frac{4500}{20\,000} = 22\frac{1}{2}$¢ per hour.

The full depreciation schedule is as follows:

End of Year	Production Hours	Yearly Depreciation	Accumulated Depreciation	Book Value
0	0	0	0	5000
1	5000	1125	1125	3875
2	4400	990	2115	2885
3	4000	900	3015	1985
4	3400	765	3780	1220
5	3200	720	4500	500

Depletion

Certain kinds of assets, such as mines, gravel pits, oil wells, timber tracts, and sources of natural gas diminish in value because the natural resources they originally held become used up. This gradual loss in value due to the using up of an asset is called **depletion**. While any of the preceding methods of calculating depreciation expense could also be used in calculating depletion expenses, the normal method of calculation used is similar to the physical-service method as the following example will illustrate.

EXAMPLE 5   A mine has an original acquisition cost of $1 000 000. It is estimated to hold 50 000 grams of recoverable silver. After the mineral worth is exhausted, the land will be sold for $80 000. If, in the first year 10 000 grams are recovered and in the second year 15 000 grams are recovered, determine the depletion deduction in years one and two.

Solution   The depletion base of the asset is $1 000 000 – $80 000 = $920 000.
The depletion rate is $\frac{920\,000}{50\,000}$ = $18.40 per gram.
The depletion deduction in year one: $18.40 × 10 000 = $184 000.
The depletion deduction in year two: $18.40 × 15 000 = $276 000.

Comparison of Methods

The tables and graphs below are for the preceding Examples 1 and 3 which use the same data.

Straight-Line Method

End of Year	Yearly Depreciation	Accumulated Depreciation	Book Value
0	0	0	5000
1	900	900	4100
2	900	1800	3200
3	900	2700	2300
4	900	3600	1400
5	900	4500	500

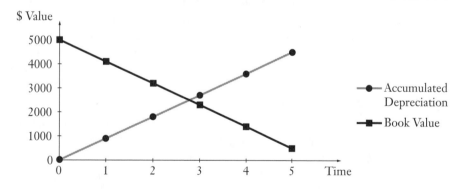

Constant-Percentage Method

Year	Yearly Depreciation	Accumulated Depreciation	Book Value
0	0	0	5000.00
1	1845.21	1845.21	3154.79
2	1164.25	3009.46	1990.54
3	734.59	3744.05	1255.95
4	463.50	4207.55	792.45
5	292.45	4500.00	500.00

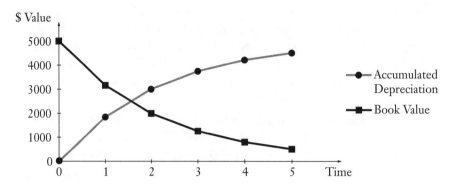

As pointed out earlier, the straight-line method is used mainly because of its simplicity. As a method of allocating the cost of an asset, however, its merits are more limited. This level allocation of the cost of the asset assumes that the services of the asset are consumed uniformly over its estimated lifetime. Further, it assumes that there is no decrease in the efficiency or quality of the service received as the asset ages. These two assumptions often may not be true.

The constant-percentage method can be referred to as an accelerated depreciation method, since it allows for larger depreciation allowances in the early years and smaller ones later on. If maintenance costs of an asset increase with time, or if the use of the asset decreases with time, this may result in a better matching of revenues with expenses throughout the life of the asset.

The constant-percentage method is popular since it is the prescribed method for most assets when it comes to determine taxable income. For companies wishing to keep only one set of records, it may be easier to use the constant-percentage method throughout.

The physical-service method is set up to match the revenue and the expenses of the asset as closely as possible. That it is not possible to draw a general graph for the method should be clear after completing several exercises that follow (Exercises 7.4, Part A: 9, 10, 11, and 12).

Exercise 7.4

Part A

1. Equipment costing $60 000 is estimated to have a useful lifetime of 5 years and a scrap value of $8000. Prepare a depreciation schedule using
   a) the straight-line method;
   b) the constant-percentage method (you must find d).

2. A machine costing $26 000 is installed. Its expected useful lifetime is 6 years. At the end of that time it will have no scrap value. In fact, it is estimated that it will cost the company $1000 to remove the old machine (i.e., $S = -\$1000$). Prepare a depreciation schedule using

   a) the straight-line method;
   b) the constant-percentage method (with $d = 25\%$).

3. A machine costing $50 000 has an estimated useful lifetime of 20 years and a scrap value of $2000 at that time. Determine the accumulated depreciation and the book value of this asset at the end of 8 years, along with the depreciation expense for the eighth year, using
   a) the straight-line method;
   b) the constant-percentage method (you must find d).

4. A machine costing $20 000 has an estimated lifetime of 15 years and zero scrap value at that time. At the end of 6 years, the machine becomes obsolete because of the development of a better machine. What is the accumulated depreciation and the book value of the asset at that time using
   a) the straight-line method;
   b) the constant-percentage method (with $d = 30\%$)?

5. A machine costing $45 000 depreciates 20% of its remaining value each year. Make out a depreciation schedule for the first 5 years.

6. A machine that costs $40 000 will depreciate to $3000 in 12 years. Determine its book value at the end of 7 years and the depreciation expense for the eighth year using the constant-percentage method.

7. Equipment worth $30 000 depreciates 10% of its remaining value each year. How many years will it take before the equipment is worth less than $15 000?

8. A machine costing $28 000 depreciates to $4000 over 15 years. How long does it take for the machine to depreciate to less than half of its original value under the constant-percentage method?

9. A machine costing $50 000 will last 5 years, at which time it will be worth $5000. In that time it is expected to produce 90 000 units. If its production follows the pattern outlined below, prepare a depreciation schedule.

Year	Units Produced
1	23 000
2	16 000
3	21 000
4	17 000
5	13 000

10. An airplane costing $10 000 000 is purchased and will be used for 3 years by a company. At the end of that time it is estimated that it can be sold for $6 000 000. The accountant sets up a depreciation schedule based on miles flown and estimates that the plane will fly 450 000 miles in the next 3 years. Given the following, prepare a depreciation schedule.

Year	Miles Flown
1	130 000
2	210 000
3	110 000

11. A mine is purchased for $300 000 and has an expected reserve of 400 000 units of ore. After mining is complete, the land will be worth $20 000. If 100 000 units of ore are extracted in the first year, determine the depletion deduction in year one.

12. Petro Canada purchases some land containing oil wells for $20 000 000. The total reserves of crude oil are estimated at 4 000 000 barrels. After the oil is gone, the land can be sold for $140 000. If Petro Canada removes 400 000 barrels in year one and 560 000 barrels in year two, determine the respective depletion deductions.

13. An $18 000 car will have a scrap value of $800 9 years from the date of purchase.
   a) Use the constant-percentage depreciation method to determine the book value of the car at the end of 3 years.
   b) An identical car can be leased for 3 years at a cost of $390 paid at the beginning of each month. If money is worth $j_1 = 9\%$, determine whether it is more economical to lease or buy the car over a 3-year period. Assume the car can be sold at the end of 3 years for its book value found in (a) if the car is bought.

14. An automobile with an initial cost of $24 000 has an estimated depreciated value for tax purposes of $4033 at the end of 5 years. Our tax system uses the constant-percentage method of depreciation.
   a) Determine the annual rate of depreciation allowed.
   b) Show the depreciation schedule.

Part B

1. Under the straight-line method, the book value at the end of k years is

$$B_k = C - k\left(\frac{C - S}{n}\right)$$

Because of the straight-line nature of this depreciation method, it is also possible to determine the book value at the end of year k

by linear interpolation between C, the original cost of the asset, and S, the salvage value of the asset, at the end of n years. Thus,

$$B_k = \left(1 - \frac{k}{n}\right)C + \frac{k}{n}S$$

Prove this formula is equivalent to

$$B_k = C - k\left(\frac{C - S}{n}\right)$$

and try this formula on questions 3 and 4 of Part A.

2. Use mathematical induction to prove formula **(19)**

$$B_k = C(1 - d)^k$$

3. Show that

$$d = 1 - \left(\frac{S}{C}\right)^{\frac{1}{n}}$$

where n is the estimated lifetime of the asset.

4. An office machine is being depreciated over 10 years to an eventual scrap value of $50, using the constant-percentage method. If the book value after four years is $457.31, what was the original value of the machine?

5. A company buys two machines. Both machines are expected to last 14 years. Machine A has a scrap value of $1050. Machine A costs $2450 and Machine B costs Y dollars. The depreciation method used for Machine A is the straight-line method, whereas the depreciation method used for Machine B is the constant-percentage method with $d = 25\%$. The present value, at $j_1 = 10\%$, of the depreciation charges made at the end of each year for Machines A and B are equal. Calculate Y.

Section 7.5   **Summary and Review Exercises**

- The net present value (or NPV) of a project over n periods with estimated net cash flow F_t at the end of period t, at interest rate i per period, is given by

$$NPV = \sum_{t=0}^{n} F_t(1 + i)^{-t}$$

If NPV > 0, the project will be profitable based on the estimated cash flows.

- The rate of interest that produces a zero net present value is called the internal rate of return (or IRR) and is calculated by solving the equation

$$NPV = \sum_{t=0}^{n} F_t(1 + i)^{-t} = 0$$

- The capitalized cost, K, of an asset with original cost C, scrap value S, annual maintenance cost M at the end of each year, and useful life of n years is defined as the present value at annual interest rate i of the total costs to own and operate the asset indefinitely and is given by

$$K = C + \frac{C - S}{(1 + i)^n - 1} + \frac{M}{i}$$

- The annual interest, Ki, on the capitalized cost K is called the annual cost and may be regarded as the sum of the annual interest cost Ci, the annual sinking fund deposit required for the asset's replacement $\dfrac{C - S}{s_{\overline{n}|i}}$, and the annual maintenance cost M.

- Notation for depreciation methods:

C = original cost
S = salvage value

$C - S =$ depreciation base

$n =$ estimated useful lifetime in years

$R_k =$ depreciation for the kth year

$D_k =$ accumulated depreciation at the end of k years; $D_0 = 0$, $D_n = C - S$

$B_k =$ book value at the end of k years; $B_0 = C$, $B_n = S$

For each depreciation method we may construct a depreciation schedule, listing k, R_k, D_k, and B_k. For each $k : D_k + B_k = C$.

● Straight-line method:

$$R_k = \frac{C - S}{n} \qquad\qquad D_k = k\frac{C - S}{n} \qquad\qquad B_k = C - k\frac{C - S}{n}$$

● Constant-percentage (Declining-balance) method:
(Assume $S > 0$, $d =$ annual rate of depreciation)

$$R_k = dB_{k-1} \qquad\qquad B_k = C(1 - d)^k \qquad\qquad D_k = C - C(1 - d)^k$$

The annual rate of depreciation, d, can be found by solving $C(1 - d)^n = S$ for unknown d to obtain

$$d = 1 - \left(\frac{S}{C}\right)^{\frac{1}{n}}$$

Review Exercises 7.5

1. A pension fund can earn $j_1 = 6\%$ with investments in government securities. Determine which of the following investments the fund should accept if the initial investment required is $100 000 in each case.

Estimated Year-End Net Cash Flow

Project	Year 1	Year 2	Year 3	Year 4	Year 5
A	25 000	25 000	25 000	25 000	25 000
B	10 000	30 000	40 000	30 000	10 000
C	–80 000	40 000	50 000	60 000	70 000
D	70 000	50 000	30 000	—	–30 000

2. Calculate the internal rate of return for a project that costs $100 000 and returns $30 000 at the end of each of the next 4 years. Compare this rate with the internal rate of return for the following alternative projects.

Estimated Year-End Net Cash Flow

Alternative	Year 1	Year 2	Year 3	Year 4
1	60 000	—	—	60 000
2	—	60 000	60 000	—
3	—	—	—	120 000
4	120 000	—	—	—
5	140 000	–100 000	130 000	–50 000

3. A company is considering buying a certain machine. One machine costs $6000, will last 15 years and will have a scrap value of $800 at that time. The cost of maintenance is $500 a year. The second machine costs $10 000, will last 25 years and will have scrap value of $1000 at that time. The cost of maintenance is $800 a year. If money is worth $j_1 = 11\%$, which machine should be purchased?

4. After 10 years of service, a machine costing $20 000 has a scrap value of $2500. It produces 1000 units a year. The annual maintenance cost is $750. How much can be spent to double its output if its scrap value, lifetime and maintenance costs remain the same? Assume $j_1 = 7\%$.

5. An asset with an initial value of $10 000 has a salvage value of $1000 after 10 years. Determine the difference between the depreciation expense entered in the books in the seventh year under the straight-line method and under the constant-percentage method.

6. a) An asset is being depreciated over an expected lifetime of 10 years at which time it will have no salvage value ($S = 0$). If the depreciation expense in the third year is $2000, determine the depreciation expense in the eighth year by the straight-line method.

b) Determine the original value of the asset C in a).

7. An $18\,000 car will have a scrap value of $2000 6 years from now. Prepare a complete depreciation schedule using
a) the straight-line method;
b) the constant-percentage method;
c) the physical-service method, given the following:

Year	km Driven
1	12 500
2	14 700
3	11 800
4	16 200
5	13 800
6	11 000

8. A gravel pit is purchased for $150\,000 and has expected usable gravel equal to 30 000 truck loads. After excavation is completed the land will be worth $25 000. Given the following shipments, produce a depletion schedule for the gravel pit.

Year	Truck Loads of Gravel
1	8000
2	9100
3	7300
4	5600

9. A machine sells for $100 000 and is expected to have a salvage value of $10 000 after 5 years. The maintenance expense of the machine is estimated to be $2000 per year payable at the end of each year.
a) Construct a depreciation schedule using the constant-percentage method.
b) Determine the capitalized cost of the asset.
c) What is the total annual cost of this asset assuming an investment rate at $j_1 = 6\%$?

10. An asset with an initial value of $100 000 is being depreciated by the constant percentage method over a 50-year period. If the book value after 30 years is $15 000 and the depreciation charge in the 31st year is $1000, determine the book value of the asset at the end of 41 years.

11. A tool is bought for $1000 and has a salvage value of $50 at the end of 8 years. Calculate the difference in book values at the end of 6 years between the straight-line and declining-balance methods of depreciation.

12. Equipment with a cost of $80 000 has an estimated salvage value of $10 000 at the end of its expected lifetime of 7 years. Determine the book value of the equipment at the end of 5 years, using
a) the straight-line method;
b) the constant-percentage method with $d = 25\%$.

13. An asset with an initial value of $15 000 has a salvage value of $2000 after 10 years. Determine the difference between the depreciation expenses entered in the books in the seventh year under the straight-line method and under the declining-balance method.

14. A machine costing $50 000 has an estimated scrap value of $5000 after 10 years. It produces 2000 units of output per year. The annual maintenance cost is $2000. How much can be spent on increasing its output by 25% and extending its service life by 30%? Assume that the salvage value and maintenance costs remain the same and that money is worth $j_i = 6\%$.

15. A machine sells for $80 000 and is expected to have a salvage value of $10 000 after 5 years. The maintenance expense of the machine is estimated to be $2000 per year payable at the end of each year.
a) What is the capitalized cost of this asset, assuming $j_1 = 10\%$?
b) Construct a depreciation schedule using the constant-percentage method.

16. A machine is purchased for $108 000 and is expected to last 8 years. The book value of the machine at the end of the second year is $44 091 by the declining-balance method. Determine the difference between the book values at the end of the fourth year using the straight-line method and the declining-balance method.

CASE STUDY 1   *A water heater*

a) A tankless water heater costs $700 and has a projected life of 25 years. The cost of replacement will increase at an annual effective rate of 4% due to inflation. Determine the capitalized cost of buying a tankless water heater if interest rates are $j_2 = 6\%$.

Disregard inflation in the prices of energy and conventional water heaters in parts b), c), d).

b) A conventional water heater has an estimated cost of $200 with a life of 15 years. Calculate the capitalized cost of owning a conventional water heater at $j_2 = 6\%$.

c) The tankless heater should save $8 per month in energy costs when compared to a conventional one. Is it cost effective to buy a tankless heater? Use $j_2 = 6\%$.

d) For a conventional heater, what is the most that should be spent on additional tank insulation if this insulation will save $4 per month in energy costs? Again use $j_2 = 6\%$.

CASE STUDY 2   *Buy or lease*

An $18 000 car will have a scrap value of $500, 9 years from the date of purchase.

a) Using the constant-percentage depreciation method, determine the book value of the car at the end of 4 years.

b) If money can be invested at $j_{12} = 6\%$, what is the monthly sinking-fund deposit necessary to replace the car if it is sold for its book value in (a) after 4 years and the price of new cars has increased at an annual rate of $j_1 = 5\%$?

c) An identical car can be leased for 4 years at a cost of $405 paid at the beginning of each month. The contract calls for the driver to pay for fuel, repairs, licences, and maintenance (but *not* for insurance). If the car is bought, there will be a cost of $800 at the time of purchase for 1 year's insurance, with insurance costs increasing by 4% at the beginning of each of the next 3 years. Still using $j_{12} = 6\%$, determine whether it is more economical to buy or lease the car over a 4-year period. Assume that it can be sold for the book value found in a) if you buy the car.

CASE STUDY 3   *Depreciation*

The XYZ Company bought a machine on January 1, 2001 for $30 000. At that time it was decided by the accountants to depreciate the machine over 20 years using the straight-line method and a salvage value of $3000. However, starting on January 1, 2007, it was decided to change to the declining-balance (constant-percentage) method to take advantage of changes in income tax laws.

a) What was the amount of the depreciation charge for 2005?

b) There are two possible ways of making the change:
    I – Take the value of the machine on December 31, 2006, and depreciate it over the remaining period using the new method; or
    II – Recalculate the depreciation schedule for the entire period using the new method and file amended tax returns for 2001 to 2006.

    i) If method I were used, what would the depreciation charge be in 2010?

    ii) If method II were used, what would be the difference between the total depreciation reported on the six income tax returns for years 2001 to 2006?

Contingent Payments

Learning Objectives

In the first seven chapters, we discussed various types of financial assets or investments, from corporate bonds to annuities, from mortgages to other types of loans. The one thing they all have in common is the assumption that future payments (or future cash flows) are guaranteed. When calculating the price of a bond, we assumed that all future coupons, along with the redemption value, were going to be paid. For a mortgage with a 5-year guaranteed interest rate, we assumed that all 60 monthly payments would be made and that the outstanding balance at the end of the 5 years would be paid. For a 10-year loan with semi-annual payments, we implicitly assumed that all 20 payments would be paid in full. In buying a 25-year annuity at age 65, we assumed that all 300 payments would be received by the individual annuitant.

However, in any investment where a lump sum is invested today and future cash flows are returned over time, there is always the possibility that not all cash flows will actually be received. For example, interest payments and the redemption value of a corporate bond will be paid only if the corporation is in a good financial position so that it can afford to honour its financial obligations. If a corporation gets into financial trouble, it may have to default on an interest payment. In extreme cases, if the corporation goes bankrupt, it may fail to make any further payments of interest or pay any redemption values.

For most investments, future cash flows are *contingent* upon the financial position of the company issuing the investment. When determining the price to be paid for an investment, how do you take into account that not all future cash flows are guaranteed? There are several ways.

One way is to determine the risk associated with buying the investment and adjusting the price paid. For corporate bonds, the price they sell at is partially determined by the market's assessment of the risk of holding a bond from a particular company. That is, the market assesses the likelihood of the company fulfilling its future financial obligations. The more likely they will be able to meet their future obligations, the lower is the perceived risk. This means the required yield rate will be lower which in turn leads to a higher price of the bond.

How do you determine the risk of holding a particular company's bond? There exists a rating system for companies that issue debt in the form of bonds. Companies that are rated in the highest category are deemed to be financially sound with minimal chance of default.

Lower ratings imply higher levels of risk, which translates into an investor requiring a higher yield rate to purchase the bond, which in turn means a lower price for the bond. Government bonds have the lowest yield rates (everything else being equal) since it is assumed that the government will always be able to honour its commitments. For this reason, government bonds may be known as "risk-free." The riskiest bonds are referred to as "junk" bonds and sell at prices well below their face values.

Another way to determine the price paid for an investment is to estimate the probability that future cash flows will not be paid and then bring these probabilities into our calculation of present values. This approach will be demonstrated in this chapter.

To begin, we first need to introduce the basic concepts of probability. This is done in section 8.1. Next we need to understand how to determine the weighted average of future contingent cash flows, where the weights are the probabilities of the cash flow actually being made. This is the process of *mathematical expectation* and is referred to as the *expected value* of a series of payments. This is discussed in section 8.2.

Finally, we extend the concept of mathematical expectation to include a rate of interest in section 8.3. When we combine interest theory and mathematical expectation, we are in effect discounting future contingent cash flows with interest. The resulting present value will be the price to pay for an investment where we have specifically estimated the probabilities that future cash flows will not be paid.

Section 8.1

Probability

Benjamin Franklin once noted jokingly that "nothing is certain except death and taxes." To all other events, it is possible to assign a probability value.

We are now used to the weather reporter telling us that there is a "20% chance of rain" for example. What do phrases such as this mean?

Classical Probability

Some probabilities are easily determined. For example, we know that the probability of obtaining any spade by randomly drawing one card from a standard 52-card deck is 13/52 or 25%. Similarly, the probability of rolling a "2" with a fair die is 1/6. These probabilities can be determined before the event occurs because we know ahead of time what all the possible outcomes are. This allows the following definition:

If an event can happen in h ways, and fails to happen in f ways, all of which are equally likely, the probability p of the occurrence of the event is

$$p = \frac{h}{h + f}$$

and the probability the event will fail to occur is

$$q = \frac{f}{h + f}$$

In the fair die example, we know ahead of time that there are 6 different sides. Thus $h + f = 6$. Only one side has the number 2, so $h = 1$. Thus $p =$ probability of rolling a "2" = 1/6.

We can see that

$$p + q = \frac{h}{h + f} + \frac{f}{h + f} = \frac{h + f}{h + f} = 1$$

That is, any event either occurs or fails to occur. Furthermore when $f = 0$, $p = 1$ and when $h = 0$, $q = 1$. That is, if an event is certain to occur, the probability of its occurrence is unity. Finally, if an event occurs with probability p, the probability that the event will not occur is $q = 1 - p$. For example, if in any time period a system survives with probability, p, then the system will fail (the complement of survival) with probability, q.

Events are said to be **mutually exclusive** if the occurrence of one event precludes the occurrence of any other events. For example, in flipping a coin, the two possible outcomes are heads and tails. Since the occurrence of a head precludes any possibility of a tail (and vice-versa) these events are said to be mutually exclusive.

If you were interested in the event that a callable bond issued by company A will be called before the end of 10 years or the event that a callable bond issued by company B will be called before the end of 5 years, these are not mutually exclusive events since both events can happen because they are two different bonds. However, for a callable bond issued by company A, if you were interested in the event that it will not be called before the end of 10 years or the event that it will be called before the end of 5 years, these are mutually exclusive events because the occurrence of one of them precludes the occurrence of the other.

Given n mutually exclusive events $E_1, E_2, \ldots, E_n$, the probability of occurrence of at least one of the n events (i.e., E_1 or $E_2 \ldots$ or E_n) is the sum of the respective probabilities of the individual events. That is,

$$P(E_1 \text{ or } E_2 \text{ or } E_3 \ldots \text{ or } E_n) = P(E_1) + P(E_2) + \cdots + P(E_n)$$

Events are said to be **independent** if the occurrence of one event has no effect on the occurrence of any other event. The occurrence of a head or tail on any one toss has no effect on the occurrence of a head or tail on any other toss. Life insurance companies assume that policyholders' deaths are independent events. That is, it is assumed that the time when one policyholder dies will not affect the time when another policyholder dies. In some situations (e.g., a husband and wife) this assumption may not be completely valid, but it is made nevertheless.

The probability of the occurrence of all of a set of independent events, $E_1, E_2, \ldots, E_n$, is the product of the respective probabilities of the individual events.

That is,

$$P(E_1 \text{ and } E_2 \text{ and } \ldots \text{ and } E_n) = P(E_1)P(E_2) \ldots P(E_n)$$

When the order in which events occur is important, you may need **conditional probability** to solve problems. For example, if you want the probability that events E_1 and E_2 occur in that order, where the probability of E_2 depends on whether E_1 has occurred, then

P(E_1 and E_2) = P(event E_1) × P(event E_2, given that event E_1 has occurred)

This can be written as:

$$P(E_1 \text{ and } E_2) = P(E_1)P(E_2 \mid E_1)$$

Conditional probability questions can also be solved using a **probability tree**. This is illustrated in Example 2.

EXAMPLE 1   You roll two fair die. Determine the probability a) the total of the two die is 7; b) the total of the two die is 6 or 7.

Solution a   There are 36 possible outcomes when rolling two fair die, all equally likely.

(1, 1)	(1, 2)	(1, 3)	(1, 4)	(1, 5)	(1, 6)
(2, 1)	(2, 2)	(2, 3)	(2, 4)	(2, 5)	(2, 6)
(3, 1)	(3, 2)	(3, 3)	(3, 4)	(3, 5)	(3, 6)
(4, 1)	(4, 2)	(4, 3)	(4, 4)	(4, 5)	(4, 6)
(5, 1)	(5, 2)	(5, 3)	(5, 4)	(5, 5)	(5, 6)
(6, 1)	(6, 2)	(6, 3)	(6, 4)	(6, 5)	(6, 6)

Thus, $h + f = 36$.

Let event E_1 = total of two die is 7. E_1 occurs when the values of the two die are (1, 6), (2, 5), (3, 4), (4, 3), (5, 2), and (6, 1). Thus $h = 6$.

$$P(E_1) = \tfrac{6}{36} = \tfrac{1}{6} = 0.16666 = 16.67\%$$

Solution b   Let E_2 = total of two die is 6. E_1 and E_2 are mutually exclusive events, since obtaining a total of 6 cannot happen at the same time as obtaining a total of 7. Obtaining a total of 6 occurs when the values of the two die are (1, 5), (2, 4), (3, 3), (4, 2), and (5, 1). Thus $h = 5$ and $P(E_2) = \tfrac{5}{36}$.

$$P(E_1 \text{ or } E_2) = P(E_1) + P(E_2) = \tfrac{5}{36} + \tfrac{6}{36} = \tfrac{11}{36} = 30.56\%$$

EXAMPLE 2   One day 20 people show up at an investment information session. The people are categorized by their income level. It turns out that 5 people have an income less than $50 000, 9 people have an income between $50 000 and $80 000, and 6 people have an income greater than $80 000. Two people are chosen at random to win a free weekend at a resort. What is the probability that a) both people chosen have an income less than $50 000; b) at least one of the winners has an income greater than $80 000?

Solution   It is helpful here to draw what is referred to as a probability tree.

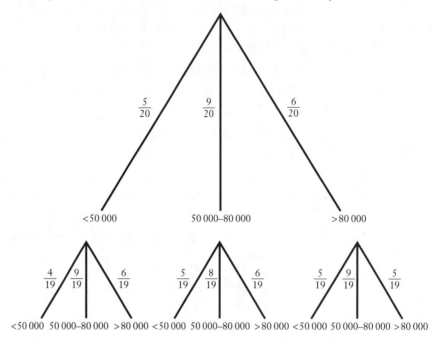

Solution a   Let E_1 = first person chosen has an income less than \$50 000 and let E_2 = second person chosen has an income less than \$50 000. Using the probability tree, the probability of E_1 followed by E_2, in that order, is

$$P(E_1 \text{ and } E_2) = P(E_1)P(E_2|E_1) = \frac{5}{20} \times \frac{4}{19} = \frac{20}{380} = 5.26\%$$

Solution b   To obtain at least one person with an income greater than \$80 000, here are the possible outcomes of the two people chosen and the associated probabilities taken by following the appropriate branches of the probability tree:

Less than 50 000, Greater than 80 000	$\frac{5}{20} \times \frac{6}{19} = \frac{30}{380}$
Between 50 000 and 80 000, Greater than 80 000	$\frac{9}{20} \times \frac{6}{19} = \frac{54}{380}$
Greater than 80 000, Less than 50 000	$\frac{6}{20} \times \frac{5}{19} = \frac{30}{380}$
Greater than 80 000, Between 50 000 and 80 000	$\frac{6}{20} \times \frac{9}{19} = \frac{54}{380}$
Greater than 80 000, Greater than 80 000	$\frac{6}{20} \times \frac{5}{19} = \frac{30}{380}$

The 5 possible outcomes are mutually exclusive events. To obtain the probability that at least one of the winners has an income greater than \$80 000, we sum the five probabilities. Our final answer is $\frac{198}{380} = 52.11\%$.

In our tree diagram, we first compute the probability of each path in the event by multiplying together the probabilities of each branch in the path. Then we add the probabilities of each path in the event together to get the total probability of the event.

EXAMPLE 3   A bag contains 5 white, 3 black, and 4 red balls. Determine the following probabilities:
  a) drawing a red ball;
  b) drawing a white or a black ball;
  c) drawing 2 white balls (no replacement);
  d) drawing a black ball twice (with replacement);
  e) drawing a white ball followed by a red ball (no replacement);
  f) drawing a red ball followed by a black ball (with replacement).

Solution   a) Probability $= \frac{4}{12} = \frac{1}{3}$
Since there are 4 red balls and 12 balls in total.

  b) Probability of white $= \frac{5}{12}$

Probability of black $= \frac{3}{12}$

Since you cannot draw a white and a black ball at the same time, these are mutually exclusive events.

Then, probability of white or black $= \frac{5}{12} + \frac{3}{12} = \frac{8}{12} = \frac{2}{3}$

  c) Probability of 1st white ball $= \frac{5}{12}$

Probability of 2nd white ball $= \frac{4}{11}$

When you do not put the first ball chosen back in the bag, the order in which the balls are chosen is important. Thus, we must use conditional probability. The probability that the second ball is white depends on whether the first ball chosen is white (had the first ball not been white, the probability of the 2nd ball being white would have been $\frac{5}{11}$, not $\frac{4}{11}$).

Probability of two white balls with no replacement $= \frac{5}{12} \times \frac{4}{11} = \frac{5}{33}$

  d) Probability of 1st black ball $= \frac{3}{12} = \frac{1}{4}$

Probability of 2nd black ball $= \frac{1}{4}$ (replacement)

When you put the first ball chosen back in the bag, you are restoring the bag to its original composition. Thus, you have independent events.
Probability of drawing black twice $= \frac{1}{4} \times \frac{1}{4} = \frac{1}{16}$

  e) Probability of white1st $= \frac{5}{12}$

Probability of red 2nd $= \frac{4}{11}$

Then, probability $= \frac{5}{12} \times \frac{4}{11} = \frac{5}{33}$

  f) Using same reasoning as above,

Probability $= \frac{4}{12} \times \frac{3}{12} = \frac{1}{12}$

Empirical Probability

Not all events allow for a priori ("before the fact") calculation of probability. For example, if a community has 1000 birth events per year, how many of these will be multiple births (twins, triplets)?

Similarly, we could ask "What is the probability of rolling a '2' with a loaded or unfair die" or "What is the probability of a company defaulting on their bond interest payments?"

The only method of solution here is to observe a large number of occurrences and to develop empirically, and after the fact, an estimate of the true underlying probability.

For example, we could roll our unfair die 100 times. If we count sixteen 2s, then an approximation to the true underlying probability of rolling a 2 is 0.16. If we roll the same die 10 000 times and observe 1715 2s, then we would refine our previous estimate and say that the "probability" of rolling a 2 is 0.1715.

Most real-life situations, including all insurance situations, require this type of estimated probability. It is important to note that this value for the probability is determined from past experience, and its use for prediction of future events involves the assumption that the future can be predicted by events in the past.

Also, if we say that the probability of an event occurring is $\frac{2}{3}$, this does not mean in 60 trials, there will be exactly 40 occurrences. Rather it means that as the number of trials is increased, the ratio of occurrences will approach $\frac{2}{3}$. This is known as the Law of Large Numbers. Formally, it states that: as the number of trials n increases, the probability that the average proportion of successes deviates from the true underlying number p tends toward zero.

In real life, however, we are usually forced to use the "best estimate," based on a relatively small number of observations, to predict future events.

EXAMPLE 4   In a study of bond default, 5865 10-year bonds issued by companies with a medium-risk rating over a 5-year period were observed. A total of 65 of them defaulted on an interest payment in the first 3 years, another 88 defaulted on an interest payment between 3 years and 6 years, while 118 more defaulted on their obligations at some point after 6 years.

If you decided to purchase a 10-year bond from a company with a medium-risk rating, what is the probability that you would receive a) less than 3 years' worth of bond interest payments; b) more than 6 years' but less than 10 years' worth of bond interest payments; c) less than the full 10 years' worth of bond interest payments?

Solution a   Using the data provided in the study, the probability of default in the first 3 years is

$$\frac{65}{5865} = 0.01108269 \doteq 1.11\%$$

Solution b   The probability of default in the last 4 years is

$$\frac{118}{5865} = 0.02011935 \doteq 2.01\%$$

Solution c   To obtain the probability of default at some point over the 10 years, we sum the data because defaulting in any of the three time periods are mutually exclusive events. Thus

$$\frac{65 + 88 + 118}{5865} = 0.04620631 \doteq 4.62\%$$

EXAMPLE 5   Based on a recent study of callable bonds, we are told that the probability of a 15-year bond not being called in the first 5 years is 0.9, not being called between 5 and 10 years is 0.8, and not being called after 10 years is 0.7. Determine the following probabilities:

    a) The probability of a just issued 15-year bond not being called before maturity.

    b) i) The probability of a just issued 15-year bond being called before 5 years; ii) between 5 and 10 years; iii) between 10 years and maturity.

    c) The probability that three 15-year bonds, one of them just issued, one of them 5-years old, and one of them 10-years old, will not be called in the next 5 years.

Solution   In answering these questions, we are forced to assume that these probabilities will remain constant and that the rates derived from past events can be used to predict future probabilities of being called.

The following tree diagram will assist us.

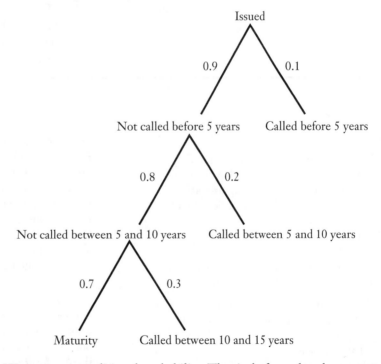

    a) We must use conditional probability. That is, before a bond can mature, it must first not be called before 5 years, then it must not be called between

5 and 10 years, and then it must not be called between 10 years and maturity. Therefore, using the tree diagram,

Prob(not called before = Prob(not called before 5 years)
maturity) × Prob(not called between 5 and 10 years)
× Prob(not called between 10 and 15 years)
= (0.9)(0.8)(0.7)
= 0.504

b) i) Prob(called before 5 years) = 1 − Prob(not called before 5 years) = 0.10
ii) For the probability of being called between 5 and 10 years from issue, the bond would first have to be not called before 5 years, followed by being called before 10 years. Thus, using the tree diagram,

Prob(called between 5 and 10 years) = (0.9)(0.2) = 0.18

iii) For the probability of being called between 10 years and maturity, the bond would first have to be not called before 10 years, followed by being called before maturity. Thus, using the tree diagram,

Prob(called between 10 and 15 years) = (0.9)(0.8)(0.3) = 0.216

c) The three bonds are called or not called independently of each other. Therefore the events of each bond not being called in the next 5 years are independent. Thus we take the product of the probability of each event.

Prob(all 3 are not called in the = Prob(1st bond is not called)
next 5 years) × Prob(2nd bond is not called)
× Prob(3rd bond is not called)
= (0.9)(0.8)(0.7)
= 0.504

Exercise 8.1

Part A

1. Given that the probability of having a male baby is equal to the probability of having a female baby, determine the following probabilities:
   a) the probability of having 2 boys in a family of three children;
   b) the probability of all boys in a family of four children;
   c) the probability of 2 boys and then a girl;
   d) the probability of a girl and then 2 boys.

2. A businessman must change planes three times in a long trip. If the probability of making any one connection successfully is 4/5, what is the probability that
   a) he completes his trip successfully?
   b) he does not complete his trip successfully?
   (Assume the changes are independent events.)

3. On your way to work, you must pass through three intersections with traffic lights. The probability that the first light you arrive at is red is 1/3. The probability of future red lights is 1/4 if the previous light was red and 1/2 if the previous light was green (ignore yellow lights). What is the probability that
   a) all traffic lights are red on the way to work?
   b) exactly one light is red on the way to work?

4. In any one year, there is a 5% chance of a bond defaulting on its bond interest payment. If you purchase a 5-year bond with annual coupons, what is the probability that you will receive all bond interest payments? (If a coupon is defaulted, then all future coupons will not be paid.)

5. A study of the default rates of 3-year bonds with semi-annual coupons concluded that the

probability of default of coupon n is $0.01n - 0.005$, $n = 1, 2, \ldots, 6$. What is the probability that
a) all 6 coupons (plus the redemption value) will be paid?
b) you will receive only the first 4 coupons?

6. The probability of team A winning a game is 3/5 (i.e., they presently have a 0.600 record). They are just starting a three game series. What is the probability that
a) they win the first two, but lose the third game?
b) they win two of three?
c) they win at least one game?
(Assume the games are independent events.)

7. The probabilities of A, B, C, and D surviving a certain period are 3/4, 4/5, 5/8, and 9/10 respectively. What is the probability that
a) all four die in the period?
b) all four survive the period?
c) at least one survives the period?
d) at least one dies in the period?
(Assume the deaths are independent events).

8. We have the following data:

Age	Probability of Surviving 10 Years
50	0.75
60	0.60
70	0.50

Determine the following probabilities:
a) someone aged 50 lives to age 80;
b) someone aged 50 dies between age 70 and 80.

9. The probability of a 40-year-old surviving to age 80 is 1/4. The probability of a 40-year-old dying between age 65 and 80 is 1/10. Calculate the probability of a 40-year-old surviving to age 65.

10. A jar contains 4 white marbles, 2 blue marbles, and 1 red marble. Determine the following probabilities (for multiple drawings, assume no replacement).
a) You draw out one marble and it is blue.
b) You draw a blue or red marble.
c) You draw out two marbles that are white.
d) You draw two marbles, the first is red and the second is blue.
e) You draw two marbles, the first is white and the second is blue.
f) You draw out two marbles of the same colour.

11. Given a normal deck of 52 cards, determine the following probabilities:
a) drawing the ace of spades;
b) drawing an ace or a king;
c) drawing the ace of spades in two draws, with no replacement;
d) drawing the ace of spades in two draws, given replacement of the first draw;
e) drawing the ace of spades on the second draw, with no replacement;
f) drawing a 2, then a 3, then a 4, if there is no replacement.

12. Given a fair die, determine the following probabilities:
a) rolling a 2;
b) rolling an even number;
c) rolling a prime number;
d) in two rolls, rolling numbers whose sum equals 9;
e) in two rolls, rolling numbers whose sum exceeds 5.

13. Given two fair die, determine the following probabilities:
a) rolling a total equal to 3;
b) rolling a total equal to 9;
c) rolling a total that exceeds 5;
d) rolling an even number, in total;
e) rolling a prime number, in total;
f) in two rolls, getting an overall total equal to 23.

14. Given a fair coin, determine the following probabilities:
a) the probability of 2 heads in three tosses;
b) the probability of all heads in four tosses;
c) the probability of 2 heads and then a tail;
d) the probability of a tail and then 2 heads.

Part B

1. What is the probability that a 3-card hand, drawn at random and without replacement from an ordinary deck, consists entirely of black cards?

2. An unbiased die is thrown twice. Given that the first throw resulted in an even number, what is the probability that the sum obtained is 8?

3. A bowl contains three red chips numbered 1, 2, 3 and three blue chips numbered 1, 2, 3. What is the probability that two chips drawn at random without replacement match *either* as to colour *or* as to number?

Section 8.2 Mathematical Expectation

A term that most students are familiar with is "average." If you take six courses, your average mark is found by taking your total mark and dividing by six. If there are 34 students in your class, the class average can be found by totalling all marks and dividing by 34.

We can look at the latter problem in another manner. Let's say the mark distribution was as follows:

Mark	# of Students
40	4
50	6
60	8
70	10
80	4
90	2

Thus, the teacher could find the class average using the following formula:

$$\frac{[4(40)+6(50)+8(60)+10(70)+4(80)+2(90)]}{34}$$

$$= 40\left(\frac{4}{34}\right)+50\left(\frac{6}{34}\right)+60\left(\frac{8}{34}\right)+70\left(\frac{10}{34}\right)+80\left(\frac{4}{34}\right)+90\left(\frac{2}{34}\right) = 62.94$$

It should not trouble us that the class average was a mark that was not achieved by anyone and, in fact, could not have been achieved by anyone.

In statistics, the class average would be called the mean of the distribution of marks. This can also be called the expected value or mathematical expectation. Formally, we say that

---

If X represents possible numerical outcomes of an experiment which can take the values $x_1, x_2, \ldots$ with corresponding probabilities $p(x_1), p(x_2), \ldots$, the **mathematical expectation** or **expected value** or **mean value** of X is defined by

$$E(X) = x_1\, p(x_1) + x_2\, p(x_2) + x_3\, p(x_3) + \cdots$$

EXAMPLE 1 If, in a dice game, one wins a number of dollars equal to the number showing on the die's upward face, what is the mathematical expectation of any participant?

Solution You can win $1, $2, $3, \ldots up to $6 each with probability 1/6 (assuming a fair die). Let X be the number of dollars won by a participant. Then,

$$E(X) = 1\left(\frac{1}{6}\right)+2\left(\frac{1}{6}\right)+\cdots+6\left(\frac{1}{6}\right) = \frac{21}{6} = \$3.50$$

Again, it should not trouble us that the expected value is an amount that cannot be won on any throw during the game.

If a person has to pay $3.50 to enter this game, then:

$$E(\text{total winnings}) = E(X - 3.50) = E(X) - 3.50 = 0.$$

Such an entry fee would make this game a "fair" game, i.e., a game in which the expected winnings are zero.

EXAMPLE 2   Two players participate in the game described in Example 1. Player A wins ($1, $2, or $3) if the face showing is 1, 2, or 3; and player B wins ($4, $5, or $6) if the face showing is 4, 5, or 6. How much should each player place in the pot (i.e., wager) if the game is to be fair?

Solution   If each player in this game wagers exactly his expectation with respect to winnings, then the game will be fair. That is, in the long run in this game, the players should expect to neither win nor lose. Thus, we find each player's expectation of winnings.

$$E(A) = \$1(1/6) + \$2(1/6) + \$3(1/6) = \$1$$
$$E(B) = \$4(1/6) + \$5(1/6) + \$6(1/6) = \$2.50$$

Therefore, if A wagers $1 and B wagers $2.50, this game will be fair.

EXAMPLE 3   Charlie pays $1 to enter a betting game. If Charlie can get three heads in a row by flipping a fair coin, he wins $5. Otherwise, he loses his $1. What is his expectation?

Solution   Coin tosses are independent events and the probability of obtaining a head on any one coin toss is 1/2. Therefore,

$$\text{Probability of winning} = \left(\frac{1}{2}\right)\left(\frac{1}{2}\right)\left(\frac{1}{2}\right) = \frac{1}{8}$$
$$\text{Probability of losing} = 7/8$$

Therefore, expectation $= \$5(1/8) - \$1(7/8) = -25\text{¢}$.

EXAMPLE 4   A local lottery sells 5 million $1 tickets each week. The cash prizes awarded are listed below. Also 250 000 people can win "Win Fall" Prizes, which entitle them to 5 tickets in the next draw. These 1 250 000 free tickets will have the same mathematical expectation as the ticket you purchase. Determine the "value" of a $1 lottery ticket.

Prize	No. Awarded	Probability
$100 000	5	$\frac{1}{1\,000\,000}$
$ 25 000	20	$\frac{1}{250\,000}$
$ 5 000	45	$\frac{9}{1\,000\,000}$
$ 1 000	100	$\frac{1}{50\,000}$
$ 100	1 950	$\frac{39}{100\,000}$
$ 10	24 500	$\frac{49}{10\,000}$

Solution   Let W be the "value" of a lottery ticket.

$$W = \$100\,000\left(\frac{1}{1\,000\,000}\right) + \$25\,000\left(\frac{1}{250\,000}\right)$$

$$+ \$5000\left(\frac{9}{1\,000\,000}\right) + \$1000\left(\frac{1}{50\,000}\right) + \$100\left(\frac{39}{100\,000}\right)$$

$$+ \$10\left(\frac{49}{10\,000}\right) + W\left(\frac{1\,250\,000}{5\,000\,000}\right)$$

Solving for W we obtain $W \doteq 47\cent$.

That means that a \$1 lottery ticket has a "value" of $47\cent$.

In general, lotteries in Canada have an expected return of $41\cent$ to $49\cent$ on the dollar. This compares to an expected return of $87\cent$ on the dollar at the horse races and a $93\cent$ to $95\cent$ expected return on the dollar at Las Vegas.

EXAMPLE 5   You invest \$10 000 for one year with the ABC company who promises to make two payments of \$5569.28, the first in 6 months and the second at the end of 1 year. What is the expected value of your investment if a) the payments are guaranteed to be made; b) the probability of default for the first payment is 2%; and the probability that the first payment is made, but the second payment is not is 5%?

Solution a   If the payments are guaranteed, the probability of receiving each payment is 100%. Thus, the expected value is

$$E(X) = 5569.28(1.00) + 5569.28(1.00) = \$11\,138.56$$

Thus you will earn \$1138.56 in interest.

Solution b   The probability of receiving the first payment is 98% and the probability of receiving both the 1st and 2nd payment is 95%. Thus, the expected total amount is
$$E(X) = 5569.28(0.98) + 5569.28(0.95) = \$10\,748.71$$

Thus you expect to earn \$748.71 in interest.

In the above example, we did not take into account that the two payments were made at different times. That is, we did not take into account the time value of money. When we combine the time value of money (that is, discount future payments with interest) and mathematical expectation, we will be discounting future contingent cash flows. Or, in other words, we will be able to determine what price we should pay for an investment when the future payments are not guaranteed. This is explored in the next section.

Exercise 8.2

Part A

1. Allan is willing to bet \$1 that he can flip a coin 3 times and not get any heads. How much should Bob wager to make the game fair?

2. A box contains four \$10 bills, six \$5 bills, and two \$1 bills. You are allowed to pull two bills at random from the box. If both bills are of the same denomination, you can keep them. What

is the maximum amount you can afford to pay to take part in this game without expecting to lose some money?

3. On a TV game show, a contestant has won a boat and motor valued at $13 000. He can continue to play by relinquishing his prize. If he continues to play, he can choose between curtains A or B. Behind curtain A is a gag prize worth nothing. Behind curtain B is a car valued at $35 000. What should he do to maximize his mathematical expectation?

4. Students who take driver education have probability 0.03 of having an accident in one year. Students without driver education have probability 0.08 of having an accident in one year. Statistics show that the cost of any one accident averages $6000. If car insurance were not available, should a student pay $280 for a driver education course? (Assume no one has two accidents in one year.)

5. Jane and Gilles play a dice game. Jane wins if, when the dice are thrown, the two faces showing are identical. Otherwise, Gilles wins. If Jane wagers $15, how much should Gilles wager to make the game fair?

6. For $1 a lottery offers the following prizes:
   - 1 prize of $25 000
   - 20 prizes of $1000
   - 168 prizes of $25
   and 1701 prizes of 5 free tickets.
   If 100 000 tickets are sold, find the expectation per ticket.

7. A 25-year-old man wants to buy insurance on his life for one year; it would be worth $100 000 in the event of his death. Ignoring any effect of compound interest and expenses, what is a fair price for this coverage if, on the average, 158 men out of each 100 000 die at age 25?

8. A rock-concert promoter wants to insure her next outdoor concert against the possibility of bad weather. She estimates that if it doesn't rain, 10 000 people will pay $5 each to attend the concert. If it does rain, only 5000 people will attend. Based on weather statistics for the day of the event over the past several years, it is determined that there is a 12% chance of rain. Ignoring any effect of compound interest and expenses, what is a fair price for the insurance?

Part B

1. When P plays Q, P wins, on the average, 1 out of 3 games. If P and Q agree to play until Q wins, but no more than 3 games, and if at the close of each game the loser pays the winner $1, what are Q's expected winnings?

2. A current quiz program gives the contestant six true-or-false statements and awards $5 for each correct answer. If he answers all six correctly, he gets $1000 extra. What is the value of his expectation assuming he guesses every answer?

3. Ruth wins a dollar if the coin she tosses comes up heads, and loses a dollar if it comes up tails. She tosses once and quits if she wins, but tries only once more if she loses. What is her expectation?

4. A perishable product is purchased by a retailer for $6 and is sold for $8. Based on past experience, the following probability table has been derived. If an item is not sold on the first day, the retailer absorbs a $6 loss. Determine the number of units the retailer should purchase to maximize daily profits.

Daily Demand	Probability
20	0.12
21	0.30
22	0.25
23	0.18
24	0.15

5. A manager of an insurance agency is interested in trying to develop a strategy for next year. She can choose one of the following three possible courses of action:
   a) stay with the present sales staff;
   b) hire additional agents, all untrained;
   c) hire additional agents, all trained.
   The net payoffs for these actions are

	Agents		
Next Year's Sales	Same Staff	Hire Untrained	Hire Trained
No change	0	−40 000	−65 000
Moderate increase	25 000	40 000	70 000
Large increase	70 000	110 000	150 000

The probability predicted for next year's sales are
same as this year 0.60
moderate increase 0.25
large increase 0.15
Which course of action should she choose?

Section 8.3 | Contingent Payments with Time Value

We started this chapter by pointing out that future cash flows from an investment are not always guaranteed to be made. For example, in a corporate bond there is a chance that the company issuing the bond may default on future interest payments.

The risk of holding a bond is determined by the investor using information provided by companies that rate the ability of bond issuers to pay off their obligations. This risk is reflected in the yield rate required by the investor, which in turn affects the price to be paid for the bond. Two bonds that are identical with respect to face value, coupon rate, and maturity date may sell for very different prices because the potential investors do not place the same probability on receiving all payments in full.

To determine the price an investor is willing to pay for a bond, an estimate is needed for the probability of actually receiving each bond interest payment. Once that is done, we are now in a position to mathematically analyze such situations, which can be referred to as contingent payments. All that is required is a combination of compound interest theory and the theory of mathematical expectation.

Suppose we receive amount S with probability, p, and amount zero with probability, $(1 - p)$. This is a special case of $E(X)$ as defined in section 8.3. The expected value of the amount we receive is:

$$E(X) = x_1 p(x_1) + x_2 p(x_2) = Sp + 0(1 - p) = pS$$

The discounted value or the present value of the expected value, pS, to be received n periods from today, assuming money is worth i per period, is

$$pS(1 + i)^{-n}$$

EXAMPLE 1   Mr. Wright goes to a finance company and borrows \$1000 for 1 year. If repayment were certain, the finance company would charge Mr. Wright 18% per annum. After doing a credit check on Mr. Wright, they determine that there is a 10% chance of default in which case no money will be repaid at all.
  a) How much should he repay?
  b) What rate of interest should the finance company charge Mr. Wright?
  In this example, we assume that if the borrower defaults at some time, the lender gets nothing at all from the time of default. This is seldom true in reality, but is a necessary assumption for ease of analysis.

Solution a   If repayment were certain, the finance company would charge 18% and Mr. Wright would repay \$1180. But, the finance company places a 90% probability of repayment. (That is, if 100 such loans are made, 90 will be repaid and 10 will not.)
  Let the amount to be repaid be X dollars. The expected value of repayment is $X(0.90)$ dollars. The present value of this is $X(0.90)(1.18)^{-1}$ dollars.

$$X(0.90)(1.18)^{-1} = 1000$$
$$X = \frac{1000}{(0.90)(1.18)^{-1}}$$
$$X \doteq 1311.11$$

Solution b   If Mr. Wright does repay the loan, the rate of interest he pays is i such that

$$1000 = 1311.11(1+i)^{-1}$$
$$(1+i) = 1.3111$$
$$i = 31.11\%$$

While Mr. Wright experiences a very high rate of interest, if the finance company lends $1000 to 100 people and only 90 repay the loan, they make only 18% on their total investment.

EXAMPLE 2   Ms. Wolnitz is approached by an agent selling a special university scholarship award. If Ms. Wolnitz's newborn daughter survives to age 18, qualifies for and enters a Canadian university, she will be awarded a $10 000 scholarship on her 18th birthday. The cost for this plan is $2500.

Ms. Wolnitz realizes that she can make 5% per year on her investments. She also determines from statistical tables that the probability of a newborn female surviving to age 18 is 0.9767. What probability must Ms. Wolnitz attach to her daughter entering university before the scheme is worthwhile?

Solution   Let the unknown probability be p. The payment of $10 000 will be paid only if Ms. Wolnitz's daughter survives to age 18 and ends up going to university. Thus, the expected value of the payment is $10\,000(0.9767)p$. For the scheme to be worthwhile, the present value of this must be at least $2500.

$$2500 = 10\,000(0.9767)p(1.05)^{-18}$$
$$p = 0.6160$$

If the probability exceeds 61.60%, the plan would be worthwhile.

EXAMPLE 3   An insurance company issues a one-year insurance policy that pays $100 000 at the end of the year if the policyholder dies during the year. If the probability that a 35-year-old female dies in the next year is 0.00086, what is a fair price for this policy, ignoring expenses and assuming $j_1 = 5\%$?

Solution   Expected Payment = $100\,000(0.00086) = \$86.00$
Price = $(86.00)(1.05)^{-1} = \$81.90$

These last five examples will illustrate the method that can be used to determine a fair price to be paid for an investment where the future cash flows are not guaranteed. We begin by taking another look at Example 5 of section 8.2.

EXAMPLE 4   You invest $10 000 for one year with the ABC company which promises to make two payments of $5569.28, the first in 6 months and the second at the end of 1 year. If ABC is paying interest at $j_2 = 15\%$, what is the fair price you should pay for these two payments if a) the payments are guaranteed; b) the probability of default for the first payment is 2% and the probability that the first payment is made, but the second payment is not is 5%?

Solution a The expected value of the first and second payment is $5569.28(1.00)$. To determine the fair price, discount the expected value of each payment back to the date of the investment.

$$A = 5569.28(1.075)^{-1} + 5569.28(1.075)^{-2}$$
$$= \$10\,000.00$$

Solution b The expected value of the first payment is $5569.28(0.98)$ and of the second payment is $5569.28(0.95)$. Thus,

$$A = 5569.28(0.98)(1.075)^{-1} + 5569.28(0.95)(1.075)^{-2}$$
$$= 5077.1111 + 4578.3156$$
$$\doteq 9655.43$$

We see that if we take into consideration the probability of default, we end up putting a lower value on the investment. In order to earn $j_2 = 15\%$ while actually investing \$10 000, we need to receive the following two payments of X,

$$10\,000 = X(0.98)(1.075)^{-1} + X(0.95)(1.075)^{-2}$$
$$X = 5768.03$$

EXAMPLE 5 Mr. Rozema, who is in very poor health, is to receive \$1000 at the end of each year as long as he is alive. The probability he will live n years is given in the following table.

n	Probability of Surviving n Years
1	0.80
2	0.45
3	0.00

If $j_1 = 8\%$, what value should Mr. Rozema place on these series of payments now?

Solution The solution follows directly from the data given, and can be derived by using the following time diagram:

The discounted value of the expected payment is

$$A = 1000(0.8)(1.08)^{-1} + 1000(0.45)(1.08)^{-2} + 1000(0)(1.08)^{-3}$$
$$\doteq \$1126.54$$

EXAMPLE 6 How much would you lend a person today if he promises to repay $1000 at the end of each year for 10 years but there is a 10% chance of default in any year and $j_1 = 12\%$. If default occurs, no money will be received beyond the time of default.

Solution The fact that there is a 10% chance of default in any year means that there is a 90% probability of receiving the first payment; an 81% chance, $(0.9)^2$, of receiving the second payment; a 72.9% chance, $(0.9)^3$, of receiving the third payment, and so on.

One method of solution is to sum the following geometric series (as outlined in Appendix 2). The discounted value of the expected series of payments is

$$1000(1.12)^{-1}(0.9) + 1000(1.12)^{-2}(0.9)^2 + \cdots + 1000(1.12)^{-10}(0.9)^{10}$$

An easier method of solution is to determine a new rate of interest j_1 that covers both the standard rate of interest and the probability of default. That is,

$$1 + j_1 = \frac{1.12}{0.9}$$
$$1 + j_1 = 1.2444\dot{4}$$
$$j_1 = 24.44\%$$

Now we calculate the discounted value of a simple annuity of $1000 a year for 10 years at $j_1 = 24.44\%$

$$1000a_{\overline{10}|0.2444} = 1000\frac{1 - (1.2444\dot{4})^{-10}}{0.2444\dot{4}} \doteq \$3631.64$$

EXAMPLE 7 A 20-year $1000 bond is offered for sale January 1, 2008. The bond interest is $j_2 = 10\%$ and the bond matures at par.
  a) Determine the purchase price to yield $j_2 = 8\%$.
  b) Determine the purchase price to yield $j_2 = 8\%$ if the probability of default in *any* six-month period is 5%.

Solution a
$$P = Fra_{\overline{m}|i} + C(1+i)^{-n}$$
$$= 50a_{\overline{40}|0.04} + 1000(1.04)^{-40}$$
$$= 989.64 + 208.29$$
$$\doteq \$1197.93$$

Solution b First we calculate a new interest rate, i per half-year, that automatically includes the probability of default.
$$(1+i) = \frac{1.04}{0.95}$$
$$1 + i = 1.094736842$$
$$i = 0.094736842$$
and then calculate the purchase price
$$P = Fra_{\overline{m}|i} + C(1+i)^{-n}$$
$$= 50a_{\overline{40}|i} + 1000(1+i)^{-40}$$
$$\doteq 513.65 + 26.77$$
$$= \$540.42$$

While it appears that a relatively small probability of default leads to a large difference in price, a 5% default probability each half-year for 20 years gives only a 12.9% probability of full repayment of the debt. Further, we have assumed there is no value at all beyond the point of default, which is not the norm.

EXAMPLE 8   You are considering purchasing a 3-year $1000 par value junk bond paying interest at $j_2 = 18\%$. The following are the probabilities that the nth coupon is defaulted, given that the previous $n - 1$ coupons were paid:

n	1	2	3	4	5	6
Prob	0.05	0.05	0.10	0.10	0.15	0.20

What price should you pay to yield $j_2 = 10\%$?

Solution   The semi-annual coupon is $90 and the redemption value is $1000. The price to be paid can be solved using the following time diagram:

The discounted value of the expected payments is

$$A = 90(0.95)[(1.05)^{-1} + (1.05)^{-2}] + 90(0.90)[(1.05)^{-3} + (1.05)^{-4}]$$
$$+ 90(0.85)(1.05)^{-5} + 1090(0.80)(1.05)^{-6}$$
$$\doteq \$1006.23$$

Note: If we assumed that all coupons along with the redemption value were guaranteed, the price, using formula (**15**) or (**16**), would be $1203.03.

Exercise 8.3

Part A

1. The Friendly Finance Company could lend out their money at 12% per year if everyone repaid their loans in full. From past experience, however, 5% of all loans are not repaid. What rate of interest, j_1, should Friendly Finance Company charge for 1-year loans?

2. Mr. Fitzpatrick wants to borrow some money. He can repay the loan with a single payment of $8000 in one year's time. The lending institution determines that there is a 10% chance that Mr. Fitzpatrick will not repay the loan. The normal lending rate at that time is $j_1 = 9\frac{1}{2}\%$. How much will they lend Mr. Fitzpatrick? If he repays the loan in full, what rate of interest was realized?

3. Mrs. Chang wants to borrow $4000. She will repay the loan with one single payment at the end of one year's time. The lending agency estimates that there is a 5% chance of default on this loan, in which case they receive nothing at all. How much will they ask Mrs. Chang to repay if their "risk-free" rate of interest is a) $j_1 = 10\%$; b) $j_2 = 10\%$?

4. For loans repayable with single payments at the end of one year if repayment is assumed, $j_1 = 9\%$. If the XYZ Finance Company charges $j_1 = 16\%$ for the same loan, what is their expected default rate?

5. Mr. Saujani dies and leaves an estate valued at $500 000 in a bank account earning 8% per annum. He has two children: Robert, aged 8, and Tammy, aged 3. The estate will be divided among the survivors 18 years from now, when Tammy turns 21. Determine the expected value of the inheritance for each child given the probability an 8-year-old boy survives for 18 years is 0.95 and the probability a 3-year-old girl survives 18 years is 0.97, and assuming independence of events. Why is your total not $500 000(1.08)^{18}$?

6. How much would you lend a person today if she promises to repay $5000 at the end of each year for 5 years and there is a 5% chance of default in any year? Assume $j_1 = 9\%$ when payment is assured.

7. An investment of $15 000 is made today and it returns X dollars at the end of each of the next 4 years. If $j_1 = 8\%$, what is the value of X if
a) the probability of default in any year is 2%?
b) the probability that a payment is defaulted, given that all previous payments were made, is 2%?

8. An insurance company sells an annuity to a person who has the following probability of survival in the future:

Year "n"	Probability of Survival to end of Year "n"
1	0.85
2	0.65
3	0.35
4	0

If $j_1 = 5\%$ and we ignore expenses, what is a fair price for an annuity paying $2000 at the end of each year?

9. A 20-year $1000 bond is offered for sale. The bond interest is $j_2 = 7\%$ and the bond matures for $1050. Determine the purchase price to yield $j_2 = 8\%$ if the probability of default in any six-month period is 1%.

10. In Exercise 9, determine the purchase price to yield $j_2 = 8\%$ if the probability of any payment

being defaulted is 1%, given that all previous payments were paid.

11. A $1000 bond with coupons at $j_2 = 6\%$ and redeemable at par has exactly 10 years left to run. Determine its price if the probability of default in any six-month period is 2% and the desired yield rate is $j_2 = 5\%$.

12. In Exercise 11, determine the purchase price to yield $j_2 = 5\%$ if the probability of any payment being defaulted is 2%, given that all previous payments were paid.

Part B

1. Mr. Cameron buys a $1000 20-year bond with coupons at $j_2 = 6\%$ redeemable at par. He determines his purchase price to yield $j_2 = 7\%$ and to allow for a semi-annual default probability of 2%. Exactly 5 years later Mr. Cameron sells the bond to Mrs. Yutzi, who determines her purchase price to yield $j_2 = 5\%$ but to allow for a semi-annual default probability of 3% in the remaining period. Determine
a) the original purchase price;
b) the selling price;
c) the yield j_2 to Mr. Cameron.

2. The XYZ finance company experiences a 90% repayment rate (a 10% default rate) on one-year loans. The ABC Bank across the street experiences a 95% repayment rate (a 5% default rate) on its one-year loans. If the ABC Bank charges $j_1 = 11\%$ on loans, what rate, j_1, should the XYZ finance company charge to have the same return on loans?

3. Mrs. Langille dies and leaves an estate valued at $50 000 in a bank account earning interest at rate $j_{12} = 4\%$. She has three children: Jim, aged 7, Fred, aged 5, and Sandra, aged 4. The estate will be divided among the survivors 14 years from now, when Sandra turns 18. Determine the expected value of the inheritance for each child given the following chart, and assuming independence:

Age Today	Probability of Survival for 14 Years
7	0.95
5	0.97
4	0.98

4. Mr. McMahon pays $880 for a $1000 bond pay-ing bond interest at $j_2 = 9\%$ and redeemable at $1000 in 20 years. If his desired yield was $j_2 = 8\%$, what semi-annual probability of default did he expect?

5. Mr. Stockie wants to borrow some money and repay the loan with a single payment at the end of one year. Based on past experience, the bank has the following probability distribution of repayments:

Proportion of Total Debt Repaid	Probability
0	5%
50%	5%
75%	10%
90%	10%
100%	70%

If the "risk-free" rate of interest the bank uses is $j_1 = 10\%$, what rate of interest will they charge Mr. Stockie?

Section 8.4	**Summary and Review Exercises**

Chapter 8 introduced the concept of risk to the evaluation of future payments.

● $E(X) = x_1 p(x_1) + x_2 p(x_2) + \cdots$ is the expected value of x.

● pS is the expected value of a payment, S, to be paid with probability, p.

● $pS(1 + i)^{-n}$ is the present value of pS.

● When the probability of default is $(1 - p)$ every period, the probability, p, and the present value factor, $(1 + i)^{-1}$, can be combined by finding a new rate of inter-est, j_1, such that:

$$1 + j_1 = \frac{1 + i}{p}$$

A series of contingent payments can now be evaluated using basic compound interest theory at rate j_1.

Review Exercises 8.4

1. A card is drawn at random from a well-shuffled deck. What is the probability that the card will be
a) an ace or a king;
b) a red face card (jack, queen, or king)?

2. On a particular assembly line, 8 parts in 1000 are defective. Assuming statistical indepen-dence, determine the probability that
a) out of 100 parts, none are defective;
b) two parts in a succession are defective;
c) the first two parts are not defective but the third is.

3. A coin is weighted such that the probability of a head is 2/3 and the probability of a tail is 1/3. Determine
a) the probability of 3 heads in a row;
b) the probability of no heads in two tosses;
c) the probability of a head followed by two tails.

4. Three cards are drawn from a deck of 52. If these cards are not replaced, what is the proba-bility of a queen followed by a king followed by an ace?

5. A consumers association tests batteries to see how long certain brands will last. Compare 100 batteries of Brand X and Brand Y below by look-ing at their expected lifetimes.

Time (hours)	Brand X	Brand Y
	(# having failed)	
3	5	6
4	15	18
5	30	22
6	20	35
7	20	12
8	10	7

6. A gambling game is played wherein a single card is pulled from a deck of 52. For pulling the cards 2 to 10 one wins the face value of the card (i.e., $2 to $10); for a jack, queen, or king, one wins $20; and for an ace one wins $25. How much would one be expected to place in the pot to make this a fair game?

7. Perishable goods are purchased by a retailer for $10 and sold for $15 each. These goods last only one day. Given the following table determined from past experience, how many items of this good should the producer purchase to maximize his profit? What is his expected profit given that purchase?

Daily Demand	Probability
70	0.05
71	0.35
72	0.40
73	0.15
74	0.05

8. Miss O'Connor goes to the Family Trust Company to borrow some money. Family Trust charges $j_1 = 9\frac{1}{2}\%$ for customers with an established credit rating. Otherwise, they assume a 5% probability of default (in which case they get nothing). For a loan to be repaid with one payment at the end of one year, what interest rate should they charge Miss O'Connor, who has no credit rating?

9. An insurance company issues a special retirement savings policy whereby they will pay the policyholder $100 000 on his 65th birthday if he is alive at that time. If the probability that a 40-year-old male lives to age 65 is 0.810 and if $j_1 = 6\%$, what is a fair price for this policy, ignoring expenses?

10. How much would you lend a person today if he promises to repay $1000 at the end of each year for 10 years, there is a 5% chance of default in any year and $j_1 = 7\%$? (If default occurs, no payment will be made beyond the time of default.)

11. A 20-year $1000 par value bond with semi-annual coupons at $j_2 = 11\%$ is issued by a company that is not financially strong. In fact, the probability of bankruptcy is 5% in any six-month period with no value if that happens. Determine the purchase price of this bond if $j_2 = 10\%$. What would be the purchase price if the probability of bankruptcy in any period is 5%, given that there was no bankruptcy in any previous period?

CASE STUDY 1 *Risky bonds*

Review the Bond Quote Table on pages 217 and 218. Short-term government bonds are as close to a risk-free asset as one can find. At the time of publication, their yield was approximately $j_2 = 4.00\%$. Corporate Bonds, on the other hand, have higher yields reflecting a positive default probability. For example, at the time of publication, a BCE Inc. bond due Oct. 30, 2007 was yielding $j_2 = 4.46\%$. Based solely on these two yield rates (i.e., ignoring the complications of timing of coupon payments and redemption), what probability of default, in any six-month period, do investors assume for BCE Inc.?

APPENDIX **1**

Exponents and Logarithms

Exponents

The product $a \cdot a \cdot a \cdot a$ may be abbreviated to a^4, which is known as the fourth power of a. The symbol a is called the **base**, the number 4, which indicates the number of times the base a is to appear as a factor, is the **exponent**. For a first power we have $a^1 = a$, a second power is called a *square*, a third power is a *cube*.

EXAMPLE 1

a) $243 = 3 \cdot 3 \cdot 3 \cdot 3 \cdot 3 = 3^5$

b) $(1 + i)^3 = (1 + i)(1 + i)(1 + i)$

c) $625 = 5 \cdot 5 \cdot 5 \cdot 5 = 5^4$

Laws of Exponents

If m and n are positive integers and $a \neq 0$, $b \neq 0$, we have

1. $a^m \cdot a^n = a^{m+n}$
2. $a^m \div a^n = a^{m-n}$
3. $(a^m)^n = a^{mn}$
4. $(ab)^n = a^n b^n$
5. $\left(\frac{a}{b}\right)^n = \frac{a^n}{b^n}$

We illustrate law (1) below:

$$a^m \cdot a^n = (a \cdot a \ldots \text{ to } m \text{ factors})(a \cdot a \ldots \text{ to } n \text{ factors})$$
$$= (a \cdot a \ldots \text{ to } m + n \text{ factors}) = a^{m+n}$$

EXAMPLE 2   a) $2^3 2^6 = 2^{3+6} = 2^9$

b) $\frac{x^5}{x^2} = x^{5-2} = x^3$

c) $(a^3)^2 = a^6$

d) $(2x^3)^4 = 2^4 x^{12} = 16 x^{12}$

e) $(\frac{a^2}{b})^3 = \frac{(a^2)^3}{b^3} = \frac{a^6}{b^3}$

Section A1.3   Zero, Negative and Fractional Exponents

We extend the notion of an exponent to include zero, negative integers and common fractions by the following definitions:

$$a^0 = 1, \ a \neq 0$$

$$a^{-n} = \frac{1}{a^n}, \ n \text{ a positive integer}$$

$$a^{\frac{m}{n}} = \sqrt[n]{a^m}, \ m \text{ and } n \text{ positive integers.}$$

It can be shown that the laws of exponents (1) to (5) hold when m and n are rational numbers (i.e., zero, positive and negative integers, and common fractions).

EXAMPLE 3   a) $1 = \frac{3^4}{3^4} = 3^{4-4} = 3^0$

b) $4^{-2} = \frac{1}{4^2} = \frac{1}{16}$

c) $(27)^{1/3} + (25)^{1/2} = \sqrt[3]{27} + \sqrt{25} = 3 + 5 = 8$

d) $(9)^{3/2} = (9^{1/2})^3 = (\sqrt{9})^3 = 3^3 = 27$

e) $\frac{a^3}{a^{-2}} = a^3 a^2 = a^5$

f) $\sqrt{\frac{x^{-2}}{y^6}} = (\frac{x^{-2}}{y^6})^{1/2} = \frac{x^{-1}}{y^3} = x^{-1} y^{-3}$ or $\frac{1}{xy^3}$

EXAMPLE 4   Using a pocket calculator, calculate

a) $\sqrt[5]{3} = 3^{1/5} = 1.2457309$

b) $\sqrt[3]{\frac{6034 \times 0.4185}{1.507}} = (\frac{6034 \times 0.4185}{1.507})^{1/3} = 11.87761303$

c) $15\ 000(1.068)^{-3} = 12\ 313.3862$

d) $\frac{3}{\sqrt[4]{608}} = \frac{3}{(608)^{1/4}} = 3(608)^{-1/4} = 0.604150807$

| Section A1.4 | **Exponential Equations — Unknown Base** |

Applying the laws of exponents and definitions of the rational exponents, we may solve exponential equations with the unknown in the base using a pocket calculator.

EXAMPLE 5 Solve the following equations:

a) $100(1+i)^8 = 200$

$$(1+i)^8 = 2$$
$$1+i = \sqrt[8]{2}$$
$$1+i = 2^{1/8}$$
$$i = 2^{1/8} - 1$$
$$i = 0.090507733$$

b) $8800(1-d)^{10} = 1500$

$$(1-d)^{10} = \frac{1500}{8800}$$
$$1-d = \sqrt[10]{\frac{1500}{8800}}$$
$$1-d = \left(\frac{1500}{8800}\right)^{1/10}$$
$$d = 1 - \left(\frac{1500}{8800}\right)^{1/10}$$
$$d = 0.162160447$$

c) $(1+i)^{12} = (1.055)^4$

$$1+i = \sqrt[12]{(1.055)^4}$$
$$1+i = (1.055)^{4/12}$$
$$i = (1.055)^{1/3} - 1$$
$$i = 0.01800713$$

| Section A1.5 | **Basic Properties of Logarithms** |

Since logarithms are exponents, the rules for exponents will be used to prove the rules for logarithms. Let $A = 10^a$ and $B = 10^b$ so that $\log A = a$ and $\log B = b$. Since

$$A \cdot B = 10^a \cdot 10^b = 10^{a+b}$$
$$\frac{A}{B} = \frac{10^a}{10^b} = 10^{a-b}$$
$$A^k = (10^a)^k = 10^{ka}, \text{ a real number,}$$

it follows that

$$\log A \cdot B = a + b = \log A + \log B$$
$$\log \frac{A}{B} = a - b = \log A - \log B$$
$$\log A^k = ka = k \log A$$

We have shown the three fundamental laws of logarithms.

1. The logarithm of the product of two positive numbers is the sum of the logarithms of the numbers.

$$\log A \cdot B = \log A + \log B$$

2. The logarithm of the quotient of two positive numbers is the logarithm of the numerator minus the logarithm of the denominator.

$$\log \frac{A}{B} = \log A - \log B$$

3. The logarithm of the kth power of a positive number is k times the logarithm of the number.

$$\log A^k = k \log A$$

EXAMPLE 6   Given $\log 2 = 0.301029996$ and $\log 3 = 0.477121255$, then

a) $\log 6 = \log(2 \times 3) = \log 2 + \log 3 = 0.301029996 + 0.477121255$
$$= 0.778151251$$

b) $\log 1.5 = \log \frac{3}{2} = \log 3 - \log 2 = 0.477121255 - 0.301029996$
$$= 0.176091259$$

c) $\log 8 = \log 2^3 = 3 \log 2 = 3(0.301029996) = 0.903089988$

d) $\log 200 = \log 2 \times 10^2 = \log 2 + \log 10^2 = 0.301029996 + 2$
$$= 2.301029996$$

e) $\log 0.003 = \log 3 \times 10^{-3} = \log 3 + \log 10^{-3} = 0.477121255 + (-3)$
$$= -2.522878745$$

f) $\log \sqrt[3]{2} = \log 2^{\frac{1}{3}} = \frac{1}{3} \log 2 = \frac{1}{3}(0.301029996) = 0.100343332$

Section A1.6   **Computing with Logarithms**

The importance of logarithms in computations has diminished with the development of calculators. Students now can quickly perform operations such as long multiplication or division; taking powers or roots; and using pocket calculators without the aid of logarithms.

However in some cases, such as solving exponential equations for an unknown exponent (see section A1.7 of this appendix), logarithms must still be used.

In the following examples we shall illustrate the use of logarithms in situations where they provide an alternative method of solution. We assume the use of calculators with a built-in logarithmic function so that logarithms or antilogarithms can be found quickly without using logarithmic tables. We also show direct solutions without the aid of logarithms.

EXAMPLE 7   The following equation comes from a compound interest problem. Determine i, which represents the interest rate per interest conversion period, if

$$800(1 + i)^{20} = 5000$$

Using logarithms, we have

$$\log 800 + 20 \log(1 + i) = \log 5000$$
$$20 \log(1 + i) = \log 5000 - \log 800$$
$$20 \log(1 + i) = 3.698970004 - 2.903089987$$
$$20 \log(1 + i) = 0.7895880017$$
$$\log(1 + i) = 0.039794001$$
$$(1 + i) = 1.095958226$$
$$i = 0.095958226$$
$$i \doteq 9.60\%$$

Direct solution without the aid of logarithms.

$$800 (1 + i)^{20} = 5000$$
$$(1 + i)^{20} = \tfrac{5000}{800}$$
$$1 + i = \left(\tfrac{5000}{800}\right)^{1/20}$$
$$i = \left(\tfrac{5000}{800}\right)^{1/20} - 1$$
$$i = 0.095958226$$
$$i \doteq 9.60\%$$

EXAMPLE 8   The following equation comes from a depreciation problem. Determine d, the annual compounded rate of depreciation, if

$$83\,000(1 - d)^{10} = 10\,500$$

Using logarithms, we have

$$\log 83\,000 + 10 \log(1 - d) = \log 10\,500$$
$$10 \log(1 - d) = \log 10\,500 - \log 83\,000$$
$$10 \log(1 - d) = 4.021189299 - 4.919078092$$
$$10 \log(1 - d) = -0.897888793$$
$$\log(1 - d) = -0.089788879$$
$$1 - d = 0.813225748$$
$$d = 0.186774252$$
$$d \doteq 18.68\%$$

Direct solution without the aid of logarithms.

$$83\,000(1 - d)^{10} = 10\,500$$
$$(1 - d)^{10} = \tfrac{10\,500}{83\,000}$$
$$(1 - d) = \left(\tfrac{10\,500}{83\,000}\right)^{1/10}$$
$$d = 1 - \left(\tfrac{10\,500}{83\,000}\right)^{1/10}$$
$$d = 0.186774252$$
$$d \doteq 18.68\%$$

Section A1.7   **Exponential Equations — Unknown Exponent**

In solving exponential equations for an unknown exponent there is no direct solution available and logarithms provide an efficient method of solution.

EXAMPLE 9   The following equation comes from a compound interest problem. Determine n, which represents the number of interest conversion periods, if

$$250(1.015)^n = 750$$
$$(1.015)^n = 3$$
$$n \log 1.015 = \log 3$$
$$n = \frac{\log 3}{\log 1.015}$$
$$n = 73.78876232$$

EXAMPLE 10   The following equation comes from an annuity problem. Determine n, which represents the number of payments, if

$$\frac{1 - (1.01)^{-n}}{0.01} = 5$$
$$1 - (1.01)^{-n} = 0.05$$
$$(1.01)^{-n} = 0.95$$
$$-n \log 1.01 = \log 0.95$$
$$n = -\frac{\log 0.95}{\log 1.01}$$
$$n = 5.154933554$$

This result means that there will be 5 full payments and a reduced 6th payment.

Section A1.8   **Exercises — Appendix 1**

1. Simplify.

   a) $a^3 \cdot a^6$

   b) $a \cdot a^2 \cdot a^3$

   c) $\frac{a^8}{a^4}$

   d) $(a^2)^3$

   e) $\frac{(a^3)^2 a}{a^5}$

   f) $(a^2 b^3)^2$

   g) $\left(\frac{aa^2}{b^2 b}\right)^3$

   h) $(1.05)^3 (1.05)^{12} (1.05)^4$

2. Simplify.

   a) $a^{1/2} a^{1/3}$

   b) $a^{1/2} \div a^{1/3}$

   c) $\frac{aa^{-2}}{a^3}$

   d) $a^{(2/3)3/2} \cdot a^{-1}$

   e) $25^{-1/2}$

   f) $\left(\frac{a^3}{b^2}\right)^{-1/4}$

3. Simplify using rational exponents

   a) $\sqrt{a}\sqrt[3]{a}$

   b) $\frac{a \cdot \sqrt[3]{a}}{\sqrt{a^3}}$

   c) $\left(\frac{\sqrt{a^4}\sqrt[3]{b^2}}{\sqrt{ab^3}}\right)^{-3}$

4. Using a pocket calculator, calculate

a) $\sqrt[3]{0.0468}$

b) $\sqrt[15]{\dfrac{24.60}{396}}$

c) $\dfrac{37(23.3)^2}{\sqrt[3]{111.3}}$

d) $\dfrac{(1.065)^{15} - 1}{0.065}$

e) $375(1.03)^{-2/3}$

f) $\sqrt[4]{\dfrac{21.2}{(0.082)^2}}$

g) $\sqrt{3}\,\sqrt[3]{5}\,\sqrt[4]{7}$

h) $\dfrac{1 - (1.11)^{-13}}{0.11}$

5. Solve the following exponential equations

  i) directly without the aid of logarithms;

  ii) using logarithms.

a) $3500(1 + i)^8 = 5000$

b) $823.21(1 + i)^{60} = 15\,000$

c) $17\,800(1 - d)^{20} = 500$

d) $8000(1 - d)^{11} = 800$

e) $1000(1 + i)^{-20} = 35$

f) $(1 + i)^{-10} = 0.9490$

g) $(1 + i)^{1/4} = 1.0113$

h) $(1 + i)^{20} - 1 = 80$

i) $(1 + i)^4 = (1.01)^{12}$

j) $(1 + i)^{12} = (1.05)^2$

6. Solve the following exponential equations

a) $50(1.035)^n = 200$

b) $500 = 20(2.06)^x - 150$

c) $808(1.092)^{-n} = 90$

d) $(1.0463)^{-n} = 0.3826$

e) $(1.02)^n - 1 = 0.5314$

f) $3^x = 5(2^x)$

g) $126(0.75)^x = 30$

h) $1 + 2^x = 81$

i) $\dfrac{3^x + 1}{2} = 21$

j) $\dfrac{2^x - 1}{3} = 12$

7. Solve the following equations for n and check your answer by substitution.

a) $\dfrac{(1.083)^n - 1}{0.083} = 21$

b) $\dfrac{(1.11)^n - 1}{0.11} = 11$

c) $\dfrac{(1.005)^n - 1}{0.005} = 10$

d) $\dfrac{1 - (1.087)^{-n}}{0.087} = 4.5$

e) $\dfrac{1 - (1.0975)^{-n}}{0.0975} = 6$

f) $\dfrac{1 - (1.025)^{-n}}{0.025} = 3$

APPENDIX **2**

Progressions

Section A2.1 ## Arithmetic Progressions

Any sequence of numbers with the property that any two consecutive numbers in the sequence are separated by a common difference is called an **arithmetic progression**. Thus,

3, 5, 7, 9, ... is an arithmetic progression with common difference 2.

20, 17, 14, 11, ... is an arithmetic progression with common difference –3.

Let us look at the first few terms of an arithmetic progression whose first term is t_1 and whose common difference is d.

1st term: t_1
2nd term: $t_1 + d$
3rd term: $t_1 + 2d$
4th term: $t_1 + 3d$, etc.

We notice that the coefficient of d is always one less than the number of the term. Thus, the 40th term would be $t_1 + 39d$.

In general, the nth term on an arithmetic progression, denoted by t_n, with first term t_1 and common difference d is given by

$$t_n = t_1 + (n - 1)d$$

Given any three of the four parameters, we can solve for the fourth.

EXAMPLE 1   In an arithmetic progression
a) Given $t_1 = 3$, $t_n = 9$, $n = 7$, determine d and t_{10}.
b) Given $t_4 = 12$, $t_8 = -4$, determine t_1 and d.

Solution   a) We have $t_7 = t_1 + 6d = 3 + 6d = 9$ and calculate $d = 1$ and
$$t_{10} = 3 + 9 = 12.$$

b) We have $t_4 = t_1 + 3d = 12$
$t_8 = t_1 + 7d = -4$

and solve these equations for t_1 and d. Subtracting $t_8 - t_4$ we get $4d = -16$ and $d = -4$. Substituting for d in the first equation we obtain $t_1 = 12 - 3d = 12 - 3(-4) = 24$.

Section A2.2 The Sum of an Arithmetic Progression

Let S_n denote the sum of the first n terms of an arithmetic progression. We may write

$$S_n = t_1 + (t_1 + d) + (t_1 + 2d) + \cdots + (t_n - 2d) + (t_n - d) + t_n$$

and

$$S_n = t_n + (t_n - d) + (t_n - 2d) + \cdots + (t_1 + 2d) + (t_1 + d) + t_1$$

Adding the above expressions for S_n, term by term, we obtain

$$2S_n = (t_1 + t_n) + (t_1 + t_n) + (t_1 + t_n) + \cdots$$
$$+ (t_1 + t_n) + (t_1 + t_n) + (t_1 + t_n)$$
$$= n(t_1 + t_n)$$

and

$$\boxed{S_n = \frac{n}{2}(t_1 + t_n)}$$

Thus,

$$3 + 5 + 7 + 9 + 11 + 13 = \tfrac{6}{2}(3 + 13) = 48$$

and

$$20 + 17 + 14 + 11 + 8 + 5 + 2 + (-1) + (-4) = \tfrac{9}{2}(20 + (-4)) = 72$$

It is easy to see that the sum of the first n integers is

$$S_n = \frac{n}{2}(1 + n)$$

Thus,

$$1 + 2 + \cdots + 100 = \tfrac{100}{2}(1 + 100) = 50(101) = 5050$$

EXAMPLE 2   A woman borrows $1500, agreeing to pay $100 at the end of each month to reduce the outstanding principal and agreeing to pay the interest due on any unpaid balance at rate 12% per annum (i.e., 1% per month). Determine the sum of all interest payments.

Solution   Interest payments are calculated as 1% of the progression 1500, 1400, ... , 100. The sum of all interest payments is the sum of 15 terms of an arithmetic progression 15, 14, 13, ... , 1

$$S_{15} = \tfrac{15}{2}(15 + 1) = \$120$$

Geometric Progression

A sequence of numbers with the property that the ratio of any 2 consecutive numbers in the sequence is constant is called a **geometric progression**. Thus,

2, 4, 8, 16, 32, ... is a geometric progression with common ratio 2.
3, $3x$, $3x^2$, $3x^3$, $3x^4$, ... is a geometric progression with common ratio x.

Let us look at the first few terms of a geometric progression whose first term is t_1 and whose common ratio is r.

1st term: t_1
2nd term: $t_1 r$
3rd term: $t_1 r^2$
4th term: $t_1 r^3$, etc.

We notice that the exponent of r is always one less than the number of the term. Thus, the 20th term would be $t_1 r^{19}$.

In general, the nth term of a geometric progression, denoted by t_n, with the first term t_1 and common ratio r is given by

$$t_n = t_1 r^{n-1}$$

Given any three of the four parameters, we can solve for the fourth.

EXAMPLE 3   In a geometric progression if $r = 10$ and the eighth term is 2000, calculate the first and the fifth term.

Solution   We have $t_8 = t_1 (10)^7 = 2000$. Thus, $t_1 = 2000(10)^{-7} = 0.0002$ and $t_5 = t_1 (10)^4 = 0.0002(10^4) = 2$.

The Sum of a Geometric Progression

Let S_n denote the sum of the first n terms of a geometric progression. Thus,

$$S_n = t_1 + t_2 + \cdots + t_n$$
$$= t_1 + t_1 r + t_1 r^2 + \cdots + t_1 r^{n-1}$$

Also,

$$r \cdot S_n = t_1 r + t_1 r^2 + \cdots + t_1 r^{n-1} + t_1 r^n$$

Subtracting the above expressions for S_n and rS_n, term by term, we obtain

$$(1-r) S_n = t_1 - t_1 r^n$$

and

$$S_n = t_1 \frac{1 - r^n}{1 - r} \quad \text{or} \quad S_n = t_1 \frac{r^n - 1}{r - 1}$$

Thus,

$$2+4+8+16+32+64 = 2\frac{(1-2^6)}{1-2}$$
$$= \frac{2(2^6-1)}{2-1}$$
$$= 2(2^6-1)$$
$$= 2(63)$$
$$= 126$$

and

$$3+3x+3x^2+\cdots+3x^n (n+1 \text{ terms}) = 3\left(\frac{1-x^{n+1}}{1-x}\right)$$
$$= 3\left(\frac{x^{n+1}-1}{x-1}\right)$$

EXAMPLE 4 A person starts a chain letter and gives it to 4 friends (step one) who pass it to 4 friends each (step two), etc. If there are no duplications, how many people will have been contacted after 10 steps?

Solution We have a geometric progression

$$4, 16, 64, \ldots$$

with $t_1 = 4$, $r = 4$, $n = 10$; we calculate

$$S_n = 4\frac{(4^{10})-1}{4-1} = 1\,398\,100$$

After 10 steps, 1 398 100 people will have been contacted.

Section A2.5 Applications of Geometric Progressions to Annuities

In Chapter 3 we used geometric progressions to derive

$$s_{\overline{n}|i} = \frac{(1+i)^n-1}{i} \quad \text{and} \quad a_{\overline{n}|i} = \frac{1-(1+i)^{-n}}{i}$$

In Chapter 4 we used geometric progressions to solve annuity problems where payments vary.

In the following examples we illustrate how geometric progressions can also be used in the ordinary general annuity problems of Chapter 4.

EXAMPLE 5 Calculate the accumulated and discounted value of $1000 paid at the end of each year for 10 years if the interest rate is 10% compounded quarterly.

Solution From first principles, using geometric progressions, we calculate the accumulated value S

$$S = 1000[1+(1.025)^4+(1.025)^8+\cdots 10 \text{ terms}]$$
$$= 1000\frac{(1.025)^{40}-1}{(1.025)^4-1} = \$16\,231.74$$

and the discounted value A

$$A = 1000[(1.025)^{-4} + (1.025)^{-8} + (1.025)^{-12} + \cdots 10 \text{ terms}]$$
$$= 1000(1.025)^{-4} \frac{1 - (1.025)^{-40}}{1 - (1.025)^{-4}} = \$6045.20$$

Section A2.6   Infinite Geometric Progressions

Consider the geometric progression

$$1, \frac{1}{2}, \frac{1}{4}, \frac{1}{8}, \frac{1}{16}, \cdots$$

whose first term is $t_1 = 1$ and whose ratio is $r = \frac{1}{2}$.

The sum of the first n terms is

$$S_n = \frac{1 - (\frac{1}{2})^n}{1 - \frac{1}{2}} = \frac{1}{1 - \frac{1}{2}} - \frac{(\frac{1}{2})^n}{1 - \frac{1}{2}} = 2 - (\frac{1}{2})^{n-1}$$

We note that for any n the difference $2 - S_n = (\frac{1}{2})^{n-1}$ remains positive and becomes smaller and smaller as n increases. We say, as n increases without bound (as n becomes infinite), the sum S_n of the first n terms approaches 2 as a limit. We write

$$\lim_{n \to \infty} S_n = 2$$

For the general geometric progression

$$t_1, t_1 r, t_1 r^2, \ldots$$

we can write the sum of the first n terms

$$S_n = t_1 \frac{1 - r^n}{1 - r} = \frac{t_1}{1 - r} - \frac{t_1 r^n}{1 - r}$$

When $-1 < r < 1$, $\lim_{n \to \infty} S_n = \frac{t_1}{1 - r}$ and we call $\mathbf{S = \dfrac{t_1}{1 - r}}$ the **sum of the infinite geometric progression**.

EXAMPLE 6   Calculate the sum of the infinite geometric progression

$$100, 100(1.01)^{-1}, 100(1.01)^{-2}, 100(1.01)^{-3}, \ldots$$

Solution   We have $t_1 = 100$, $r = (1.01)^{-1} < 1$ and calculate

$$S = \frac{100}{1 - (1.01)^{-1}} = \frac{100}{1 - \frac{1}{1.01}} = \frac{101}{0.01} = 10\,100$$

Section A2.7   **Exercises — Appendix 2**

1. Determine which of the following progressions are arithmetic and which are geometric, then write the next term of each and find the term and the sum as indicated.

   a) $1, -\frac{1}{2}, \frac{1}{4}, \ldots$ Determine the 8th term and the sum to 10 terms.

   b) $-1, 2, 5, \ldots$ Determine the 15th term and the sum to 12 terms.

   c) $19, 31, 43, \ldots$ Determine the 9th term and the sum to 10 terms.

   d) $40, \frac{120}{7}, \frac{360}{49}, \ldots$ Determine the 7th term and the sum to 12 terms.

   e) $\frac{1}{3}, \frac{1}{12}, -\frac{1}{6}, \ldots$ Determine the 8th term and the sum to 10 terms.

   f) $9.2, 8, 6.8, \ldots$ Determine the 10th term and the sum to 15 terms.

2. Calculate the sum of
   a) the first 300 positive integers;
   b) the first 100 positive even numbers;
   c) all odd integers from 15 to 219 inclusive;
   d) all even integers from 18 to 280 inclusive.

3. Determine the 10th term and the sum of the first 10 terms of the progressions
   a) $2, 4, 6, \ldots$
   b) $625, 125, 25, \ldots$
   c) $1, 1.08, (1.08)^2, \ldots$
   d) $(1.05)^{-1}, (1.05)^{-2}, (1.05)^{-3}, \ldots$

4. In an arithmetic progression
   a) Given $t_1 = 2$, $d = 3$, $n = 10$, determine t_n and S_n.
   b) Given $t_n = -11$, $d = -4$, $n = 7$, determine t_1 and S_n.
   c) Given $t_3 = 18$, $t_6 = 42$, determine t_1 and S_6.
   d) Given $t_1 = 7$, $t_n = 77$, $S_n = 420$, determine n and d.
   e) Given $t_1 = 13$, $d = -3$, $S_n = 20$, determine n and t_n.

5. In a geometric progression
   a) Given $t_1 = 5$, $r = 2$, $n = 12$, determine t_n and S_n.
   b) Given $t_1 = 12$, $r = \frac{1}{2}$, $t_n = \frac{3}{8}$, determine n and S_n.
   c) Given $t_5 = \frac{1}{20}$, $r = \frac{1}{4}$, determine t_1 and S_5.
   d) Given $t_2 = \frac{7}{4}$, $t_5 = 14$, determine t_{10} and S_{10}.
   e) Given $t_1 = 1.03$, $r = 1.03$, determine t_{15} and S_{15}.

6. A man borrows $5000, agreeing to reduce the principal by $200 at the end of each month and to pay 15% interest per annum (i.e., $1\frac{1}{4}$% per month) on all unpaid balances. Calculate the sum of all interest payments.

7. In buying a house a couple agrees to pay $3000 at the end of the 1st year, $3500 at the end of the 2nd year, $4000 at the end of the 3rd year, and so on. How much do they pay for the house if they make 20 payments in all?

8. In drilling a well the cost is $5.50 for the first 10 cm, and for each succeeding 10 cm the cost is $1 more than that for the preceding 10 cm. How deep a well may be drilled for $1000?

9. The value of a certain machine at the end of each year is 80% as much as its value at the beginning of the year. If the machine originally cost $10 000, determine its value at the end of 10 years.

10. Each stroke of a vacuum pump extracts 5% of the air in a tank. What decimal fraction of the original air remains after 40 strokes?

11. A rubber ball is dropped from a height of 50 metres to the ground. If it always bounces back one-half of the height from which it falls, determine
   a) how far it will rise on the 8th bounce;
   b) the total distance it has travelled as it hits the ground the 10th time;
   c) the total distance it has travelled before coming to rest.

12. If a person were offered a job paying 1 cent the first day, 2 cents the second day, 4 cents the third day, and so on, each day's salary being double that for the preceding day, how much would she receive
   a) on the 30th day;
   b) for a 30-day working period;
   c) for the each of the three consecutive 10-day working periods?

13. Determine the accumulated and the discounted value from first principles, using geometric progressions,
   a) of $100 paid at the end of each month for 10 years if the interest rate is 12% compounded semi-annually;
   b) of $500 paid at the end of each half year for 5 years if the interest rate is 12% compounded monthly.

14. Determine the sum of the infinite geometric progressions
   a) $1, -\frac{1}{3}, \frac{1}{9}, -\frac{1}{27}, \ldots$
   b) $3, 0.3, 0.03, 0.003, \ldots$
   c) $1, 0.8, (0.8)^2, (0.8)^3, \ldots$
   d) $(1 + i)^{-1}, (1 + i)^{-2}, (1 + i)^{-3}, (1 + i)^{-4}, \ldots$

Linear Interpolation

The first use of linear interpolation in the text is Example 3 of section 2.5. In this appendix, we expand upon the solution from section 2.5 to show, in general, how linear interpolation should be applied.

EXAMPLE 1 How long will it take $500 to accumulate to $850 at $j_{12} = 12\%$ if the practical method of accumulation is in effect?

Solution As shown in section 2.5, this reduces to asking: Determine n given $(1.01)^n = 1.7$. Solving this equation by logarithms we calculated $n = 53.3277$. Using a calculator, we find:

$$(1.01)^{53} = 1.6945$$
$$(1.01)^n = 1.7000$$
$$(1.01)^{54} = 1.7114$$

This can be shown graphically as follows:

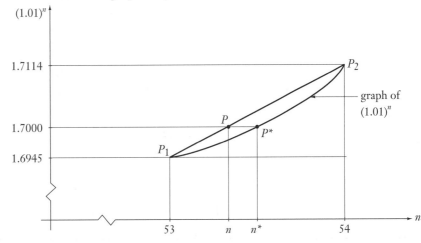

The true value n^* corresponds to the point P^* where the curve gives the value $(1.01)^n = 1.7$. Using logarithms we can calculate this exact value of n^*. Otherwise, we are forced to make some approximating assumption.

Under the method of linear interpolation, we assume the graph is linear between the points P_1 and P_2, as indicated by the straight line. The method of interpolation will determine the value n corresponding to the point P on the straight line. Clearly n is an approximate value of n^*.

To calculate the value n we use the fact that the three points $P_1 = (53, 1.6945)$, $P = (n, 1.7000)$ and $P_2 = (54, 1.7114)$ lie on a straight line, i.e.,

$$\frac{n-53}{54-53} = \frac{1.7000-1.6945}{1.7114-1.6945}$$

Solving for n we obtain

$$\frac{n-53}{1} = \frac{0.0055}{0.0169}$$
$$n = 53.32544379$$
$$n \doteq 53.33$$

This linear approximation, called **linear interpolation**, may be illustrated schematically by the following diagram:

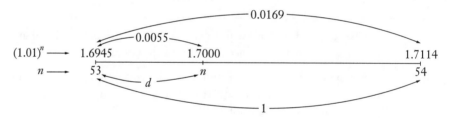

The value n lies the same distance between 53 and 54 as the value 1.7000 between 1.6945 and 1.7114.

Thus,

$$\frac{d}{1} = \frac{0.0055}{0.0169}$$
$$d = 0.32544379$$
$$\text{and } n \doteq 53.33$$

The data needed for linear interpolation is usually given in tabular form, called an **interpolation table**, shown below.

		$(1.01)^n$	n		
		1.6945	53		
0.0169	0.0055	1.7000	n	d	1
		1.7114	54		

$$\frac{d}{1} = \frac{0.0055}{0.0169}$$
$$d \doteq 0.33$$
$$\text{and } n = 53 + d = 53.33$$

In section 3.6 we used linear interpolation to determine the interest rate (see Examples 1 and 2 of section 3.6).

EXAMPLE 2   Determine the interest rate j_4 at which deposits of \$275 at the end of every 3 months will accumulate to \$5000 in 4 years.

Solution   As shown in section 3.6, Example 1, this reduces to solving the equation below for unknown rate i.

$$s_{\overline{16}|i} = \frac{(1+i)^{16} - 1}{i} = 18.1818$$

Using a calculator we calculate

For $j_4 = 6\% \ (i = 0.015) \quad s_{\overline{16}|i} = 17.9324$
For $j_4 = 7\% \ (i = 0.0175) \ s_{\overline{16}|i} = 18.2817$

We want to use a linear approximation to calculate the value of $j_4 = 4i$ such that $s_{\overline{16}|i} = 18.1818$. This linear approximation, called linear interpolation, may be illustrated schematically by the following diagram:

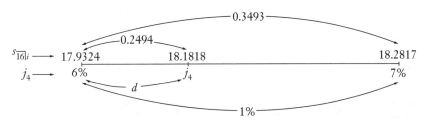

The value j_4 lies the same distance between 6% and 7% as the value 18.1818 does between 17.9324 and 18.2817. Thus,

$$\frac{d}{1\%} = \frac{0.2494}{0.3493}$$
$$d \doteq 0.7140$$
$$\text{and } j_4 = 6.71\%$$

Usually we arrange our data in an interpolation table, as below.

		$s_{\overline{16}|i}$	j_4	
		17.9324	6%	
0.3493	0.2494	18.1818	j_4	d
		18.2817	7%	

$$\frac{d}{1\%} = \frac{0.2494}{0.3929}$$
$$d \doteq 0.7140$$
$$\text{and } j_4 = 6.71\%$$

In section 6.6, we used linear interpolation to determine the yield rate of a bond (see Examples 2 and 3 of section 6.6).

EXAMPLE 3   A \$500 bond paying interest at $j_2 = 9\frac{1}{2}\%$, redeemable at par on August 15, 2018 is quoted at 109.50 on August 15, 2006. Determine the yield rate, j_2, to maturity by the method of linear interpolation.

Solution   As shown in section 6.6, Example 2, this results in linear interpolation between two market prices.

$$Q \text{ (to yield } j_2 = 8\%) = \$557.18 \text{ and}$$
$$Q \text{ (to yield } j_2 = 9\%) = \$518.12$$

The linear interpolation may be illustrated schematically by the following diagram:

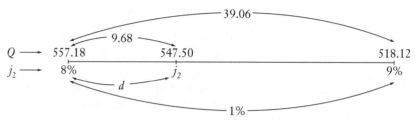

The value j_2 lies the same distance between 8% and 9% as the value 547.50 does between 557.18 and 518.12. Thus,

$$\frac{d}{1\%} = \frac{9.68}{39.06} \text{ or } d \doteq 0.25\% \text{ and } j_2 = 8.25\%.$$

Section A3.1   **Exercises — Appendix 3**

In the following exercises, illustrate linear interpolation schematically on a diagram and also set up the interpolation table.

1. Solve the following equations for n using linear interpolation.
   a) $(1.05)^n = 2$ d) $(1.045)^{-n} = 0.5$
   b) $(1.025)^n = 3.8$ e) $(1.0125)^{-n} = \frac{1}{4}$
   c) $800(1.03)^n = 1100$ f) $1000(1.0225)^{-n} = 700$

2. Solve the following equations for i using linear interpolation.
   a) $\frac{(1+i)^{12}-1}{i} = 15$ c) $\frac{1-(1+i)^{-20}}{i} = 10$
   b) $\frac{(1+i)^{100}-1}{i} = 200$ d) $100 + .90\frac{1-(1+i)^{-6}}{i} = 600$

3. Determine the interest rate j_{12} at which deposits of \$100 at the end of each month will accumulate to \$4000 in 3 years.

4. An insurance company will pay \$100 000 to a beneficiary or monthly payments of \$1150 for 15 years. What rate j_{12} is the insurance company using?

5. A \$1000 bond paying interest at $j_2 = 10\frac{1}{4}\%$ matures at par on August 1, 2024. If this bond is quoted at 105.50 on August 1, 2007, determine the yield rate j_2 using the method of interpolation.

6. A \$1000 bond that pays interest at $j_2 = 11\%$ matures at par on November 1, 2013. If this bond is sold on May 1, 2008, at a market quotation 78.25, calculate the yield rate j_2 that the buyer will realize using the method of linear interpolation.

Glossary of Terms

Accumulated Depreciation   The total depreciation allocated to accounting periods at any point in the life of an asset.

Accumulated Value   The total of the amount of money originally invested plus the interest earned.

Accumulated Value (of an Annuity)   The equivalent dated value of the periodic payments at the end of the term of the annuity.

Accumulation of Bond Discount   The periodic increase in the book value of a bond bought at a price below redemption so that the book value will equal the redemption value at maturity.

Amortization Schedule   A schedule showing in detail how a debt is repaid by the amortization method.

Amortize   To repay a debt by means of equal periodic payments of interest and principal.

Amortizing a Bond Premium   The periodic reduction of the book value of a bond bought at a price above redemption, so that the book value will equal the redemption value at maturity.

Annual Cost (of an Asset)   The annual interest on the capitalized cost of an asset including operating expenses and repair costs.

Annuity   A series of payments made or received at regular intervals of time.

Annuity Certain   A series of payments involving a fixed number of such payments.

Annuity Due   A series of payments in which the payments are made at the beginning of each interval of time.

Balloon Payment   An extra payment made at the same time as the final regular payment of an annuity in order to have equivalence.

Bond   A certificate of indebtedness agreeing to reimburse the purchaser and to pay periodic interest payments, called coupons.

Bond Interest Rate   The interest rate specified in a bond, upon which the actual periodic interest payments are based. Also called the coupon rate.

Book Value (of an Asset)   The difference between the original cost of an asset and its accumulated depreciation.

Book Value (of a Bond)   The value of a bond, at any particular time, according to its purchaser's accounting records.

Call Price   A lump sum of money paid to the purchaser to redeem a bond earlier than its maturity date.

Capitalized Cost (of an Asset)   The present value of the total costs involved with an asset for an infinite term.

Compound Interest   Interest that is earned upon previously earned interest.

Contingent Payment   A payment that will be made only if some predesignated condition is met, such as the company being able to make the payment.

Coupon   A detachable portion of a bond that represents the bond interest payment.

Deferred Annuity   A series of payments that has its first payment postponed for one or more periods.

Demand Loan   A loan for which repayment in full or in part may be required at any time.

Depreciation   A periodic charge to income to measure the consumption of an asset.

Depreciation Schedule   A chart showing the details of allocating the consumption of an asset to the various accounting periods.

Discount (Bond Purchased at)   The amount by which the purchase price of a bond is less than its redemption value.

Discounted Value   The amount of money that must be invested on the evaluation date in order to accumulate a specified amount at a later date.

Discounted Value (of an Annuity)   The equivalent dated value of the periodic payments at the beginning of the term of the annuity.

Discounting   Calculating the discounted value at a specified rate of interest or discount of an amount due in the future.

Drop Payment   A smaller concluding payment made one period after the final regular payment of an annuity in order to have equivalence.

Effective Interest Rate   An annual interest rate that produces the same accumulated values as the nominal rate compounded more frequently than annually.

Equation of Values   The equation obtained when comparing the dated values of the original payments at a focal date to the dated values of the replacement payments at the same focal date.

Equivalent Rates   Two rates of interest that produce the same accumulated value in the same period of time.

Equivalent Single Payment   One payment that can replace several other payments because it equals the dated value of the other payments.

Face Value (of a Bond)   The amount that is stated on a bond, upon which the interest payments and redemption price are based.

Face Value (of a Promissory Note)   The amount of money specified on the promissory note.

Flat Price (of a Bond)   The total purchase price of a bond, including any accrued interest.

Focal Date   A specific point in time selected to compare the dated values of sets of payments. Also called the valuation date.

Grace Period   The period of time (usually 3 days) following the date a payment of a short-term promissory note is due; during that time payment may be made without the loss of any rights.

Indexed Bond   A bond where the coupon and redemption value increase with a specific index such as the consumer price index (CPI).

Interest Conversion Period   The period of time between interest compoundings.

Internal Rate of Return   The rate of interest for which the net present value of a capital investment project is equal to zero.

Maturity Date (of a Note)   The legal due date, which includes 3 days of grace, for a short-term promissory note in Canada.

Maturity Value (of a Note)   The face value plus interest that must be paid on the legal due date.

Nominal Interest Rate   An annual interest rate that is quoted with the understanding that interest is compounded more than once a year.

Noninterest-Bearing Promissory Note   A note that does not require the payment of interest (the maturity value of such a note is the same as its face value).

Ordinary Annuity   A series of payments in which the payments are made at the end of each interval of time. Also called an immediate annuity.

Periodic Cost (of a Debt)   The sum of interest paid and the sinking-fund deposit when a debt is retired by the sinking-fund method.

Perpetuity   An annuity for which the payments continue forever.

Premium (Bond Purchased at)   The amount by which the purchase price of a bond exceeds its redemption value.

Probability   The likelihood of an event occurring.

Proceeds (of a Promissory Note)   The amount of money for which a promissory note is sold.

Promissory Note   A written promise to pay a specified amount of money after a specified period of time with or without interest, as specified.

Quoted Price (of a Bond)   The price of a bond without accrued bond interest.

Real Rate of Interest   The net rate of interest after taking inflation into account.

Redemption Value (of a Bond)   A lump sum of money paid to the bondholder to redeem a bond on or after the day of maturity.

Rule of 70   A quick method that can be used to approximate how long it will take to double an investment.

Scrap Value (of an Asset)   The value of an asset at the end of its useful life. Also called the salvage or the residual value.

Serial Bond   A bond whose principal is repaid by a series of payments rather than by a single redemption.

Sinking Fund   A fund that is being accumulated by periodic payments for the purpose of attaining a certain amount by a certain date.

Sinking Fund Deposit   A regular periodic payment into a sinking fund.

Strip Bond   A bond that has its coupons removed and sold separately.

Treasury Bill   A short-term security issued by the federal government.

Yield Rate   The interest rate that an investor will actually realize on an investment.

Answers to Problems

Exercise 1.1

1. a) $2950   b) $1234   c) $10 122.74
2. a) 16.8%   b) 14.29%   c) 12%
3. 1328 days   4. $131.25; $129.45   5. 60%
6. $4880.38   7. $547.59   8. $1011.74 ; $1011.58
9. $1042.11   10. $80.14   11. 10.37%
12. $28.28; $19.63; $11.54; $1.78; total interest = $61.23
13. $65.75; $198.90; $175.89; $110.13; $24.04; total interest = $574.71
14. 37.24%   15. 18.62%   16. 56.44%
17. a) 16.55%   b) $19.79

Exercise 1.2

1. February 6; $3000; 67 days; $2944.60
2. November 3; $1211.39; 27 days; $1207.15
3. June 27; $518.70; 185 days; $500.93
4. April 7; $4000; 37 days; $3965.83
5. a) $2038.11   b) 13.64%   c) 11.94%
6. $5108.29; $6.24; $102.05   7. $801.69
8. $1025.48   9. $5094.13
10. $1935.88; $435.88   11. $1960.09
12. a) $1508.62   b) 3.88%   c) 8.59%
13. a) $3333.33   b) $3333.42; $166.58
14. a) $4957.36   b) $4978.44   c) 3.88%
15. a) 4.65%   b) 6.07%; 2.29%

Exercise 1.3

1. $1169.25   2. $238.60   3. $988.31
4. $532.94   5. $409.11   6. $739.93
7. a) $1153.68   b) $1193.79   c) $1235.58

8. $428.19   9. $529.41; $529.81   10. $1173.09
11. $161.87; $161.96   12. $3332.70; $3010.95
13. a) $543.05   b) $541.57
14. $121.19; $121.29; $121.26, $121.13

Exercise 1.4

1. $463.95; $461.50   2. $369.26; $367.07   3. $1067.50; $1066.67
4. $334.30; $327.67   5. $478.07   6. $1233.03; $1229.35

Exercise 1.5

1. a) $1941.23   b) $1939.45
2. a) $4552.88   b) $5491.03   c) 13.18%
3. $6.90; $693.10   4. 5.72%   5. $814.05
6. $143.51; $51 611.99   7. 245 days   8. 9.24%   9. $1971.52

Review Exercise 1.6

1. a) 20 months   b) 541 days
2. Ordinary interest: $1010.69; $989.42
   Exact interest: $1010.55; $989.56   3. 123.87%
4. a) 37.63%   b) $163.46   5. a) 28.22%   b) $107.48
6. $691.87   7. $1395.35   8. $842.31
9. $957.50; $965.08   10. a) $1580.17   b) $1579.82
11. $124.15; $124.57   12. a) $926.67   b) $1079.14
13. a) $1523.29   b) 10.90%   c) 13.19%   d) 13.30%
14. a) $2021.36   b) 6.50%   c) 7.01%
15. $12.23; $809.78   16. 175 days   17. $20.21   18. $2.72
19. $1487.57   20. a) $1030.97   b) $1032.39

Exercise 2.1

Part A

1. $130.70; $30.70   2. $625.51; $125.51   3. $285.65; $65.65
4. $1695.88; $695.88   5. $63.52; $13.52   6. $1687.57; $887.57
7. $381.30; $81.30   8. $1221.37; $221.37
9. a) $520.37   b) $541.50   c) $563.41   10. $2462.88
11. a) $146.93   b) $148.02   c) $148.59   d) $148.98   e) $149.18
12. $2936.77   13. $39.658 billion; $164 200   14. a), b), c), d) $1061.36

Part B

1. a) $61.83   b) $60.90   c) $61.69
4. $6920.22; $7037.62; $7098.19; $7139.29; $7155.26; $7159.38

Exercise 2.2

Part A

1. a) 7.12%   b) 16.99%   c) 8.24%   d) 12.75%   e) 9.38%
2. a) 5.91%   b) 8.71%   c) 9.57%   d) 15.70%   e) 4.40%
3. a) 7.92%   b) 6.05%   c) 18.27%   d) 9.96%   e) 8.08%
   f) 4.04%   g) 5.19%   h) 12.59%

4. 6.02%   **5.** 9.04%   **6.** 23.14%   **7.** $j_2 = 8.9\%$

8. a) $j_2 = 15\frac{1}{2}\%$ is best; $j_{365} = 14.9\%$ is worst

b) $j_2 = 6.5\%$ is best; $j_{365} = 5.9\%$ is worst   **9.** $m = 4$

Part B

5. a), b), c) $26 764.51; $26 878.33; $26 937.10; $26 977.00; $26 996.51

6. a) 6%   b) 6.70%   c) 6.53%   **7.** 6.14%   **8.** $j_2 = 12.37\%$

Exercise 2.3

Part A

1. $83.64   **2.** $42.21   **3.** $655.56   **4.** $306.96   **5.** $688.57

6. $672.97   **7.** $1465.93   **8.** $978.85   **9.** $306.56   **10.** $1564.14

11. $393.55   **12.** $291.71   **13.** $1054.12

14. The cash plan is better by $10 657.22.   **15.** $2735.69   **16.** $3258.08

Part B

1. $62.19   **2.** $362.84; $367.39; $369.72; $371.29; $371.91; $372.06

3. Select proposal A with higher net present value.

Exercise 2.4

Part A

1. $142.92; $142.93   **2.** $1150.16; $1150.21   **3.** $2631.55; $2631.94

4. $198.99; $199.21   **5.** $1046.53   **6.** $1466.97

7. $6810.12   **8.** $628.82   **9.** $1278.66; $149.93

Part B

3. $2111.09; $1224.25

Exercise 2.5

Part A

1. $j_4 = 10.96\%$ **2.** $j_{12} = 8.88\%$ **3.** $j_1 = 7.60\%$

4. $j_2 = 13.54\%$ **5.** 3 years 4 months 26 days

6. 2 years 11 months 23 days   **7.** 7 years 10 months 8 days

8. 2 years 6 months 12 days   **9.** $j_1 = 7.18\%$ **10.** $j_4 = 10.27\%$

11. 14.77%   **12.** $j_{365} = 13.52\%$

13. a) 15 years 199 days   b) 9 years 330 days

c) 15 years 129 days; 10 years

14. 6 years 208 days   **15.** 8 years 41 days

Part B

1. a) $1542.21   b) $2378.41   **2.** 9 years 186 days

4. 8.5486117 years   **5.** $(1 + j_1)^2 - 1$ **6.** 21 years 31 days

7. 19 years 233 days   **8.** 7 years 128 days

Exercise 2.6

Part A

1. $1709.14   **2.** $809.40   **3.** a) $1678.58   b) $3370.45

4. $2468.20   **5.** a) $972.00   b) $1567.09   c) $2526.49

6. $550.21	**7.** $1533.25	**8.** $888.02	**9.** $232.13
10. a) $706.89	b) $459.58	**11.** $226.78	**12.** $193.61
13. $22 593.42	**14.** $840.04	**15.** $932.32	

Part B

2. $3951.33	**3.** $3611.27	**4.** $2504.12	**5.** $106.67

Exercise 2.7

Part A

1. $6273.74   2. $654.06   3. $646.28; 5.27%
4. $3810.26; $1810.26; 6.55%   5. $3612.72
6. $2067.29   7. $81 638.36   8. They should not accept the offer.
9. a) The payments option.   b) The cash option.   10. 7.57%

Part B

2. $686.76; $2.48; 8.26%   3. $2958.57   4. $15 903.69
5. $3494.79; 5.83%   6. 5.98%   7. 7.83%

Exercise 2.8

Part A

1. 87 645   2. 345   3. 6.50%
4. 6.6374573 years   5. $17 520.57   6. $217 324.45
7. a) 3.92%; i real AT = 2.39%   b) 3.85%; i real AT = 1.85%
   c) 3.77%; i real AT = 1.32%   8. $n = 1.61$ days

Part B

1. a) 76 501   b) 0:47 a.m.
2. 36 886   3. $0.7968 U.S. = $1 Cdn.

Exercise 2.9

Part A

1. a) $1706.99   b) $1715.94   c) $1716.81
2. a) $5383.77   b) $5362.80   c) $5362.56
3. 13.52%; 14.47%   4. a), b) November 8, 2011
5. 7.9248125 years   6. She should accept offer c).

Part B

1. 8.38%   2. 14.624063 years   3. 4.0612599 years
4. 6.1250454 years   5. $328.59   6. 6.85%

Review Exercise 2.10

1. $1892.94   2. $3996.16   3. $466.10
4. a) $2191.67; $2192.04   b) $1825.10; $1825.41
5. $827 323.97   6. $57.92   7. $228.04
8. j_2; j_4; j_{12} 9. $2276.06   10. 15 years 100 days
11. 11.14%   12. $7801.58   13. September 3, 2003
14. $877.83   15. a) 11.04%   b), c) 10.99%

16. $1338.23

17. Cash option is better by $1709.88.

18. $2199.72; $146.06

19. $715.95; 6.17%

20. $1213.12

21. a) $1349.87

b) $1348.85

c) $1349.86

d) $1350.88

e) $1362.58

22. $2584.47

23. a) $6253.15

b) $6253.11

24. $1618.57

25. a) $850.27

b) $850.46

26. a), b) 6 years 340 days

c) 7 years 7 days

d) 7 years 38 days

Rule of 70: $n = 7$ years

Exercise 3.2

Part A

1. a) $11 969.42

b) $12 832.52

2. $28 760.36

3. $3280.87

4. $334.12

5. $606.03

6. a). $47 551.33

b) $78 806.67

7. $13 031.63

8. $62 284.13

9. $12 833.69

10. $29 477.01

11. a) $8111.34

b) $9281.38

12. $204.56

13. $5522.36

14. $278.03

15. $49 702.20

Part B

1. $25 732.82

2. $15 448.11

4. 14.2; 30

5. $3515.68

6. $\dfrac{(1+i)^{20} s_{\overline{21}|i} - 21}{i}$

7. $24 527.91

9. $n + \dfrac{n(n-1)i}{2}$

11. a) $165.56

b) $195.18

12. $529.37

13. a) $2546.43

b) $3312.68

14. $103 343.97

Exercise 3.3

Part A

1. a) $3992.71

b) $3274.29

c) $3535.33

2. a) $1992.01

b) $2058.53

c) $1917.10

3. $27 737.28

4. $15 569.49

5. $6160.42

6. $6450.04

7. $670.04

8. $7019.27

9. $22 096.92

10. $12 269.34

11. $13 869.21

12. a) $12 795.73

b) $1016.81

c) $8085.63

d) $7218.90

13. $84.39

14. $2014.79

15. $33.94

16. $118.95, $2137; $111.22, $1673.33; $103.79, $1227.40

17. a) $1012.63

b) $1217.12

18. $182.08

Part B

2. 50; 12

4. $17.\dot{7}$

5. 6.57

6. $(1 + i)^{-1} + (1 + 2i)^{-1} + \cdots + (1 + ni)^{-1}$

7. $a_{\overline{2n}|i} - a_{\overline{n}|i} = s_{\overline{n}|i} - a_{\overline{2n}|i} = \frac{1}{4i}$

8. Ratio $= (1 + i)^n$

9. $(1 + i)^n$

10. a) $7758.83

b) $1065.88

c) $8034.50

d) $4717.02; smaller, since 9% > 6%

11. $13 559.93

12. $6526.63

13. The company should purchase Machine A.

14. $35 632.60

15. $12 181.80

16. $13 589.73

17. $1169.92

Exercise 3.4

Part A

1. $7066.97; $15 484.60   2. $508.79   3. $10.23   4. $5057.63
5. $1080.31   6. $576.61   7. $73 868.88   8. $910.98
9. $4566.77   10. $4291.72   11. $1842.32   12. $40 416.40
13. $2338.80   14. $2532.43   15. $4357.35   16. $59.16
17. $276 963.65

Part B

1. $32 868.66   2. a) $4883.88   b) $5006.92   c) $2203.59
5. $17 531.17   8. $9639.42
9. $a_{\overline{7}|i}(1+i)^{-3}$; $a_{\overline{7}|i}(1+i)$; $s_{\overline{4}|i} + a_{\overline{3}|i}$; $s_{\overline{7}|i}(1+i)$; $s_{\overline{7}|i}(1+i)^4$
10. a) $\ddot{s}_{\overline{3}|i}[3(1+i)^6 + 2(1+i)^3 + 1]$ b) $2s_{\overline{3}|i}(1+i)^2 + 3a_{\overline{3}|i}(1+i)$
11. $13 566.11   12. $228.91   13. $6461.63   14. $3096.92

Exercise 3.5

Part A

1. 13; $9.94   2. 185; $382.13; $133.11   3. 31; $474.56; $77.93
4. 7; $1410.28   5. 6; $192.99   6. 32; $345.58
7. 3; $1694.97   8. 24; $192.57 on July 1, 2012
9. a) 58; $4732.82   b) $7411.23
10. a) 11; $789.92 on January 1, 2013   b) $858.07
11. 15   12. $947.09

Part B

1. August 1, 2003; $16.18
2. a) 81   b) $1298.20   c) $1311.76
3. a) 43   b) $853.53   c) $938.88
4. $151 158.86   5. 7; $1494.19   6. $n = \dfrac{\log(\frac{S}{R}i+1)}{\log(1+i)}$
7. $n = -\dfrac{\log(1-\frac{A}{R}i)}{\log(1+i)}$ 8. 20; $798.39   9. 48

Exercise 3.6

Part A

1. 7.98%   2. 18.40%   3. 8.70%   4. 19.61%; 21.47%
5. 35.07%   6. 19.48%   7. 10.82%

Part B

1. 21.20%   2. 35.07%   3. 16.22%   4. 17.97%; 19.53%
5. Option 1: $j = 22.73\%$; Option 2: $j = 19.98\%$ is better.
6. $24.19 a month to borrow and buy a TV set
7. 20.86%   8. 7.61%

Review Exercise 3.7

1. a) $96 757.14; $39 470.85   b) $333 943.43; $55 572.48
2. a) $1984.65   b) $2332.09   3. $3571.94
4. a) $2050.63   b) $8649.69   5. $9.57

6. $14 631.36; $7214.18   **7.** $71 580.38   **8.** $96 435.44
9. $51 893.87   **10.** $1973.95   **11.** $14 329.99
12. $2569.15   **13.** $28 630.72   **14.** 69; $2310.56; $323.66
15. 15; $140.88   **16.** February 1, 2008; $41.01
17. 65.66%   **18.** 21.55%   **19.** 17.97%
20. 70.04%   **21.** 14; $111.97 on January 1, 2007
22. $376.91   **23.** May 1, 2004; July 1, 2010
24. $14 796.40   **25.** $11 487.31
26. a) $7.01   b) $2172   c) 28 months; $473.74
27. 17; May 10, 2002; $61.08   **28.** 19.91%
29. a) $618.26   b) $694.53   c) $4551.60
30. $253.07   **31.** a) $7520.60; $19 816.34 b) June 1, 2013; $253.07
32. 16.47%   **33.** $4055.39

Exercise 4.1

Part A

1. $1199.86   **2.** $5119.84   **3.** $2286.27
4. a) $11 469.92 b) $11 386.59   c) $11 629.86   d) $11 300.85
5. a) $2314.08   b) $2312.37   c) $2304.96   d) $2314.94
6. a) $74.56   b) $74.70   **7.** $1133.07
8. a) $221.85   b) $219.36   **9.** $161.71
10. a) $222.93   b) $223.25   c) $222.87
11. $330.67   **12.** $5843.61   **13.** a) $15 059.01   b) $15 058.46
14. a) $6781.37   b) $6782.71   **15.** Buying is cheaper.
16. $23 691.40   **17.** 14.86%   **18.** 16.62%   **19.** 112; $9.80
20. $239.89   **21.** a) $7078.18   b) $21 983.75   c) $7281.59
        d) $22 615.51 e) $4498.31   **22.** a) $17 991.16   b) $1426.50
23. $114.33   **24.** 36; $71.19   **25.** a) $582.07   b) $582.08

Part B

4. a.) $1019.62   **2.** $246.95   **5.** a) $330.85   b) $4106.23
8. $15 495.16   **9.** 11%   **10.** 29.70%   **11.** $4567.34
12. $111 188.52   **13.** a) $47 915.51   b) $49 393.59
14. a) $7804.35   b) $2058.21

Exercise 4.2

Part A

1. $687.48   **2.** $1177.89   **3.** $1534.67   **4.** $1579.05
5. a) $581.60   b) $700.42   c) $827.98
6. $1451.28; $1367.04; $1320.54; $198 307.20; $260 112; $325 394.40
7. They would be better off with the government mortgage at $j_2 = 6\%$.
8. $219.47   **9.** 243; $240.13   **10.** They should take the seller's offer.
11. a) $407.97; $444.83; $512.01   b) 15.7 years
12. a) $292.15;   b) $633.48

Part B

1. $134 296.84   **2.** 8.00%   **3.** 15 years 8 months   **4.** $606.90
5. $945.56; $217.73   **6.** $179 085.59   **7.** 11 years; $286.81

Exercise 4.3

Part A

1. a) $10 000   b) $8333.33   c) $6666.67
2. a) $5000   b) $3205.13
3. a) $25 000   b) $26 500   c) $19 802.34
4. $2775.15   b) $3373.21   5. a) $2380.95   b) $2894.06
6. $13 333.33   7. a) $58 125.94   b) $57 142.86   c) $43 618.37
8. $20 959.18   9. 12.5%;12.89%   10. a) $131.16   b) $1508.88
11. $2523.65   12. 11%   13. $20 548.18   14. $1461.10

Part B

3. a) 12%   b) $200 000   c) 18
4. $54 514.58   5. 20 months; $182.88   6. $88 506.21   7. $1652.63
8. $161.29   9. 68 months; $103.32   10. a) $4912.66   b) $5764.96
11. a) $3920.63   b) $4600.83   12. $2222.49   13. $623.50
14. 14.654614 years   15. $1989.36.

Exercise 4.4

Part A

1. $7332.70   2. $1 167 898.49   3. $20 180.04   4. $59 561.47
5. $8323.06   6. $137 500   7. $8973.78   8. $113 990.19
9. $16 082.70   10. $2504.44   11. $7797.87   12. $60 673.97
13. $4780.77   14. $15 754.79

Part B

2. b) $100 000   3. $22 620.20   4. $97 489.02   5. $435.84
9. $4932.95   10. $16 090.80   11. She should choose fund A.
12. $\dfrac{1}{is_{\overline{2}|i}}\left(p+\dfrac{q}{is_{\overline{2}|i}}\right)$ 14. At the end of the 24th year.
15. $442.88; $2708.61   16. $147 928.85

Review Exercise 4.5

1. a) $603.73   b) $99.42   2. $4892.00; $3281.39
3. $4046.12   b) $4045.61
4. a) 27; $88.29   b) 27; $0   5. $1273.45   6. 28; $38.03
7. 15.74%; 16.36%   8. $22 830.71   9. $7006.36; $5202.01
10. a) $9380.77   b) $7606.79   c) $15 705
11. Lease option is cheaper.   12. a) $41 884.02   b) $60 795.57
13. a) $610.31; $717.10; $1086.31   b) 15 years; $835.77
14. $123.65   15. $2256.98   16. $848.07
17. a) $16 435.51   b) $16 517.69   c) $14 654.25   18. $1352.74
19. $165.88   20. a) $10 716.74   b) $13 048.26
21. a) $187 500   b) $93 309.97   22. $14 012.21
24. $10 442.13; $100 727.85   25. $380 000   26. $6358.35
27. $338 971.64   28. $449.21   29. $31 787.13   30. $335.92
31. $1118.60   32. $25 542.66

Exercise 5.1

Part A

1. a) $336.04   b) $335.53
2. a) $626.62   b) $623.85
3. $758.05   4. $155.30   5. $133.63
6. Last payment is $3226.91.   7. Last payment is $1842.92.
8. Debt at the end of 5 months is $2076.13; last payment is $117.38.
9. Last payment is $26.95   10. $472.82   11. $424.91
12. $1190.71; $1297.74   13. $2072; $78.75

Part B

1. a) $43.75   b) $1639.45   2. $131.08
3. $1373.79   b) $343.45   c) 19 years 51 weeks
4. $1516.06   5. 16th   6. 8%   7. $8524.76
8. a) $274.75   b) 0.0082071   c) 10%   d) $29 738.47
   e) 22 years   9. $100(\frac{n}{a_{\overline{m}i}} - 1)$ 10. U.S. uses j_{12}, bank statement is correct
11. a) $1241.97   b) 24 years 39 weeks   c) $209.54
13. 8.17%   14. 8%   15. 16.99%   16. $1314.67
17. 43rd   18. Mortgage A: $111 192.62; Mortgage B: $97 256.92
19. 8.87%

Exercise 5.2

Part A

1. $5607.30; $5607.50   2. $5200.37   3. $3750.17; $950.33
4. $1708.84   5. $1281.01; $245.39   6. $1210.01; $82.29
7. $108 166.95   8. $184 618.15; $141 381.85
9. $41 738.99; $38 261.01   10. $8334.94   11. $15 849.33
12. $18 137.44   13. $481.02   14. $22 626.01

Part B

1. $105 400.67   2. Take out $125 000 mortgage at $j_{12} = 7.25\%$
3. $153 975.41   4. 17 years and 9 months; $98.36   5. $2126.40
6. a) 8 years and 5 months; $236.76   b) 7 years and 8 months; $150.40
7. a) $197 015.20   b) $71 082.21   c) $64 572.63
9. November 30, 2007   10. $3076.26
11. 11; $93.46   12. $123.54
13. a) $915.86   b) $154 754.41   c) i) 17 years and 2 months
   ii) $99 091.38   iii) $108 711.27   iv) $202.91

Exercise 5.3

Part A

1. $154.25; $4.75   2. $3.11   3. He should not refinance.
4. They should refinance.   5. $1009.23   6. $82 974.21
7. $422.02   8. $3787.21   9. $479.18
10. a) $188.68   b) $3580.97
   c) They should refinance and save $7.42 per month.

Part B

1. a) $1114   b) $871.41   c) $15 682.65   d) $97 554.57
2. $125.26; $243.76   3. $2062.74
4. a) January 1, 2001   b) $442.62   d) $399.84   e) $389.35
5. 1.836017314
6. a) $1291.55; $1281.44 b) $146 666.52; $140 349.12
   c) $1331.73; it would not pay to refinance.
7. a) $1339.65; $1337.86 b) $590 010.50   c) $180 910.94 d) $12 402.25
8. $2974.13   9. Choose Mortgage B.

Exercise 5.4

Part A

1. $155.30   2. $87.46   3. $5469.48
4. $11 928.33   5. $154.67; $4.33   6. $1.85
7. a) At the end of 2 years: $10 412.37; $9584.29
   b) At the end of 5 years: $10 023.71; $8674.92
8. She will save money by refinancing the loan.

Part B

1. Take option 2.
2. b) $131.66; $90.11   c) $15 766.21; $15 489.54   d) Do not refinance.
3. $14 700.94

Exercise 5.5

Part A

1. $3428.87   2. $17 045.65   3. $241.38
4. $374.21; $84.26; $458.47; $6075.77   5. $1392.44
6. $184.27; $8711.54   7. $7958.92   8. $119.14
9. No final deposit needed; after 9.5 years the account will have $203 263.82
10. $41 971.91

Part B

1. $1290.02   3. $5168.85

Exercise 5.6

Part A

1. $706.63; $3919.24   2. $12 956.27; $36 706.27
3. a) $28 277.87   b) $164 182.71
4. a) $122 036.72   b) $1 070 154.78
5. $100.96   6. $1370.79
7. a) $325.12   b) $505.12   c) $1618.57   8. $5606.85

Part B

1. a) $24 394.59   b) $1 519 331.88   2. 3 years and 7 months; $95.61
3. $13 082.32   4. $4460.37   5. 6.5%   6. 14.74%
7. a) $846.42   b) $17 458.03   8. a) $6366.56   b) $789.34

Exercise 5.7

Part A

1. a) $7791   b) $7791   c) $8293.40
2. The sinking fund plan is cheaper by $302.25 per year.
3. Amortization is cheaper by $559.32 semi-annually.
4. 10.04%   **5.** 9.48%   **6.** 7.45%
7. a) $15 196.71   b) 8.92%
8. The amortization method is cheaper by $56.52 a month.

Part B

1. Amortization will save $117.61 a month.   **2.** 13.03%   **3.** $810.00
4. 7.25%   **5.** $1278.04 at the end of 12 years.   **6.** 8.35%

Review Exercise 5.8

1. a) $190.01   b) i) $11 810.25; $88.58; $101.43
ii) $12 125.07; $90.27; $99.74   **2.** $966.73; $243.08
3. $4736.06   **4.** 8.96%   **5.** $349.41
6. a) $536.70   b) $57 262.74   c) $69.16   d) $23 024.34
7. Do not refinance.
8. a) $703.79   b) $98 820.18   c) $818.59   d) $178.49; $640.10
9. $1198.27   **10.** Sinking fund will save $10.02 annually.
11. $3900   **12.** $14.36
13. a) $889.19   b) $41 870.31   c) i) $152.88; $736.31
ii) −$51.93; $941.12   d) $992.59
14. a) $47.60   b) $63.54
15. a) $65.81   b) $3540.41
16. $429 476.31   **17.** 1795.80
18. a) $662.40   b) $642.66   c) $6754.97
d) i) 22 months sooner   ii) $12 173.89   **19.** $7548.01
20. a) $2718.46   b) $14 718.46   c) 13.57%
21. a) $5489.74; $5489.52   b) $445.04   c) $37 277.73
22. a) Amortization: $14 144.72; sum-of-digits: $15 492.96
b) Do not refinance.

Exercise 6.2

Part A

1. $549.48   **2.** $923.14   **3.** $1897.17   **4.** $5857.95
5. $792.96   **6.** $2539.30   **7.** $13 454.97   **8.** $6287.08
9. $1 068 973.16   **10.** $940.36; $1164.03   **11.** $107.25
12. a) $893.22   b) $1000   c) $1125.51

Part B

3. $6000   **4.** $1209.28   **5.** $1049   **6.** $846.28
7. $860.20   **8.** 10 years   **9.** $60.08
10. a) $957.88   b) 12 years   **11.** 7 years   **12.** $95

Exercise 6.3

Part A

1. Premium; $1025.79
2. Discount; $4866.79
3. Premium; $2046.13
4. Discount; $995.24
5. Premium; $2104.42
6. Discount; $10 599.34
7. $5.25; $1094.75
8. $102.34

Part B

1. $16.32
2. $9.01
3. $1360
4. a) $1052.76   b) $1068.52
5. $909.91
6. $1019.14
7. $31.28
8. $881.53
9. a) $2216.30
10. $1801.07
11. $886.82
12. a) $925   b) Discount   c) $0.50; $0.53
13. b) $10 408.88

Exercise 6.4

Part A

1. a) $2345.84   b) $1699.07
2. a) $5627.57   b) $4466.12
3. a) $1098.96   b) $914.20
4. a) $n = 10$ or 20 b) $n = 20$ c) $n = 10$
5. a) equal 8%   b) exceed 8%   c) less than 8%   d) equal 8%

Part B

1. a) $1689.13   b) $2260.08
2. a) $1133.76   b) $883.17
3. $5419.36
4. a) $1092.77   b) i) Premium = $80   ii) Premium = $12.77   c) 13 years.

Exercise 6.5

Part A

1. $857.26; $829.19
2. $550.69; $535.36
3. $1905.10; $1865.97
4. $9655.77; $9502.10
5. $1172.84; $1164.96
6. $1885.95; $1881.14
7. $1501.71
8. $1591.55
9. $1548.01
10. $1742.68
11. $128.84
12. $116.71
13. $97.29
14. $113.43
15. $1012.31

Part B

2. a) $1003.60   b) $1167.10
3. October 4, 2006
4. $1886.02
5. a) $1087.03; $1074.02   b) 1094.17; $1081.17
6. a) $4521.50   b) $4543.09   c) 121.15
8. a) $815.98   b) $823.34   c) i) $1109.16
   ii) $634.48   iii) 90.56
9. a) $4581.84   b) 107.87   c) 94.29

Exercise 6.6

Part A

1. 11.42%
2. 6.11%
3. 10.64%
4. 7.82%
5. 11.48%; 11.466%
6. 6.09%; 6.0824%
7. 10.55%; 10.5346%
8. 7.97%; 7.9669%
9. a) 7.44%   b) 7.50%
10. a) 9.87%   b) 9.86%
11. a) 10.96%   b) 10.50%
12. $j_2 = 10.20\%$
13. 6.76%
14. 8.62%

15. a) $913.54   b) $1074.39   c) 10.44%
16. 12.04%   **17.** a) Y2006: $80   b) Y2007: $110

Part B

1. a) $802.71   b) 9.33%   **3.** 9.63%
4. a) $795.37   b) $1058.36   c) 12.32%
5. a) $944.61   b) 7.61%
6. a) $5\frac{1}{2}$%   b) $4\frac{1}{2}$ years   **7.** $7\frac{1}{2}$%
8. 28.50%   **9.** 8.69%
10. a) $1497.89   b) Discount; $2.11   c) 1.76%

Exercise 6.7

Part A

1. $11 926.56   **2.** $111 898.48   **3.** 8.99%   **4.** $301.23   **5.** $95.40

Part B

2. $29 861 132.58   **3.** $242 773.02   **4.** a) $9614.46   b) $10 343.62
5. 9.20%

Review Exercise 6.8

1. a) $11 155 738.60   b) $148 362.33   **2.** $10 691 791.51
3. a) $1200.00   b) 7.47%   **4.** a) $1007.98   b) Discount
5. a) $2156.30   b) 7.44%   c) 108.48
6. a) $907.99   b) $1093.68   c) 12.35%   d) $1100.04
7. $2334.76   **8.** a) $901.04   b) 20 years   c) 8.36%
9. a) 7.97%   b) 7.95%   **10.** a) 7%   b) 17.5 years
11. $1092.01   **12.** $8881.54   **13.** $4785.17
14. a) $1146.23   b) $34.27   c) $1272.38   d) 8.65%
15. a) Discount ($119.50)   b) Premium ($107.12)
16. $1023.41   **17.** $2240.50   **18.** $2224.13
19. $4693.99   **20.** 92.53   **21.** 13.12%

Exercise 7.1

Part A

1. + $11 700.02; proceed   **2.** + $15 461.25; proceed
3. –$4061; not proceed   **4.** + $25 170.46; proceed
5. At $j_1 = 4$%: NPV(A) = $22 591.12; NPV(B) = $56 572.77; choose B
    At $j_1 = 7$%: NPV(A) = $5009.87; NPV(B) = $29 217.93; choose B
6. NPV(A) = –$548.58; NPV(B) = + $2865.55; choose B
7. NPV at 16% = $481 522; the company should proceed with the project
8. NPV = + $9874.62; the fund should proceed with the investment
9. NPV at 7% = + $135.29; proceed

Part B

1. NPV = –$130.81; do not borrow
2. NPV of investment 1 = + $11 626; NPV of investment 2 = + $11 358;
    investment 1 provides the company with the highest profit
3.

Rate	2%	4%	6%	8%	10%	12%
NPV	$22 923.25	16 445.44	10 502.14	5037.15	1.24	–4648.79

Exercise 7.2

Part A

1. 15.5% **2.** 16.5% **3.** 10.5%
4. 29% **5.** 11% **6.** 12%

Part B

1. IRR(A) = 20.5%; IRR(B) = 20%. At 15%: NPV(A) = + $985.63
NPV(B) = + $1609.89. At 25%: NPV(A) = –$757.12; NPV(B) = –$1217.92;
At 15%, project B should be chosen
2. a) 20% b) 19%

Exercise 7.3

Part A

1. $23 824.08
2. K_1 = $266 601.48; K_2 = $259 867.53; build the cement block warehouse
3. K_1 = $238.88; K_2 = $223.21; the company should purchase the second battery
4. Capitalized cost per widget; A = 6.037, Z = 6.005; machine Z should be purchased
5. $29.41 **6.** Save $225.27 per year by buying the $700 000 roof
7. $11 679.69 **8.** $182 607.41 **9.** $23 996.81
10. a) $1666.67 b) $2650 **11.** $120 000

Part B

1. Purchasing the $25 000 car saves $4571.34 in capitalized costs
2. $1 905 412.60 **5.** $4433.49 **6.** i = 2.26% **7.** 15 months
8. a) $570.42
b) Total monthly costs = $279.52; the heat exchange is cost effective
9. $55.72 **10.** $1 000 000

Exercise 7.4

Part A

1. a) R_k = $10 400 b) d = 0.331674938 **2.** a) R_k = $4500
3. a) $19 200; $30 800; $2400 b) $36 202.70; $13 797.30; $2409.27
4. a) $8000; $12 000 b) $17 647.02; $2352.98
5. B_5 = $14 745.60 **6.** B_7 = $8827.66; R_8 = $1713.88
7. 7 years **8.** 6 years
9. Per-unit depreciation = $.50 **10.** Per-unit depreciation = $8.88
11. $70 000 **12.** $1 986 000; $2 780 400
13. a) $6375.95 b) Leasing the car is more economical. **14.** a) d = 30%

Part B

4. $2000.04 **5.** $942.00

Review Exercise 7.5

1. Accept all (D is best)
2. IRR of the project is 7.5%; for alternative projects: IRR (1) = 8%,
IRR (2) = 7.5%, IRR (3) = 4.66%, IRR (4) = 20%, and IRR (5) = 18%
3. Buy machine 1 **4.** $23 996.82 **5.** $383.38
6. a) $2000 b) $20 000
7. a) R_k = $2666.67 b) d = 0.306638726 c) Depreciation per km = 20¢

8. Depletion per truck load = $4.16

9. a) $d = 0.369042655$ b) $352\,145.18$ c) $31\,693.07$

10. $5908.92   **11.** $181.76

12. a) $30\,000   b) $18\,984.38

13. $482.87   **14.** $27\,747.57

15. a) $214\,658.24   b) $d = 0.340246045$

16. $i = 0.12$ **17.** $37\,500

Exercise 8.1

Part A

1. a) $\frac{3}{8}$ b) $\frac{1}{16}$ c) $\frac{1}{8}$ d) $\frac{1}{8}$

2. a) $\frac{64}{125}$ b) $\frac{61}{125}$ **3.** a) 2.083%   b) 54.17%   **4.** 77.38%

5. a) 83.22%   b) 4.15%   **6.** a) $\frac{18}{125}$ b) $\frac{54}{125}$ c) $\frac{117}{125}$

7. a) $\frac{3}{1600}$ b) $\frac{27}{80}$ c) $\frac{1597}{1600}$ d) $\frac{53}{80}$

8. a) 0.225   b) 0.225   **9.** $\frac{7}{20}$

10. a) $\frac{2}{7}$ b) $\frac{3}{7}$ c) $\frac{2}{7}$ d) $\frac{1}{21}$ e) $\frac{4}{21}$ f) $\frac{1}{3}$

11. a) $\frac{1}{52}$ b) $\frac{2}{13}$ c) $\frac{1}{26}$ d) $1-\left(\frac{51}{52}\right)^2$ e) $\frac{1}{52}$ f) $\frac{8}{16\,575}$

12. a) $\frac{1}{6}$ b) $\frac{1}{2}$ c) $\frac{1}{2}$ d) $\frac{1}{9}$ e) $\frac{13}{18}$

13. a) $\frac{1}{18}$ b) $\frac{1}{9}$ c) $\frac{13}{18}$ d) $\frac{1}{2}$ e) $\frac{5}{12}$ f) $\frac{1}{324}$

14. a) $\frac{3}{8}$ b) $\frac{1}{16}$ c) $\frac{1}{8}$ d) $\frac{1}{8}$

Part B

1. $\frac{2}{17}$ **2.** $\frac{1}{6}$ **3.** $\frac{3}{5}$

Exercise 8.2

Part A

1. $8   **2.** $4.12   **3.** He should go on.

4. Students should take driver training.   **5.** $75

6. 54¢   **7.** $158   **8.** $3000

Part B

1. $\$\frac{13}{27}$ **2.** $\$\frac{1960}{64}$ **3.** $0

4. 21 units   **5.** She should stay with the present sales staff.

Exercise 8.3

Part A

1. 17.89%   **2.** $6575.34; 21.67%

3. a) $4631.58   b) $4642.11   **4.** 6.03%

5. Robert will receive $977\,526; Tammy will receive $1\,017\,487

6. $16\,865.74   **7.** a) $4752.88   b) $4621.24   **8.** $3402.87

9. $742.74   **10.** $902.33   **11.** $794.57   **12.** $1056.39

Part B

1. a) $586.94   b) $619.12   c) 11.08%   **2.** 17.17%

3. $28\,402.12; $29\,294.14; $29\,753.26   **4.** 1.18%   **5.** 23.60%

Review Exercise 8.4

1. a) $\frac{2}{13}$ b) $\frac{3}{26}$ **2.** a) 0.4479   b) 0.000064   c) 0.007873
3. a) $\frac{8}{27}$ b) $\frac{1}{9}$ c) $\frac{2}{27}$ **4.** $\frac{8}{16\,575}$
5. $E(X) = 5.65$; $E(Y) = 5.50$ **6.** $10.69   **7.** 71 items; $354.25
8. 15.26%   **9.** $18 872.89   **10.** $5 507.09   **11.** $531.22; $1031.51

Appendix Exercise 1

1. a) a^9 b) a^6 c) a^4 d) a^6
  e) a^2 f) $a^4 b^6$ g) a^9/b^9 h) $(1.05)^{19}$
2. a) $a^{\frac{5}{6}}$ b) $a^{\frac{1}{6}}$ c) a^{-4} d) 1
  e) $\frac{1}{5}$ f) $a^{-\frac{3}{4}}/b^{\frac{1}{2}}$
3. a) $\sqrt[6]{a^5}$ b) $1/\sqrt[6]{a}$ c) $a^{-3} b^7$
4. a) 0.36036999   b) 0.830901089   c) 4175.88482   d) 24.18216933
  e) 367.6826338   f) 7.493367615   g) 4.817537887   h) 6.749870404
5. a) 0.045593188   b) 0.049565815   c) 0.163574046   d) 0.188869169
  e) 0.182487607   f) 0.005248373   g) 0.045971928   h) 0.24573094
  i) 0.030301   j) 0.008164846
6. a) 40.29758337   b) 4.816952038   c) 24.93728565   d) 21.22762776
  e) 21.52150537   f) 3.969362296   g) 4.988439193   h) 6.321928095
  i) 3.380238966   j) 5.209453366
7. a) 12.65507765   b) 7.598623985   c) 9.782407637
  d) 5.954792501   e) 9.453195311   f) 3.157282008

Appendix Exercise 2

1. a) Geometric; $t_4 = -\frac{1}{8}$; $t_8 = -\frac{1}{128}$; $S_{10} = 0.666015625$
  b) Arithmetic; $t_4 = 8$; $t_{15} = 41$; $S_{12} = 186$
  c) Arithmetic; $t_4 = 55$; $t_9 = 115$; $S_{10} = 730$
  d) Geometric; $t_4 = \frac{1080}{343}$; $t_7 = 0.24785591$; $S_{12} = 69.99731233$
  e) Arithmetic; $t_4 = -\frac{5}{12}$; $t_8 = -\frac{17}{12}$; $S_{10} = -\frac{95}{12}$
  f) Arithmetic; $t_4 = 5.6$; $t_{10} = -1.6$; $S_{15} = 12$

2. a) 45 150   b) 10 100   c) 12 051   d) 19 668
3. a) 20; 110   b) 0.00032; 781.24992
  c) 1.999004627; 14.48656247   d) 0.613913254; 7.721734929
4. a) 29; 155   b) 13; 7   c) 2; 132   d) 10; $\frac{70}{9}$ e) 8; −8
5. a) 10 240; 20 475   b) 6; 23.625   c) 12.8; 17.05
  d) 448; 895.125   e) 1.557967417; 19.1568813
6. $812.50   **7.** $155 000   **8.** 400 cm   **9.** $1073.74
10. 12.85%   **11.** a) 19.5 cm   b) 149.8046875 m   c) 150 m
12. a) $5 368 709.12   b) $10 737 418.23
  c) $10.23; $10 475.52; $10 726 932.48
13. a) $22 616.89; $7052.05   b) $6637.64; $3653.68
14. a) 0.75   b) $3.\dot{3}$ c) 5   d) $\frac{1}{i}$

Appendix Exercise 3

1. a) 14.20   b) 54.06   c) 10.77   d) 15.74   e) 111.59   f) 16.03
2. a) 3.97%   b) 1.21%   c) 7.77%   d) 2.25%
3. 7.12%   **4.** 11.22%   **5.** 9.60%   **6.** 17.29%

Index

Accrued bond interest, 215

Accumulated depreciation, 254

Accumulated value
    annuities, where payments vary, 134–138
    of annuities due, 92
    of an ordinary simple annuity, 76
    approximate accumulated value, 45, 46
    at compound interest, 30
    exact accumulated value, 44, 46
    for fractional period, 44–46
    per period, 78
    at simple interest, 1

Accumulation
    of bond discount, 205
    future value, compounded interest, 32
    at a simple interest rate, 2

Accumulation factor
    continuous compounding, 68–69
    fundamental compound interest formula, 32
    at a simple discount rate, 24
    at a simple interest rate, 2

Allowance for depreciation expense. See Accumulated depreciation

Amortization
    of a bond premium, 203
    buyer's equity, 158
    of debt, 145–153
    and interest payment, 146–153
    mortgage payment, 126
    outstanding balance, 156–159
    payment, 146
    refinancing a loan, 162–167
    schedule, 147–152
    seller's equity, 158
    vs. sinking-fund method, 183–185

Amortization method, outstanding balance, 147–152

Amount (accumulated value), 1

Annual cost of physical assets, 249–250

Annual effective rate
    at changing interest rate, 60–61
    compound interest, 37–39
    continuous compounding, 70–71

Annual simple discount rate, 23

Annuities. *See also* Simple annuity
    annuity certain, 76
    annuity due, 76, 91–94
    arithmetic progression, payments vary in, 135–138
    common ratio, payments vary in terms of a, 134–135
    contingent annuity, 76
    deferred annuity, 76, 94–97, 98
    defined, 75
    discounted value of, 76
    general annuity, 76, 115–121
    geometric progressions, applications of, 300–301
    mortgages, 124–127
    ordinary annuity, 76
    payment interval, 75
    where payments vary, 134–139
    perpetuities, 128–132
    term, 76, 100–103

Annuity due, 76, 91–94, 97–98

Approximate method
    of accumulating, 45–46
    of discounting, 45, 46
Arithmetic progression, 297–298
Averages, method of, 220–221

Balloon payment, 100
Banker's Rule, 3. *See also* Ordinary interest
Base, 287
"Blocking technique"
    accumulated value of an annuity, 80–81
    discounted value of an annuity, 88
Bonds
    accrued interest, 215
    accumulation schedule, 205
    alternative purchase-price formula, 198
    amortization schedule, 203
    bond market, 194, 213
    bond rate, 194
    bond tables, 214, 217–218
    book value, 203, 206
    callable at par, 211
    callable bonds, 194, 210–212
    discount, purchased at, 196, 204–209
    extendible bonds, 212
    face value, 194
    flat price, 214–215
    indexed bonds, 229–230
    inverted yield curve, 225
    junk bonds, 267
    marketable bonds, 194
    market quotation, 216
    market (quoted) price, 215
    maturity date, 194
    modified coupon rate, 209
    notation, 195
    par, redemption at, 194
    premium, purchased at, 196, 202–204
    premium, redemption at a, 194
    price, 195–200, 206
    purchased between interest dates, 213–218
    purchase price formula, 196
    redemption date, 194
    redemption value, 194, 195
    retractable bonds, 212
    "riding the yield curve," 225
    risk, 266–267, 280
    serial bonds, 230–231
    strip bonds, 231
    taxable income, 203, 205
    trading of, 213–214
    writing down, 203
    writing up, 205
    yield rate, 194, 201, 220–226
    zero-coupon bonds, 231
Book value
    of an asset, 254
    of a bond, 203
    of a debt, 180
Business decision making
    capitalized costs, 248–251
    discounted values, 42
    future cash flows, 42
    internal rate of return, 243–245
    net present value, 237–238
Buyer's equity, 158, 159

Callable bonds, 194, 210–212
Canada Savings Bonds, 212, 228–229
Canada Tax Act, 256
Capital budgeting, 249
Capitalized costs, 248–251
Cash discounts, invoice, 6–7
"Change of payment" approach, 119–120
"Change of rate" approach, 116, 118, 120
Classical probability, 267–271
Comparison date, 16, 55
Compound amount. *See* Accumulated value
Compound discount, 41
Compounding period, 30–31
Compound interest
    accumulated value, 32
    annual effective rate, 37–39, 60, 68–69
    at changing interest rates, 59–62
    continuous compounding, 68–71
    dated value of the set, 55
    defined, 30
    discounted value, 41–46
    equations of value, 53–58
    equivalent rates, 37–40
    fundamental formula, 30–36
    multiplicative growth, 63–64
    notation, 31
    time value of money, 33
    unknown rate, 47–49
    unknown time, 49–52, 301–302
Computer spreadsheets
    amortization schedule, 149–150, 151
    compound interest, 34
    interest rate of simple annuities, 107–109
    internal rate of return, 244
    net present value, 239–240

purchase price of a bond, 208–209
sinking-fund schedule, 177–178
term of simple annuity, 103
yield rate, 222–223
Conditional probability, 269–270
Constant-percentage method of depreciation, 255–257, 260
Consumer Price Index (CPI), 65
Contingent annuity, 76
Contingent payments, with time value, 280–284
Continuous compounding, 68–71
Conversion frequency, 37
Conversion period, 31
Cost of capital, 238, 245
Coupon rate, 194
Credit, invoice cash discounts, 6–7
Cube, 287

Dated value of the set, 15, 55
Dated values, 14
    dated value of the set, 15, 55
    equations of value, 14–18, 53–58
    equivalent dated values, 15
    partial payments, 20–22
    time value of money, 14–15
Debt
    book value of, 180
    periodic expense of, 180, 183
Debt repayment
    amortization method, 145–153, 162–167
    amortization method vs. sinking-fund method, 183–185
    buyer's equity, 158, 159
    outstanding balance, 156–159
    refinancing, 162–167, 169–174
    sinking funds, 176–178
    sum-of digits method, 169–174
Declining Balance Method, partial payments, 20–21, 22
Declining-balance method of depreciation. See Constant-percentage method of depreciation
Deferred annuity, 76, 94–97, 98
Demand loans, 5–6
Denomination. See Face value, of a bond
Depletion, 258–259
Depreciation
    accumulated depreciation, 254
    base, 254

comparison of methods, 259–260
constant-percentage method of depreciation, 255–257, 260
defined, 253
notation, 254
physical-service method, 258, 260
rate of, 256
schedule, 254, 255, 256, 258, 259
scrap value, 254
straight-line method, 254–255, 259–260
tax, 253, 255–257
Discount
    bonds, 196, 204–209
    cash, 6–7
    factor, 8, 23
    simple discount, 23–26
Discounted loans, 23–26
Discounted value
    annuities, 76
    of annuities due, 92
    of an ordinary simply annuity, 83–89
    applications, 42–43
    approximate discounted value, 45, 46
    at compound interest, 41–46
    of deferred annuities, 95
    exact discounted value, 44, 46
    over fractional period of time, 44–46
    and future cash flows, 430
    of ordinary simple perpetuity, 129, 130–131
    promissory notes, 9–12, 42–43
    at simple interest, 8–12
    Treasury bills, 12
Discount factor
    for payments, 84
    at a simple discount rate, 23
    at simple interest, 8
Discounting, 41
    of promissory notes, 10
Drop payment, 100
Due date of a note, 10

Equations of value
    changing interest rates, 61–62
    at compound interest rate, 53–58
    at simple interest rate, 14–18
Equivalence. See also Dated values
    comparison date, 14–18
    compound interest rates, 37–40
    defined, 14
    equation of, 16, 55
    interest rates, 25–26, 39
    property of transitivity, 17, 54

Equivalent dated values, 15

Exact interest, 3

Exact method of accumulating, 44, 46

Exact method of discounting, 44, 46

Expected value, 276. *See also* Mathematical expectation

Exponential equations
    unknown base, 291
    unknown exponent, 294–295

Exponents
    defined, 289
    fractional exponents, 290
    Laws of Exponents, 289–290
    negative integers, 290
    zero, 290

Extendible bonds, 212

Face value
    of a bond, 194
    of a note, 10

Financial calculator method
    accumulated values of simple annuities, 81, 97–98
    annuities due, 97–98
    bond price, 197
    deferred annuities, 98
    discounted values of simple annuities, 89, 97–98
    interest rate of simple annuities, 107
    nominal interest rate, 48–49
    periodic payment of simple annuities, 81, 89, 97–98
    term of simple annuity, 103
    yield rate, 222

Flat price of a bond, 214–215

Focal date, 16, 55, 56

Fractional exponents, 290

Frequency of compounding, 31

Fundamental compound interest formula
    accumulation factor, 32
    compound amount, 30
    future value, 32
    notation, 31

Fundamental formula
    compound interest, 30–36
    discounted value at compound interest, 41

Future cash flows, 43, 266–267

General amortization schedule, 152

General annuity, 76, 115–121
    "change of payment" method, 119–120
    "change of rate" method, 116, 118, 120
    defined, 115
    where payments more frequent than interest
        compounded, 119–121

problem-solving procedure, 116
    unknown interest rate, 118

General perpetuity, 131–132

Geometric growth, 63–64

Geometric progression
    annuities, applications to, 300–301
    defined, 299
    infinite geometric progressions, 301
    sum of, 299–300

Grace period of a note, 10

Immediate annuity. *See* Ordinary annuity

Independent events, 268

Indexed bonds, 229–230

Infinite geometric progression, 129, 301

Inflation
    indexed bonds and, 229–230
    and "real" rate of interest, 65–67

Initial public offering (IPO), 42

Interest. *See also* Compound interest in
        advance, 19
    defined, 1
    in early times, 2
    exact interest, 3
    on mortgages, 124
    ordinary interest, 3, 4
    simple interest, 1–12

Interest period. *See* Compounding period

Interest rate
    changing, 59–62
    defined, 1
    of demand loans, 5
    equivalent rates, 25–26, 39
    and inflation, 65–67
    mortgage, 124
    "real" rate of interest, 65–67
    rounding off, 40
    simple annuity, 105–109, 303

Internal rate of return, 243–247

Interpolation, method of, 221–222. *See also* Linear
    interpolation

Interpolation table, 302

Investment rate. *See* Yield rate of a bond

Invoice cash discounts, 6–7

Junk bonds, 267

Law of Large Numbers, 272

Laws of Exponents, 289–290

Legal due date of a note, 10

Legal value date of a note, 10

Linear interpolation, 305–308
    unknown rate of simple annuity, 106, 307
    unknown term of an investment, 49–50, 305–306
    yield rate of a bond, 221, 308
Loans
    amount (accumulated) value, 1
    demand loans, 5–6
    discounted loans, 23–25
    interest, 1
    principal, 1
Logarithms
    basic properties of, 291–293
    computing with, 292–293
Long-term promissory notes, 9–12, 26, 42–63

Maker of a note, 9
Marketable bonds, 194
Market price of a bond, 215
Market quotation, 216
Mathematical expectation, 276–278
Maturity date
    of a bond, 194
    of a note, 10
Mean value, 276
Merchant's Rule, 21–22
Modified coupon rate, 209
Mortgages
    amortization period, 126, 163
    interest on, 124
    interest rates, 124, 163
    penalty for early refinancing, 163, 166
    periodic payment, 124–127
    refinancing, 163–166
    total interest paid, 125
Multiplicative growth. See Geometric growth
Mutually exclusive events, 268

Negative exponents, 288

Ordinary annuity, 76
Ordinary deferred annuity. See Deferred annuity
Ordinary interest, 3, 4
Ordinary simple perpetuity, 128–132
Outstanding balance
    amortization method, 147–153
    prospective method, 157–158
    retrospective method, 156–157, 159
    seller's equity, 158
Outstanding principal balance, 148. See also
        Outstanding balance
Owner's equity. See Buyer's equity

Par value of a bond, 193
Payee of a note, 9
Payment interval, of an annuity, 75
Periodic expense of the debt
    amortization method, 183
    sinking-fund method, 180, 183
Periodic payment
    annuities due, 97
    ordinary simply annuity, 79, 87–88, 89
Perpetuities
    defined, 128
    discounted value, 129, 130–131
    general perpetuity, 131–132
    ordinary simple perpetuity, 129–131
    perpetuity deferred, 129
    perpetuity due, 129
Physical-service method, 258, 260
Practical method of accumulating. See Approximate
        method, of accumulating
Practical method of discounting. See Approximate
        method, of discounting
Premium, of a bond, 194, 196, 202–204
Present value. See Discounted value
Principal, of a loan, 1
Probability
    classical probability, 267–271
    conditional probability, 269–270
    probability tree, 270
Proceeds. See Discounting
Progressions
    arithmetic progression, 297–298
    geometric progression, 299–300
Promissory notes, 9–12
    defined, 9
    discounting of, 10
    due date, 10
    face value, 10
    legal due date, 10
    long-term notes, 42–43
    maker of, 9
    payee, 9
    simple discount, application of, 26
    term, 10
Property of transitivity, 17, 54

Quoted price of a bond. See Market price of a bond

Real interest rate, 56–67
Real rate of return, 66–67
Real Return Bonds. See Indexed bonds
Redemption date, 194

Redemption value, 194, 195
Refinancing
    amortization method, 162–167
    mortgage, 163–166
    penalty, 162
    reasons for, 162
    sum-of-digits method, 169–174
Retractable bonds, 212
Risk assessment, 267–268, 280
Rounding off
    amortized payments, 146, 147
    of final answer, to nearest cent, 33
    interest rate per compounding period, 35
    total payout of a loan, 147
    unknown yearly rates of interest, 40
Rule of 78. *See* Sum-of-digits method

Salvage value, 254
Savings bonds, 194
Scrap value. *See* Salvage value
Seller's equity, 158
Serial bonds, 230–231
Simple annuity
    accumulated value of, 76–81
    discounted value, 76, 83–89, 92, 95
    interest rate, 105–109, 303
    periodic payment, 79, 87–88, 89
    term, 76, 100–103
Simple discount, 23–26
    accumulation factor, 24
    annual simple discount rate, 23
    discounted loans, 23–25
    discount factor at a simple discount rate, 23
    equivalent rates, 25–26
    promissory notes, 26
Simple interest, 1–12
    accumulation at, 2
    accumulation factor, 2
    defined, 2
    demand loans, 5–6
    discounted value, 8–12
    discount factor at, 8
    discounting, 8
    exact interest, 3–4
    for fractional period, 45
    invoice cash discounts, 6–7
    ordinary interest, 3–4

promissory notes, 9–12
    Treasury bills, 12
Simple perpetuity. *See* Ordinary simple perpetuity
Sinking-fund loan, 179, 184
Sinking-fund method
    of retiring a debt, 179–181
    vs. amortization method, 183–185
Sinking funds, 176–178
Sinking-fund schedules, 176, 177–178
Spreadsheet. *See* Computer spreadsheets
Square, 287
Straight-line method of depreciation, 254–255, 259–260
Sum
    of arithmetic progression, 298
    of geometric progression, 299–300
    of infinite geometric progression, 301
Sum-of-digits method, 169–174

Taxable income, 203
Tax deduction, 146–147, 147
Term
    of an annuity, 76, 100–103
    of a note, 10
Theoretical method. *See* Exact method of accumulating; Exact method of discounting
Time value of money, 14–15, 33
Total debt, 173
Treasury bills, 12
2/10, *n*/30 credit terms, 6

Useful life of an asset, 253–254

Valuation date, 16, 55

Writing down a bond, 203
Writing up a bond, 205

Yield curve, 225
Yield rate of a bond, 194, 201
    method of averages, 220–221
    method of interpolation, 221, 305

Zero-coupon bonds, 231
Zero exponent, 289

SUMMARY OF NOTATIONS

Chapter 1

P = principal = present value of S = discounted value of S
I = simple interest
r = annual simple interest rate
S = accumulated value of P = future value of P
t = term of the investment in years
D = simple discount
d = annual simple discount rate

Chapter 2

n = term of the investment in compounding periods
m = number of compounding periods per year
j_m = nominal rate of interest per year
i = effective rate of interest per compounding period
j = annual effective rate of interest = j_1
i_{real} = real rate of return
$i_{\text{real after-tax}}$ = real after-tax rate of return
$j_\infty = \delta$ = nominal rate of interest compounded continuously = force of interest

Chapters 3 and 4

A = present value of an annuity = discounted value of an annuity
S = accumulated value of an annuity = future value of an annuity
R = periodic payment of an annuity
n = term of an annuity in compounding periods
i = annuity interest rate per compounding period
$s_{\overline{n}|i}$ = accumulated value of an ordinary annuity consisting of n-payments of \$1
$\ddot{s}_{\overline{n}|i} = s_{\overline{n}|i}(1+i) = s_{\overline{n+1}|i} - 1$ = accumulated value of an annuity-due consisting of n-payments of \$1
$a_{\overline{n}|i}$ = present/discounted value of an ordinary annuity consisting of n-payments of \$1
$\ddot{a}_{\overline{n}|i} = a_{\overline{n}|i}(1+i) = 1 + a_{\overline{n-1}|i}$ = present/discounted value of an annuity-due consisting of n-payments of \$1

Chapter 5

A = original loan amount
R = periodic loan payment
n = term of loan = number of periodic payments during term of loan
I = total interest paid over term of loan = total payments − loan amount
i = interest rate on the loan per payment period
I_k = interest portion of the kth payment
$\quad = iB_{k-1}$ (amortization method)
$\quad = \dfrac{n-k+1}{s_n} I$ (sum of digits method)
P_k = principal portion of the kth payment = $R - I_k$
B_k = outstanding balance immediately after the kth payment = $B_{k-1} - P_k$
$s_n = 1 + 2 + 3 + \cdots + n$

Chapter 6

F = face value of a bond
C = redemption value of a bond ($C = F$ for a par value bond)
r = bond interest rate per compounding period = coupon rate
Fr = bond interest payment = bond coupon
i = yield rate per compounding period
n = term of the bond = number of compounding periods until the redemption date
P = purchase price of a bond to yield i = flat price of a bond
P_0 = purchase price of a bond on the coupon date before the date of sale
k = fractional part of coupon period elapsed since preceding coupon date
I = accrued bond interest = $k\,Fr$
Q = quoted price of a bond between coupon payments = $P - I$

Chapter 7

NPV = net present value of an investment
IRR = internal rate of return of an investment
i = annual interest rate = cost of capital
K = capitalized cost of an asset
Ki = annual cost of an asset
C = original cost of an asset
n = estimated useful lifetime of an asset
S = scrap value of an asset at the end of n-years
M = annual maintenance costs of an asset
$C - S$ = depreciation base of an asset
R_k = annual depreciation expense of an asset
D_k = accumulated depreciation of an asset at the end of k-years
B_k = book value of an asset at the end of k-years

Chapter 8

$P(E)$ = probability that event E occurs
$P(E_2 | E_1)$ = probability that event E_2 occurs, given that event E_1 has occurred
$E(X)$ = expected value of X